BE CIVIL!

BE CIVIL!

A guide to learning civil litigation and evidence

VIRGINIA DUNN

Worth Publishing

First published 2011 by Worth Publishing Ltd
www.worthpublishing.com

Second Edition published 2014 by Worth Publishing Ltd

Third Edition published 2015 by Worth Publishing Ltd

Forth Edition published 2023 by Worth Publishing Ltd

Printed and bound in Great Britain by Grosvenor Group (Print Services) Ltd

British Library Cataloguing in Publication Data
A catalogue record for this book is available from the British Library

ISBN 9781903269411

Design by Anna Dadswell

Preface to the first edition

If you are reading this, my guess is you are getting ready to sit a professional examination. Whether you are at the beginning or end of your course or, having already qualified, are embarking on a change of direction in early practice, this book is intended to help. Its purpose is to make civil litigation easier and more fun to understand, so that when the time comes, you really know what you are talking about.

My experience of teaching has shown me that most students look upon civil procedure, not so much as a Cinderella subject, but as one of the ugly step-sisters. It often seems to them like an avalanche of apparently disjointed rules and regulations, so that what is covered in class one week is forgotten the next. And anyway (they think) crime is *so* much more fun. This attitude makes it hard to get to grips with the subject. My approach is intended as an antidote.

The key to learning civil litigation is to see the big picture. If, for example, you are putting together a jigsaw puzzle, it is much more difficult if you do not know what it should look like when it is completed. That is what I hope to provide. You have been (or are about) to look at all the individual pieces of the civil litigation puzzle in some detail on your course. This book is the picture on the box.

It is intended to augment, not replace, your own learning. It can assist with classroom preparation, by allowing you to focus intelligently on the subject matter, research more knowledgeably and contribute intelligently to discussions, rather than merely writing down everything you see and hear. It should be especially helpful as you prepare for examinations by reinforcing the bigger picture while reviewing the essential individual concepts. I also offer many revision tips. This book should also remind you of the value of common sense (an under-rated commodity) in learning how to think about and understand any aspect of the law, including civil procedure and evidence.

This book is the product of many years of helping students to learn and enjoy its subject. In particular it is an elaboration of the revision notes they had access to when I taught full-time at the Inns of Court School of Law/City Law School. I am grateful to all of my students - past and present - for teaching me to teach them better. Many colleagues at City Law School were also very supportive of this enterprise, in particular: Lisa Laurenti (who keeps me teaching and learning), Catherine Hill (who keeps me in touch with my roots), Ros Carne (who tried, with limited success, to curb my enthusiasm for exclamation marks), Robert McPeake (whose library extended to *Hart's Rules*) and especially Stuart Sime, who spent time he did not have to make some very useful editorial suggestions. My most grateful thanks, however, go to Ronnie Lachkovic (who runs the BPTC Civil Litigation course at City Law School) and Sir Peter Coulson, who kindly wrote the Foreword. Ronnie (who doubles as Lady Coulson) not only took a personal interest in the book (and its author), but also the time to read virtually all of the manuscript, which is very much improved as a result. Neither she, nor anyone else of course, should be held accountable for any of its content, and any errors which remain are mine alone.

I should also thank my supportive daughters, Eden, Kate and Rachael Sanders, who have become adept at making their own or ready-meals (which they sometimes like better than mine, if the truth be told) while I was chained to my desk. Finally, I should like to pay tribute to Martin Wood and Andrea Perry at Worth Publishing for their help in producing this book. It took patience, professionalism and good humour, which they have in abundance.

The dedication is to two people very close to my heart, always: my husband Ray Sanders, a social security appeal judge, who died in 2002, and Rosie Samwell-Smith, former BVC course director at the ICSL, who died in 2010. How I wish they were here to see this.

VVD

London, March 2011

For Ray and Rosie

About the author

Virginia V Dunn, BA, MA, Barrister began practice in civil and family law and has spent more than 35 years teaching students training for the Bar at the Inns of Court School of Law, now the City Law School. She has taught a range of skills and knowledge subjects there, including procedure and evidence. For much of that time, she co-ordinated the civil litigation course, and has first-hand knowledge of how the subject is taught and assessed. She is currently a Visiting Lecturer at the City Law School. She edited and contributed to City Law School's Law in Practice manuals supporting training for the Bar, and has written for the Institute of Legal Executives. For many years she has supervised students advising clients as part of City Law School's pro bono programme. This book is the culmination of many years helping students to enjoy learning civil litigation and evidence. She has also published a companion guide for criminal procedure entitled *It's Criminal!: Guide to learning criminal litigation, evidence and sentencing.*

Preface

Since the last edition of this book, there has been more change to the teaching and assessing of its subject matter, than to the subject matter itself. *Be Civil!* is primarily written with trainee barristers in mind, and following a major review, new approved 'pathways' to Bar training were created in 2019 to replace what had until then been a more uniform course. Training for solicitors has undergone its own revolution.

The curriculum of the Civil Procedure component of Bar training continues to be centrally set and assessed by the Bar Standards Board (BSB), but much else has changed. The syllabus is now very particularly based around specific material in two named texts - the White Book and Jackson's ADR Handbook - and requires both breadth and depth of knowledge. Only one type of question format - the so-called Single Best Answer Question - is used, but there are now two papers, each with its own set of challenges. *Be Civil!* is intended not only to help you gain a good understanding of the examinable material, but also the confidence to prepare for and successfully navigate the assessments. Chapter 1, by way of introduction, sets out some preliminary information and important ground rules, and Chapter 20, which is well worth looking at now before you begin, ends the book by focusing on examination content, preparation and technique. It is important not only to 'know your stuff' when you sit these (or indeed any) exams, but also to be well aware of the sorts of questions you will have to answer. As all lawyers come to learn - good preparation is critical.

To this end it is very important to treat your course syllabus with respect! This book is not updated annually, but your syllabus will be, not necessarily very dramatically but you always want to be focused on the current examinable material. It is vital to to use your exam syllabus as a serious 'to-do' list, ensuring that you have learned, understood and revised the required topics (question-spotting is not a good strategy for the Bar examinations). Remember too that your course leaders and teachers want you to succeed, so follow their lead and take advantage of all learning opportunities on offer.

Meanwhile both the Civil Procedure Rules Committee and the Editor-in-Chief of the White Book are on something of a mission to streamline and modernise both the content of the CPR, and the explanatory commentary paragraphs in the White Book which accompany them. A current trend is to absorb a Practice Direction (which follows its corresponding part of the rules) back into the rules themselves, and dispense altogether with the Practice Direction in question. So suddenly a part of the rules has some extra paragraphs, but no Practice Direction. Or a decision is taken to 'tidy up' the numbering of a part of the rules or to completely re-write a section of the commentary. Certainly many of the changes in the last few years have been more cosmetic than substantive, but this does mean that some of my references to the CPR and so forth will in time be overtaken by editing events.

And sometimes, of course, more major developments take place. During the pandemic, for example, special arrangements were put in place (and then removed again). When Elizabeth II died, suddenly the Queen's Bench Division became the King's Bench Division. Important changes have been and continue to be made to the rules governing case management and costs. A new allocation track is due to be added soon. So things can and do change. I have tried my utmost to ensure (at something like the 11th hour) that this fourth edition of *Be Civil!* is up-to-date to April 2023. But I have to stop somewhere, which is where you will need to start. And note that the BSB will give you a cut-off date beyond which any changes to the law will not be tested in that year's examinations.

As always, I am grateful to family and friends, and Worth Publishing, for their continued support in producing this fourth edition. As always, special mention must go to my editor Andrea Perry, the book's designer Anna Murphy, and to City Law School's Ronnie Lachkovic, all of whom remain committed to this project, despite having many other demands on their time and energy. All have helped to improve this edition - as usual, however, any errors of content are mine alone. Finally, my thanks for the constructive and helpful comments from the many students and practitioners who have both enjoyed and benefitted from this book - which, after all, is the point of it.

VVD
London, April 2023

Foreword

One of the complaints that I regularly receive as the Editor-in-Chief of the White Book is that it is too long and, in places, impenetrable. It is difficult to disagree with the first criticism; as to the second, my answer is that civil procedure has, for better or for worse, become much more complicated than Lord Woolf ever imagined, with a corresponding increase in both the rules and the authorities which address those rules.

That is why a shorter, simpler guide to civil procedure is always so welcome. *Be Civil!* ticks all the necessary boxes. It is concise, but it does not omit or ignore anything of importance. It focuses on the principal areas of civil procedure, and stays well clear of the undergrowth. And it is written in a very clear and focused way, allowing everyone (be they students, young practitioners or even crusty judges) to understand the essential elements of each stage in the process.

Whilst it is always a little unfair to single out particular chapters, I should commend in particular Chapter 15, dealing with Part 36 and Offers of Settlement. That is one area of the CPR that, despite the attempts to clarify it, seems to defy all the best efforts of the Civil Procedure Rules Committee. Chapter 15 is the best possible guide to its critical components.

A good deal has happened since the first edition of *Be Civil!* but it appears that Virginia's enthusiasm for civil procedure has not abated over the last 12 years. I wish this fourth edition every success.

Lord Justice Coulson
Editor-in-Chief of the White Book
Formerly Deputy Head of Civil Justice

Glossary of terms

Actions	Before the CPR, this is what 'claims' were called. Both expressions are still sometimes used. 'Action' will appear in older legislation and case law.
Affidavit	This is a written, sworn statement containing evidence. It was at one time commonly used to support interim applications, so will still be referred to in older cases. Affidavits are still used for freezing and search orders, but most interim applications nowadays present their supporting evidence by means of witness statements.
Alternative Dispute Resolution (ADR)	This is a collective description for methods of resolving disputes otherwise than through the normal litigation process.
Civil Procedure Rules (CPR)	One of the primary sources of procedural law in England and Wales. It was brought in as a new procedural code in 1999.
Cross-examination *(compare with examination-in-chief)*	Questioning of a witness by a party other than the party who called the witness.
Damages	A sum of money awarded by the court as compensation to the claimant. 'Exemplary' damages are awarded to punish the defendant's objectionable behaviour, and 'aggravated' damages compensate a claimant for it. These are exceptional and if sought should be specifically claimed in the Particulars of Claim: CPR, r 16.4(1)(c).
Disbursements	In a legal context, money paid by solicitors on behalf of their client.
Evidence-in-Chief	The evidence given by a witness for the party who called him.
Examination-in-Chief	The questioning process by which a party's evidence-in-chief is elicited orally.
Joint liability *(see also several liability)*	Parties who are jointly liable share a single liability and each party can be held liable for the whole of it.

Overriding Objective	The principal aspiration of the CPR, which is to deal with cases justly and at proportionate cost.
Obiter	Judicial observation in a case which is not strictly binding, as it is not the point to be decided in the case.
Plaintiff	Pre-CPR description for a Claimant.
Pleadings	This is an old-fashioned way of referring to statements of case.
Practice Form	Form to be used for a particular purpose, as specified by a practice direction.
Quia timet	Literally, 'because he fears'. Used to describe an injunction restraining a threatened wrong.
Set aside	Cancelling a judgment or order or step taken by a party in the proceedings.
Several liability *(see also joint liability)*	A person who is severally liable with others may remain liable for the whole claim even where judgment has been obtained against others.
Stay	A stay imposes a halt on proceedings, apart from taking any steps allowed by the rules or the terms of the stay. Proceedings can continue if, but only if the stay is lifted.
Tort	A civil wrong, other than breach of contract, which is compensated by damages.
Tortfeasor	A person who has committed a tort.
Westlaw	An online legal resource.

Abbreviations and references

ADR	Alternative Dispute Resolution
BCP	Blackstone's Civil Practice
BSB	Bar Standards Board
CFA	Conditional Fee Agreement
CH	Chancery Division (of the High Court)
Ch, Chs	Chapter, chapters
CJEU	Court of Justice of the European Union (formerly European Court of Justice/ECJ)
CPR	Civil Procedure Rules
CRU	Compensation Recovery Unit
DBA	Damages Based Agreement
ECHR	European Court of Human Rights
GLO	Group Litigation Order
LAA	Legal Aid Agency (replacing Legal Services Commission)
LEI	Legal Expenses Insurance
MIB	Motor Insurance Bureau
MR	Master of the Rolls
para/s.	paragraph/s in CPR and BCP and WB etc
PD	Practice Direction
PI	Personal Injuries
PSLA	Pain, suffering, loss of amenity element of personal injuries damages
r/rr.	rule/s
RSC	Rules of Supreme Court (predecessor to CPR)
RTA	Road traffic accident
SI	Statutory Instrument
s/ss.	section/s
TCC	Technology and Construction Court
WB	The White Book (Civil Procedure)

Case References

AC	Appeal Court
All ER	All England Law Reports
BCC	British Company Cases
BLR	Business Law Reports
CostsLR	Costs Law Reports
CPLR	Civil Procedure Law Reports (Westlaw)
EWCA	Neutral case citation for Court of Appeal case
EWHC	Neutral case citation for High Court case
FSR	Fleet Street Reports
KB	Kings Bench (pre-1952 Law Report citation)
LS Med	Medical Law Reports
LSG	Law Society Gazette
NLJ	New Law Journal
PIQR	Personal Injuries Quantum Reports
QB	Queen's Bench Division of the High Court
QBD/KBD	Queen's Bench Division of the High Court, which became the King's Bench Division after the death of Queen Elizabeth II in 2022.
RPC	Reports of Patent, Design and Trade Mark cases
RTR	Road Traffic Reports
UKHL	Neutral case citation for House of Lords case
UKPC	Neutral case citation for Privy Council case
WLR	Weekly Law Reports
[ ]	Indicates para/section of judgment

Statute References

AJA 1999	Access to Justice Act 1999
CCA 2013	Crime & Courts Act 2013
CCA 1984	County Courts Act 1984
CEA 1972	Civil Evidence Act 1972
CEA 1995	Civil Evidence Act 1995
CJJA 1982	Civil Judgments and Jurisdiction Act 1982
FAA 1976	Fatal Accidents Act 1976
HRA 1998	Human Rights Act 1998
LA 1980	Limitation Act 1980
LASPO 2012	Legal Aid, Sentencing and Punishment of Offenders Act 2012
LDA 1986	Latent Damage Act 1986
MCA 2005	Mental Capacity Act 2005
SCA 1981	Senior Courts (formerly Supreme Court) Act 1981
SoGA 1979	Sale of Goods Act 1979

County Court Remedies Regulations 2014

County Court Jurisdiction Order 2014

Contents

BE CIVIL!

Introduction

This book sets out the nuts and bolts of the way in which disputes are resolved in the civil courts of England and Wales. It is written primarily for students training to be barristers, and who are preparing for the assessments centrally set by the Bar Standards Board (BSB). But it will also be of assistance to solicitors and other practitioners. It can be used both as an overview, as your course progresses, and a revision guide, as you prepare for your professional examinations or experience early practice. What it is not is a substitute for your own learning. This book can do a lot for you, but it cannot do everything.

So there are some ground rules. *The first is that you must learn your way around the accepted practitioner texts.* More specifically, if you are engaged in Bar training you must become intimately familiar with what is known in the trade (for obvious reasons if you are looking at a copy) as the 'White Book'.[1] This is because the BSB sets most[2] of its examination syllabus by reference to it, principally because it is still the favoured reference work of many judges. Your course should provide it to you, in hard copy as well as on-line. You must familiarise yourself with it, and know how to use it. But take it gradually - you do not need to go all the way on the first date!

And let's be honest - no one reads the White Book for pleasure. It is a reference work for practitioners who understand the subject and need to keep up-to-date. Its

1 There is also a 'Green Book' (yes, it is green). There was a time when this was used only for civil procedure in the County Court, and the White Book only for that in the High Court, but because the rules are largely the same for both jurisdictions, this division of labour no longer exists (although solicitors and County Court practitioners may be a little more apt to use the Green Book). Both books are set out in similar ways, so if you can use the one, you can use the other.

2 The other Bar exam syllabus source is Jackson's ADR Handbook ('Jackson'), which I will cite from time to time. But my book does not cover in detail ADR outside of the litigation context.

primary purpose is to inform, not teach. Updating is not always executed with learners in mind, and some of the commentary can be quite opaque and long-winded. So, you do not have to love the White Book, or even learn the essentials of the topics you are studying from it, but you do need to know *how to use it* and find answers by reference to it. The better you understand the subject matter, the easier this will become.

The White Book is updated annually (with supplements in between) and comes in two weighty volumes. The first contains the relevant rules and other primary source material, accompanied by explanatory notes as appropriate. This 'commentary' is, of course, a secondary source of information, although it will lead you to relevant case law. One of the advantages of this lay-out is that the primary and secondary source materials appear side-by-side, and are easily distinguished one from the other,[3] so it is easy to move from one to the other, although at times the volume of the commentary seems to swamp the (often much) shorter recital of the actual rules. Volume II contains procedural legislation (more primary source material), specialist information, and some useful general guidance in Sections 11 to 15. Both volumes have helpful calendars on the very back pages. Have a look inside the front cover to each volume for a guide to its contents. When I refer to the White Book in my footnotes, I will use the abbreviation 'WB'.

You may also have been given (or have access to) *Blackstone's Civil Practice* ('BCP'). It has performed a similar function to the White Book. The 2023 edition has dropped most of the primary source material (which can be found elsewhere) and is essentially only commentary, which is something of a cross between a textbook and reference work. It seeks to introduce and explain the rules and case law developments, rather than simply providing practitioner-focused notes, and for this reason can feel more accessible to students. BCP also covers some areas of interest which the White

3 For example, the rules are all in bold, and the font size is different when you move to the commentary.

Book does not (for example, guidance on drafting statements of case), includes useful tables and examples, and you may find its procedural checklists more user-friendly than the White Book's. Again, look at the contents summary for a quick guide to what is inside.

The hardback editions of both works contain print which is getting so vanishingly small (although I think the White Book wins the prize here) that at times you will wish you had a magnifying glass (I am sure I have seen 'terms and conditions' in a bigger font!). Similarly, both are printed on paper which you may fear will dissolve in your hands, but it won't. It is surprisingly resilient! You just need to be patient and in the right frame of mind when you use these books.

Because of the BSB's nearly complete focus on the White Book for its Bar examination syllabus, this is the practitioner work I too will almost always cite here.[4]

You may also have been provided with other textbooks and learning materials for your course, which you should use as required or needed. Make the most of what works best for you. Stuart Sime's *A Practical Approach to Civil Procedure* ('Sime')[5] is a comprehensive and knowledgeable work, regularly updated and with lots of useful examples of various documents and court forms. He rather charmingly manages to marry up many of his chapter numbers with the Parts of the CPR they are discussing. His is a popular textbook, to which I will refer from time to time, but remember that it is not a practitioner text, as such - do not confuse the two.[6]

The second ground rule is that you yourself must engage with the primary source material. It is nothing to be afraid of. The Civil Procedure Rules are generally written in clear, straightforward language (the same might not always be said of the practitioner commentary). There aren't so many statutes to deal with (unlike criminal procedure), and what there is you will know intimately by the completion of your course (for example, the Limitation Act 1980). At the end of the day, you

4 The 2023 edition of the White Book was released just as this book was going to print, and I have tried my best to ensure that all references to it are to the 2023 edition. References to Jackson are to the 3rd edition (2021). References to BCP are to the 2023 edition.

5 Oxford University Press, 2022, 25th edition.

6 Although Stuart Sime is one of the editors of BPC, so he can, and does, publish both! At times the two sound very similar on that account.

must not simply rely on what someone else tells you the law is - go that one step further and have a look yourself.

In particular, I want you to *read some cases.* By that I do not mean the headnotes or summaries or a précis or a case analysis (although read those too if you wish) - I mean *actual judgments given by actual judges!* This, of course, is another primary source of the law. For some reason students tend to come to their professional training courses, if not with an aversion to reading cases, then with a very strong desire to find a way to avoid doing so. I do not know whether this is because they were made to read *Re Diplock*[7] as a punishment or what, but such an attitude is short-sighted and utterly counter-productive. *There is no better way* to learn about the law than to see it in operation, and that is just what the cases do. The BSB examination syllabus requires students to know and be able to apply a handful of named cases. But beyond this, a well-written judgment, which sets out the facts and relevant law clearly, and explains why the case has been decided the way that it has, will teach you a whole lot more about the rules and principles involved than any secondary source - and it is usually much more interesting to read.[8]

To encourage you in this endeavour, at the end of most chapters I have suggested you read a judgment[9] in one or two cases. They are all accessible on-line.[10] It will not necessarily be the leading case in the subject, nor the most recent, nor the most talked-about[11] - I have tried to choose cases which are particularly well written, or fun to read, or even a bit bizarre, so that you can see how useful they are. All of them will tell you a lot about civil litigation and should show you that, contrary to the popular belief of many students, *cases are your friends.*

Finally, remember that even when major change is not being implemented, the civil procedure rules continue to evolve and it is important to know how to keep up to date (for example by keeping your eyes and ears open and always checking

7 A very old and very long case!

8 The WB commentary is often updated in such a piecemeal way as to make it less rather than more readable, at least until it is completely re-written. The current Editor-in-Chief is committed to making the commentary more 'digestible' and has succeeded to an extent: See Preface to WB 2022 Vol 1

9 And I mean the judgment - you can skip the preliminaries and go straight there. Some reports set out the legal argument as well, which can be interesting too but I want you to focus on what the judge says.

10 Through Westlaw or other online legal resource service, provided by most teaching institutions for their law students.

11 These will be referred to in the relevant chapters themselves, so feel free to read them too.

the most recent supplement to the practitioner texts). Your course tutors will give crucial guidance and any exam syllabus will test you on the state of play up to a given date.[12] The examinations may be your endgame, but don't forget that life, and the law, do not end there.

So if you do your part, I will do mine. This book, including footnotes, will boost your understanding of civil litigation and evidence, principally by showing you how the various pieces of the 'procedural puzzle' fit together. This is the key to understanding the subject. If you can see the big picture clearly, the smaller detail will more easily fall (and fit) into place.

You must never try to learn rules in an intellectual vacuum. Think of all the games you know. Football. Monopoly. Even Snakes and Ladders has rules. As a general proposition, such rules will always be based on consistency, predictability, fairness and the purpose of the game. Those governing civil litigation are not really very different. To help you understand these rules, I use a thematic approach, which might be a little different from the way in which your course (or even the BSB syllabus) is designed. I hope this will help reinforce what you have been learning and give you further insight into the subject. Similarly, this book may well cover areas which are not on your particular examination syllabus: but naturally, the focus throughout is on litigation. There are some study tips at the end of most chapters, and I close the book with a brief guide to your learning and revision in preparation for the Bar examinations (which would be worth reading at the outset), and the nature of the questions which you will encounter there.

The main rules of the civil litigation game are, of course, the Civil Procedure Rules ('CPR'), which originally came into being in 1999 - additional detail about implementation is sometimes set out in Practice Directions ('PD'), which immediately

12 Given that this book is not updated annually, it is particularly important to note any significant changes which might occur between editions.

follow the rules to which they relate. These embody what became known as the Woolf reforms, named for the judge whose task it was to devise what was then a completely new and modern system. The principal impetus behind the CPR was a desire to take the pace and direction of litigation out of the hands of the parties (for which read 'the lawyers') and place them firmly in the hands of the court. This was a radical departure at the time.[13] The idea was that litigation (where this is, as a last resort, necessary) should become:

- more efficient, both in terms of costs and time, because it proceeds more quickly and only real contests get to trial;
- more accessible, to the extent it is less legalistic and easier to understand;
- more proportionate, so that cases proceed in a manner and at a pace commensurate with their complexity;

and so …

- more *just* overall than was the case before the CPR.

The CPR transformed the procedural landscape (from which other areas of litigation, notably family and criminal law, have borrowed). But the costs of litigation still proved difficult to control (and at times eye-watering in amount) and so Lord Justice Jackson was asked to 'review' this aspect of the process and suggest changes which would better promote access to justice, but at proportionate cost. This he did, and the upshot is what are now known as the 'Jackson reforms', which made significant changes to several aspects of the rules - most of which were brought into effect in April 2013. In a nutshell, what these amendments did was to boost the importance of proportionality in the rules (both in spirit and in practice), especially where case

13 The vocabulary of litigation was also (and continues to be) updated. For example, 'plaintiffs' became 'claimants', 'claim forms' replaced 'writs' which started off proceedings in the High Court, and so on. So be prepared when reading older cases. For the sake of consistency, I shall use the modern vocabulary even when referring to events which occurred before the CPR.

and costs management is concerned, and place more emphasis on the importance of compliance with the rules and court orders, as well as encouraging parties to solve their difference without recourse to a courtroom. Amendments are regularly made to the CPR, so keep alert.

But to begin at the beginning: the aspirations of both the Woolf and Jackson reforms are manifested and expressed in the *'overriding objective'* of the CPR, which is to enable the court 'to deal with cases *justly and at proportionate cost*'. What this means in practical terms is explained in CPR, r 1.1(2). It is worth setting this out in full.

> 'Dealing with a case justly and at proportionate cost includes,[14] so far as is practicable -
> (a) ensuring the parties are on an equal footing;
> (b) saving expense;
> (c) dealing with the case in ways which are proportionate -
> (i) to the amount of money involved;
> (ii) to the importance of the case;
> (iii) to the complexity of the issues; and
> (iv) to the financial position of each party;
> (d) ensuring that the case is dealt with expeditiously and fairly;
> (e) allotting to it an appropriate share of the court's resources, while taking into account the need to allot resources to other cases; *and*
> (f) enforcing compliance with rules, practice directions and orders.

Tape a copy of CPR, r 1.1 to your fridge or bathroom mirror, because the overriding objective and its constituents are of primary importance to understanding civil

14 Note the use in the rule of the word 'includes'. The list is not exhaustive.

litigation. *They give the rules purpose and also dominate their content. It is essential always to bear them in mind.* Everyone, the parties as well as the court, by actively managing cases, is under a duty to further the overriding objective.[15] So CPR can also stand for -

> **C**ourt control and compliance with rules and court orders ...
> **P**roportionality ...
> **R**esolution by efficient and cost-effective means.

If you begin by eating, sleeping and dreaming about the overriding objective (within reason), then you will have made a good start.

Civil jurisdiction is exercised mainly[16] by the High Court, which has some regional outposts, but is based at the Royal Courts of Justice and the Rolls Building in London, and by the County Court (which is a single court, sitting at various locations in the country). The High Court, along with the Crown Court (a criminal court) and the Court of Appeal used to be known together as the Supreme Court of England and Wales, but when the House of Lords (the highest appellate court in the land) was re-branded 'The Supreme Court', this meant that suddenly there were too many chiefs. So the High Court, Crown Court and the Court of Appeal became the Senior Courts.[17]

The High Court, which deals with the more important and complex civil cases, is itself divided into three divisions:

(i) The Chancery Division ('ChD'), which specialises in land, trust, probate and such cases;
(ii) Family Division, where matrimonial and related cases are assigned;

15 CPR, r 1.2 - 1.4

16 Some civil jurisdiction is exercised by magistrates' courts (for example, on regulatory matters) and some specialist tribunals (for example, employment tribunals).

17 And the Supreme Court Act 1981, which is the primary source of their procedural powers, became the Senior Courts Act 1981.

(iii) The King's Bench Division ('KBD'), where most tort and contract cases appropriate for the High Court are started. This division was, of course, until Queen Elizabeth II's death in September 2022, known as the Queen's Bench Division (and after 70 years of habit you may find the odd slip of the tongue still being made!). The Administrative Court, which hears judicial review cases, is part of the KBD.

There are other specialist courts in the High Court, including the Commercial Court (part of the KBD), the Companies Court (part of the ChD) and the Technology and Construction Court ('TCC'),[18] but this book concentrates on mainstream litigation, which will tend to proceed either in the County Court (for the more straightforward and lower value cases) or the King's Bench Division of the High Court.

So off we go. But before we start, there is one *final ground rule*, and that is: *you should have fun* reading this book. And if, by the end of it, you have *understood* what you have read, both in principle and in application (as opposed to merely memorising or 'learning' it), and if you have also abided by my ground rules, then you should be well able to meet the challenge that awaits you.

18 These tend to have their own special way of doing things. For further information on these specialist courts, see BCP, para 2.16ff

revision tips

- You might find it useful to print off (or otherwise save in e-form) a 'clean' copy of *only* those Rules, PDs, statutory provisions, and WB commentary paragraphs as are included on your examination syllabus, both as you learn a topic but especially for revision purposes so you know by the end of the day that you have covered all the examinable material (no more and no less). For some topics, all that will be tested are rules and PD's. You can find these on: justice.gov.uk/courts/procedure-rules/civil/rules.
- You can do the same for the Jackson Handbook paras, although this is a much lighter/smaller/more accessible book than the White Book!

PART ONE

getting started

Litigation lite:
pre-action conduct

Courtroom drama may make good television, but by and large it is a costly, time-consuming and forbidding way to resolve disputes. Parties who can settle their differences on sensible and agreed terms will retain ownership of, and some faith in, the outcome. For that reason, it has always been a matter of common sense as well as good practice that litigation should be seen as a last and not a first resort.

An important innovation of the CPR was the introduction of a formalised system for the early exchange of information about legal disputes, which is intended to increase the opportunities for a fair settlement without proceedings ever having to be issued. This manifests itself in the various pre-action protocols, which exist for, and are tailored to the needs of certain specific types of disputes, including personal injuries claims ('PI Protocol').[1] In addition, the principles underpinning pre-action behaviour generally and the guidance to be followed in cases *not* covered by an existing protocol are set out in the generic Practice Direction: Pre-action Conduct ('Pre-action PD').[2]

Pre-action conduct tends to be the expertise of solicitors, who are there on the front line from the beginning. After all, the idea is to avoid, not incur legal costs! Nevertheless, it is important for barristers to have a clear grasp of the fundamentals because compliance (or lack of compliance) with proper pre-action behaviour can

1 For the complete list of protocols currently in force see WB, Vol 1, para C1-010

2 The protocols are stand-alone documents, and indeed many of them pre-date the Pre-action PD, but are now set out in the WB, Vol 1, as part of a unitary Section C: Pre-Action Conduct and Protocols.

have serious consequences down the line, especially where case management and costs orders are concerned.[3]

The various Protocols are set out in all practitioner texts. This chapter will focus (as the Bar examination syllabus does) on the PI Protocol and the Pre-action PD (which is only 17 paragraphs long).[4] BCP also includes a helpful one-page procedural checklist for both of these.[5] It is important to grasp the essential framework and function of appropriate pre-action conduct. The necessary detail will fall into place so long as you understand the two main objectives:

(1) to empower and equip the parties to resolve their dispute fairly and at proportionate cost without having to start proceedings if possible;

and

(2) in cases where going to court cannot be avoided, to ensure that the case proceeds as quickly and efficiently as possible when it gets there.[6]

The PI Protocol was one of the trailblazing protocols. Unless some other specialist protocol applies (for example, that governing clinical negligence), the PI Protocol was designed and is primarily intended for contested personal injury claims of between £10,000 and £25,000 in value (these are cases which, if litigated, would usually end up on the fast track), but it is *'equally appropriate'* for larger claims. It is important to note that 'the spirit, if not the letter', of the PI Protocol should still be followed for personal injury claims which could potentially be allocated to a higher value track.[7]

At the other end of the spectrum, there are a number of special protocols dealing with low value personal injury claims arising from road traffic or work accidents, where liability is admitted and/or where litigation costs are to be severely

3 See Pre-action PD, paras 13-16 and examples at WB, Vol 1, para C1A-006. And see Chs 13 (case management) and 18 (costs) below.

4 Always check your course syllabus for the current examinable material.

5 Procedural checklists 1 and 2

6 Pre-action PD, para 3 and PI Protocol, para 2.1

7 PI Protocol, para 1.1.2 and see WB para C2A-001. Track allocation is covered in Ch 8

8 See Sime, Ch 9 for more information. Unsurprisingly, the detail of these are not on the BSB syllabus, but the most recent addition is discussed briefly at Ch 8 because of its impact on the track allocation rules.

9 PI Protocol, para 1.2 and WB para C2A-002

10 The PI Protocol also makes special reference to the possibility that a claimant may wish to 'notify' the defendant of the claim before sending the more official letter of claim.

restricted. These basically provide a streamlined, fixed-price and highly prescriptive procedure to keep legal costs down and discourage 'ambulance chasing'.[8] Claims sometimes 'exit' one of these prescriptive protocols and when that happens, they should continue under the PI Protocol.[9]

The PI Protocol was something of a prototype for some of the other specialist protocols which came after, including the Pre-action PD itself. There are similarities and differences to note between the PI Protocol and the more generic Pre-action PD, but they both have four essential elements.

A. LETTER DETAILING THE NATURE OF THE CLAIM

The PI Protocol refers to this as a 'letter *of* claim', but it is also known (perhaps more descriptively) as a letter *before* claim. Previous communications between the parties may well have made clear the prospective claimant's concerns and expectations,[10] but it is sending this specific letter which starts off the formal pre-action process (in PI claims, two copies should be sent - one for the defendant and one for any insurer[11]). The letter before claim should be concise but include a clear summary of the facts and sufficient detail (what went wrong, what and/or how much the claimant wants from the defendant, on what basis the claim is made and so forth) so that the defendant can understand and investigate the issues raised without having to ask for more information.[12] The level of detail will vary depending on the type and value of the case. In personal injury cases, the nature and impact of the injuries complained of, including an indication of heads (and amounts) of damage claimed (if practicable) should be included.[13] In the spirit of openness, the letter before claim should include, and seek from the defendant, any relevant documents 'key' to any disputed issues,[14] and should be professional, not spiteful in tone. A fill-in-the-blanks example is appended to the PI Protocol.[15] Most solicitors would have something similar on their template database.

This might happen where the claimant is incurring significant expense and hopes for an early offer of an interim payment from the defendant or the defendant has no idea at all about the incident giving rise to the claim. Such a letter of notification should be responded to within 14 days of receipt, but does not start the protocol timetable running as such: PI Protocol, para 3

11 The defendant should send the copy to the insurer within 7 days. See PI Protocol, para 5.1. Although strictly speaking no-one is being sued yet, it is common to refer to the parties as 'claimant' and 'defendant' once the pre-action process, (which is now very much 'part of the architecture' of the litigation system) has got underway. See WB, Vol 1, para C1A-002

12 Pre-action PD, para 6(a) and PI Protocol, para 5.2

At one stage the Pre-action PD required that letters before claim sent to unrepresented defendants should refer explicitly to the practice direction, draw attention to the risks of non-compliance and warn that ignoring the letter may result in proceedings being issued and increase the defendant's liability to costs. Although no longer a specific requirement, this is probably still a good idea, especially as the PI Protocol makes clear that litigants in person are required (so far as practicable) to comply with it.[16]

B. RESPONSE AND IDENTIFICATION OF ISSUES

The PI Protocol has prescribed time limits for responding to the letter before claim. The defendant must 'reply' (essentially acknowledge receipt of the letter) within 21 calendar days of the date the letter was posted.[17] Thereafter, the defendant has a 'maximum of three months' from the date of acknowledgment to investigate and respond to the claim.[18]

The generic Pre-action PD needs to be more flexible. It thus simply requires the defendant to respond 'within a reasonable time', which will vary depending on the complexity of the allegations. It could be 14 days in a simple debt action, but no more than three months in a very complex contract case.[19] The Pre-action PD does not require (as the PI Protocol does) an acknowledgement of receipt of the letter prior to a considered response to the claim, but if that full response will take some time, it might be sensible to alert the claimant to this.

In responding, a defendant should confirm whether any aspect of the claim is accepted and where it is not, make clear what aspects of the claim are denied and on what factual or legal basis.[20] This would include making clear if contributory negligence is being alleged or the defendant intends to counterclaim. The PI Protocol specifically requires that where liability or causation is denied, the defendant should

13 PI Protocol, para 5.3

14 See WB, Vol 1, para C1A-005, Pre-action PD, para 6(c) and PI Protocol, para 7.1.1

15 Which must include additional information specific to the individual types of actions. See, e.g., PI Protocol, Annex B.

16 PI Protocol, para 1.7

17 PI Protocol, para 6.2. It is unusual to have to respond to anything from the 'date of posting', so I can see some over-eager examiner trying to catch you out on this. See generally the service rules discussed in Ch 4. If there is some obvious or immediate issue which needs addressing (e.g., a wrong defendant) this should be raised in this letter of reply.

18 These time periods are extended for defendants out of the jurisdiction. Once the defendant has responded and confirmed the identity of any insurer (and not before!),

set out their 'version of events' and enclose supportive documentary evidence.[21] This would be a sensible thing to do in any event; the idea is that each side understands the other's position and can make informed decisions about what to do next.[22]

In personal injuries actions, *both* sides should consider, as early as possible, whether the claimant requires *rehabilitation* treatment.[23] This should be an on-going process. With personal injuries cases, clearly the earlier rehabilitation is factored into the equation (and indeed begun), the better for everyone.

C. EARLY EXCHANGE AND CONSIDERATION OF RELEVANT EVIDENCE, INCLUDING EXPERT EVIDENCE

We have seen that relevant documents are exchanged almost from the outset, as they often accompany the letter before claim or the formal response. In personal injuries claims, different types of cases call for the disclosure of different kinds of documentary evidence.[24] For example, a current MOT certificate might be relevant to a serious collision claim, but not to a workplace accident case, where health and safety compliance documents would be more to the point.

The prompt exchange of what the Pre-action PD refers to as 'key' documents is intended to help clarify, if not resolve the matters in dispute. The hope is that very early on, both sides should be in a position to assess the strength (or weakness) of their respective cases - and proceed accordingly. Expert evidence can be a crucial component of this picture, although not every case needs expert evidence and the parties are reminded that expert evidence can only be relied upon at trial if the court gives permission.[25]

There are several ways in which expert evidence can be exchanged and/or presented, both before and after proceedings are issued in civil cases. The various protocols differ in their requirements, depending on what the nature of such cases usually requires. Reducing costs of resolving disputes is a stated aim of the

details of the claimant's date of birth and national insurance number should be supplied to the insurer. This makes it possible to identify which aspects of any damages payable are to be sent directly to the State, in effect as repayment of relevant benefits paid to the claimant: PI Protocol, paras 6.3 and 5.4

19 Pre-action PD, para 6(b)

20 Pre-action PD, para 6(b) and PI Protocol, para 6.5. If liability is admitted in a personal injury claim, the claimant must send the defendant any relevant medical reports and a Schedule of loss and damage, and not issue proceedings for 21 days (unless limitation is about to expire) so the parties can determine whether the quantum aspects of the claim are capable of being settled: PI Protocol, para 8.1.1/2

21 See PI Protocol, para 6.5. In

Pre-action PD.[26] Where expert evidence really is required, one important way expense is saved is by the use of a single expert on an issue (rather than one for each party), which can come about in a number of ways. Put generally (and assuming one claimant and one defendant), a single expert can be:

- jointly *agreed/selected* (where both sides participate in the selection of, but only one side pays for and gives instructions to the expert, calls the evidence and retains legal professional privilege over the evidence, unless and until it is disclosed to the other side);

or

- jointly *instructed* (where both parties instruct the expert who will send each side a copy of the report. Generally the costs of such reports are shared. This is the norm in fast track cases which *litigate*)[27];

or

- the claimant could get expert evidence independently and hope its use can be agreed by the other side and/or sanctioned by the court.

The PI Protocol shows something of a preference for the first of these where quantum (and some liability) evidence is concerned.[28] The Pre-action PD reminds parties that many disputes can be resolved *without* expert evidence, but if such is necessary (especially in a low value claim) the jointly *instructed* single expert is to be preferred.[29]

The third option tends to arise with *medical* evidence in personal injuries actions. The PI Protocol recognises that a patient may well seek, or have already obtained, a medical opinion from his or her own doctor in the process of formulating a cause of action. It therefore anticipates, indeed 'promotes'[30] the practice of a claimant, having obtained an informal medical report, disclosing this to the defendant, who

effect the defendant should disclose documents which a court would order to be disclosed either pre-action or during litigation. For disclosure rules see Ch 9

22 See Pre-action PD, para 6(b) and 3(a), (b)

23 See detail at PI Protocol, para 4. Any documents or reports in support of setting out a claimant's rehabilitation needs will not be used in any future litigation except by consent and is not treated as admissible expert evidence.

24 PI Protocol, para 7.1 and see examples at Annex C of the PI Protocol.

25 See Pre-action PD, para 7

26 See *ibid*, para 3(f)

27 See generally Ch 17. The terminology distinguishing joint selection from joint instruction can be confusing. 'Single joint expert' is not particularly descriptive but in the context of litigation refers to

can then query the report and/or agree it without the need for obtaining his own or selecting another expert. Such an expert would, again, remain the claimant's expert. This is the cheapest option, but is probably only viable when the medical evidence is relatively uncontroversial. Even at this stage, a defendant may not find the claimant's own doctor to be completely free of bias.

A claimant wanting to use his own (that is, the treating) doctor as the single expert *at trial*, however, may well find that the defendant and/or the court would consider this expert insufficiently objective for those purposes, resulting in the evidence being excluded. Care should thus be taken from the outset, since, even if the claimant wins, the costs for such (unusable) reports may not ultimately be recoverable.

D. TAKING STOCK AND THE IMPORTANCE OF ALTERNATIVE DISPUTE RESOLUTION

The protocols and PD all reinforce the message (which permeates the entire system) that litigation should always be seen as a last resort. They stress the importance of 'reality checks' and giving *continual* thought to whether there might be some other, alternative, way to resolve the dispute (known colloquially as 'ADR') - even after proceedings have started.[31] As Sir Rupert Jackson put it: 'The aim is that, in general, no case should come to trial without the parties undertaking some form of ADR to settle the case'.[32] In most cases 'the court will want to know what steps' the parties have taken to settle their differences[33] and it would certainly be frowned upon if proceedings were started while meaningful negotiations were on-going, unless there were good reasons. One very good reason for doing this would be where the limitation period in the cause of action is about to expire. Indeed, the fact that the parties are in the middle of pre-action steps is *not* a good reason for failing to issue proceedings within the limitation period. In this situation, what the claimant should

the expert whom both sides instruct: CPR, r 35.2(2). The pre-action protocols are a little less precise in their vocabulary although the Pre-action PD defines its terms: see para 7

28 Joint selection of an expert under the PI Protocol works like this: the claimant sends the defendant a list of experts, and is free to instruct any who are mutually acceptable to both parties. If the defendant objects to all the names listed, the parties can instruct experts of their choice but both will have to explain their choices and objections to the court, who might decide one or other has acted unreasonably. See PI Protocol, para 7.2-7.11. Whiplash evidence now involves dedicated rules, but these are not on the Bar examination syllabus.

29 Pre-action PD, para 7

30 *Ibid*, para 7.2

do (having explained the need to do so to the defendant) is issue proceedings and (if necessary) seek a stay (a sort of 'time out') from the court while the pre-action steps are completed.[34]

Alternatives to litigation as a means of resolving a dispute come in many shapes and sizes. The most common of course is *negotiation*, which is essentially the parties and/or their lawyers sorting things out between themselves. This is usually the cheapest, if not always most cheerful option. To really work, it requires negotiable points on both sides and a willingness to compromise. If assistance in negotiating a settlement is needed, then parties might consider *mediation*, which introduces a neutral third party (the mediator) to facilitate the negotiation process. This increases the costs, but a talented and experienced mediator (who has no skin in the game) can assist parties to reassess (and move away from) what may have become entrenched views and help them find a way forward both can live with. It is commonly used in family and commercial disputes. If a dispute largely turns on a specific issue requiring specialist expertise, the parties might well benefit from a form of ADR known as *early neutral evaluation* (ENE). This essentially involves the parties asking a neutral independent person with the relevant expertise to provide them with an opinion on the specific contentious point(s). The idea is that, with this information both parties can reassess the strength (or weakness) of their own case, which might then 'unlock' the impasse and allow the parties to more fruitfully engage in finding a negotiated settlement. What these three methods of ADR have in common is that they are 'non-adjudicative', that is to say they do not impose any outcome on the parties.

There are other forms of ADR (known as 'adjudicative') which do impose an outcome. The most well-known is *arbitration*, which is a contract-based route to an imposed resolution to a dispute. Like court hearings, arbitration is formal and expensive and leads to a binding decision, but unlike litigation it is a private

31 Pre-action PD, paras 8 and 9 and PI Protocol, para 9

32 Pre-action PD, para 10. The Jackson ADR Handbook referenced there now forms part of the Bar examination syllabus.

33 *Ibid*, para 11

34 A claimant has 4 months to serve a claim form, so this may provide enough time to complete any steps. If not, a claimant should issue and serve the claim form and seek a stay from the court. See WB para C1A-005 (para 3), and Jackson, para 8.24

process, tailoured to the needs of the particular dispute. Commercial contracts commonly include arbitration clauses. Where the outcome of a case will turn on an issue requiring expert knowledge, it is also possible for the parties to appoint an expert to make (or assist in the making of) a binding decision. This is known as *expert determination*. Again where parties use expert determination to resolve a dispute, they usually agree that the determination is final and binding on them.

There are other methods of ADR (and indeed variations on some of the methods discussed above), so parties have a lot of choice, depending on the circumstances and needs of the dispute. In the round, ADR should have lots of advantages (cheaper, quicker, more private) but each method will have its own benefits and drawbacks, which will dictate which form most suits the parties.[35]

It is important to note, however, that the duty on the parties is to give ADR (or the offer of ADR) serious *consideration*, not necessarily to initiate or engage in it. Parties cannot be compelled to use ADR to settle their dispute, and not all issues or cases are suited to it. But an unreasonable rejection of an offer to participate in ADR can result in a costs penalty. Moreover, silence in the face of an invitation to engage in ADR can itself be considered unreasonable, so reasons for refusing such an offer should always be given.[36]

To an extent, the Pre-action Practice Direction and protocols create a system of pre-litigation litigation, but without the wigs and gowns, expense and bad tempers that flare when the bureaucracy bears down and parties begin to lose control over the outcome. You might think of it as 'litigation-lite'. Certainly if, despite everything, proceedings are issued, the groundwork will have been laid for the expeditious conduct and progress of proceedings. Many of the steps of the litigation process, especially where disclosure, choice of expert and exchange of evidence is concerned, will often have already taken place.

35 See relevant paragraphs in Jackson's ADR Handbook included on the BSB's Bar examination syllabus.

36 Pre-action PD, paras 11 and 14(c) and see discussion in ***Helsey v Milton Keynes General NHS trust*** [2004] and EWCA Civ 576 in Jackson, paras 11.07-11.37

Compliance and proportionality

Finally, remember that compliance with proper pre-action conduct is a cornerstone of the CPR and is viewed very seriously. Non-compliance by one party is no excuse for non-compliance by another.[37] The court will not look kindly on someone who approaches the protocol in the wrong spirit (as a tactical device or to gain an unfair advantage)[38] and it has an armory of effective penalties for willful non-compliance.[39] In particular, it will not be pre-disposed to assist a party seeking a helpful direction or extension of time who has failed, in some fundamental and inexcusable way, to engage with the ethos of the PD and protocols. Adverse costs orders are another important sanction. Note that only 'reasonable and proportionate' steps should be taken during the pre-action phase. Disproportionate costs may not be recovered.[40]

However, the court will not concern itself with minor or technical infractions. The protocols are codes of best practice to be followed 'generally but not slavishly'. Sometimes, circumstances will justify a departure from the protocol, especially if mediation is in progress or being attempted. The court will expect 'substantive' compliance, but will always make allowances bearing in mind the 'need for proportionality, saving costs and the efficient progress' of the litigation. And any punishment for non-compliance should, of course, be in keeping with the overriding objective, but should also fit the crime.[41]

37 See Jackson, para 8.25

38 Pre-action PD, para 4, 13, 14

39 *Ibid*, para 15 and see WB, Vol 1, para C1A-006 and Jackson, para 11.05. For example, in ***King v Telegraph Group Ltd*** [2005] 1 WLR 2282, the court penalised the claimant by putting a cap on the costs which the defendant might have to pay because the letter before claim was written 'in a vituperative tone calculated to raise the temperature and inflate the parties' costs.'

40 Pre-action PD, para 5

41 *Ibid*, para 13 and ***ADD2 Research and Development Ltd v DSpace Digital Signal Processing and Control engineering GmbH*** [2020] EWHC 912 (Pat), cited at WB, para C1A-005

revision tips

- At the time of writing the BSB syllabus focuses squarely on the Personal Injuries Pre-action Protocol (but not the dedicated whiplash rules), as well as the generic Pre-action Conduct Practice Direction, which applies when no specific protocol does (e.g., many basic contract cases). Always double check your current exam syllabus to ensure that you have the required understanding of what is being tested. Solicitor's examinations, for example, may well test a wider knowledge of pre-action procedure and conduct.
- Remember the court cannot ultimately force a party to *engage* in ADR, because everyone is entitled to fair access to the courts (Art 6 ECHR), but it can penalise a party for not giving it serious *consideration*. Not every case is suitable for ADR (e.g., where the merits are obviously all on one side), and sometimes urgency or secrecy makes some recourse to the courts necessary initially, but litigation should always be viewed as a last (and not very pleasant) resort.

It is worth reading ...

Lightman J's judgment in ***Hurst v Leeming*** [2002] EWHC 1051 (Ch). This is something of a cautionary tale, I suppose, given that the claimant is a solicitor and the defendant, a barrister, but don't let that put you off. It is short and to the point and a precursor of sorts to the (more important) ***Halsey*** case. Too bad we could not have been there for the 'frank exchange of views' between the judge and the defendant on the merits of the latter's utterly hopeless case. Counselling might have been more appropriate than mediation!

Chapman v Tameside Hospital NHS Foundation Trust [2016] 6 WLUK 356. This is a pretty easy judgment to follow (although there are a couple of typos) and contains all sorts of procedural goodies, including a bit of back and forth with the judge making a summary assessment of costs. You might also want to come back to it when you've covered costs, but you get the message. The defendant did not follow the spirit or the letter of the pre-action protocol and quite literally paid the price.

CHAPTER 3

Proceedings and parties

If a dispute does not settle in the pre-action phase, then it will become necessary, if the case is to be pursued, to commence proceedings.[1] This raises questions of where and how to start an action, and against whom. This is also a convenient chapter for discussing special rules about joining parties to proceedings.

1. WHERE TO START?

An important effect of the CPR was to end, generally speaking, the distinction between High Court and County Court procedure. The latter had been created in the image of the former, and so, despite some significant differences, there were always many similarities.[2] The CPR instituted a unitary code of practice, which applies to all civil courts, although some specialist areas, such as family law (which has its own CPR-like procedure), are specifically excluded. Whether a party brings a civil action in the High Court or the County Court will depend both on rules about jurisdiction (which court is capable of dealing with the claim) and rules about commencement (where to start off a claim). It is important not to confuse the two concepts.

1 The focus here, as on the Bar Course, is on mainstream County Court and High Court actions.

2 County Court jurisdiction is entirely the creature of statute: The County Court Act 1984, as amended ('CCA 1984'). The High Court has a longer pedigree and an inherent jurisdiction, but the primary source of its powers is governed by the Senior Courts Act 1981 ('SCA 1981'). In 2014, what was once a localised County Court system became, like the High Court, one national court (sitting in various locations) and thus became a more equal, if still junior partner in dispensing civil justice.

There are certain types of cases where only the High Court has jurisdiction. These include libel, judicial review, certain specialist and human rights claims, and equity cases exceeding £350,000.[3] There are even a very few cases where only the County Court has jurisdiction, for example certain unlawful discrimination and lower value consumer credit claims.[4] But in the *general run* of contract and tort cases,[5] the High Court and County Court have *concurrent* jurisdiction, which is to say that either has the power to deal with such cases.

Although *jurisdiction* is concurrent in such cases, there are, nevertheless, important rules about *commencement* which dictate where certain actions must be started.[6] In particular:

(i) Cases seeking damages for *personal injuries and death*: if less than £50,000 such claims *must* be commenced in the County Court.[7] There are two points to note here:

   (a) The amount sought must be one which a claimant can 'reasonably expect' to recover. Many personal injury claims are, realistically, worth less than £50,000.

   (b) When calculating a claim for these purposes, certain features of a case (for example costs, interest, and aspects, such as a finding of contributory negligence, which might reduce how much the claimant will get in the end) are to be disregarded.[8]

(ii) Generally, as regards *all other types* of money claims: those which do not exceed £100,000 *must* be commenced in the County Court.[9]

Bear in mind that these are fundamentally rules about *commencement, not jurisdiction.* Their purpose is to force litigants to begin 'smaller' claims in the County Court, where

3 See BCP, para 11.2. In some very limited instances (e.g., libel) the parties can agree in writing to confer jurisdiction on the County Court: PD 7A, para 2.9

4 See BCP, para 11.3

5 CCA 1984, s 15

6 See CPR PD 7A, para 2. If an enactment requires a claim to be issued in a particular court, then the claim must be commenced there: PD 7A, para 2.3

7 CPR, PD 7A, para 2.2. The actual wording is 'proceedings which include a claim for damages for personal injuries', so the latter need not be the only claim being made for the rule to be applicable.

8 CPR PD 7A, para 2.2 and see list at CPR, r 16.3(6). Recoupment or recovery of benefit (referenced at r 16.3(6)(d)) refers to any amount the state may have to be 'repaid' out of the claimant's damages

they will most likely be tried (if the case gets that far). Note, too, the possible sanctions for non-compliance with these commencement rules. Deliberate or tactical flouting can result in the claim being struck out. More usually, there will be a penalty in costs, either at the end of the trial, assuming the case litigated all the way in the High Court when it should have been brought in the County Court[10] - or when the case is transferred from the High Court to the County Court where it belongs.[11]

Further, it is important to understand that it does *not* follow from these rules that claims crossing the relevant thresholds must be started in the High Court. Such actions *may* also be commenced in the County Court, and indeed should be if the claim is otherwise straightforward. But where the claimant has a choice and believes that the High Court could better deal with the claim because of its size, complexity or its public importance, then the case should be started there. Such considerations would also dictate where claims for remedies other than money (for example, an injunction) should most appropriately be commenced.[12]

And as you might expect, the court, for the same sorts of reasons, can transfer cases from the High Court to the County Court (and vice versa!) as part of its extensive case management powers, either on its own initiative or on application by any party. Thus, where appropriate, a high value claim may be transferred to the County Court even if properly started off in the High Court. Moreover, where it is likely a case may ultimately be tried is another factor which will influence where a claimant, with a choice, decides to start off his action.

for sums paid out to the claimant by way of relevant social security benefits.

9 CPR, PD 7A para 2.1

10 A winner's costs could be reduced by up to 25% to reflect the fact that the case could have litigated more cheaply in the County Court: SCA 1981, s 51(8),(9). This would now be an unlikely scenario given active case management by the courts.

11 This is the most typical outcome. See, e.g., ***Restick v Crickmore*** [1994] 1 WLR 420, CA

12 CPR, PD 7A para 2.4

2. HOW TO START?

Civil proceedings involving run of the mill factual disputes (for example, negligence, breach of contract, breach of trust) are started by means of the issue of a Part 7 claim form, which comes in one standard form (to be adapted as necessary).[13] The claim form is issued by the court at the request of the claimant, whether personally or, more usually, acting through his or her solicitor. The claim form is the lead document in what are known generically as statements of case. It is only valid for service on the defendant for 4 months; a failure to serve it in this time can cause real problems (as discussed in Chapter 12).

The claim form kicks off the proceedings, although it need not recite all the specifics of the case against the defendant. This is done in the particulars of claim, which should set out in detail the cause of action, the facts relied upon by the claimant and the remedy sought.[14] In personal injuries actions, a medical report and schedule of past and future loss and expense ought to accompany the particulars of claim.[15]

The particulars of claim itself can either be (a) *contained on* the claim form itself, (b) come as a separate document *with* (or 'attached' to) the claim form, or (c) follow *within 14 days* of service of the claim form (and in any event while the claim form is still valid for service). However they are served, the particulars of claim must be accompanied by a so-called 'response pack', for use by the defendant.[16]

Where practicable the particulars of claim should be set out on the claim form[17] (typically where it is short) or accompany the claim form. However, where neither is possible (for example because the draft is long or complicated or time is a factor), the claim form itself must give concise details of the nature of the claim, remedy sought and (where money is at stake) contain a statement of value (that is, less than £10,000; £10,000-£25,000; more than £25,000; or don't know). These values, as you can

13 Some specialist courts like the Commercial Court use their own special forms.
14 CPR, r 16.4
15 See CPR PD 16, para 4.1-4.3
16 CPR, r 7.4(1) and (2) and r 7.8
17 See example in Sime figure, 6.1

probably tell, are for track allocation purposes.[18] If commenced in the High Court, the claim form must state that the relevant threshold has been crossed, or that it is a specialist High Court case.[19]

If the particulars of claim are not actually contained on the claim form, the latter should state whether they are 'attached' to (that is, included with) the claim form or will follow later. If the claim form and particulars of claim are distinct documents, then both will need to be verified by a statement of truth.[20]

Not all disputes, of course, are fact-based. Those which are essentially about legal questions or issues are initiated by using a Part 8 claim form. Typically such actions ask the court to construe a document such as a Will or a deed. In such cases, the so-called 'weapons of litigation',[21] used in contentious disputes of fact, are not generally deployed. No particulars of claim or defences are exchanged. Written evidence is filed and served with the Part 8 claim form and with the defendant's acknowledgement of service. Any trial will essentially involve legal submissions and argument based on that evidence, rather than cross-examination of witnesses of fact.[22]

So, for example, *compare*:

- claim for breach of contract (Part 7) versus asking the court to answer the legal question, 'What does this contractual term mean?' (Part 8)
- claim for breach of trust (Part 7) versus asking the court to construe a Will so the trustees know to whom to give the estate's assets (Part 8)

Certain procedural applications also use Part 8 claim forms as required by relevant rules, statutes and practice directions.[23] Broadly speaking, where no claim has been brought, but an issue requires a judge's determination, then Part 8 is the usual

18 CPR, r 16.3(2). Relevant information regarding the value of the PSLA claim in personal injuries actions will also be required: r 16.3(2)

19 CPR, r 16.3(5)

20 PD 22, para 1.1. If the particulars of claim are served separately from the claim form, a copy (and certificate of service) of the particulars may need to be filed with the court. See r 7.4(3)

21 Especially orders for disclosure of documents, and testing of oral evidence at trial.

22 See generally CPR, r 8.1-8.6

23 For example, the approval of children's settlements per CPR, r 21.10(2). And see WB, Vol 1, para 8.0.1

mechanism to bring the matter to the court's attention. Part 8 is also used for specialist proceedings. If the court, either on application by the defendant or on its own initiative, feels that a Part 8 claim involves a substantial dispute of fact, it can order that it continue as a Part 7 claim and give directions as appropriate.[24]

The vast majority of claims, of course, are factually based: (in other words, Part 7 claims) and are for money - and most of these are started in the County Court. Money only claims in the County Court, whether for a specific sum or not (and unless special procedures apply), should be sent to the Money Claims Centre. Claimants should indicate on the form which hearing centre they would prefer to deal with their case, and this is where *undefended* cases will often be sent for matters (such as the amount or rate of payment) to be finalised.[25] *Defended* cases tend to go to the *defendant's* preferred or local hearing centre, if the defendant is an individual, but will usually not end up there until after directions questionnaires have been filed (or any stay of proceedings pending attempts to settle has expired), when it will be clearer what steps next need to be taken in the case.

Not surprisingly, claimants can now make money claims online these days, so long as certain basic conditions are met - for example, neither party must be a child or protected party[26] and the fixed amount claimed must be less than £100,000. The claim form is issued and the fees paid on-line using the court service portal at moneyclaim.gov.uk. The particulars of claim can be contained on the form if short enough (no more than 1080 characters) - otherwise they may be filed and served separately. Service is effected by the court and defendants can respond electronically, or by traditional (hard copy) methods if they prefer.[27]

24 See CPR, r 8.1(4)
25 See CPR, PD 7A, para 5
26 See discussion below.
27 See generally CPR, PD 7C

3. WHOM TO SUE: PARTIES AND JOINDER

A. PARTIES

When starting proceedings, one needs to make clear who is suing whom[28] - and for what. This is often fairly obvious, but thought must be given to the rules regarding special types of parties, as well as to what happens when there is more than one party on each side.

As regards the first of these, the following merit special mention, if only because they commonly feature in litigation and regularly crop up in examinations.

(i) Children

An individual attains full age at 18. Until then, a person is, legally speaking, considered to be 'acting under a disability'.[29] In the past (and in older cases) such people have been referred to variously as minors or infants, but the CPR now uses the more modern description 'child' or 'children'.

Children must sue and defend by their *'litigation friend'*, although the court may order that a child is able to conduct proceedings on his or her own behalf.[30] Remember that the child is the party (for example, claimant or defendant), but he or she litigates by *means of a* litigation friend. The title of proceedings brought by a child would reflect this in the following way:

MISS WENDY DARLING Claimant
(a child by MR GEORGE DARLING, her litigation friend)

A person assuming the role of a child's litigation friend usually does so voluntarily and so *without* the need for a court order. Typically such a person would be the child's parent or guardian, but in any case it must be someone with no conflicting interests,

28 This needs to be made clear on the statements of case. The 'full name' of individual parties must be given, including the title by which they are known: see CPR PD 16, para 2.4, which sets out how various types of parties are named in proceedings, which is usefully summarised in BCP at table 14.1 and in Sime at table 19.2. The title should set out the court and case number: PD 7A, para 4

29 As are persons lacking mental capacity to conduct proceedings, who are now called 'protected parties' in accordance with the Mental Capacity Act 2005 ('MCA 2005'). *See below*.

30 CPR, r 21.2(2) and (3). This is uncommon, but might be appropriate for an older child in certain circumstances.

who is capable of acting fairly and competently and who, *if the child is a claimant*, will undertake to pay any costs ordered against the child (subject to any right to be repaid from the assets of the child).[31] The litigation friend must file a certificate of suitability with the court.[32] In the rare instances where no appropriate person steps forward to be a child's litigation friend, the court can make an order that one is appointed.[33] Note that if a claim is made *against* a child, no pre-action applications can be made nor any litigation steps taken *beyond issuing and serving proceedings* until that child has a litigation friend (unless the application is for the appointment of a litigation friend or the court gives permission).[34] This is a sensible rule designed to ensure that child *defendants* are also properly protected and represented as early as possible.

It is important to note that settlements of monetary claims made by a child require special attention. There are two principal reasons for this: children need protection from exploitative, ill-advised or disadvantageous settlements, and defendants need to be confident that a settlement made in good faith is effectively final.[35] The court should always be asked to approve the proposed settlement as being in the child's best interests (in view of the strengths and weaknesses of the case, the risks of and expected delays in litigation and so forth). If it does so, the court will also give relevant directions to ensure the money is used and applied properly.[36]

The procedure for seeking court approval varies depending on whether the offer of settlement is made before or after proceedings have started. Thus -

(a) If *no action has yet been commenced* in respect of a child's claim, a Part 8 claim form is the mechanism used for seeking the court's approval for the settlement. It should set out the details of the claim, the terms of the proposed compromise, all advice received in respect of the settlement and so forth. As this case has not been in front of the court until now,

31 CPR, r 21.4(3) and see e.g., ***Nottingham County Council v Bottomley*** [2010] MedLR 407. Note that litigation friends to children who are defendants are not required to give this undertaking as to costs. This is because claimants choose to become claimants; defendants do not.

32 CPR, r 21.5, see example in Sime, Fig 19.1

33 CPR, r 21.6

34 CPR, r 21.3

35 See editorial introduction, at WB, para 21.10.1 for a neat description of the purpose of CPR, rr 21.10 and 21.11

36 CPR, r 21.11

the court will need to start from scratch, as it were, to determine whether the proposed settlement is in the child's best interest.[37]

(b) If *proceedings have been commenced*, no settlement is valid without court approval. As a Part 7 claim form will already have been issued, the application for approval is, like all interim applications, made under CPR, Part 23.[38]

In either event, the critical point is that whether proceedings have been started or not, until a proposed children's settlement is approved by the court, there is no binding agreement, and either party can resile from it.[39]

(ii) Persons suffering mental incapacity

Persons lacking the mental capacity[40] to conduct litigation are known as 'protected parties' and, like children, they are treated as persons 'acting under a disability'. Thus the rules discussed in (i) above also apply to such litigants,[41] with appropriate adaptations - for example, the protected person would not be described in the court documents as a child (unless he or she was also a child) and it will be clearer when a child, by virtue of his having reached 18, ceases to be acting under the (legal) disability of childhood. But otherwise, like children, protected persons are considered vulnerable and thus require a litigation friend to sue and be sued, and court approval should be sought for any settlement of claims made by such litigants. One important procedural difference to note, however, is that protected parties must *always* litigate by means of a litigation friend; the court has no power (as it has with children) to order otherwise.[42]

(iii) Partnerships and sole traders (trading in the jurisdiction)

A partnership is the association of two or more persons who co-own a business for

37 CPR, r 21.10(2). The court will need a lot of information before it to make such a determination, especially if the claim is for personal injuries. See list at CPR, r 21.10(3)

38 CPR, r 21.10(1): for interim applications see Ch 4

39 Court approval gives the defendant a valid discharge from liability. See e.g., *Drinkall v Whitwood* [2004] 1 WLR 462

40 There is a presumption of mental capacity, which is displaced when it is shown that an individual has an impairment which prevents them from making the necessary decisions. See formula set out in MCA 2005, s 3, at WB para 21.0.2

41 CPR, Part 21 is entitled 'Children and Protected Parties'.

42 Compare CPR r 21.2(1) with r 21.2(2) and (3). This distinction makes sense, since the older a child gets

profit. A partnership typically trades under a firm name. Generally speaking, it is 'one for all and all for one' in partnerships; in most situations each partner, who was a partner at the relevant time, will be bound by acts done on behalf of the firm and liable in respect of them.[43]

Unless it is inappropriate to do so, claims by or against a partnership must use the firm name under which the partnership carried on business at the time the cause of action arose.[44] There was a time when this was merely an alternative to suing in the name of all of the individual partners (which could be very tiresome if there were a lot of them), but it was so routinely preferred that it seemed sensible to make it the rule, rather than a matter of choice. As to when it might be 'inappropriate' to sue or be sued in the name of a firm, your guess is as good as mine - like the proverbial elephant, such a situation may be difficult to describe, but you will probably know it when you see it.

In the title to proceedings, the fact that a partnership is named is signified by putting the words 'a firm' in brackets after the name, as in *Warner v Penningtons (a firm)*.[45]

Compare the rules about naming partnerships in proceedings (whether as claimant or defendant) with those about suing a sole trader. The latter is merely an individual carrying on business whether in his own or another name. Such individuals, if not trading in their own name,[46] may be sued in their 'business name as if it were the name of a partnership'.[47] This option helps the claimant who might not know the name of the person behind the business name. Whether the individual's name is known or not, the title should reflect the status of sole trader. For example, a defendant might be described as 'BITS 'N' BOBS (a trading name)' or (if both names are known) 'MR ROBERT SMITH t/a BITS 'N' BOBS'. A sole trader who *brings* a claim presumably knows his own name, so it is unnecessary to give him this choice!

---

the more capable he or she might (not necessarily will) be to conduct litigation on their own, and the closer they get to the clear end of their legal disability. The same cannot be said for mental incapacity.

43 See generally Partnership Act 1890

44 Assuming it has a name. See PD 7A, para 7.3. Presumably if a partnership had no name (which would be rare) it could be sued in the name of the individual partners.

45 [2010] EWHC 1753 (Admin). See suggested reading in Ch 17

46 PD 7A, para 9.1. These provisions also require that the individual carries on business in the jurisdiction (even if that individual is not personally in the jurisdiction).

47 PD 7A, para 9.2

(iv) Companies

Limited companies registered under the Companies Act 2006 (or a predecessor) *must sue and be sued using the full, registered company name.*[48] If the company does not end its name with the traditional 'Ltd', 'plc', or 'LLP' (the hybrid 'limited liability partnership', which in the UK is more a corporate body than a partnership), then its name should be followed by an accurate description of how its liability is limited. Different companies can have similar sounding names, and it is important to be accurate.

The essential difference between a partnership and a limited company, technically speaking, is that the latter is a legal artifice, created so as to limit the liability of its owners.[49] It is capable of suing and being sued.[50] A partnership is, in a sense, the sum of its human parts, whereas a registered company has its own legal personality, which is distinct from the human individuals through which it must act. One sues in the name of a firm because it is convenient (and the rules say so); one sues in the name of a limited company because there is no alternative.

(v) Bankrupts, trusts and deceased persons

When a person becomes bankrupt, generally speaking, all causes of action (other than for personal injuries and defamation) vest in the 'trustee in bankruptcy', whose official name appears, for example, as 'the trustee of the estate of MR JUSTIN PENNY, a bankrupt'.[51] If a claimant becomes bankrupt in the course of proceedings, the trustee in bankruptcy may carry on with it, if the court agrees to substitute the name of the trustee for the bankrupt's name.[52] If, on the other hand, it is the defendant who goes bankrupt, this is obviously very bad news for the claimant. Whether the case proceeds really depends on the circumstances,[53] but if there is no money to be had from the defendant, a claimant would have to be very wary of throwing good money after bad.

48 Note that just because a business calls itself 'Jones and Co' does not make it a registered company. Full registered names are filed at Companies House. If the company is in liquidation, the words ('in liquidation') should indicate this.

49 This is why 'limited' is part of the description!

50 Compare this with the status of unincorporated associations which have no separate legal personality, some of which may nevertheless sue or be sued in their names (e.g., trades unions can, but most social and sports clubs cannot). Where a charity is unincorporated, proceedings may be brought against it by suing an officer of the charity 'on behalf of' the (named) charity. Alternatively, the trustees of the charity may be named as parties. See generally Sime, 19.32ff and 19.41/ BCP para 14.35-14.41

Claims involving trust property generally may be brought by or against the trustees (in that capacity) without joining the beneficiaries. Trustees should act jointly and so all should be named in any proceedings. Importantly, even though the beneficiaries are not named, any judgment or order made in the claim will bind them unless the court orders otherwise.[54]

If a party to litigation dies, this causes logistical problems, since the dead litigant no longer exists and needs to be replaced. Similarly where one was intending to sue someone, but that person dies before proceedings are issued - who does one sue now? In this context, it is important to remember that, generally speaking, most causes of action subsisting for or against an individual survive that person's death, and vest in his or her personal representatives. If the latter are known, then CPR r 19.2(4) can be used to substitute the one for the other in on-going proceedings. But it can take some time for personal representatives to be formally put in place. CPR, r 19.12, which can come across as rather impenetrable, is designed to deal with the various permutations which can arise when a party (or intended party) dies and there are (at that moment anyway) no personal representatives.[55]

A claim which *has been brought* will only cease upon the death of a claimant if the cause of action is personal to him or her, such as a libel action.[56] Otherwise the deceased's personal representatives can take over the claim. Similarly with the death of an existing defendant - the case can continue against the deceased's personal representatives.[57] If at the time of death, the deceased (whether a claimant or defendant) has no personal representatives, the court can order that the case proceed in the absence of anyone representing the deceased's estate (which would be rare) or appoint (for the time being, effectively) a person to 'represent the estate of the deceased'. The idea behind this power is to allow a case to continue without having to wait for a formal grant of probate or letters of administration, where this would be

---

51 The trustees in bankruptcy do not have to disclose their own names: Insolvency Act 1986, s 305(4)

52 This is a good example of the use of the court's powers under CPR, r 19.2(4) or, if limitation has expired, r 19.6(3)(c). *See below* at Ch.11

53 It could be 'stayed' or could continue on conditions. See Insolvency Act 1986, s 285

54 CPR, r 19.10. The rule, which refers to 'trustees, executives or administrators,' applies to trusts in various contexts.

55 'Personal representatives' is a generic description for those who have been appointed to deal with and distribute a deceased's estate. If there was a Will, it is the executor(s) who do this once probate has been granted; if there was no Will, letters of administration will appoint administrator(s).

56 Law Reform (Miscellaneous Provisions) Act 1934, s 1(1)

disproportionate or unnecessary in the circumstances.[58]

If a *claimant dies before* proceedings are issued, the claim must be brought by the deceased's personal representatives. Where a *potential defendant dies before* proceedings are issued, then:

(a) If probate or administration *has been* made, the claim must now be brought against the personal representatives of the deceased.[59]

(b) If probate or administration *has not been* made, then the claim must be brought against 'the estate of' the deceased *and* the claimant must also apply to the court for an order appointing a person to represent the estate.[60]

If a claim is brought against someone who, unbeknownst to the claimant, was in fact dead when proceedings were issued, then the case will be treated as having been brought against 'the estate of' the deceased, and an application will have to be made to the court for an order appointing a person to represent the estate (or substituting the personal representatives for the deceased if they are known).[61]

B. JOINDER OF PARTIES AND CAUSES OF ACTION

If you, as a claimant, want to sue one person or one firm or one company in respect of one cause of action, that is straightforward enough. But what if you have more than one person you want to sue ... or there is more than one of you who wants to sue ... or you have more than one cause of action in respect of which you want to sue? The CPR give claimants very wide latitude to combine - or 'join', as it is called - causes of action or parties into one claim form without seeking permission, although the court will always have the last case management word on which claims will be heard together and which will not.

57 Changing a dead party for a living one to whom the dead party's interest has passed is a good example of the use of CPR, r 19.2(4). Substitution of personal representatives in proceedings started before limitation expired does not infringe the limitation rules, whether the death occurred before or after limitation expired: ***Roberts v Gill & Co*** [2011] 1 AC, 240 at [103]. See generally Ch 10

58 See CPR, r 19.12(1)(a) and (b). Obviously the ideal appointment would be the person most likely to become the estate's formal representative. See WB para 19.12.1

59 CPR, r 19.12(2)(a). The capacity of the executor or administrator must be made clear in the description of the party on the claim form.

60 CPR, r 19.12(2)(b). Again, an appointment under r 19.12(2)(b)(ii) would only subsist for the duration of the

Common sense will very much dictate decisions on this, taking account of the overriding objective, especially the need to save expense and deal with cases expeditiously and fairly.

It is useful to distinguish between joining causes of action and joining parties to proceedings, particularly as these two things may be happening simultaneously! It also helps to differentiate between what claimants and defendants can do in this context.

(i) Joining causes of action

(a) By claimant

A claimant may use a single claim form to start *all* claims which can be 'conveniently disposed of' in the same proceedings.[62] No permission of the court is necessary. This is a nice, simple rule, ostensibly giving the claimant wide scope for making common sense decisions about combining causes of action in one claim form.[63] Although there need not be any special connection between the actions, the wording of the rule suggests some link between them: even if it might be 'convenient' to a claimant to use only one form to bring various, possibly disparate, claims against a single defendant, the wording of the rule refers to how convenient it would be to 'dispose' of the actions together. The court will focus on this too - ultimately it will be the one to decide, by reference to the overriding objective, whether to hear cases together or separately.[64]

(b) By defendant

A defendant with a claim against the claimant can raise it by way of a *counterclaim*. This is one type of 'additional claim' referred to in CPR Part 20, which is discussed in detail below. Thus, a defendant can join a cause of action to the one(s) brought

proceedings. But note that where someone has been appointed to represent the estate under CPR, r 19.12, then any decisions made in the claim will bind the estate. For this reason, before it makes any orders under r 19.12, the court may direct that notice be given to any other person with an interest in the claim, which it would do, for example, if it would assist in discovering the most appropriate person to be ordered to represent the estate. See r 19.12(4) and (5)

61 CPR, r 19.12(3). The same applies if the case is started against personal representatives when there had not yet been a formal grant.

62 CPR, r 7.3

63 A typical example might be where the claimant's case against the defendant can be formulated in alternative ways, for example negligence and occupier's liability.

against him by 'countering' with his own claim against the claimant, no matter what the cause of action or remedy sought. No permission is required if the counterclaim is against the claimant *alone* and is filed at the *same time as the defence*, at the end of which document it typically appears.[65] No connection between the claim and counterclaim is required, although if they are completely unrelated, the court may well separate the two in due course.

(ii) Joining parties

(a) By claimant

CPR, r 19.1 says that 'any number of claimants or defendants may be joined as parties to a claim'. In conjunction with CPR, r 7.3, referred to above, this gives a claimant the freedom, when starting all claims which can be 'conveniently disposed of' on the one claim form, to join as many parties to those claims as are relevant so to dispose of them. Again, as a matter of common sense, it follows that 'convenience' will require, when deciding whether to join various claimants or defendants to one or more causes of action, a degree of interrelationship between the parties and the claim(s). Suppose, for example, a claimant had building work done which went badly wrong, both because of poor workmanship on the part of the builders, but also because of the lack of supervision of those builders by the architects overseeing the project. It would make sense to sue both the builders and the architects in the one claim because, even though there are two separate contracts or causes of action, the allegation is that both parties, in their own ways, were responsible for the loss and damage.

CPR, r 7.3 and 19.1 are very open-ended and together give the claimant a great deal of latitude as regards joinder at this initial stage.[66]

In this context, however, it is important to remember that no-one can be forced to be a claimant.[67] This is a sensible proposition, since litigation always involves an

64 In its case management capacity. See generally CPR, r 3.1(2)

65 CPR, r 20.4(2). If permission is required because the defence has already been filed, the application should be supported by evidence as required by PD 20, para 2.1. If a claimant serves a reply and defence to a counterclaim, this too should normally form one document. In this sense it mirrors the defence and counterclaim. See PD 20, para 4

66 Here we are discussing the rules about deciding whose names to put on the claim form, and in respect of which claims, when *commencing* proceedings. Usually no permission of the court is needed. Adding parties at a *later stage* (after the claim form is served) always requires the permission of the court. See generally at Ch 11

67 See, e.g., CPR, r 19.4(4)

element of risk, and no-one should be compelled to litigate claims if they do not wish to (it is different for defendants, who have fewer options!). However, the rules say that where two or more persons are 'jointly entitled' to a remedy (e.g., as joint owners of a property), they *must* all be parties to the litigation, unless the court orders otherwise.[68] If everyone is willing, as they usually are, then they would all be co-claimants. But what if one of those jointly entitled with the others does not want to be a claimant? In that case, the solution (unless the court orders otherwise) is to make the unwilling person a defendant. This is no judgment on that unwilling person but merely a procedural device to comply with the requirement that the jointly entitled person must be made 'a party' - if that person is unwilling to be a claimant, then we can make them a defendant.[69]

(b) By defendant

Defendants can bring parties into proceedings in two ways. First, if a defendant is counterclaiming against the existing claimant, he can join another person to that counterclaim, but *only with the permission* of the court.[70] Secondly, defendants can bring in parties by way of third party proceedings, another form of 'additional claim', which is discussed below.

It is always important to remember that what the parties have joined together, perfectly appropriately under the rules, the court can always put asunder. The court, as part of its case management mandate, will be the ultimate arbiter of what is and is not 'convenient' to be disposed of together, and will *sever* causes of action and order separate trials whenever it believes that this will further the overriding objective. To a great extent, of course, both solicitors and barristers should anticipate when this might happen - and act accordingly.

68 CPR, r 19.3(1). This rule does not apply to probate proceedings.

69 CPR, r 19.3(2). Often when the unwilling person in this scenario discovers that they have to be involved in any event (as a 'defendant'), they are often persuaded to agree to be a co-claimant.

70 CPR, r 20.5. For example, suppose a claimant brings an action against a defendant for payment for (lawful) services rendered. This defendant is in fact owed money by the claimant and his brother (which may explain the lack of payment). The defendant will no doubt want to counterclaim in respect of the debt, but if he wants to claim from both debtors, he will need permission to 'join' the brother to the counterclaim against the existing claimant. It might be quite straightforward, but still requires permission (and some consequential

Equally, where two actions have been started separately, the court has the power to order that they be *consolidated* into one action, if this would further the overriding objective. In one sense consolidation is the mirror image of severance.[71] But do not confuse consolidation with 'representative' actions[72] or 'group litigation'.[73]

Finally, *once litigation has started*, the court has equally wide powers to put right situations where, say, a potential party was not joined at the outset or one party needs to be replaced by another. Thus the court has a wide discretion to add, substitute or indeed remove a party, after the action has started, where to do so is 'desirable' in order to 'resolve' the matters in dispute.[74] The court can do this on its own initiative or on application, but remember that the permission of the court is *always* required to add or substitute parties once the claim form has been served. Note too that this area of litigation also impinges on matters of limitation and amendment, discussed below.[75]

4. THIRD PARTY PROCEDURE AND OTHER ADDITIONAL CLAIMS

A. THIRD PARTY CLAIMS

A defendant in an action can make certain linked claims against a person *not yet* a party to the action brought against him. Such have historically been called third party claims and the party brought into the action, a 'third party'. The CPR lumps these sorts of claims in with counterclaims and claims between existing defendants, referring to them globally as 'Additional Claims'.[76] The expression 'third party', however, continues to be used in advocacy and in the title of proceedings to distinguish third party claims from the other types of additional claims (so that the various parties are described as *Claimant v Defendant v Third Party*[77]) and I will use it here.

Let's start with a given set of facts:

directions) because so far the brother has apparently had nothing to do with the litigation.

71 Both possibilities are on the long list of the court's case management powers at CPR, r 3.1(2) at (e),(g) and (i)

72 These are rare, but maybe a convenient way of litigating a dispute where otherwise a large number of persons would have to be named as parties (either as claimants or defendants), which would be inefficient both in terms of time and expense. If all the people represented have the same interest in the outcome, then one or more persons can bring (or be allowed to continue to pursue or defend) the action as representatives of all the others. See generally WB, para 19.8.3. At the time of writing these are not on the Bar exam syllabus.

73 This is rather like the class action in the USA. Group

C is injured in an accident while a passenger in D's car. C sues D. Let's call the driver of the other car involved in the accident T.

Before the introduction of the CPR, there were only four types of claim which a defendant could initiate against a third party, namely:

(i) A 'contribution' claim

This is a claim that the third party is wholly or partly to *blame* for the claimant's loss.[78] Thus, in our example, D could bring in T as a third party claiming that T (who, like D, owed C a duty of care) was wholly or partly to blame for the accident through his poor driving, and seek a 'contribution' from T (commensurate with his actual contribution to the accident) to anything that D may have to pay C in the main action. A contribution claim is thus *fault* based.

(ii) An 'indemnity' claim

This is a claim that the third party is under an *obligation* to the defendant, usually arising in contract, to reimburse the defendant for some or all of what the defendant may be ordered to pay to the claimant. Note that this is *not* an allegation that the third party shares responsibility for what happened to the claimant. It is a different animal from a contribution claim and the two should not be confused. A simple example of an indemnity claim involves insurance. Insurance companies rarely pay out on the whole of a claim, since there is usually an 'excess' to be paid by the policy holder or not all losses may be covered by the policy; so it is dangerous to think of an indemnity as being equivalent to a 100% contribution. But so-called indemnity clauses are common in building contracts, where a total indemnity will be more usual. It all depends on the extent of the obligation!

In our example, if the defendant's motor insurance company denied their

Litigation Orders (and an order of the court is required) are intended to assist in multi-party claims where there are common questions of law or fact, and other existing procedures are incapable of providing a cost-effective way of dealing with the action. They are typically used in cases where a large number of people have been affected (albeit in different ways) by a disaster of some kind, e.g., industrial accident, damaging side-effect of drugs. Funding of such cases can be very problematic. See generally CPR, PD 19B. At the time of writing, GLO's are not on the Bar exam syllabus.

74 CPR, r 19.2(2)-(4). This wide discretion does not apply where limitation in the action has expired: rr 19.2(1) and 19.6

75 See Chs 10 and 11

76 The title of CPR, Part 20 is

obligations to him under his policy, he could join the insurers as a third party and claim an indemnity from them. In effect, the defendant would be saying to the third party: *"Under our contract of insurance, you promised you would pay if I was found liable in these circumstances, so if I have to pay anything in damages to the claimant in respect of this accident, I want you to meet your obligation to indemnify me under my insurance policy"*.

It may be useful to think of these two third party claims as defensive in nature because they are dependent on the claimant succeeding against the defendant. If the main action settles, with the defendant agreeing to pay something to the claimant, there will still be a question of what, if anything, the third party should pay to the defendant.[79] *But if the defendant is not liable to pay anything to the claimant in the action, there is nothing to contribute to or in respect of which to indemnify.*

(iii) A claim for the defendant's own remedy

A defendant can also claim his own remedy or relief against a third party so long as it is the same or similar to that claimed by the claimant and it arises out of the same or similar facts. So, in our example, D, having sought a contribution from T, might also go on to say, in effect: *"... and by the way, T, while you were injuring C, you also injured me in that accident, and I want damages from you for my own injuries and losses caused by your negligent driving."*

This type of claim might usefully be thought of as offensive in nature because it is not dependent on the claimant's claim succeeding against the defendant. Although it commonly goes hand-in-hand with a contribution claim, regardless of what happens to the main action, this claim for the defendant's own remedy can continue in its own right, just as if it had been brought separately. *This is an important distinction, which is often tested in assessments.*

'Counterclaims and Other Additional Claims.' An early attempt to completely re-brand third party claims as 'Part 20 claims' led to confusing terminology and was soon abandoned. An 'additional claim' is defined at CPR r 20.2(2)(a) as being any claim other than a claim by the claimant against the defendant.

77 If a defendant needs to bring in more than one new party against whom he has *separate* claims (or if a third party wants to make an additional claim against a new party) these will be called 'Fourth Party', 'Fifth Party', and so on. If such a claim were to be made against two new parties jointly, they would be referred to as the 'First Named Third Party' and the 'Second Named Third Party': PD 20 para 7

78 A right to a contribution arises where liability is

(iv) A connected question of law or fact

Finally, there has traditionally been a 'safety net' category of third party claims, which caters for situations where there are questions or issues needing adjudication which are common to both the main claim *(C v D)* and the third party claim (*D v T*). Such may not fall neatly into categories (i) to (iii) above, but the original and third party claims are so inter-related that it would be silly not to deal with them together.

Suppose, for example, I was sued by someone who claims ownership of the White Book which I use and think is mine. The cause of action against me would be the tort of conversion or trespass to property (the civil law's answer to the theft, in effect). As the defendant, I could bring in the person who sold me the disputed White Book as a third party because if the claimant were to succeed against me, it would mean that I paid money for something that belongs to someone else. My cause of action against the third party would be breach of contract. The issue or question common to both claims is *"Who has good title?"* It obviously makes sense to deal with the two cases together, because the answer to that question will determine the outcome of both cases. Otherwise I might be running up and down the hallway giving evidence in two cases in different rooms with two different judges, but telling both courts the same thing. And what would happen if one judge decided the book was mine, but the other decided it wasn't?!

Indeed, the whole point of third party proceedings has always been to avoid this sort of multiplicity of action and the risk of different results where the logical connection between the main action and third party claim dictates that the two matters be heard together. This is still the purpose of Part 20 procedure under the CPR, which is stated as being to enable additional claims 'to be managed in the most *convenient and effective* manner'. But because Part 20 is not simply about third party claims, one gets to essentially the same destination as under the old rules, but by a slightly different route.

---

joint or 'joint and several', i.e.where two or more persons are liable to the same claimant for the 'same damage.' See the Civil Liability (Contribution) Act 1978, s 1(1) and BCP, para 29.2 or Sime at 20.07

79 See ***Stott v West Yorkshire Road Car Ltd*** [1972] 2 QB 651. There might even be an issue as to whether the settlement is legitimate. This is why, when people are insured against claims, the insurance company (who *will* be picking up the tab) wants to be in charge of how the case is handled, and in particular whether to settle or not (and for how much).

80 See CPR, r 20.2(b), which refers to such additional claims by a defendant against 'any person, whether or not already a party.' If not already a party, that person would become a third party (or a fourth party if the claim

The old rules had mandated that only claims (i)-(iv) mentioned above were capable of getting off the ground as third party claims. The CPR specifically refers only to (i) and (ii) (contribution and indemnity claims), but not to (iii) and (iv) as such. Instead it gives a defendant free rein to claim (in addition to a contribution or indemnity) 'some other remedy' from a third party.[80] It then leaves it to the court, in the exercise of its discretion and case management powers, *to detach*, as it were, such of those claims as it decides should not be heard together with the main action. CPR, r 20.9 specifically uses the language of the old rules in describing the 'matters to which the court should have regard' in deciding whether a third party claim should be 'dealt with separately' from the main claim, including (but not limited to) references to whether the defendant is seeking from the third party 'substantially the same remedy' as the claimant (as in (iii) above) or whether there is a 'question connected with the subject matter' of the main action to be determined (as in (iv) above).[81]

In effect, as regards third party claims (iii) and (iv) as described above, these are now simply factors which the court will look at when deciding whether or not to let the claim continue as a third party claim. Practitioners, of course, ought to be able to predict when a claim by a defendant would appropriately be tried with the main action as a third party claim, but ultimately it is for the court to decide this.[82] In the normal course of events, both common sense and the overriding objective would dictate that claims falling within categories (iii) and (iv) mentioned above ought to be heard together with the main action as third party claims.

is being made by a third party!). As we will *see below*, such claims can also be made by one defendant against another.

81 CPR, r 20.9(2). In addition it adds a more generic consideration, i.e. the degree of 'connection' between the main and third party claim, thus opening up possibilities and giving the court a bit more discretion than it had under the old rules.

82 We have noted that under CPR, r 19.2 the court may add, substitute etc a party to ongoing litigation if this would help determine all of the issues in dispute or there is some other relevant connection between the claim against the party to be added and the ongoing litigation. *Do not confuse this* with defendant's ability to make (or seek permission to make) third party claims under Part 20

Procedural points

When bringing in a third party, an 'additional claim' form (also sometimes referred to as a Part 20 claim form) must be issued and served on the third party within 14 days of issue. If the third party claim is issued *before or at the same time* as the defence is filed, *no permission* of the court is needed.[83] It is because the defence and the third party claim interact with one another[84] that the filing of the defence is the procedural point around which the question of permission turns. If, for example, a defence has already been filed and served, and the defendant later seeks to add a third party to the proceedings, the defence document which is in the hands of any existing party/ies will, in effect, need to be amended and re-served to incorporate the name and relevant act, obligation or omission of the third party.[85]

Where permission is required to bring an additional claim, then again the matters set out at CPR, r 20.9, referred to above, will be relevant to the court's decision. Such applications may be made *without notice* (unless the court directs otherwise) and must be supported by evidence. If permission is given, the court can make case management directions as necessary.[86]

You will remember that permission is always required when a defendant wishes to add another person as a defendant to a counterclaim (in addition to the claimant). If the court gives permission for this, you might wonder what this additional party is to be called. 'Co-defendant to the counterclaim' is a bit of a mouthful, so the best solution the CPR could come up with (somewhat confusingly) was to call such a party a 'third party' as well.[87]

Finally, with some specific (and fairly obvious exceptions), you will notice that much of third party procedure mimics that for the main action. Claim forms are issued, particulars are served, a response pack must accompany the additional claim form, defences are filed and so on. But be aware of the differences as well as the similarities.[88]

83 CPR, r 20.7(2) and 20.8(1)(b)

84 For example, the name of the third party will need to be added to the title of the proceedings/defence.

85 The same logic applies to defendants seeking to make a counterclaim against the claimant after the defence has been filed, which is why permission is then required: CPR, r 20.4(2)(b)

86 See CPR, r 20.8(3) and PD 20, especially paras 1-3

87 PD 20, para 5.3(c)

88 For example, default judgment under CPR, Part 12 applies to counterclaims but not to third party claims. See generally CPR, r 20.3

B. ADDITIONAL CLAIMS AGAINST CO-DEFENDANTS

So far, two types of 'additional claim' under Part 20 have been discussed: counterclaims and third party claims. There is one more that needs mentioning. Where two or more defendants have been sued by a claimant, so that they are *already parties* to the action, they can make the same sorts of claims against one another that a defendant can make when bringing in a third party (who until then is *not* a party to the action).[89]

If the claim is for a *contribution or indemnity*, then such a claim may be made by filing and serving a *notice*, rather than an additional claim form. As the protagonists are already parties to the litigation, a notice setting out the nature and grounds for the claim is thought to be cost effective and sufficient to put everyone in the picture. Such notices are sometimes referred to as 'contribution notices' (even when the claim is for an indemnity and not a contribution!). A defendant does not need permission to do this so long as (yes, you guessed it) he files and serves the notice with his defence.[90]

Note however, that if a co-defendant wants to make some *other* additional claim against a co-defendant, then a claim form will be required, and the provisions of CPR, r 20.7 will apply.

89 The same would apply to any existing party against whom an addition claim can be made, so if there are third and fourth etc parties involved, the possibilities multiply.

90 CPR, r 20.6(2). If a new co-defendant is added after a defendant has already filed his own defence, then he has 28 days from the filing of the new defendant's defence to file his notice seeking a contribution or indemnity against that new defendant.

revision tips

- If the main action folds or is otherwise unsuccessful, whether the third party proceedings can continue independently essentially depends on whether the third party claim is 'defensive' or not. If it is 'defensive', it will die a death with the main claim. To the extent that it is 'offensive' in nature, or there is otherwise a live issue to be determined between the parties, then the third party claim can carry on independently. With claims involving 'connected questions' of law or fact, you will need in each case to look at the relationship between the main action and third party claim - they often stand or fall together.
- Remember that, subject to the court's case management powers, *only claimants* decide who the defendants will be. And *only defendants* bring in third parties.
- *Note too that a claimant cannot obtain judgment against a third party. Claimants only recover from defendants.* If a claimant suspects that the third party might conceivably be the entire villain, then that claimant should turn the third party into a defendant!! He can do that by amendment (see Ch 11).

It is worth reading ...

The judgment of Denning MR in ***Stott v West Yorkshire Road Car Ltd*** [1971] 3 WLR 282. It is an old case and much has changed (including the value of money!). The relevant legislation has also changed, and so too some of the descriptions used (claimants were called plaintiffs and District Judges were called Registrars back then). But it is a good example of a straightforward third party scenario. Anyway, if you have never read a Denning judgment, then you are in for a treat. He loves setting the scene and wrote with admirable clarity.

It may also be worth dipping into PD 16 to remind yourself of matters which should be included (in various circumstances) on statements of case, some (but not all) of which I cover at various points in this book and much of which students on bar or solicitor training courses will have come across in drafting classes.

CHAPTER 4

Interim applications and service

1. MAKING INTERIM APPLICATIONS

Issue of the claim form begins the *interim* phase of the proceedings which, despite sounding rather temporary, in effect covers all the preparatory stage(s) through which a case passes until trial or settlement.[1] In most defended cases, directions will be given at the track allocation stage, which is usually some weeks after proceedings have been served. These deal with requirements common to almost every case as it litigates (such as disclosure of documents and the exchange of evidence). Somewhere along the line, however, a party may still need or want to ask the court to make some other (or different) order prior to the trial of the action. These are known as interim applications.

It has always been true that most cases are concluded pre-trial, which is why the focus of any civil litigation course (and indeed this book) is on what does (or does not) go on in this interim period between the initiation of a claim and (if the case does not settle) the trial of the substantive action. The CPR rules are designed to control this aspect of litigation to such an extent that even fewer cases reach trial than did before, and those which do, get there much more quickly.

CPR, r 25.1 sets out a rather long list of various interim orders and remedies which the courts are commonly asked to make. It is not an exhaustive list.[2] You will

1 If you think of litigation as a linear continuum, with commencement of proceedings at one end, and trial at the other, everything in between (and sometimes even pre-action) is the interim phase.

2 CPR, r 25.1(3). You do not need to know about all of the possibilities set out in this list. Just focus on those on your examination syllabus.

see that most are *not* linked to the final remedy sought by the claimant, but rather are geared to the conduct of the litigation.[3] In any event r 25.1(4) makes it very clear that an interim remedy may be granted whether or not there has been a claim for a final remedy of that same kind.

CPR Part 23 sets out the general rules about making interim applications, to which reference is often made in other parts of the rules.[4]

In High Court actions, *most* interim applications are made to a '*Master*', who is essentially a procedural judge, with no significant trial jurisdiction.[5] It is the High Court *judge* who tries cases there. In the County Court, the equivalent of a Master is a *District Judge*.[6] Unlike Masters, County Court District Judges have a certain amount of trial jurisdiction; they can try cases where the claim *does not exceed* £25,000.[7] Otherwise it is the Circuit Judge who tries cases in the County Court. Most interim applications can[8] and will be dealt with by Masters and District Judges, although most seeking an interim injunction will be heard by a trial level judge.[9]

Not surprisingly, the person making the application is called the 'applicant' and the person responding is called the 'respondent'. These terms might be used interchangeably with claimant and defendant, where the claimant is also the applicant. But sometimes the defendant in the main action is the one applying for the interim order, so you must be careful with your terminology - both in your own mind and for the benefit of the court.

Interim applications should be made as soon as it is necessary or desirable to do so, and as the rules allow. Most interim applications are made by filing an *application notice* with the court (usually, but not inevitably, the same court where the action was started), setting out what order is sought and why.[10] More importantly, it is an important general rule that the person(s) against whom the order is sought must be given *notice* of the application by being served with a copy of the application notice

3 But some of them are linked to the final remedy sought. For example, interim injunctions (r 25.1(a)) and interim payments (r 25.1(k)), which are discussed below at Ch 6

4 There is some repetition and overlap between some of Parts 25 and Part 23 insofar as this aspect of procedure is concerned.

5 'Master' is a curiously archaic judicial title, which the CPR did not modernise. But from December 2022, in a welcome change, Masters are now to be addressed in court not as 'Master' but as 'Judge'. Masters sit in London at the Royal Courts of Justice in London. Their out-of-London equivalent is the more prosaically titled High Court District Judge.

6 Out of London, it is not uncommon for one person to act as both a High Court and County Court District Judge, as the case arises.

(an 'inter partes' application, in the old jargon).[11] The reason for this is obvious - where the matter is of any importance, all interested parties are entitled to be alerted and have their say on the issue. This is just natural justice.

Notice should be given as soon as practicable after the application has been filed, and in any event (for most interim applications) at least *three clear days* before the date on which the matter is to be dealt with (a hearing date is commonly known as the 'return date' since this is when everyone returns to have the court deal with the application).[12] For telephone hearings, the period is extended to *five clear days* (presumably because it takes a bit more organising to ensure everyone will be technically available to be on the call).[13] Some applications, which are thought to be more complex, involve longer notice periods (for example, summary judgment and interim payment applications). These are discussed in more detail in later chapters.

Some interim applications will be heard (and an order granted) without the other side having been given notice ('ex parte', in the old jargon), but this is very much *the exception* and *not* the rule.[14] Sometimes this happens out of necessity, for example when there is no defendant on record or the matter does not essentially concern the defendant at that time.[15] Otherwise, the main justifications for applying without notice are because *secrecy* is vital or, more commonly, where the matter is so exceptionally *urgent* that there is *no time* to give formal notice.[16] Indeed, an application and order could even be made pre-action (before a claim has been issued) if the matter was so urgent that the circumstances warranted it.[17]

It is important to note that (except where secrecy is required) where the matter is so urgent that there is not time to give the other side proper notice, it is still incumbent on the applicant to give such notice at he can, either by giving 'short' notice (serving the notice late) or by giving informal notice (telling or phoning the other party).[18] With some notice, the respondent may even still be able to attend the

District judges are also now to be addressed in court as 'Judge': see judiciary.uk/guidance-and-resources/what-do-i-call-a-judge

7 In other words, small claims or fast track cases. District judges can also hear certain specialist cases, e.g., some landlord and tenant claims. See CPR, PD2B, para 11

8 See generally CPR, PD2B and PD25A, para 1

9 Interim injunctions are discussed in Ch 6

10 CPR, r 23.2(1) and 23.3. It is worth looking at Form N244 as to what should be included on the notice (as required by CPR, r 23.6 and PD23A, para 2)

11 CPR, r 23.4(1)

12 CPR, r 23.7(1) and PD 23A, para 4.1. As to the meaning of 'clear days' see CPR, r 2.8, which includes examples.

13 CPR, PD 23A, para 4.1

14 If permitted by a rule, practice direction or court order an application may be made

hearing. An applicant who fails to give proper notice will have to explain to the court both why this was so *and* what steps were taken to give informal notice. The court takes this very seriously - in this day and age of mobile devices and instant communication, judges take the view that there is unlikely ever to be a practical reason why an applicant could not, at the very least, give informal notice to the other side.[19]

Equally important is the applicant's duty to 'make full and frank disclosure' when applying without notice for an interim order. This means that the applicant *must* disclose to the court all material facts or law, including those adverse to the application. In effect, the applicant is obliged to *compensate* for the other side's absence, not *exploit* it. It is a crucial and continuing duty in any application made without notice, and sanctions for a failure to comply can be severe, including the discharge of any order which was made, however meritorious the application might otherwise have been.[20]

Note that this duty of full and frank disclosure also applies if the respondent attends the hearing after short notice (even if legally represented) since it is assumed that less than the required notice may well not give sufficient time to prepare properly, although this does not mean that the applicant must duplicate any points which the respondent has been able to make clearly, and it is open to the court to treat the notice given as sufficient in the circumstances and conduct the hearing accordingly.[21]

Most interim applications must be supported by *written evidence*, which should be filed and served with the application notice.[22] The rules allow such evidence to be provided in several ways.[23] It can either be:

(i) included on the notice of application itself, if it contains a statement of truth;
(ii) found in any statement of case served in the proceedings, which should already contain a statement of truth;

without notice: CPR, r 23.4(2). In short, there has to be a very good reason to depart from the general principle of giving notice: see first sentence of WB, para 25.3.5

15 For example, an application to extend the validity of the claim form (see Ch 12). These are made by means of filing an application notice, but without serving a copy to the other side. Do not get confused by the jargon: an application made *by* notice refers to the document used to make the application whereas an application made *on* or *with* notice refers to letting the other side know about the application by serving a copy of the application notice on them.

16 CPR, PD 23A, para 3 and para 4.2. Other more generic possibilities are set out in para 3, but either they do not often arise (e.g., where it 'best furthers the overriding objective' not to give notice)

(iii) contained in a witness statement (that is, statement of evidence of a relevant person), including a statement of truth, to be served with the notice of application;

or

(iv) contained in an affidavit (that is, a sworn statement) to be served with the notice of application.

Because affidavits cost rather more than witness statements (due to the costs of being 'sworn'), a litigant will not generally recover the costs of making an affidavit. The 'statement of truth' now performs much the same function as swearing to the truth of an affidavit, but more cheaply. Thus, most interim applications are supported by witness statements, except where affidavits are specifically required by the rules.[24] If applying without notice, it is in the supporting written evidence that the reasons for this should be set out.

Unless the application is a very simple one, a draft of the order sought should also be included. If long and/or complex, the draft should be provided electronically as well as in hard copy (which makes it easier for the court to adapt it to its own liking!).[25]

The rules seek to encourage dealing with interim applications 'on the papers', that is to say without the need for parties to attend a (costly) hearing. This furthers the overriding objective by saving time and money. Thus, the court may determine an interim application without a hearing either if the parties agree or the court considers that a hearing would be unnecessary.[26] A party who is not happy about the latter may apply to have that decision set aside, varied or stayed.[27]

The court's case management powers are extensive. They include keeping the scope of what goes on during an interim hearing within proportionate bounds, agreeing to virtual hearings,[28] conducting short hearings by telephone,[29] and making

or the party already knows or does not care much about the application (e.g., where 'all the parties consent'). Secrecy arises with special kinds of injunctive orders (e.g., search orders) discussed in Ch 7. CPR r 25.3 refers to the court being able to grant an interim remedy if there are 'good reasons' for not giving notice, but presumably if the reason is not covered by the list in PD 23A it is not likely to be a good one.

17 CPR, r 25.2. If an order is made pre-action, the court will (if granting the order) require the applicant to commence proceedings.

18 CPR, PD 23A, para 4.2

19 CPR, r 25.3(3) and see observations at WB para 25.3.2

20 See WB, para 25.3.5 and 25.3.6, which is focused on interim injunctions (see Ch 6), but makes clear the importance of full and frank

orders when no-one has even asked for one.[30] Again, in this last situation, an unhappy party can trigger a hearing by applying to set aside the order, but may have to pay for the costs of doing so.

If a hearing is listed and either the applicant or respondent fails to attend, the court can still proceed without the absent party. If an order is made, the court also has the power to 're-list' the application so that it can reconsider the matter (with both parties there ideally!).[31]

If an order is made by the court on a without notice application, a copy of that order must be served on the other party, along with a copy of the application notice itself and evidence in support. More importantly, the order must inform the respondent of his right to apply (within seven days) to have the order set aside or varied, which is only fair since this may be the first he has heard of it![32]

If a completely unmeritorious application is dismissed by the court, it must record this fact and go on to *consider* whether it should make a civil restraint order.[33]

There are the obvious exceptions, but generally speaking hearings on interim applications are heard in public. Most are pretty mundane, however, and would not be apt to draw in the crowds. The more complicated the matter, the more apt one would be to instruct counsel, file and exchange chronologies, skeleton arguments and so forth[34]. Disputes of *fact* on interim applications[35] raise the question of how the court should deal with these, given the lack of oral testimony and opportunity to test the evidence, which after all is just set out on pieces of paper.[36] It is generally thought that such questions are decided by asking whether the applicant has established a 'good arguable case' on the matter - a middling sort of standard, which in essence amounts to saying that the court should be as satisfied as it can be in the circumstances, given the limitations inherent in hearings based on written evidence but at the same time wanting to avoid mini-trials of matters raised on interim applications. Where

disclosure in *without notice* applications.

21 See WB, para 25.3.5.1

22 CPR, r 23.7(2)/(3) and see PD 23A, para 9

23 See WB, para 25.3.3

24 For example, when applying for freezing and search orders - see Ch 7. But watch out when reading older cases. At one time all interim applications were supported by affidavit evidence.

25 CPR, PD 23A, para 12.1

26 CPR, r 23.8

27 CPR, r 3.3(5)(a)

28 See CPR, PD 23A, para 7

29 See CPR, PD 23A, para 6.2

30 This is known as the court 'acting on its own initiative', and is an important part of the court's ability to control proceedings before it. See CPR, r 3.3

31 CPR, r 23.11

32 CPR, r 23.9/10

33 CPR, r 23.12. Civil restraint orders are usually reserved for vexatious litigants who persist in bringing actions

interim applications are dealt with in less than a day (as most are), the court will normally make a summary assessment of costs immediately after making its order. To assist the judge in doing this, parties are required to file and serve on each other a statement of their costs for the hearing not less than 24 hours before it takes place. [37]

2. SERVICE IN THE JURISDICTION[38]

A. SERVICE OF THE CLAIM FORM

Service of the claim form is the next procedural step after issuing proceedings. A claim form issued for service inside the jurisdiction remains valid for four months.[39] It must be served during this time, unless an extension (sometimes called a renewal) is granted.[40]

The service rules include considerations of *how, where* and *by whom* service is to be effected. The first thing to remember is that generally, any document prepared or issued *by the court*, which includes the claim form, will be served by the court. This is the most stress-free form of service. But there are times when this does not happen. One is the rare occasion when the rules or the court require that the defendant be served personally.[41] Another, much more commonly invoked insofar as service of the claim form is concerned, is where a claimant notifies the court of a desire to serve the claim form himself.[42] In such circumstances, CPR, r 6.3 provides a variety of permissible methods:

(i) Personal service

This is effected by leaving the claim form with the relevant *person*.

(ii) First class post, DX or other 'next business day' delivery service

The claim form may be sent to an appropriate address by first class post or other

or applications without any merit. They effectively bar the person from making applications or bringing proceedings without court permission.

34 Skeleton arguments are usually required for applications before Circuit and High Court Judges, unless the matter is very simple or time is short. These provide a concise summary of the party's submissions and give the opportunity for pre-reading. They are in their own way a piece of written advocacy, but they are not a substitute for oral argument.

35 Do not confuse a factual dispute in this context with the merits of the substantive action. As we shall see, how strong the latter must be shown to be at the interim stage varies depending on the nature of the interim application.

36 It is always worth remembering that it is not

method of mail transmission (it need not be the Royal Mail), which provides for delivery on the *next business day*. This includes using the document exchange (DX) system, which is commonly used to transport documents between business offices, and also normally arrives the next business day. DX is permissible only if the defendant has provided a DX number for service or the relevant information otherwise appears on correspondence and no unwillingness to be served in this way has been stated.[43]

(iii) Leaving the claim form at an address

The claim form may be left at the place for service (e.g., delivered through the letter box at the appropriate address).

(iv) Fax or email

Before service is permitted by fax or other electronic means, the party who is to be served, or his legal representative, must have '*indicated in writing*' a willingness to be served in this way and provided a fax-number, email address or other electronic identification as appropriate. This willingness must be *explicitly* given by an *unrepresented party*. But where service is to be made on the party's *solicitors*, the willingness to be served by *fax* is sufficiently indicated by including the relevant fax number on the solicitor's writing paper (it is sort of assumed that solicitors' offices are geared up for and expected to look at their incoming faxes). However, a litigant's solicitor's willingness to be served by *e-mail* must, *in addition*, actually state that the e-mail address provided on the writing paper may be used for this purpose (this is because e-mail is rather more personal than the office fax machine). A party seeking to serve by electronic means should in any case first ask whether the recipient has any limitations on such transmission (for example, on the size of an attachment to an e-mail).[44]

---

the advocate's role to give evidence. His or her job is to get the court to view the available evidence in a particular way.

37 See Ch 18 for costs.

38 In previous editions, service of proceedings out of the jurisdiction was covered in outline. This has been removed from the current edition in view of the evolving state of affairs post-Brexit and the fact that the topic is not now on the Bar Examination syllabus.

39 CPR, r 7.5(1)

40 This is an important topic, dealt with in Ch 12

41 CPR, r 6.5(1). An example is a claim form relating to committal proceedings.

42 See CPR, r 6.4. If the court is to serve the claim form, the claimant must provide additional copies for every defendant to be served.

43 CPR, PD 6A, para 2

Where to serve

All of these service options require the claimant to do something (i.e. take the 'required step'), as set out in CPR, r 7.5(1). For example, if serving by first class post, the step required is the *act* of posting the claim form (putting it in the post box, for example). Having chosen a method, it is important that service is made to the *right person or place.* One *very important rule* is that where the defendant's *solicitor* is *authorised* to accept service on the defendant's behalf and the claimant has been given written notice of this (by the defendant or the solicitors) and supplied with the solicitor's business address, then the claim form *must* be served at that address.[45]

Otherwise, service may be effected at an address where the defendant lives or carries on business and which the defendant has given for the purpose of service.[46] Failing that, where a defendant has provided no such address, the claim form may be served at the defendant's '*usual or last known address*.' The defendant's *last known* address can be used, even if the claimant knows the defendant no longer lives there, so long as the claimant took reasonable steps to discover a current address, and was unable to do so (or to serve in some other way).[47]

When did service occur?

Once service has been effected on the right person/place and in an appropriate way, the next question is when service of the claim form will have occurred. Previously this was calculated on a rather piecemeal basis, depending on the service option selected. Now it is dealt with by a strict, but generic and uniform rule, which says that service of the claim form takes effect on the 'second business day' after completion of the required step.[48] This even applies to personal service, which in real time is instantaneous! So regardless of what step is required/taken, and regardless of when or indeed whether the claim form might actually have arrived at its destination,

44 *Ibid*, para 4
45 CPR, r 6.7(1). Note the word 'must' - this is not optional in these circumstances.
46 CPR, r 6.8
47 CPR, r 6.9 and *Mersey Property Holdings v Kilgour* [2004] EWHC 1638 (TCC). As to alternative service, read on.
48 CPR, r 6.14.

service of the claim form is *deemed* to have taken place on the second *business* day after the relevant step was taken. Watch out for holidays and weekends - they are not business days![49]

The effect of deeming provisions

It is important to understand the effect of such deeming provisions. Where they apply, service takes effect on the deemed date *and no other.* They create, in effect, an irrebuttable presumption of law[50] and no evidence is admissible to prove that the claim form arrived on some other date, or even not at all. This may sound severe, but the deeming provisions inject some predictability into this aspect of litigation, and only very rarely does the outcome of a case turn on service of the claim form.[51]

The advantage of letting the court serve the claim form is obvious - the claimant does not need to provide a certificate of service or otherwise prove, or worry about being responsible for service, as is the case when a DIY option is chosen.[52] The latter, however, can give the litigant some control over when and how service is effected and for that reason some claimants prefer to do it themselves.

B. SPECIAL CASES

You want to be aware of special rules about serving claim forms on particular types of parties[53] and what to do if none of the sanctioned methods of serving the claim form seem to work. Pay attention, in particular, to the following:

Serving children and protected parties

Where the defendant is a child (but not also a protected party), the claim form must be served on one the child's parents or guardians or (if no such person exists) on an adult

49 CPR, r 6.2(b). So, if the relevant step is taken on a Friday, service is deemed to occur on the following Tuesday (assuming Monday is not a Bank Holiday).

50 See generally below at Ch 17

51 But where limitation is at issue, whether the claim form was served in time can suddenly become very important. See generally Chs 10 and 12

52 If the claimant serves the claim form, a certificate of service must be filed within 21 days, unless all the defendants have acknowledged service by then: CPR, r 6.17(2)

53 As discussed in Ch 3

with whom the child resides or in whose care the child is. Analogous provisions apply to protected parties.[54] These are the sorts of persons who would typically assume the role of 'litigation friend' once proceedings are brought. Once the litigation friend is identified, then any document which would otherwise be served on the child or protected party must be served on the litigation friend.[55]

Serving partnerships

As discussed in Chapter 3, partnerships should generally be sued in the name of the firm. Special refinements to the service rules thus become necessary, because a firm is not a single entity and so poses some service quandaries. A firm is not a person, so how, for example, would you serve a firm 'personally'?

If the court effects service on a partnership, it will normally do so by first class post to the firm's address (or other address given for service). For a claimant wishing to serve the claim form himself the possibilities are as follows:

(a) If the claimant has been notified of *solicitors who are authorised* to accept service on the firm's behalf, the claimant must serve the defendant firm at this address. This can be effected by whatever method is appropriate.

Otherwise:

(b) The partnership can be served '*personally*' by leaving the claim form with any of the partners or leaving it with a person who, at the time of service, has the control or management of the partnership business at its principal place of business,

or

(c) Service (other than personal service) can be effected by sending the claim form to the address provided by the defendant firm or, if no such

54 CPR, r 6.13(1) and (2)
55 CPR, r 6.25(2)

address was provided, to the usual or last known residential address of a partner or to the *principal or last known place of business* of the firm.[56]

Sole trader

Note that a proprietor of a business, even if a sole trader (and not a firm) can be served either at his own usual *or* last known residence or the address of his principal or last known place of business.[57]

Serving claim forms on companies

Companies dance to a slightly different drummer. They can be served either under the CPR rules, or they can be served at their registered offices under the Companies Act 2006. Assuming no address for service is given or mandated, the CPR allows for service at the 'principal office' or any place of business of the company which has 'a real connection with the claim' or (if this is an option) personal service on a 'senior person' in the company. This sometimes provides rather more latitude for place of service, than simply the registered office. It is worth noting that it would seem that if serving the claim form under the Companies Act 2006, the CPR deeming rules would not apply.[58]

Contractually agreed service

The rules also allow for a contractually agreed method of service of the claim form. If the action is based solely on a contract, one of whose terms specifies the manner of and place for serving a claim form (should the need arise), then the claim form may be served in this way.[59] This option, when applicable, essentially gives the claimant another choice when serving the claim form.

56 CPR, r 6.5(3)(c), r 6.8, r 6.9(2)
57 CPR, r 6.9(2)
58 See CPR, r 6.5(3)(b) and 6.9(2), and see WB, Vol 1, para 6.14.4. Limited Liability Partnerships are treated similarly to Companies.

Alternative service

In many ways a claimant is spoiled for choice when serving the claim form; it is not often that at least one of the available methods of service will not work.[60] But it does happen sometimes, especially if a prospective defendant is elusive or actively evading service. So, if the court is persuaded that there is a 'good reason' to authorise service by 'a method or at a place not otherwise permitted' by the rules, it can make an order permitting service by an 'alternative method or at an alternative place.' This provision also applies to service of other court documents.[61]

The claimant's application to the court for such an order must be supported by written evidence, which would typically explain what attempts to serve have been made (or would have been made were they not impractical), as well as what method of service is being put forward as more likely to bring the claim form to the defendant's notice. Dealing with cases fairly and efficiently and in keeping with the overriding objective will also be relevant considerations for the court - the most important thing is that the contents of the document come to the attention of the defendant.[62] If the court makes an order for alternative service, it should go on to specify not only how service is to be effected, but when such service is deemed to be served and how long the defendant has to respond.[63] Alternatively, the court can order that steps which a claimant has already taken to bring the claim to the attention of the defendant, constitutes good service.[64]

It is also worth noting that this is a good example of an interim application which, out of necessity, would be made without giving the other side notice. If the claimant could serve the defendant for the purposes of the application, it is unlikely he would need the order at all!

59 CPR, r 6.11(1)
60 This was not always the case.
61 CPR, r 6.15(1) and 6.27
62 See discussion at WB, para 6.15.3
63 CPR, r 6.15(4)
64 CPR, r 6.15(2)

Dispensing with service

In *exceptional* circumstances, the court may dispense altogether with the need to serve the claim form.[65] This might happen where there has been a very minor, technical fault with service, and it is no longer possible to try again to serve properly.[66] But the court will use this power *very sparingly* indeed; otherwise it would undermine the rules themselves. Service is not that hard to achieve, so it will be *rare* for the court to excuse a claimant for not managing to do it.

3. SERVICE OF DOCUMENTS OTHER THAN THE CLAIM FORM

You will notice that CPR, Part 6 is divided into distinct sections, so that there is, in effect, one set of rules for service of the claim form (Part II) and a second set for service of documents other than the claim form (Part III). There are many similarities between the two, and often the same or similar wording is used.[67] For example, when any party is acting through solicitors, and their business address has been provided, all documents in a case should be served on that address.[68] But there are also some discrepancies. For example, notice the somewhat subtle difference in the deeming provisions as regards service by post of documents other than the claim form ('second day after posting if that day is a business day; or if not, the next business day after that day'). And insofar as electric service of such documents, where a fax number or e-mail address has been included on a statement of case or response to a claim filed with the court, then this itself is sufficient indication of a willingness to be served in this fashion. Remember too that there is no generic overarching deeming provision for service of documents other than the claim form (like there is for service of the claim form itself) and so as the method of serving such other

65 CPR, r 6.16(1)

66 As in *Cranfield v Bridgegrove Ltd* [2004] 1 WLR 2441

67 This is partly because only the rules about serving the claim form were overhauled in 2008, leaving service of other documents to be covered by the pre-existing rules.

68 CPR, r 6.23(2)

documents becomes more instantaneous in nature, then service is equally deemed to occur more quickly (for example, service by email or indeed personal service).[69]

Normally, service of other documents is even less controversial than service of the claim form in the general run of the case, but you still want to be aware of the fact (and basic detail) of the differences. It can easily crop up in exams. There is a very useful table (with comparative examples) at WB, PD 6A, para 10.1.

revision tips

- Do not let the minutiae of the service rules prevent your gaining a confident understanding of the system. Get a grasp of the basics and the rest will follow.
- Appreciate that, despite similarities, the service rules for service of the *claim form* can differ from the rules about service of *other* documents. In particular know how the deeming provisions differ. In an exam question requiring application of these provisions, think to yourself: are we talking about service of a claim form here, or service of some other document?
- Despite the various options for serving the claim form (in the jurisdiction), remember that this choice is sometimes constrained by the rules. It might help to remember what is sometimes called the 'hierarchy' of service by asking:

  - Is personal service required? (this is rare)
  - If not, has C been notified in writing by D or his solicitors that service should be at the solicitor's business address? If so, the claim form must be served there.
  - If not, then you have some options: is the place and method of service governed by contract? Has D given C an address for service (which is where

continues ...

69 CPR, r 6.26

continued ...

he resides or carries on business)? Do you want to serve personally for some reason?
- If all else fails, then C can serve the claim form at D's usual or (if reasonable attempts have been made but failed to find a current address) at D's last known address.

- You may need to apply both concepts, so do not confuse the deemed date of service with the more general computation of time rules (CPR, r2.8/9). As to the latter, know what is meant by 'clear days' and note that when computing short periods (5 days or less) for doing an act (e.g., giving notice), holidays and weekends are excluded from the calculation. This is not the case with longer notice periods. For example, if a notice of application must be served 3 clear days before a hearing date on Tuesday 14th February 2023, the 3 clear days would be the previous Thursday, Friday and Monday (assuming this is not a bank holiday), so that the last day for service (to be deemed to have occurred) would be Wednesday, 8th February.

It is worth reading ...

Judgment of ***Munby J*** (as he then was) in ***R (Lawer) v Restormel Borough Council*** [2007] EWHC 2299 (Admin); [2008] HLR 20. This is not a mainstream case (it involves the Local Authority's obligation to house the homeless), but it is easy to follow the story. At this point it is the judge's comments about the without notice interim application (which was made over the telephone!) which you should take on board.

CHAPTER 5

Early judgment without trial

Even if matters are not resolved pre-action and it is necessary to commence proceedings, it is still the case that most civil suits never get to trial. Some never even get to first base. Not only do the rules contain certain carrots to encourage the early settlement of cases with some merit, they also include several sticks to ensure that claims with no merit are thrown out well before the expense of a full trial. The most lethal of these sticks are *striking out*[1] and *summary judgment*.[2] These can be deployed against *both* claims and defences, and are draconian but important weapons in the court's armoury for keeping control over its proceedings and achieving the overriding objective. Where claims are thus lost, then of course to that extent the defendant wins and the claimant, as the loser, will usually have to pay both side's legal costs.[3]

Claimants have the *additional* procedural stick of obtaining *judgment in default* under CPR Part 12, which in effect penalises defendants who do not make clear their desire to defend a claim.[4] A claimant who succeeds through any one of these methods in defeating the defendant's case will get judgment (on liability anyway) without the aggravation and expense of a trial of the action.

The two most common procedural devices claimants use to get early judgment without having to go to full trial are *judgment in default* under CPR Part 12 and *summary judgment*.

1 See Ch 13
2 *See below*.
3 See generally Ch 18 on the costs rules.
4 Judgment can be entered in default of compliance with other procedural requirements, but CPR, r 12.3 is the first opportunity for a claimaint and is the form of default judgment discussed in this chapter.

1. DEFAULT JUDGMENT

Default judgment applies where a defendant does not want, or (more accurately) does not indicate that he wants to contest a claimant's action. Since it would be silly to carry on any further in those circumstances, the claimant may in such cases obtain judgment 'in default' of the defendant's manifesting an intention to defend. Where the claim is for *money* only, default judgment is *usually an administrative*, not a judicial, process and is available 'on request' from the relevant court office by merely filling out a form. No application or appearance before a judge is needed. However, non-money claims (for example, injunctions), *always* require an *application to the court.*

Availability of default judgment

With some *limited* specialist exceptions (for example, certain consumer credit cases, Part 8 claims, contentious probate cases), a claimant may obtain default judgment in respect of *any* sort of claim.[5]

Meaning of default judgment

It is important in this context to remember that the document to which the defendant must respond is the *particulars of claim*, and not the claim form as such.[6] When the particulars of claim are served, they must be accompanied by a 'response pack' containing forms of acknowledgement of service, admission and defence/ counterclaim.[7] These give the defendant a range of options for responding to the claim. Silence is not really one of them!

Once the particulars of claim have been served, a defendant wanting to defend a claim should manifest this intention in one of two ways:

5 See CPR, r 12.2

6 CPR, r 9.1(2). You will remember that the particulars of claim can be put directly on the claim form, arrive with the claim form or be served within 14 days of service of the claim form (and in any event while the claim form is still valid for service). See Ch 3

1. by acknowledging service of the particulars of claim within 14 days of service and thereafter filing a defence (so long as this is within 28 days of service of the particulars of claim);

or

2. by skipping the acknowledgment stage altogether and filing a defence from the outset within 14 days of service of the particulars of claim.[8]

You will notice that filing an acknowledgment of service 'buys' the defendant a little more time to file his defence. It is worth noting also that the parties can agree to extend the time for filing the defence for up to (*at most*[9]) a further 28 days. The defendant should notify the court of the agreed extended period.[10]

Not surprisingly, default judgment is therefore possible in two basic situations:

(a) where the defendant has failed to file either an acknowledgement of service or defence in time (in effect, where there has been no response at all from the defendant);

or

(b) where, having filed an acknowledgement of service, the defendant has nevertheless failed to go on to file a defence in time.[11]

PROCEDURAL PREREQUISITES

The procedural requirements for entering judgment in default all have to do with ensuring that a defendant who intends to defend an action has had every opportunity, but has nevertheless failed to respond to the claim in an appropriate manner consistent with defending. First of all, the court must be satisfied that the defendant was served with the particulars of claim. If the court itself has not been responsible

7 CPR, r 7.8. See Court Form N9 (available online).

8 CPR, rr 10.1(3) and 15.4. Note that any document 'intended to be a defence' is sufficient for these purposes: CPR, r 12.1(b)

9 The expression 'up to' 28 days is used, so if more time were needed the safest course would be for the defendant to seek court approval for a further extension. The court cannot allocate the case to an appropriate track until the defence has been filed, and so will want to ensure this happens in good time.

10 CPR, r 15.5

11 CPR, r 12.3

for effecting service, then the claimant will have to prove service by means of a certificate of service. Secondly, the time for filing an acknowledgment of service or defence, as the case may be, must have expired; obviously the defendant must be given the *entire* period in which to respond.

Finally, the defendant must have failed to file an acknowledgment of service or defence (as the case may be) *and* must not have either admitted the claim and asked for time to pay,[12] satisfied the claim, or applied for summary judgment.[13] Obviously it would be rather perverse to give the claimant judgment in default where (or to the extent that) the defendant was in the process of attempting to satisfy (or indeed had already satisfied) the claim, or had made an application to the court saying the claim itself is so groundless that it is the defendant and not the claimant who should get early judgment. In essence, if, in the allotted time, a defendant wanting to defend has failed to respond in a pertinent manner, the claimant may seek to enter judgment in default.

HOW JUDGMENT IS OBTAINED

On request

In money claims only (and this includes claims for delivery of goods where the claimant will accept money instead) default judgment is available 'over the counter', as it were, unless there are exceptional features (for example, claims against a child or protected party, who require a 'litigation friend',[14] a claim in tort against a spouse, a claim served out of the jurisdiction).[15] In ordinary money cases, therefore, the claimant merely requests judgment on the prescribed standard form (including how and when payment of a specified amount of money is to be made where payment by instalments is acceptable). There is *no* hearing and *no* question of having to persuade a judge to give judgment on the merits of the case; judgment (plus costs) will be 'entered' so long as the prerequisites mentioned above have been met, which only involves court staff checking

12 And provided relevant financial information

13 And/or applied for the claimant's statement of case to be struck out. See CPR, r 12.3(3). If the defendant admits part of the claim and wants to defend part, this should be made clear by returning both the admission and defence response forms.

14 See Ch 3

15 CPR, r 12.11(a) and (b)(i)

that documents have or have not reached their relevant destinations.[16]

Thus, in standard, everyday claims for *money* (whether for a specified sum or not) and/or claims for delivery of goods where the defendant is given the alternative of paying their value in *money*, entering default judgment is purely an *administrative* act. These account for the overwhelming majority of cases.

Note, however, that although entering judgment in such cases is administrative, it is *not* automatic, so unless and until a claimant enters judgment in default, a defendant can still manifest an intention to defend, even after the initial time for doing so has expired, thereby precluding such judgment being entered. Thus a defendant who does not respond appropriately to the particulars of claim within the allotted time is *at risk* of the claimant's entering judgment against him; but the claimant actually has to *do* something to convert the risk into a reality.

On application

In money claims with exceptional features, and where the claimant is seeking a non-money remedy (for example, equitable relief), an *application* to the court is necessary.[17] The reason for requiring an application in the latter sort of case is that equitable remedies are 'discretionary' and therefore require a judge to exercise his or her judgment on the matter. The view of the person in the court office is not good enough for this purpose!

Where permission is required, the application is made in writing and usually on notice in accordance with the Part 23 procedure for interim applications. The application must be supported by written evidence relating to the nature of the claim and the meeting of the procedural requirements.[18] There will be a hearing and the court will give such judgment 'as it appears the claimant is entitled to on his statement of case'.[19]

16 Or are taken to have done so by virtue of the deemed service rules (see Ch 4). See CPR, r 12.4(1)

17 CPR, r 12.4(3)

18 No evidence need be served on a defendant who did not acknowledge service. Special cases (e.g., claims against the State) often have additional procedural requirements. See CPR, r 12.12

19 This does not mean the court should investigate the legal basis for the claim, but rather the circumstances in which the application was made so as to ensure procedural fairness: CPR r 12.12(1) and *Football Dataco Ltd v Smoot Enterprises Ltd* [2011] 1 WLR 1978].

Multiple defendants

If there are two or more defendants, a claimant may obtain default judgment *on request* against one and proceed against the others. But if the rules require a claimant to *apply* for default judgment (against one defendant and not others), then whether the judge will be able to enter judgment at that time will depend on the relationship between the claim that is the subject of the default judgment application and the claim against the remaining defendant(s). If, for example, two defendants have been sued in the alternative (where only one can be held responsible), then the court can only deal with the application for default judgment against the one at the same time as it disposes of the claim against the other, since only at that time will it be apparent which is actually liable. But if the earlier application for default judgment can safely be dealt with separately and will not impact on the later decision (for example, because the liability of all the defendants is joint and/or several and all that needs to be decided is the extent of each's responsibility), then the court can enter default judgment against the one defendant (damages to be assessed later) and the claimant can continue the proceedings against the others.[20]

TYPES OF JUDGMENT IN MONEY CLAIMS

If the claim is for a '*specified*' amount of money (plus interest), the judgment entered will be *final* as to both liability and quantum (including interest and costs). Where the claim is for an '*unspecified*' amount of money (or 'damages'), or the claimant requests that the court decide the quantum or the interest, the judgment will be partial (sometimes called 'interlocutory' judgment).[21] In other words, it will be final as to the defendant's liability to pay damages, but the *amount* to be paid will remain to be determined. The date of future hearings to decide this will be fixed (and relevant directions given) when judgment is entered.[22]

20 CPR, r 12.9 and see *Albesher v Ryan* [2015] EWHC 3058 (Comm). Note that a claimant who has obtained judgment on request against one of several defendants will not be able to enforce against that one for recovery of land or delivery of goods unless he has obtained judgment against all of the defendants or the court gives permission.

21 CPR, r 12.5

22 CPR, r 12.8

Under the old rules the distinction was made, not between specified and unspecified money claims, but between 'liquidated' and 'unliquidated' claims. A liquidated demand is one which is objectively ascertainable (usually by looking at the contract to which it relates) and not open to argument, although it might involve an element of calculation. Typical examples are debts and the price of goods sold and delivered. If you buy a Twix bar for 80p and find when you get it home that there is something basically wrong with it, in money terms your claim against the shop for a refund is for 80p - no more and no less - because that is what you paid for the Twix bar. It is a liquidated demand.

Unliquidated claims, on the other hand, are open to argument (even if nobody would bother) or require the exercise of judicial discretion in their assessment. Most claims for 'damages' are unliquidated: indeed the words are practically synonymous (although, confusingly, there is such a thing as 'liquidated damages'). Some claims are obviously identifiable as unliquidated, for example claims for pain, suffering and loss of amenity or for future financial loss - so-called 'general damages'. But others can fool you. A claim for the amount paid to have a broken watch repaired or to buy a specially adapted car is also an unliquidated claim because the defendant may want to quibble about the amount which was spent. Maybe the claimant did not need a four-wheel drive Mercedes Benz with diamond encrusted wing mirrors! Just because a claimant can put a price tag on a damage claim does not make it liquidated, although in most cases price tags are accepted as fair and accurate.

Of course, to many people the words 'liquidated' and 'unliquidated' do not convey the meaning lawyers ascribe to them. So it is not surprising that in drafting the new rules an attempt was apparently made to update these expressions with more readily understandable vocabulary. But legal concepts and terms can sometimes be difficult to modernise. Possibly the descriptions 'specified' and 'unspecified' were intended to replace (and so translate into) 'liquidated' and 'unliquidated', but this is not what happened given how easy it is to 'specify' the amount of what is strictly speaking an unliquidated claim. The result is to place the burden on defendants to indicate if they take issue with, and seek the court's determination on, the amount of a claim, which although unliquidated is one on which the claimant has put a specific price tag.[23]

SETTING ASIDE DEFAULT JUDGMENT

Because of the non-judicial nature of most default judgments, it is not something which is subject to an appeal, as such. Instead, defendants who have had default judgment entered against them (or indeed anyone who is 'directly affected' by such judgment, even if not the defendant) can apply to have it varied or 'set aside'. Such applications are made using the Part 23 procedure for interim applications.[24]

Default judgment will be set aside 'as of right' if it was wrongly entered. That is to say, it *must* be set aside if the court finds that the relevant procedural requirements of Part 12 were not met (for example, if the time for acknowledging service had not expired when judgment was entered).[25]

Otherwise default judgment *may*, and presumably will only, be set aside or varied if it appears to the court on looking at the evidence in support of the application that 'the defendant has a *real prospect of successfully* defending the claim' *or* there is some other '*good reason*' for setting side or varying the judgment, or for letting the defendant defend the claim.[26] In either case, the court must take into account whether the application to set aside was made *promptly*.[27]

23 Even so the distinction between liquidated and unliquidated claims comes up in other contexts, so it is useful to understand it.

24 The written evidence in support should address the matters which are relevant to the court's decision. Part 23 is discussed in Ch 4. See also WB para 13.3.4 for applications to set aside made by a non-party.

25 CPR, r 13.2. In ***Intense Investments Ltd v Development Ventures Ltd*** [2005] BLR 478, for example, judgment was set aside as of right because it had been entered by the request method, in circumstances where an application to the court should have been made. Wrongly entered judgments are sometimes referred to as being 'irregular'.

26 CPR, r 13.3(1). Applications under r 13.3 must be supported by

'Real prospect of success'

This is sometimes known as setting aside 'on the merits' of the case. Notice how the wording of the rule here intentionally invokes the summary judgment test, although in this context the burden of proof is always on the defendant.[28]

The purpose of the court's wide discretion here is to avoid injustice and meet the overriding objective. To this end, the court will not lightly let a defendant's case be lost simply because of an initial and isolated failure to comply with the timetable rules. The gist of Lord Atkin's sentiments expressed over 50 years ago in *Evans v Bartlam*[29] remain valid today:

> The principle obviously is that unless and until the Court has pronounced a judgment on the merits or by consent, it is to have the power to revoke the expression of its coercive power where that has ... been obtained by a failure to follow any of the rules of procedure.

On the other hand, there has to be some real point in carrying on with the case. It would be a waste of time and money to put the defendant's ship back on course when it would almost immediately - and inevitably - be sunk on the shoals of a successful summary judgment application.

'Some other good reason'

As we have seen, because of the deeming provisions, a defendant may be considered properly served with particulars of claim, even though they never in fact arrived. This is not a procedural defect, but it could amount to a 'good reason' to set aside any judgment in default entered as a result, despite there not otherwise being a real prospect of successfully defending the case. It would all depend on the circumstances. Other examples of good reasons might be where the defendant was unrepresented

evidence: r 13.4(3)

27 CPR, r 13.3(2)

28 See discussion which follows. A good articulation of the principles is set out in *Agadzhan Avanesov v Too Shymkentpivo* [2015] EWHC 394 (Comm)

29 [1937] AC 480, HL

or where the claimant failed to serve a Response Pack or where the defendant would have paid up rather than having an embarrassing judgment entered against him. Unconscionable behaviour on the part of the claimant might also amount to a good reason.[30]

The importance of promptness

How promptly an application to set aside default judgment is made (and the reasons for any delay) has always been relevant to the exercise of the court's discretion in such cases, even before the CPR. There is a public interest in the finality of litigation and a very late application might signify a sudden afterthought, or a mere delaying tactic. What the CPR did was to single out this aspect of the matter, so that while promptness is not in itself a condition to be satisfied, it is nevertheless given special prominence as something the court 'must' have regard to in exercising its discretion in such applications. Whether a delay in making an application will be fatal to it will depend on the facts and circumstances of any individual case. A court will naturally be reluctant to preclude a party with a good defence from defending a claim, however late the application to set aside. Even so, if there is a marked failure to make an application promptly, a court *might* be justified in refusing to grant relief, notwithstanding the possibility that the defendant might have succeeded at trial.[31]

Interplay between CPR, r 13.3 and r 3.9

The court's discretion to set aside default judgment is an old one. It pre-dates by many decades the advent of the CPR, r 3.9 and in particular the Jackson reforms of 2013, which highlight the importance of 'enforcing compliance with rules, practice directions and orders.' Sanctions can be imposed for 'non-compliance', and default judgment under r 12 has been said to be an example of this because the defendant

30 See, e.g., *Ahmet Erol v Global Fashion Links Ltd* [2014] EWHC (IPEC), at para 19ff, and other examples at WB para 13.3.2

31 See, e.g., *Standard Bank Plc v Agrinvest International Inc* [2010] EWCA Civ 1400, and Moore-Bick LJ at [22-23]). And see the examples at WB para 13.3.3

did not comply with the rule about how to respond to the claim if wanting to defend. When sanctions are imposed (either by the rules or by the court) there is a general discretion under CPR, r 3.9 to give 'relief' from the sanction. How the court should approach applications under r 3.9 is laid down in *Denton v TH White Ltd (Practice Note)* [2014] EWCA Civ 906. This is discussed further in Chapter 13.

The thing to note here is that the Court of Appeal has suggested that an application under r 13.3 to set aside default judgment is, at least by implication, an application for relief from the sanction within the meaning of r 3.9 and so (in addition to the principles discussed above) the *Denton* test is also said to be engaged. Contrary views have been expressed, but the point has yet to be fully argued. This is probably because it cannot be very often that applying *Denton* would bring the court to a different result after having applied r 13.3 (the tests effectively complement each other). Until the question has been finally decided on appeal, the safer option would seem to be that both should be taken into account when deciding whether to set aside a default judgment, and when explaining the court's decision.[32]

When a court in its discretion sets aside default judgment, it may impose conditions.[33] The most common is that the defendant pay the costs 'thrown away', since these will have been incurred as a result of a failure to follow the rules. Additionally, the defendant may be ordered to pay the whole, or some part, of the disputed sum into court before being allowed to continue defending the action. The court should not, however, impose a financial condition which the defendant cannot possibly meet, since this would if effect be a roundabout way of (re)giving judgment to the claimant.[34]

32 So watch out for any appeal court decisions on this. See WB para 13.3.5

33 CPR, r 3.1(3) referenced at r 13.3

34 The onus will be on the defendant to prove the impossibility of any financial condition. See also discussion of summary judgment below.

2. SUMMARY JUDGMENT

SUMMARY JUDGMENT FOR THE CLAIMANT

It is relatively easy to manifest an intention to defend a claim; in the first instance this merely involves ticking a box on a form. Sometimes a defendant will go through the motions of defending - perhaps out of desperation or as a delaying tactic - when there is in reality nothing that can be said that would prevent the claimant succeeding at the end of the day. If this is so, it is really rather pointless to wait until the end of the day.

The rules provide two important means of ensuring that cases without merit are quickly laid to rest. One is the 'striking out' procedure. A defence must be set out with clarity and precision, and make clear where issue is being taken with the claim. Incoherent or meaningless defences would be liable to be struck out by the court.[35]

Summary judgment is a related, and to some extent overlapping, procedure.[36] It is used for situations where whatever a defendant says, however clearly or logically set out, it is incapable of succeeding as a defence (or is inherently implausible) and there is no other compelling reason why the case (or issue) should continue on to trial. The point of summary judgment for the claimant, therefore, is to provide early judgment in those cases where the defendant has no realistic hope of success and any defence raised will merely have the effect of delaying the inevitable judgment for the claimant.

Availability of summary judgment for the claimant

With a *very few* exceptions (notably certain residential possession proceedings), summary judgment *for the claimant* may be given in any type of case.[37]

35 Claims can similarly be struck out: CPR, r 3.4 and see Ch 13

36 Summary judgment and striking out can be applied for in the alternative: CPR, PD 3A, para 1.2. See, e.g., ***Clancy Consulting Ltd v Derwent Holdings Ltd*** [2010] EWHC 762 (TCC) where the court struck out certain paragraphs in a defence and then granted summary judgment in respect of the claim which, as a result, was no longer defended.

37 CPR, r 24.3(1)

Claimant's application for summary judgment

Unless the court gives permission (or a practice direction provides otherwise), the claimant may only apply for summary judgment after the relevant defendant has responded to the particulars of claim by filing an acknowledgement of service or defence[38] (a failure by the defendant to respond to the claim would, of course, mean that the claimant could request default judgment as discussed above). An application by a claimant who has failed to comply with any relevant pre-action protocol will not normally be entertained until a defence has actually been filed (or the time for doing so has expired).[39]

Otherwise, such applications for summary judgment are normally made in the period between acknowledgment of service (which precludes a claimant entering default judgment) and the filing of the applicant's directions questionnaire.[40] Indeed the first question on the directions questionnaire specifically asks if a summary judgment application is pending. Certainly applications should be made as promptly as possible. The idea is to put a hopeless case down before unnecessary time and costs are wasted. Furthermore, a delay in applying, while not necessarily fatal, might show a certain lack of conviction on the part of the applicant.

The application is made in accordance with the rules on making interim applications under CPR 23, with relevant modifications. Thus the application is made in writing. Notice must be given to the respondent(s), although the notice period is *at least 14 days* before the hearing, rather than the usual three.[41] The written evidence in support of a claimant's application must identify concisely any point of law or provision relied upon and include a stated belief that on the evidence, there is no defence with a real prospect of success and no other reason is known of as to why there should be a trial of the claim.[42] A defendant's evidence in reply, geared to showing why there ought to be a full trial of the claim or issue, must be filed at

38 CPR, r 24.4(1)
39 PD 24, para 2(6)
40 PD 26, para 5.3. See generally Ch 8
41 CPR, r 24.4(3)
42 PD 24, para 2. This 'belief' is an essential ingredient: see WB para 24.2.4

least *seven* days before the hearing. If the applicant wishes to respond to this, further evidence must be filed within *three* days of the hearing.[43] Once the application by the claimant is made, a defendant may, but need not, file a defence before the hearing.[44] If the application is made before the case has been allocated to a case management track, the application will be heard before the allocation is made.[45] If the matter arises at the allocation stage, the question of summary judgment can be dealt with at an allocation hearing.

Such applications are heard by a Master (in the High Court) or a District Judge (in the County Court).

The hearing

For the claimant to succeed, the court must consider that the defendant 'has no real prospect of successfully defending' the claim (or an issue in the claim) *and* there is no other *compelling* reason to have a trial.[46]

'No real prospect of success'

We came across this part of the test earlier in the context of setting aside default judgment. It has been said that in order to have a real prospect of success a case must carry 'some degree of conviction' and be 'more than merely arguable'.[47] If the case in question is 'at best' distinctly improbable, then it will be right to grant summary judgment. Having said that, it still remains the case that it is a serious matter to deprive a defendant of the right to put a defence case at trial, and so the 'standard of proof' at this stage is a high one. In *Swain v Hillman*,[48] the architect of the CPR, Lord Woolf, said that the words 'no real prospect of success' are self-explanatory - 'real' means realistic, not fanciful; 'possible', not necessarily probable. He emphasised the need to keep summary judgment applications in proper perspective. They are

43 CPR, r 24.5
44 Assuming no defence has already been filed when the application is made: CPR, r 24.4(2)
45 PD 26, para 5.3(2)
46 CPR, r 24.2. Note similarities and differences when compared to the test for setting aside default judgment.
47 See, e.g., ***Bee v Jenson*** [2007] RTR 9, and ***ED & F Man Liquid Products Ltd v Patel*** [2003] EWCA Civ, at [8]
48 [2001] 1 All ER 91. In this case it was the defendant who was applying for summary judgment (as discussed below). The WB commentary para 24.2.3 does not make this clear.

not, he said, meant to dispense with the need for a trial where there are issues which should be considered and tested there (in other words, what used to be called 'triable issues'). If the defendant's case has some prospects of success, summary judgment should be refused.

Nor are summary judgment applications mini-trials. They are hearings to determine whether and to what extent there *ought* to be a trial, disposing in the process of cases with no realistic[49] prospect of success or other reason to be tried. Choosing between two versions of events is the function of the trial judge, not the interim judge (unless one version is inherently implausible). The court should take into account evidence that could reasonably be expected to be available at trial, but it will not be enough that 'something may turn up.'[50] However it is described, given that justice is an integral part of the overriding objective, before granting summary judgment the court must be clear in its own mind that a trial would be a waste of time and money.

'No other compelling reason for a trial'

Sometimes the court may feel that the defence has little or no prospect of success, but there is some other compelling reason for a trial. This can arise if a case is very complex, or if there is a right to jury trial (this is rare), or if the court feels judgment should be obtained in the full glare of publicity. It can also happen when the claimant's actions appear discreditable in some way. An infamous example is *Miles v Bull.*[51] In that case a farmer sold his farmhouse to the claimant while his estranged wife was still living in it. The wife had not registered her rights of occupation before the sale and so she was not protected as against the new owner, who wanted her out of the house. The new owner sued the wife for possession and applied for summary judgment. The wife did not really have a defence in law, but the court decided

49 (In *E.D. & F. Man,* op cit, Potter LJ at [6] said the terms 'real prospect' and 'realistic prospect' were interchangeable.

50 Per Cockerill J in *King v Stiefel* [2021] EWHC 1045 (Comm), cited in WB, para 24.2.3 which includes a good readable summary of the principles.

51 [1969] 1 QB 258, referenced at WB para 24.2.5 (and see the other examples there).

that the husband and new owner had conducted their business in such a secretive, if not underhand, way that the wife ought to have access to all of the weapons of the litigation process to test the new owner's claim. In effect, the court felt that the claimant ought to be put to strict proof of the claim in order for justice to be done.

Burden of proof

CPR, r 24.2, unlike its predecessor, is not explicit about where the burden of proof lies in summary judgment cases. Assuming an application by the claimant,[52] the question is this: is it the claimant's job to persuade the court that the defendant's case has no real chance of success; or is it the defendant's job to prove that it does? The old rules had clearly put the burden on the defendant, presumably because at that time he would have known more about his own case than the claimant. And while it may have been the original intention to replicate this in the new rules, there is not now anything in CPR, r 24.2 (or its accompanying PD) which says so explicitly. And what do the judges say? The question has never been directly decided, and it does not really keep anyone up at night since cases rarely turn on the point, but the weight of judicial observation indicates that the courts now interpret the rules as placing the burden on the applicant/claimant to show that the defendant/respondent's case is not worthy of trial.[53] A defendant seeking to stop summary judgment will of course need to produce some evidence showing real prospects of success or other compelling reason for a trial,[54] but it will be for the claimant to persuade the court to give summary judgment. One logical reason for this is that the applicant is the one asking for early judgment. When the defendant applies to set aside default judgment so that he can put his case at trial, the burden is on him to show his case has a real prospect of success.[55] It would seem to follow that when it is the claimant who is making the application, then the persuasive burden should be on him.

52 Defendants can also apply for summary judgment, as discussed below.

53 In *E.D. & F. Man,* op.cit., [at 9] Potter LJ said as much when contrasting the position with setting aside default judgment. Because that case was about the latter, his view was strictly 'obiter', but other cases have taken similar approaches.

54 This is sometimes referred to as an 'evidential burden'. This is not a burden 'of proof' as such (despite the White Books's rather loose vocabulary at para 24.2.4!), but it means a claimant seeking summary judgment will find the task of discharging its burden of proof much easier if the defendant has nothing to say on the matter. See general discussion of evidential and legal burdens at Ch 17

55 As discussed above

In any event, the judge will not test or weigh up the respective merits of the cases, which are typically set out in the parties' witness statements and exhibits, except to determine whether there is some point in having a trial. Cases which therefore tend not to be amenable to summary judgment are those where a substantive defence has been pleaded (for example, frustration), a specific answer to the claim has been raised (for example, a relevant exclusion clause), a point of law requires protracted argument and/or the relevant facts are disputed.[56] Negligence claims, for example, do not usually lend themselves to summary judgment once liability has been denied and the defendant has set out his disputed version of events. But every case must be looked at individually; in *Dummer v Brown*[57] summary judgment was granted against a coach driver who had previously pleaded guilty to a charge of dangerous driving in respect of the accident giving rise to the claim. Given the difference between the criminal and civil standard of proof, it was almost inconceivable that the defendant could escape liability for negligence.[58]

It is important to remember, however, that the court is not liable to take every assertion made at face value;[59] it will reject legal argument which is erroneous or evidence which is inherently implausible, irrelevant, self-contradictory or manifestly inconsistent with other believable facts. In short, the case of the party opposing summary judgment must appear to have a certain degree of credibility; for this reason summary judgment applications will often focus on the implausibility (or not) of the parties' allegations. In *Sandhar v Sandhar and Kang Ltd*,[60] for example, a respondent's assertion that he retained a beneficial interest in property was rejected as fanciful. No supporting documentary evidence had been exhibited, nor were the circumstances (including no provision for rental income or how his interest was to be realised) consistent with it. Summary judgment was granted.

56 A lot of witness statements going back and forth in response to each other usually indicate a factual dispute worthy of a trial.

57 [1953] 1 QB 710. By way of comparison see ***McCauley v Vine*** [1999] 1 WLR 1977

58 See Ch 17 on admitting previous convictions in a civil case.

59 Or, as Lewison LJ put it in ***Calland v Financial Conduct Authority*** [2015] EWCA Civ 192 at [29], in evaluating prospects of success ... judges are 'not required to abandon' their 'critical faculties.'

60 [2008] EWCA Civ 238, LTL 14/2/2008

POSSIBLE ORDERS ON CLAIMANT'S APPLICATION

At the hearing of the claimant's application for summary judgment, the possible orders of the Master or District Judge are as follows:

Judgment for claimant

This is the appropriate order where no viable or believable defence is raised and there is no other compelling reason to have a trial. The claimant will normally get an order for the costs of the application.

Conditional order

This is an appropriate order where a defence cannot be ruled out altogether, but is 'shadowy' or of doubtful credibility; in other words where it appears to the court 'possible that a defence ... will succeed, but improbable that it will do so'.[61] This is a safety net for cases where the court feels uncomfortable about giving summary judgment, but is only willing to let the defence continue on strict conditions, the most typical of which is that the defendant 'put his money where his mouth is' by paying part or all of the amount claimed into court, failing which the claimant gets judgment. The idea is that defendants should think hard about 'throwing good money after bad' if they have no real answer to the claim. Conditions should be proportionate and effective in serving the intended purpose (to provide security against a weak defence).[62] In particular, the court must not impose a condition unless there is some prospect that the defendant can comply, since this would be tantamount to giving judgment for the claimant. Having said that, the onus is on defendant to establish an inability to meet the condition 'were he really minded to do so'. Both of these principles were established in *Yorke Motors v Edwards*[63] where the appeal court reduced the amount the defendant was ordered to pay

61 PD24, para 4

62 See WB, para 24.6.6. Note that when money is paid in under such an order, the claimant is a secured creditor for that amount if ultimately successful: *Crumpler v Candey Ltd* [2018] EWCA Civ 2256

63 [1982] 1 WLR 444

into court from over £30,000 to £4,000. The defendant wanted the condition lifted altogether, but the court felt that notwithstanding certain indicators of impecuniosity (including a legal aid certificate), a properly motivated Mr. Edwards (of whose defence the court was very sceptical) could lay his hands on the reduced amount. It is not just a question of whether the defendant personally has the funds, but whether such funds could be made available by some closely associated person, including (in the case of a corporate defendant) its beneficial owner. Requiring a defendant to take a particular step in the litigation (for example, filing a more detailed defence) could also be a condition.

Note that it might also be appropriate to make a conditional order if the defendant has a history of poor litigation conduct, although if such a defendant has a good defence the court should be cautious about imposing conditions on this account.[64] The usual costs order when a conditional order is made is 'costs in the case'.[65]

Dismissal of application

This is appropriate where the defence clearly has a chance of success or there is some other compelling reason to have a trial. The defendant's means are irrelevant here. If there is a real prospect of success at trial, there is clearly a reason for a trial and that is that. Presumably the claimant should have figured that out, so in such circumstances the costs of the interim application will normally go to the defendant.

When the claim or any part of it is proceeding to trial (that is, where the claimant's application is dismissed or a conditional order is made), the court will go on to give appropriate directions as to the future conduct of the litigation.

64 See now the principles as set out in *Gama Aviation (UK) v Taverelas Petroleum Trading DMCC* [2019] EWCA Civ 119, usefully summarised at WB para 24.6.7

65 This means that whoever wins at trial gets the costs of this interim application. See generally Ch 18

3. EXPANSION OF SUMMARY JUDGMENT

The summary judgment procedure is not limited to use by claimants against defendants. In giving the court effective case management powers, the CPR expanded summary judgment in two important ways.

(i) Defendant's application

The first is that *defendants* may apply for summary judgment to attack hopelessly weak claims (or a particular issue in the claim). Thus, summary judgment *for the defendant* will be granted when the court considers that the claimant has no real prospect of succeeding on a claim or issue and there is no other compelling reason to have a trial.[66] Defendants' applications for summary judgment are possible in *any* sort of case and again are a useful adjunct to the power to strike out (which is also available against claimants). In this context, therefore, another possible order to be made by the court in summary judgment proceedings is the striking out or dismissal of the whole of, or some issue in the claimant's action. Otherwise, the same principles, procedure and range of possible orders discussed above applies to a defendant's application for summary judgment, adapted as necessary to the circumstances of the reversed roles. A *conditional order*, for example, would be most apt to involve some specified step which the claimant is required to make in the litigation before being allowed to proceed, failing which the action will be struck out or dismissed.

(ii) Court's initiative

Secondly, the court can fix a summary judgment hearing *on its own initiative.*[67] Thus, whenever, and as soon as it scents a weak claim or defence (usually at the allocation stage), the court can itself trigger a hearing, having given adequate notice to the parties.

66 CPR, r 24.2. So the applicant/respondent roles are reversed. It is always the applicant who must satisfy the court of the weakness of the respondent's case. For an example of a defendant's application see *Akinleye v East Sussex Hospital NHS Trust* [2008] LS Law Med 216

67 CPR, r 3.3

This procedure can also be used for the purpose of obtaining a summary determination of certain issues in a case where the court is satisfied that these do not require full investigation, thus reducing the complexity and length of any trial.

4. COUNTERCLAIMS, SET-OFFS AND SUMMARY JUDGMENT

Often defendants make claims against the claimant in response to the latter's claim against them. When these are included in the same proceedings as the claimant's action they are known as cross-claims or counterclaims. A 'set-off' is a special kind of counterclaim, which historically has had an important impact on summary judgment applications.

ALL SET-OFFS ARE COUNTERCLAIMS ...

What makes a set-off special is its ability to operate as a *defence* (to the extent of the set-off). This can be highly relevant to the outcome of a summary judgment application by a claimant. Let us suppose, for example, that a claimant's claim is for £6,000 and the defendant pleads nothing else except a (not inherently incredible) set-off to the value of £4,000. There is thus a defence being raised up to £4,000, but thereafter there is no answer given to the claim. So on a summary judgment application by the claimant, the proper order would strictly be: summary judgment for the claimant for £2,000 (the part that the set-off couldn't reach, as it were) and dismissal of the claimant's application as regards the £4,000, leaving the defendant free to continue his defence (or even get summary judgment *against* the claimant as regards the £4,000 if there is no real prospect the claimant will win on that issue).

It is important to know whether a cross-claim amounts to a set-off, because the particular magic about a set-off is its *defensive capability*. It is worth remembering that while *all set-offs are counterclaims, not all counterclaims are set-offs!* In essence there are three set-off situations:

(a) Mutual Debts

If D owes C £5,000 and C owes D £3,000 (both liquidated demands), then if C sues D for the £5,000, D can set the £3,000 which C owes him off against C's claim (hence the expression 'set-off'!). The amounts need not be debts strictly speaking, so long as ascertained amounts are owed.

(b) Supply contract set-offs

This applies where goods or services supplied under the contract in respect of which the claimant sues are claimed by the defendant to be defective. So where the claimant sues for the price of goods sold or services supplied (a liquidated demand), the defendant can set-off, in diminution of the price, any claim he has for defects in the quality of those *same* goods or services (usually an unliquidated claim).[68]

(c) The equitable set-off

This is a broad and somewhat nebulous category. In essence, a defendant's counterclaim will be treated as an equitable set-off where, even though it is not technically a set-off in law, nevertheless it and the claimant's claim arise out of the same contract or transaction or are otherwise so inextricably linked that it would be unfair to uphold the one without taking into account the other. Equity in effect intervenes to treat such a cross-claim as a set-off.[69]

In the leading case of *Hanak v Green*,[70] for example, the claimant sued her builder for breach of contract for failing to complete works at her house. The defendant

68 Purists will distinguish between sale of goods cases, where the set-off derives from statute (e.g., Sale of Goods Acts 1979, s 53(1)) and cases which derive, by analogy, from the case law, but the concept is identical.

69 See discussion in *Geldorf Metaalconstructie NV v Simon Carves Ltd* [2010] BLR 401

counterclaimed for (a) extra work done for the claimant by him outside the original contract; (b) loss sustained as a result of the claimant's refusal to let the defendant's workmen onto the premises; and (c) trespass to the defendant's tools. All three cross-claims were treated as equitable set-offs.

Another classic example of the equitable set-off arises in landlord and tenant cases. Typically, a tenant who has been sued by his landlord for arrears of rent will usually be allowed to set off against that claim a counterclaim for damages for breach of the same tenancy agreement (for example, the landlord's failure to repair).[71]

... BUT NOT ALL COUNTERCLAIMS ARE SET-OFFS

Where the counterclaim is not a set-off (you might think of this as a 'mere' counterclaim), then it can have *no* defensive capability and cannot stop the claimant getting summary judgment. So, assuming the defendant is not raising any other defence, the claimant will get judgment. It may, however, be appropriate to delay, or 'stay' execution of that summary judgment (and so make the claimant wait for his money) until after the determination of the counterclaim. On the basis of the pre-CPR case law, this will be appropriate *only* where there is sufficient connection between the claim and the counterclaim, some unresolved issue between the parties and/or some other *compelling* reason to keep the claimant from the immediate fruits of his judgment. In determining whether a defendant's 'mere' counterclaim justifies a stay of execution, the court will have regard to:

(a) The degree of connection between claim and (mere) counterclaim (the closer the connection, the stronger the case for a stay)

(b) The strength of the counterclaim (the stronger the counterclaim, the better the case for a stay).

70 [1958] 2 QB 9

71 But cf *Bluestorm Ltd v Portvale Holidings Ltd* [2004] EWCA Civ 289, where the tenant's failure to pay rent had the intended consequence of impeding the landlord's ability to meet his obligations as landlord.

and

(c) the ability of the claimant to satisfy any judgment which the defendant might obtain on the counterclaim (any doubt on this matter strengthens the case for granting a stay).[72]

EFFECT OF COUNTERCLAIM ON SUMMARY JUDGMENT APPLICATIONS

It can sometimes be difficult to distinguish between the equitable set-off (which, as a defence, can stop the claimant obtaining summary judgment) and the 'closely connected' counterclaim (which does not amount to a set-off, and so, strictly, cannot stop the claimant getting summary judgment, but can justify a stay of execution of that judgment, with or without conditions).[73] You might say that one person's equitable set-off is sometimes another's closely connected counterclaim. Technically, and certainly historically, the outcomes are very different, and for this reason it is important (if only for the sake of argument) to understand how the legal effect of a set-off differs from that of a (closely connected) 'mere' counterclaim. Having said that, the practical result in both cases is much the same, since in neither is the money paid over (or at least not all of it) until after the trial (or earlier resolution) of both claim and counterclaim. Often, it is the practical rather than the technical result which matters.

Even predicting when a stay of execution will or will not be granted can be tricky. The Court of Appeal considered the 'lack of overall clarity' which existed under the old rules in *United Overseas Ltd v Peter Robinson Ltd*[74] and concluded that, all things considered it was a good thing because it gave the court useful room for manoeuvre in dispensing justice in individual cases. This approach, of course, is very much in keeping with the ethos of the CPR. Certainly, where fairness demands that no money passes hands until the defendant's cross-claim is resolved, the court will choose whatever route to that end

72 See, e.g., ***Mead General Building v Dartmoor Properties Ltd*** [2009] BCC 510, and generally ***Drake and Fletcher v Batchelor*** (1986) LSG 1232 per Sir Neil Lawson

73 So, for example, if the claim exceeds the alleged value of the (non-set off) counterclaim, the court could stay execution of the claimant's summary judgment on condition that the defendant pays that difference into court, or indeed limit the stay to the amount of the counterclaim. And see WB para 24.2.6 for the general distinction between the effect of a set-off and a (mere) counterclaim on summary judgment applications.

74 [1991] 3 WLUK 401

best accords with the facts and the need to dispense justice proportionately and fairly.

THE CHEQUE RULE

Historically, one important exception to the rule about the defensive capability of set-offs has been the so-called 'cheque rule'. This is summed up in the maxim: *There is no defence to a bad cheque.* In effect, when you pay for something by cheque, you promise that the cheque is as good as cash. This is a second and *entirely separate agreement* to the one for the sale or supply of the thing being purchased. The implications of this are important. If you buy something with cash and later discover there is a fault with it, you can try and get your money back but you cannot prevent the money changing hands because the payment will already have been made! You are not meant to be any better off if you pay by cheque, so that not honouring a cheque which you have written is only very exceptionally treated as excusable by the civil courts. Thus where a claimant sues *not* on the original contract of sale/supply (sometimes called the 'underlying' contract), but *on the bad cheque*, then nothing the defendant can say about defects in the thing sold or supplied will be allowed to operate either as a defence or a reason to stay execution of the claimant's judgment on the dishonoured cheque, except in *very* limited circumstances. These involve situations where it is alleged either that the cheque was obtained by fraud or misrepresentation[75] or the underlying contract is void or voidable. If the underlying contract is effectively nullified, then no money should have changed hands in the first instance and the method of payment then becomes irrelevant. Thus allegations of fraud, illegality, invalidity and total failure of consideration can operate, exceptionally, as a defence to an action on a dishonoured cheque. The very limited nature of these exceptions was highlighted by Sachs LJ when he said that the court will not 'whittle away [this] rule of practice by introducing unnecessary exceptions to it under the influence of sympathy-evoking stories'.[76]

75 *Solo Industries UK Ltd v Canara Bank* [2001] 1WLR 1800

76 *Cebora SNC v SIP (Industrial Products) Ltd* [1976] 1 Lloyd's Rep at 271. And see leading case of *Nova (Jersey) Knit Ltd v Kammgarn Spinnerei GmbH* [1977] 1 WLR 713, HL. And see WB para 24.2.7

The cheque rule is a very old one. Of course, writing cheques these days is getting to be as rare as handwritten letters, but the rule applies to any form of promissory note, including direct debit mandates. It has both a legal and commercial rationale. Business people expect to be paid at the end of the period for clearing cheques and so forth, and the rule was formulated with the need to promote commercial stability in mind. Legally, its operation is explained by the existence of the two separate agreements. It is precisely because the claimant is suing on the *independent* contract about payment, to which there is rarely an answer, that counterclaims relating to the *underlying* contract (of sale or supply) will be ineffective in preventing summary judgment being given and executed.

The fact that there is, as a rule, no defence to a bad cheque does not, of course, prevent the defendant complaining about the goods supplied or sold to him under the underlying contract. Indeed, it does not always prevent people stopping cheques as a bargaining tool when something has gone wrong with such contracts! What it does mean, however, is that such complaints will afford *no defence* to the *claimant's action* on the bad cheque, leaving any claim of defective goods or service to be pursued independently.

revision tips

- Be clear about the distinction - and relationship - between default judgment and summary judgment. The former rarely involves a hearing; the latter always does (as does an application to set aside default judgment). Part 12 default judgment is relevant when a defendant fails to manifest an interest in defending a claim; summary judgment against a defendant who *has* shown an interest in defending is appropriate when the claimant shows that the defence has no real prospect of success (and there is no other compelling reason to have a trial).
- Do not be fooled into thinking that a defence should necessarily be filed within 14 days after acknowledgment of service. A defendant who first acknowledges service has until *28 days after service of the particulars of claim* to file his defence. So a defendant who, for example, acknowledged service within four days would have longer from that point to file a defence than one who acknowledged service on day 12. Examiners like to test this point.

- A defendant seeking to set aside default judgment will have to convince the court that his defence has a real prospect of success or there is some other good reason to have a trial. The 'real prospect of success' test is effectively the same for claimants seeking summary judgment, although the burden is on the defendant seeking to set aside judgment to do the convincing.
- Know the significance of that special kind of counterclaim known as a set-off. Remember that all set-offs are counterclaims, but not all counterclaims are set-offs. Be able to recognise an obvious set-off and its effect in applications such as those for summary judgment.
- Don't forget the 'cheque rule'. Remember the maxim: *There is no defence to a bad cheque.* It will remind you that the principle only operates if the claimant sues on the bad cheque and not the underlying contract.

It is worth reading ...

The judgment in ***Gentry v Millar*** (Practice Note) [2016] 2696. There is a bit of to-ing and fro-ing in this story, but the gist is very easy to understand. Focus on the application to set aside the default judgment. It seems to have been accepted by everyone that the ***Denton*** principles applied in addition to CPR r 13.3 (there are differences of opinion about this, which at the time of writing remains to be fully argued). But notice that even without ***Denton***, the Court of Appeal would have let the default judgment stand, since the application to set aside was not made 'promptly'. Notice too that the court does not cut 'professional' parties much slack!

And for a creepy but fascinating case on summary judgment, read Males J's judgment in ***Sargespace Limited v Natasha Anastasia Eustace*** [2013] EWHC 2944 (QB). I doubt the former barrister-turned playboy (don't get any ideas!) will win any Prince Charming awards. Bet you can't read the first paragraph and not keep going to the end!

CHAPTER 6

Remedies pending trial:
interim injunctions/payments

An important aspect of any case is the substantive remedy or relief sought by the claimant. Courts are limited in what they can do to put right wrongs which have occurred. No amount of money can actually replace a missing leg, for example, but it pays for services and other bills and so this is the remedy which claimants seek, for lack of any other. Another common remedy is an injunction, which is an order that the defendant do, or stop doing, something.[1] Usually it is not until the end of a case that such remedies are ordered; a judge would have to have heard all the evidence before deciding, finally, who was liable - and for what.

There are occasions, however, when the court will order this sort of relief as an interim measure, either where it is obvious the claimant will win at the end of the day and it would be unjust not to grant some part of his ultimate remedy at an earlier, pre-trial stage; or where, without an order pending trial, irreparable damage may be caused to the claimant. Interim injunctions[2] and interim payments are two important forms of this kind of pre-trial order, and it is useful to think of them conceptually as interim versions of the kind of substantive remedy which the claimant ultimately seeks.[3]

1 An order to do something is called a 'mandatory' injunction; an order not to do something, a 'prohibitory' injunction

2 Somewhat confusingly, there are other specialised forms of injunction, which are also granted on interim applications but perform other functions. These are called not by the generic name, but by their more descriptive names, Freezing and search orders. See Ch 7 below.

3 Remember that not all interim orders are temporary versions of the final remedy sought by the claimant. Many are procedural remedies aimed at assisting the progress of the litigation, some of which are discussed in detail in later chapters. See possibilities listed at CPR, r 25.1

1. INTERIM INJUNCTIONS (GOING TO SUBSTANTIVE RELIEF)

Interim injunctions are temporary orders granted by the court to regulate the position between the parties to an action, pending trial. They are coercive in effect: a mandatory injunction requires the respondent to do some defined act(s); a prohibitory injunction restrains the respondent from certain specified conduct. Failure to obey is a contempt of court. Because the orders themselves, and the consequences of breach, are very serious (and unlike most other interim applications), it is usual for applications for interim injunctions to be made (or referred) to a High Court or Circuit Judge, even where the procedural judge has jurisdiction.[4]

It is important to remember that injunctions are a remedy, not a right, and so applications must be founded on an identifiable cause of action (for example, trespass, nuisance, breach of contract), over which the courts have jurisdiction. Most injunction cases involve actionable torts against named defendants committed in England & Wales. If appropriate, an interim injunction may be granted to prevent a threatened wrong before it actually occurs - these are known as quia timet injunctions. Very occasionally (for example, where some but not all of the defendants are known), interim injunctions may be granted against 'persons unknown'.[5] As with all forms of equitable relief, whether or not to grant an injunction (interim or final) is a matter within the *discretion* of the court, which should be exercised with justice and proportionality and the overriding objective in mind.[6] These aspirations are fairly easy to articulate; what is more difficult is understanding how the court, in each individual case, goes about making a decision which achieves these results.

4 Either because it is a County Court case which comes within the District Judge's trial jurisdiction (see Ch 3) or by virtue of CPR, PD 25A, para 1 and PD 2B.

5 See, e.g., ***South Cambridgeshire DC v Persons Unknown*** [2004] EWCA Civ 1280

6 See WB, Vol 1, para 25.1.10 and 11

A. GENERAL RULE: *AMERICAN CYANAMID* GUIDELINES

Given the pre-trial context, it is as well to think about what the judge is being asked to do when considering whether to grant an interim injunction. Assuming the application is made on notice and both sides are present, the judge is being asked to make a decision on written evidence alone, which is usually conflicting, some of which may be wrong, and neither of which may tell the whole story. There is no testing of oral evidence, as there would be at a trial. In effect the judge is asked to make a premature decision, on limited and untested written information, about a form of relief which even if temporary may cause one or other side enormous financial or other irreparable damage.

For this reason, *the general rule* is that so long as the action is not frivolous or vexatious, that is to say, so long as there is a 'serious' (as opposed to a silly) issue to be tried, a decision at *this interim point* should be determined by reference to what is described (with typical English understatement) as the 'balance of convenience', by which the court will ask itself which party would suffer more irreparable hardship by not getting what it wants at this stage? This is the well-known guidance set out in the leading case of *American Cyanamid v Ethicon*.[7] According to that case, beyond checking that there is a serious issue to be tried, a detailed examination of the merits of the case ought to be left to the trial, where witnesses can be heard and their credibility properly evaluated.[8] As one appeal judge put it many years later, the interim judge should not attempt to resolve 'critical disputed questions of fact or difficult points of law' on which the claim of either party may ultimately depend, particularly where the point of law 'turns on fine questions of fact which are in dispute or are presently obscure.'[9] Thus, except in the exceptional cases discussed below, it is only as a *last resort* (to help tip the balance of hardship in those rare cases where it does not obviously favour one or other party) that the court at this interim stage should consider the

7 [1975] AC 396. Balance of 'hardship' might have been a better description.

8 Before this case, the courts had always tried to make their interim decision by reference to the likely outcome at trial. Lord Diplock (at 407) made clear that this was not the right approach: 'it is no part of the court's function *at this stage* to try and resolve conflicts on (written evidence) … nor to decide difficult questions of law which call for detailed argument and mature debate.'

9 *Sukhoruchkin v Van Bekestein* [2014] EWCA Civ 399, Sir Terence Etherton C at para 32, cited in WB, Vol 1, para 25.1.11

substantive merits of the case and attempt to prejudge the ultimate outcome.

Over time a sort of DIY guide[10] was devised to help judges apply the *American Cyanamid* principles, which tends to be set out as a series of steps to take and/or questions which the court should ask itself, namely:

(i) Is there a 'serious issue' or question to be tried?

This is a *very low* hurdle. The court will therefore only investigate the merits to the limited extent of satisfying itself that the claimant's cause of action has some substance in reality. It does not matter at this stage whether the chances of success are 20% or 80%. If there is no serious issue to be tried (in other words, the chance of success is effectively 0%), the injunction will be refused.[11]

(ii) Would the claimant be adequately compensated in damages?

If there is a serious issue to be tried, the court will then consider whether the claimant would be adequately compensated in damages were the injunction not granted. This is a sensible early question, since injunctions are equitable remedies which should not in any event be awarded if damages would adequately compensate the claimant. Damages might well be an adequate remedy in some contract cases, but are often considered not adequate in circumstances where the damage is non-pecuniary (for example, nuisance, trade secrets, negative covenants), or difficult to assess, or where the loss is irreparable (for example, a loss of voting rights). Bear in mind too that the court is a little sensitive about the idea of a defendant effectively being able to 'buy' the right to commit a tort. It will also be *very relevant*, of course, when considering this question whether or not the defendant would be likely to be *able to pay* any damages which might be awarded. So, if damages would be an adequate remedy for the claimant (and the defendant

10 See for example Brown LJ's useful articulation of the principles in ***Fellows & Sons v Fisher*** [1976] 1 QB 22,CA, set out in WB Vol 2, para 15-10

11 For an amusing case which did not even get over this initial hurdle see ***Morning star Co-operative Society Ltd v Express Newspapers Ltd*** [1979] FSR 113

could pay), then, again, the injunction would likely be refused. If, however, damages would not be an adequate remedy for the claimant, then the court would look at the same issue (money as compensation) from the defendant's perspective, and ask itself the next question.

(iii) Would the defendant be adequately protected by an undertaking in damages?

An undertaking in damages is almost always required when an interim injunction is granted. This effectively is a promise which the claimant gives to the court to compensate the defendant (and any other named person affected by the order) for any loss caused by the imposition of the injunction if it later appears that it was wrongly ordered.[12] Here it is the *claimant's* ability to pay which is an important part of the equation. So if, in the circumstances, money would compensate the defendant (and any others named in the order), and the claimant could pay any damage award, then this would incline the court to grant the interim injunction.

You might think of questions (ii) and (iii) as the 'money questions'. They are specific aspects of ascertaining hardship, which are logically considered first since they are often easiest to answer. If the scales of hardship are still evenly balanced at this point (as is often the case), then the court will go on to the next step.

(iv) Other factors weighing into the 'balance of convenience'

This is the stage where most cases 'tip', when the court effectively puts into the balance all other factors in a case which are relevant to deciding whether the grant or refusal of an interim injunction would cause 'uncompensatable disadvantage' or 'irremediable prejudice'[13] to one or other side, and to what extent. Each case will be

12 See CPR, PD 25A, para 5.1(1) and 5.2 (protecting other persons)

13 'Irremediable prejudice' was the expression used by Lord Hoffmann in ***National Commercial Bank Jamaica Ltd v Olint Corporation Ltd*** [2009] 1 WLR 1405

different, but the sorts of matters which can figure into this part of the equation are: loss of employment, loss of goodwill in a business, loss of market share, disruption to non-parties, the public interest in the outcome, the length of time to trial, special factors[14] and so on. These are *essentially the sorts of things that money can't easily buy back.*

If the scales are still evenly balanced at this stage, which is rare, then the court may be assisted by asking itself the next question.

(v) What order would best preserve the status quo?

In *American Cyanamid*, Lord Diplock said: 'Where other factors appear to be evenly balanced it is a counsel of prudence to take such measures as are calculated to preserve the status quo'.[15] The status quo in this context usually means the state of affairs pertaining before the conduct complained of, unless there has been unreasonable delay since then, in which case it would be the state of affairs immediately before the application for the interim injunction. '*Immediately*' should not be taken too literally[16] but the claimant should act promptly to prevent the defendant's offending behaviour itself becoming the status quo. Sometimes it can be difficult to determine the '*status quo*' or there may be cases where preserving the status quo will itself cause injustice, in which case the court may be forced to look more closely at the merits of each party's case.

(vi) Relative strength of each party's case

In a case to which the *American Cyanamid* guidance applies, only *very rarely* will the court be justified in considering the merits of the case in detail, and very much as a *last resort.* Basically if the court gets this far, it has run out of other options. This of course is assuming that the relative strength of the parties' cases is difficult to assess, so if this aspect of a case is easy to discern, it could go into the scales with everything else.

14 Sometimes 'special factors' are listed as a final consideration which might tip the balance one way or the other, but these can just as easily (or perhaps more logically) go into the balance at this stage.

15 Op. cit., at 408

16 See, e.g., *Play It Ltd v Digital Bridges Ltd* [2005] EWHC 1001 (Ch)

The remedy is discretionary, and at the end of the day the *American Cyanamid* guidance should be applied with sufficient flexibility to give effect to the overriding objective.[17]

American Cyanamid was decided in the bad old days when 'interlocutory' warfare was common and a main cause of delay. And in one sense, this case was an early precursor to case management. Its guidance came from the court's desire to avoid getting bogged down with highly contentious issues not suitable for interim applications. Indeed it has been described as creating 'crude case management rules designed to reduce costs and delay and in particular to avoid a case being tried twice.' The CPR of course heralded a very different (and more flexible) approach to case management, with the court very much in charge. The *American Cyanamid* principles seem to have adapted pretty well.[18]

B. EXCEPTIONS TO THE *AMERICAN CYANAMID* APPROACH

It is important to understand, and be able to identify, the situations where the *American Cyanamid* test does *not* apply, either because of an historical exception,[19] the intervention of statute,[20] or because one or more of the assumptions underlying the decision in that case is missing. For example, there are two very different sorts of circumstances when the court will decide the interim injunction application on the apparent strength of the claimant's cause of action. One is where the facts are not disputed and the law is clear, and applying one to the other is easy. In such cases the court will, quite happily, decide the matter 'on the merits', as it is called, because it will be obvious even that early stage that the applicant is entitled to the injunctive relief. The other situation is where it looks as if there will in fact never be a trial of the action because the decision at this interim stage will (if the injunction is granted) effectively amount to a final remedy. Here too the courts feel compelled to decide

17 See, e.g., Laddie J's observations in ***Series 5 Software Ltd v Clarke*** [1996] 1 All ER 853, cited in WB, Vol 2, para 15-15

18 See WB, Vol 2, para 15-9

19 E.g., defamation cases

20 See, e.g., s 12(3) Human Rights Act 1998 and Trades Union and Labour Relations (Consolidation) Act 1992, s 221(2)

the matter on the strength of the claimant's case. These 'merits exceptions' are discussed at some length below.[21]

Let's look at some of these exceptions to *American Cyanamid* in more detail.

(i) Freedom of speech

(a) Defamation cases

The general principle here is that an injunction to restrain an alleged defamation will not be granted, or if granted without notice, will be discharged, where the defendant pleads (or intends to plead) justification, unless the alleged libel is obviously untrue.[22] This is an historical exception[23] to protect free speech. It pre-dates *American Cyanamid* and is unaffected by it.[24] In effect, the public interest in freedom of speech takes absolute priority over any personal right to protect one's reputation by injunction and the individual is left to his (often not inconsiderable) remedy in damages.

But note that this very strict and stark rule does not extend to trade mark infringement cases, even where the trademark is used in comparative advertising (which might be said to 'bad mouth' the competition), nor to claims for damage to reputation not based on defamation. In short, to get the benefit of this particular exception, the cause of action must be *defamation*.[25]

Bear in mind, however, that the courts will not protect purveyors of obvious falsehoods and will check to see that the justification plea is not inherently implausible. Otherwise there is no consideration of merits, no consideration of any balance of hardship; if the defendant's plea of justification is a legitimate one, then no injunction will be allowed, end of story. This ancient guardian of freedom of speech is thus extremely protective where interim injunctions are sought; even more so than the human rights legislation.

---

21 At the time of writing, the focus of the Bar exam syllabus is on the so-called 'merits' exceptions (and especially 'final disposal' cases) and so this will be covered in more detail in this chapter than the others.

22 See, e.g., ***Greene v Associated Newspapers Ltd*** [2005] QB 972. Allied defences, such as fair comment on a matter of public interest or privilege can also trigger the rule.

23 Notice the date of the leading case of ***Bonnard v Perryman*** [1891] 2 Ch 269

24 As confirmed in the amusing case of ***Bestobell Paints Ltd v Bigg*** [1975] FSR 421. Obviously it also predates the Human Rights Act 1998.

25 ***Boehringer Ingelheim Ltd v Vetplus Ltd*** [2007] FSR 29

(b) Other cases

It is with cases *other than* defamation where freedom of speech under Art 10 of the European Convention on Human Rights is at issue, that s 12(3) Human Rights Act 1998 comes into play.[26] This requires the claimant to show a case which will 'probably succeed' at trial before an interim injunction will be granted which interferes with freedom of expression.[27] This clearly involves close consideration of the merits of the case, and so is another exception to (or at least an adaptation of) *American Cyanamid.*

Applications based on a right to privacy under Art 8 can also present a conflict with Art 10. There is no cause of action for privacy, as such, and this is an evolving field jurisprudentially. Interim injunctions in such cases are determined by applying *American Cyanamid*, but specifically weighing into the balance the public interest element. In other words a court will ask itself, in each case, whether the desire to keep the information in question private ought, in the circumstances, to yield to the right to free speech under Art 10, bearing in mind that neither Art 8 nor Art 10 takes precedence over the other in principle. In *Douglas v Hello! Ltd*[28] for example, the court would have been a lot more sympathetic to the happy couple's claim that the defendant magazine's desire to publish photographs of their wedding infringed their right to privacy had they not already sold the right to do so to someone else (so in fact privacy was not really the point!).

(ii) The common law 'merits exceptions'

(a) Entitlement to injunction obvious at interim stage

There are two important assumptions which lie behind the decision in *American Cyanamid.* One is that the appropriate place to determine the merits of the case is at trial, where conflicting evidence can be properly scrutinised and tested. The interim judge does not have the tools, or the time, to consider properly the substantive merits of the case.

26 See *ibid*, applying *Cream Holdings Ltd v Banerjee* [2005] 1 AC 253

27 *McKennit v Ash* [2008] QB 73

28 [2001] QB 967

Sometimes, however, this is *not* the situation. Where the facts are not disputed and the law is clear (so that the right to the remedy is clearly established) it will be straightforward to apply the one to the other and the court will be content to determine the interim application 'on the merits of' the cause of action. In a sense there is no serious question to be tried since the outcome is *obvious* and so the testing of the evidence at trial is unnecessary.[29] Other stages of the *American Cyanamid* test would, thus, not arise. This would also be in keeping with the court's case management remit.

Typical cases falling within this exception include clear-cut breaches of confidence; clear cut sale of land cases and, generally, claims where there is no arguable defence.

These sorts of cases are analogous to a summary judgment situation (and, indeed, this may sometimes be an appropriate alternative application). And in the same sort of way, the court would have to be satisfied of the 'overwhelming' strength of the applicant's case in order to grant the interim injunction on this basis. Claimants are usually happy to come within this exception because they almost always get their injunction. But it is important to note that if the claimant's case is not 'open-and-shut',[30] then the *American Cyanamid* principles would apply (unless the case falls into the next category).

(b) Final disposal cases: interim decision effectively final

The second assumption underlying *American Cyanamid* is that there is, in fact, going to be a trial of the action. This, too, may not always be so. There will be some cases where, as a practical matter, the grant or refusal of an injunction at the interim stage will effectively 'dispose of the action' fully, in favour of whichever party is successful. This is because there may be nothing left (insofar as the injunction remedy is

29 *Office Overload v Gunn* [1977] FSR 39, CA

30 *Lawrence David Ltd v Ashton* [1991] 1 All ER 385, CA, per Balcombe LJ.

concerned) on which it will be in the unsuccessful party's interest to proceed to trial. And where the contest over the injunction at the interim stage is likely to be the *only* contest, then again different considerations apply.

This situation commonly arises when something is scheduled to happen within a relatively short time (for example, the transmission of a TV programme or a concert) and, whatever the outcome, the injunction issue will be old news (or a non-issue) by the time of any trial, or a future trial will come too late to be of any use.[31] In such cases, (and if it is not practical to proceed more quickly to trial), the court feels it *must* determine the application on the strength of the cause of action because, if there is going to be no later trial of the injunction claim, it is 'now or never.'[32] This investigation need not, and perhaps should not, amount to a mini-trial of the action - it is for the interim judge to control the extent of the investigation. What it does mean, is that to succeed, a claimant must show *far more* than a 'serious issue to be tried' (the very low threshold for classic *American Cyanamid* cases). In these sorts of cases the claimant must again have a much more 'overwhelming' case. This is because where the outcome at the interim stage for all practical purposes gives the claimant his final injunctive remedy, it also has the effect of depriving the defendent of his chance to put his full case at trial, and there must be a compelling reason to do this.[33] Claimants can very rarely meet this very high standard. It is for this reason that they dislike their case being determined on this exceptional basis (and will try hard to argue that their case should be determined on *American Cyanamid* principles).

(iii) Mandatory injunctions

Mandatory injunctions are orders which require the respondent to do something, and are sometimes considered something of an exception to *American Cyanamid*, requiring a 'high degree of assurance' that the applicant is entitled to the remedy

31 See, e.g., *Cream Holdings*, *ibid*

32 See, e.g., *Cayne v Global National Resources plc* [1984] 1 All ER 225, CA. Some restraint of trade cases might come under this category of merits exception, if not under the previous: WB Vol 2, para 15-20

33 Per Everleigh HJ, in *Cayne v Global*, *ibid*, p 233. See generally WB Vol 2 para 15-18. You might find that these 'merits cases' are described in the WB commentary either as 'exceptions' to *American Cyanamid* or 'variations' or 'adaptations' of it. Do not let this confuse you. What is important is that you can distinguish a 'final disposal' fact pattern from a classic *American Cyanamid* case.

before it is granted at the interim stage. In fact, it is pretty clear now that there is no underlying difference *in principle* between interim applications for prohibitory and mandatory injunctions, but generally speaking the latter are apt to cause greater 'inconvenience' than the former. So mandatory injunctions are harder to get on that account. The 'high degree of assurance' test lives on as a factor which, weighed in the balance, might offset the prejudice which the injunction would cause to the respondent. But it is *not* a prerequisite as such. Some acts are easier to perform than others, and so much will depend on the circumstances of the individual case, as Lord Hoffmann made clear in *National Commercial Bank Jamaica Ltd v Olint Corporation Ltd.*[34]

C. PROCEDURE

The application is much like any other under CPR, r 23. Both the High Court and County Court have jurisdiction to grant the kinds of interim injunctions we have been discussing[35], and wherever the substantive claim has been brought, then generally this is where the interim application would be made. Such applications may be made in any level of case (even one allocated to the small claims track) and are usually made *on notice*. Thus the application notice (stating the order sought and reasons for it) is issued, and served on the other side as soon as practicable and in any event at least *three clear days* before the hearing, along with the *written evidence* in support and (wherever possible) a *draft order.*[36] *Skeleton arguments* are usually required, especially in the High Court, and *costs schedules* should be filed by both sides 24 hours before the hearing.

Applications should be made as soon as the need becomes apparent. There are very few good reasons for not giving proper notice when applying for these sorts of interim injunctions. The most common justification is exceptional urgency, for example where there is an imminent threat of damage which cannot wait for what is

34 Op. cit., cited at WB, Vol 2, para 15-24

35 Some specialist injunctions (e.g., search orders) and some specialist causes of action (e.g., libel) can only be dealt with in the High Court.

36 Where possible an electronic version of the draft order sought should also be made available to the court, to be used, amended as necessary, for any order it might make. See generally PD 25A, paras 2 and 3

37 CPR, r 25.3 refers to the need for 'good reasons'. In addition to extreme urgency, interim applications may also be made without giving notice if the court gives permission, all the parties consent or if the overriding objective is furthered by doing so (e.g., because of

a relatively short notice period and requires the immediate intervention of the court.[37] Even so, where the application is made without giving formal notice to the other side (and assuming secrecy is not an issue), all reasonable attempts should be made to tell the other side what is going on.[38] This is an important requirement - the ability to send messages on mobile phones makes it very difficult these days to justify not, at the very least, giving informal notice of such applications. Sometimes with informal (or short) notice, the other side may be able to attend.

The claim form[39] should also have been issued, unless the case is so urgent there was no time to do this either, in which case an application by a claimant pre-action can be entertained.[40] Some latitude is given for cases of this degree of urgency, so that informal evidence may be relied upon. It would be very unusual for a prospective *defendant* to want to apply for an injunction pre-action, and they can only do so with the court's permission. Otherwise a defendant, who might perhaps be seeking injunctive relief on a counter-claim, must normally wait to make an application for an interim injunction until they have filed an acknowledgement of service or defence in the case brought against them.[41]

On a without notice application, full and frank disclosure must be made to the court. As you will remember, this is a critical requirement and obliges the applicant to tell the court about all known matters of fact or law, including those *adverse* to the applicant's case, which might affect the judge's decision.[42] The applicant must also explain why formal notice could not be given, and set out what was done to give informal notice. These matters should be addressed in the written evidence. The advocate should also make a note of the hearing. To grant an injunction against someone who has not had his day in court is very serious indeed. As with any without notice interim application, any order the court makes must inform the absent party of his right to apply to have the order set aside or varied. In any event, interim injunctions granted

the need for secrecy): PD23, para 4

38 PD 25A, para 4.3(3) and as discussed in Ch 4

39 Where the interim injunction is a temporary version of the final remedy sought, the latter (a final injunction, also sometimes called a 'perpetual' injunction) must be clearly set out in the claim form: CPR, r 16.2. But remember that the court has an overriding power to grant any sort of interim remedy, whether or not there has been a claim for a final remedy of that kind: r 25.1(4) and see Ch 4

40 Or it is otherwise in the interests of justice: CPR, r 25.2(2)(b). Extremely urgent applications can be made by telephone: PD 25A, para 4.5

41 CPR, r 25.2(2)(c)

42 See discussion at WB, Vol 1, para 25.3.5

in the absence of the other side will only last for such limited time as is necessary for the application to be resumed (on a stated return date) after proper notice is given to the respondent.[43]

Note that even where the other side attends, having been given informal or 'short notice', the applicant remains under this very important duty to make full and frank disclosure. This is because the respondent (whether represented or not) may not be as prepared as one would expect if proper notice had been given, and were it otherwise there would be no incentive to attend a hearing on short notice, which can save the court time and money.[44]

The court takes this obligation to give full and frank disclosure very seriously. If it is not observed, the court may discharge any interim injunction granted as a result - it may do so (and refuse a fresh application) even if, after looking at all the matters of which it should have been made aware, it would probably have granted the injunction anyway. In such situations the court has to balance the need for a deterrent (against non-disclosure in without notice applications) and the interests of justice. Having said that, litigants should not 'chance their arm' by making accusations of material non-disclosure on a flimsy basis. The court will not be interested in 'trifling errors'.[45]

Finally, it is especially important to be aware of the relevant *undertakings* (which are promises to *the court*, not to the other party) which may be necessary when interim injunctions are ordered or agreed. The mainstay, of course, is the claimant's undertaking in damages - this is a promise to compensate the other side (or affected third parties) if at the end of the day it transpires that the interim injunction should not have been granted (for example, if the claimant loses the case at trial). This is sometimes referred to as a 'cross undertaking' since it is being given in exchange for the injunction, and it is an important protection for the defendant. Strictly the court

43 CPR, r 23.9(3) and PD 25A, para 5.1(3)

44 This does not mean that the applicant needs to duplicate information or points made by the attending respondent. See Chapter 4 and WB, Vol 1, para 25.3.5.1

45 See discussion at WB, Vol 1, para 25.3.6-25.3.8

cannot order the claimant to make such a promise to it, but the willingness to do so is effectively 'the price' of getting an interim injunction. If the undertaking is not very 'meaningful' (because the applicant hasn't much money), this will not bar the applicant absolutely from the interim order, but it will be something to be taken into account in deciding whether or not to grant the injunction.[46]

The applicant may also need to give additional undertakings, depending on whether the application was made without notice and/or pre-action. In effect, whatever an applicant was unable to do procedurally because of lack of time (for example, serve the application notice and evidence in support), he will have to undertake to do as part and parcel of any order he is granted.[47]

Defendants themselves may offer the court a cross undertaking in terms similar to that sought by the claimant, instead of contesting the application for an interim injunction. Where these become incorporated into a consent order (confirming an agreement *between the parties*), they will be construed (and enforced) as any other contractual obligation.

Otherwise, breach of an undertaking is a contempt of court. And because they are promises *to* the court, *not* orders *of* the court, they cannot be appealed or varied, as such, although a different undertaking can be accepted and substituted (which more or less gets you to the same place). A party who wants to be 'released' from the undertaking (usually to be replaced by another), must however show that there has been a *significant* change of circumstances (arising since the undertaking was given). A mere change of mind or re-assessment of the facts would not normally be sufficient.[48]

Finally, it probably goes without saying that any injunction ordered by the court (interim or final!) must be worded with sufficient precision so that it is very clear what the respondent is prevented from doing or is required to do. An application by a claimant seeking injunctive relief which is vague or imprecise will not succeed.[49]

46 See WB, Vol 2, para 15-30
47 See PD 25A, para 5.1
48 A claimant who really does not wish to abide by an undertaking proposed by the court could refuse to do so, knowing that the interim injunction would thereby be refused, and then appeal that refusal. For these somewhat technical distinctions, see WB, Vol 1, para 25.1.14.1/2
49 WB, Vol 1, para 25.1.9 (para 5) and PD 25A, para 5.5

2. INTERIM PAYMENT (OF DAMAGES)

Interim payments are a means by which claimants can get some of their money remedy ('damages, debt or other sum, except costs'[50]) 'on account' as it were, before the full trial or assessment of damages. Where:

(i) the defendant has admitted liability;

or

(ii) the claimant has already got early judgment against the defendant (for example, default or summary judgment), damages to be assessed;

or

(iii) where the court is *satisfied* that (if the claim went to trial) the claimant *would* obtain judgment for *substantial* damages from the defendant,

- then the court may order the defendant to make an interim payment to the claimant.[51] Grounds (i) and (ii) speak for themselves - as to (iii), the claimant must satisfy the court that he would actually succeed on his claim (or part of it) at trial *and* that he would obtain judgment for a substantial amount of money. Substantial means not negligible or nominal, and should be judged in the overall context of the case, but it means that interim payments are not appropriate for most small claims track cases. Indeed most applications for interim payments are made in multi-track cases.

The standard of proving the claim would succeed at trial is said to be the balance of probabilities, but it will likely be more difficult for a claimant to achieve this standard on the limited written material available to the court at this interim stage than it would be at trial.[52] So it is quite a high bar. The idea behind the interim payment procedure is to make it possible for a claimant to be awarded at an early

50 CPR, r 25.1(1)(k)

51 See CPR, r 25.7. If C's claim is for possession of land, the court should be satisfied that if the case went to trial the defendant would be held liable to pay the claimant a sum of money for the occupation of that land whilst the possession action is pending: CPR, r 25.7(d)

52 *Tests Claimants in FII Group Litigation v Commissioners of HM Revenue and Customs* [2012] 1 WLR 2375

stage some of the money which it appears clear he will obtain at the end of the day, and where it would be unjust to make him wait that long. The court has a *discretion*, but if the conditions are made out it will usually make an order unless there is some good reason not to. Bear in mind that ordering an interim payment runs counter to the general notion that defendants should not have to part with any money until final judgment has been given - so it is important to get it right. Certainly no-one wants the claimant to have to sell his wheelchair because the interim payment made to him needs to be given back to the defendant!

So, for example, in the context of a summary judgment application by a claimant, where that application is dismissed, and the case continues to trial, it would be inconsistent also to grant the claimant an interim payment award. The court cannot simultaneously be satisfied to the requisite standard that the claimant would succeed at trial for interim payment purposes *and* that the defendant has a real prospect of success at trial. It might, however, be possible to have an interim payment where the summary judgment application has been dealt with by way of a *conditional* order (although this would depend on how doubtful the court is of the defendant's defence); indeed the making of the interim payment could be the condition.

Interim payments thus help tide claimants over during what can sometimes be a long period until trial or assessment of damages.[53] And there can be a benefit for the defendant too - if, for example, an injured claimant uses the money for early rehabilitative treatment, this might well reduce the overall amount of the claim. Indeed, often interim payments are made voluntarily for this purpose. And of course an interim payment would reduce the defendant's liability to pay interest at the end of the day.

It is obvious that interim payments are common and particularly useful in personal injuries actions, but it is important to note that they *are not limited* to such

53 Liability may well be admitted, but calculating damages can be very complex.

cases. Examiners sometimes like to test students on this.

Stringman v McArdle[54] (a pre-CPR case) decided that a claimant does not have to show a need for the money as a pre-condition of getting the order; only that the procedural requirements have been met. On the other hand, the relevant practice direction specifically requires the claimant to include in the written evidence supporting the application what the money will be used for.[55] This is because the interim judge will have to be very careful (and conservative) in predicting the sort of order which the trial judge might make before making an interim payment award. One has to be especially cautious as regards future losses, particularly when these might ultimately be catered for, not with a single sum, but with a periodic payments order.[56] To this extent, therefore, need (or lack of it) will be highly relevant both as to how much to order by way of interim payment and, if choices have to be made, *for what aspect* of the claimant's losses.[57]

Multiple defendants

Where there are two or more defendants, if it is clear to the court that a specific defendant will be liable to the claimant, then, assuming the other procedural requirements are met, the court can order an interim payment against that one identified defendant, regardless of the fact that there are other defendants named in the proceedings. In other words, even where there are multiple defendants, if the claimant can establish that he would recover substantial damages from one of them, the court can make an interim payment order against that one, if it sees fit.

Where, however, there are multiple defendants and it is *unclear* against whom the claimant will succeed, then an interim payment may still be ordered, but *only if* it is established that:

- The claimant will succeed against *at least one* of the named defendants,

54 [1994] 1 WLR 1653

55 CPR, PD 25B, para 2

56 These are common with catastrophic injury cases and involve regular payments over what is often a very long time. If a big chunk of money has been expended with an interim payment award (for example to buy a specially adapted house) this might mean there is not enough capital left at the end of the day to fund a long-term periodical payments award. In a sense the 'need' for the new house becomes a foregone conclusion. Coulson J (as he then was) sets out the principles well in ***Brewis v Heatherwood & Wrexham Park Hospitals NHS Trust*** [2008] EWHC 2526 (QB).

57 See ***Smith v Bailey*** [2014] EWHC 2569 (QB), building on the Court of Appeal decision in ***Eeles v Cobham Hire Services Ltd*** [2009] EWCA Civ 204. And see

even if it is not clear which;

and

- all of the defendants are *either insured, public bodies* or defendants whose liability will be met by, for example, the Motor Insurance Bureau.[58]

These additional requirements are intended to safeguard the position if the 'wrong' defendant is required to make the interim payment, which could easily happen if it is not clear who will be held ultimately liable to the claimant. Where *only* insurance companies and public bodies are involved, no great injustice will occur if one of those sorts of defendants has to reimburse another at the end of the day. Otherwise, the claimant has to point the finger of blame clearly at the defendant from whom he seeks an interim payment.

Amount of interim payment

It is important that the court does not order an interim payment greater than the amount ultimately awarded at trial. Thus an interim payment must not exceed a '*reasonable proportion*' of the likely amount of the final judgment.[59] The rules are no more specific than this, to allow the courts to exercise their discretion from case to case, although in practice the amount ordered will be apt to cover the special damage claim, plus (perhaps) some proportion of the general damage claim, taking care to be conservative and as accurate as possible about a likely final award. But the wording of the rule is left purposely wide. Counterclaims/set-offs and allegations of contributory negligence will obviously have to be taken into account.[60] The idea is that at the end of the day, the claimant recovers more by way of total damages than was awarded by way of interim payment![61]

Note that if an interim payment has been ordered, *no mention of it should be made*

below regarding amount of an interim payment.

58 See CPR, r 25.7(1)(e). The Motor Insurance Bureau (MIB) picks up the tab for uninsured drivers.

59 See CPR, r 25.7(4)

60 CPR, r 25.7(5)

61 Though the court has extensive powers to make 'adjustment' if need be, including orders that the claimant reimburse the defendant. See CPR, r 25.8

to the trial judge until all matters of liability and quantum are decided.[62] There is an obvious risk of prejudice if the trial judge knows that an interim judge thought the case so clearly favoured the claimant. This is a very important rule which is forgotten at the advocate's peril - such could result in a mis-trial and a personal costs order.

Remember, too, that unlike a Part 36 offer,[63] an interim payment has no costs implications. It is not an offer of settlement in any way. Nor is it a payment into court. Rather it is an order or agreement that a defendant pay out to a claimant now some of what the defendant will, or will almost certainly, have to pay out to the claimant at the end of the trial or other assessment of damage.

Procedure

This is a fairly typical Part 23 interim application. It is made *on notice*, with supporting *evidence in writing* to include the matters set out at PD 25B, para 2, which are specifically geared to the nature of the interim remedy. This includes the amount sought by way of interim payment, what the payment is to be used for, what the likely total judgment will be, the reasons for believing the grounds for such an order are made out, and so on. Documents in support (including medical reports) must be exhibited - defendants in personal injuries actions should obtain and file a certificate of recoverable benefits.[64]

An application for an interim payment cannot be made before the time the defendant is given to acknowledge service has expired (but otherwise should be made as soon as the desirability of doing so becomes apparent).

The application (like a summary judgment application) must be served on the defendant at least *14 days* before the hearing. A defendant should serve any evidence in reply at least *seven days* before the hearing date, and any further evidence in reply from the claimant must be filed at least *three days* before the hearing. Second or further

62 Unless the defendant does not mind, which would be rare. See CPR, r 25.9

63 *See below*, Ch 15

64 CPR, PD 25B, para 4.1: skeleton arguments and so forth will be required.

applications for an interim payment may be made in appropriate circumstances.[65]

INTERIM PAYMENTS VERSUS PROVISIONAL DAMAGES

Word of warning! Do not confuse interim payments with provisional damages.

They sound as if they could be the same thing, but they are very different. Interim payments, which can be awarded in *any sort* of case, are about a claimant getting some of his ultimate damage award *before* the trial of the action. Provisional damage claims are limited to *personal injuries claims only*, and really focus on what happens (or might happen) *after* the trial (or settlement).

Even if paid in instalments, damages are usually calculated on a one-off, once-and-for-all basis, immediately after liability is established or as soon thereafter as damages can be properly assessed. This is not always well suited to situations where, at the time of assessing loss and damage, there is merely a chance that some deterioration in health (for which the defendant would be liable) will occur in the future. If that chance is assessed on a once-and-for-all basis, it can only be calculated in percentage terms. This can result in the claimant either being over-compensated, if the disease or deterioration never happens, or (more problematically) under-compensated, when it does happen, because the damages awarded earlier reflected merely the possibility, not the actuality. The problem is particularly pronounced in cases where there is a relatively small chance of some dreadful disease occurring.

To remedy this situation, the courts are given the power to make awards of what are known as 'provisional damages'. They work like this: in assessing immediate damages on a once-and-for-all basis, it is assumed that the named disease or deterioration in question will not happen, and so is *left out of account altogether*. But if it does occur within a *specified time*, the claimant[66] can come back to

65 CPR, r 25.6

66 Or his dependents if the claimant has died. See Fatal Accidents Act 1976, s 3

court and have that aspect of his losses accurately assessed.[67]

There are essentially four conditions:

(a) Condition 1: The claim for provisional damages must be set out in the *particulars of claim*.[68]

(b) Condition 2: The possible future disease or deterioration must be '*serious*' in nature. To be serious, the condition must be something beyond ordinary wear and tear. Conditions like osteoarthritis pose problems because we all are apt to suffer them with age.[69]

(c) Condition 3: It must be '*proved or admitted*' that there is a '*chance*' of the future disease or deterioration occurring. In other words, it is only *how* the loss is to be compensated which remains at issue, not the nature of the loss, nor the defendant's responsibility for it. The chance of deterioration is usually fairly easily established by the medical evidence.

(d) Condition 4: The future development or deterioration must be of the claimant's '*physical or mental condition*'. So, provisional damages are limited to this one, albeit important, aspect of a personal injuries claim. It does not apply to the chance that a claimant might lose his job or his house in future; if causally connected, these sorts of loss continue to be assessed on a once-and-for-all basis.

Even if these conditions are all met, it is still a matter of the court's *discretion* whether to make a provisional, rather than a conventional, damage award. Common sense considerations apply, including which form of judgment would dispense better justice and how easily it will be to know when and whether a serious deterioration

67 See, Senior Courts Act 1981, s 32A: County Courts Act 1984, s 51

68 CPR, r 41.2(1)

69 See, e.g., *Willson v Ministry of Defence* [1991] 1 All ER 638

has in fact occurred.[70]

If an order for provisional damages is made, it should specify both the nature of the disease or deterioration in question and *how* long a period the claimant has to make a future application to the court should the worst happen.[71] Provisional damages are hard enough on a defendant, without the time-frame being completely open-ended. Having said that, the period can be expressed to last for the claimant's life in appropriate circumstances. A claimant making an application for the further assessment of damages must give the defendant or the defendant's insurers at least 28 days notice. Many years might have passed since the original order and it may take some time to find the files. Subsequent procedure is much like that for an interim payment, which conveniently brings me back to my initial warning: be sure you know the difference between interim payments and provisional damages!

70 *Ibid*

71 See generally CPR, r 41.2(2) and PD 41A, para 2.1 An example of a provisional damage award is given at the annex to PD41A

revision tips

- The interim remedies discussed in this chapter mirror the claimant's substantive claim. Others are aimed at assisting the litigation process. CPR, r 25.1 lumps them all together in one list but it helps to make the distinction.
- You must be able to recognise both the guidance in, and the name of, the *American Cyanamid* case. It is worth reading Lord Diplock's judgment. It is very short!
- You should have a good grasp of the situations where the principles in *American Cyanamid* do *not* apply - and *why*. Check your syllabus to know which 'exceptions' to focus on.
- The White Book commentary on interim injunctions (especially Vol 2) can sometimes seem like wading through treacle. Keep calm and carry on. Highlight the key concepts.
- Be clear about the *distinction* between interim payments and provisional damages. They sound similar, but they are very different.

It is worth reading ...

Lord Hoffmann's judgment in ***National Commercial Bank Jamaica Ltd v Olint Corporation Ltd*** [2009] UKPC 16, [2009] 1 WLR 1405. This is a Privy Council case, which might just get you feeling sorry for banks (if that is possible)! Lord Hoffmann's judgments are a pleasure to read - this one is short, and to the point, but no less enlightening for that. Note in particular what he has to say about without notice applications and the court's approach to granting (interim) mandatory injunctions. You should be getting the message now that the courts do not much favour applicants who do not give notice to the other side when they should.

The judgment in ***Brewis v Heatherwood & Wrexham Park Hospitals NHS Trust*** [2008] EWHC 2526(QB). With his usual clarity, Coulson J (as he then was) sets out the principles regarding how amounts by way of interim payments are determined in catastrophic injury cases (where there will be periodic payments over many years) - and then demonstrates how it is done.

CHAPTER 7

Making litigation meaningful: freezing and search orders[1]

There are some forms of interim injunction which are not geared to the claimant's ultimate remedy or relief, but which aim to make the litigation meaningful, either by ensuring that there are funds to enforce against if the claimant wins, or by preserving crucial evidence. These are known, respectively, as *freezing* and *search* orders, although the older case law will refer to them by their pre-CPR names of *Mareva* Injunction and *Anton Piller* Order.[2] It is important both to distinguish them from the more 'bog standard' type of interim injunction discussed in the last chapter, and also to appreciate just how draconian these forms of order are.

1. FREEZING ORDERS

Freezing orders are designed to stop defendants (or potential defendants) from wilfully turning themselves into paupers or hiding assets in order to thwart a claimant's ability, if he wins the case, to get his hands on them. If there are no assets, there will be no way to execute judgment[3] and the claimant will get no money! Freezing orders make litigation meaningful for a claimant because a 'paper' judgment is of little use. Freezing orders thus restrain defendants from 'disposing of', 'dissipating'

1 At the time of writing these forms of injunction are not on the Bar Examination syllabus. This could change in future years, so always check carefully what is being tested.

2 Named after the leading cases of *Mareva Compania Naviera SA v International Bulk Carriers SA* [1980] 1All ER 213 and *Anton Piller KG v Manufacturing Processes Ltd* [1976] Ch 55. The CPR gave them more modern and descriptive names.

3 As to enforcement of judgments generally see Ch 19. It is usually claimants who seek freezing orders against defendants, and so I use those terms here, but anyone in a 'claimant-like' position can apply, e.g., a counterclaiming defendant or defendant against a third party.

or even 'dealing with' certain of their assets so as to frustrate the enforcement of any judgment the claimant may obtain against them. The amount 'frozen' should not normally exceed the value of the claim. It is, of course, very serious to stop people using their own money before they have been judged liable to pay some of it to another person, so such orders are not granted lightly. After all, maybe it will be the defendant who wins the case! So, although the granting of such orders, like all injunctions, is discretionary,[4] the conditions for obtaining freezing injunctions are very strict. They are as follows:

(i) Jurisdiction

The claimant must show *a substantive cause of action over which the court has jurisdiction* (or in respect of which it can act). An injunction is a remedy, and thus needs a cause of action to which it relates. The order cannot 'simply be made in the air'.[5] As a general rule, therefore, an applicant must be able to point to proceedings underway or about to be commenced, so as to show where and on what basis he expects to get judgment against the defendant. It is no longer strictly necessary to show that the substantive action is to be brought in the English courts,[6] although this will usually be the case.

(ii) Strength of case

The claimant must show he has a '*good arguable case*'. This is a middling standard; higher than that required for an *American Cyanamid* type of injunction (which is about as low as it gets), but not as high as, say, summary judgment applications.

(iii) Assets

The claimant must show that the defendant *has assets in (or exceptionally out of) the*

4 S 37(1) Senior Courts Act 1981 enables the court to grant interim injunctions where it appears 'just and convenient' to do so, and 'on such terms and conditions' as it thinks just.

5 Per Lord Mustill in *Mercedes-Benz A.G. v Leiduck* [1995] 3 All ER, PC, at 929

6 See CJJA 19882, s 25 and *Fourie v Le Roux* [2007] 1 WLR 320, HL

jurisdiction. Assets come in all shapes and sizes: money, land, valuable things like cars and jewellery. So long as the asset belongs to the defendant, or he can get his hands on it, then it can be the subject of an order. Normally, the assets to be frozen must be in the jurisdiction, but in exceptional circumstances, the court will make a 'worldwide' order affecting assets both here and/or abroad.[7] The relevant assets must be identified with some degree of precision, so the court can make the order. Normally an order would freeze named assets up to a maximum value, not to exceed the most that the claimant could win in the case.

(iv) Real risk of dissipation

The claimant must show that there is a *'real risk' of the dissipation or disposal of those assets* so as to render judgment of no value. This is the critical requirement, and the most difficult to establish, in part because there is rarely direct evidence of such a risk. It is usually to be inferred from some conduct or attitude of the defendant's, but an expression of general apprehension on the part of the claimant will not be enough.[8] The ease with which a defendant could dispose of assets will be an obvious consideration, but the claimant's ability to enforce judgment is also key. Remember, too, that it is not the job of a freezing order to provide security for the claim;[9] its purpose is to obviate the risk that a defendant's actions might render himself 'judgment proof'. A useful list of factors relating to this aspect of freezing orders is set out at BCP, para 38.13.

Have a look at the standard form of freezing injunction annexed to PD 25A, which includes a version for both domestic and worldwide orders, to get a feel for what the order typically sounds like.

7 These will only be ordered, effectively, when it is shown that there are no or insufficient assets in the jurisdiction and that there are identifiable assets out of the jurisdiction. See, e.g., *Derby v Weldon (No 1)* [1990] Ch 48. CA

8 See, e.g., *O'Regan v Iambic Productions* [1989] 139 NLJ (Sir Peter Pain)

9 The order does not put the claimant in any better position than any other creditor. But note that the fact that a defendant has a dubious credit history does not in itself justify the making of an order: *Mobile Cerro Negro Ltd. V Petroleos de Venezuela SA* [2008] 1 Lloyd's Rep 684 (Walker J at para 36)

2. SEARCH ORDERS

Search orders are about preserving things of vital evidential value to the claimant's case, in circumstances where there is a *real risk* that the defendant might try to destroy or tamper with them, before the evidence can be exchanged or sought in the normal way. They make litigation meaningful because a claimant may not be able to prove his case at trial without this evidence. This form of injunction, which is a bit like a civil search and seizure order, allows a claimant, without warning,[10] to enter the defendant's premises to find, and keep safe until trial, certain named pieces or types of evidence. This obviously involves a very serious invasion of the defendant's personal (or business) space and will not be ordered lightly. Indeed, it is largely considered to be an interim remedy of last resort.

Like any other injunctive relief, whether the court grants a search order is a matter of discretion. *At a minimum*, however, the following are essential requirements:

(i) Strength of case

The claimant must have an *extremely strong prima facie case* on the merits. This is a noticeably higher standard even than the freezing order. Not as high as for summary judgment, perhaps, but getting there. If the case were just middling in strength, presumably the defendant's motivation to tamper with or destroy evidence would not be very high either.

(ii) Serious harm

The defendant's activities must be shown to cause *very serious actual or potential harm* to the claimant. This is often not difficult to establish as such. Search orders tend to be applied for in cases involving fraud, big money divorces and infringement of

10 But with safeguards, *see below*.

intellectual property rights, where either the continued conduct of the defendant or the vanishing evidence is pretty obviously at least potentially harmful.

(iii) Evidence of possession

There must be *clear evidence* that the incriminating items are in the possession (or control) of the defendant.

(iv) Real risk of tampering/destruction

It must be shown that there is a *real possibility* that the items of evidence will be tampered with or destroyed before (or if) the application were made on notice. As with the freezing order, this requirement goes to the *heart* of the application. In the normal course of litigation, evidence is exchanged as a result of appropriate pre-trial conduct, following court directions[11] or by an order of the court after a contested hearing, with both sides present. It is assumed that most people will comply with such requirements, however reluctantly. Thus, to get the search order there must be a cogent reason for believing that the defendant would disobey a request or order to preserve the evidence in question. Again, the court is usually asked to infer such a risk from the defendant's conduct, although it will be wary of 'the extravagant fears which seem to afflict claimants who have complaints of breach of confidence, breach of copyright and passing-off'.[12]

In the exercise of its discretion, the court will also ask itself whether granting the order is proportionate in the circumstances. This will be particularly important if the evidence would significantly harm the defendant or benefit the claimant over and above its preservation for trial.

There was a time when *Anton Piller* Orders (as search orders used to be called) were given out like sweets, but those days are long gone.[13] Before embarking on

11 See Ch 9

12 Per Dillon LJ in *Booker McConnell v Plascow Plc* [1985] R.P.C. 425, at 441

13 See, e.g., the court's stern words in *Columbia Pictures Industries Inc v Robinson* [1987] Ch 28

an application for a search order, it is always incumbent on a claimant to have considered whether some less draconian measure would suffice.[14]

In any case, remember that a search order is *not* a search warrant. It is directed to a named person, not a place. The defendant can refuse entry, and no one should be kicking in doors or otherwise forcing entrance. It is not a police operation! Having said that, a failure to comply with a search order would amount to a contempt of court and itself could be rather damning evidence against the defendant in the upcoming trial to which the order relates.

Given the harsh nature of search orders, there are a host of *safeguards* and rules designed to ensure that they are carried out properly and fairly, and that any property belonging to the defendant is returned as soon as its evidential value has been preserved (for example after copying). These are set out very clearly at PD25A, paras 7.2 to 7.11. In addition, an example of a search order is annexed to the practice direction. Take a careful look at these. Note especially the possibility of including what are sometimes called 'ancillary orders' which augment a search order. These typically require the defendant to disclose relevant information, either as regards the evidence in question or the cause of action itself. None of these are unusual in themselves, since they may be required or ordered in the ordinary course of litigation. In the context of a without notice search order, however, they become part and parcel of the draconian nature of the injunction.

As you might appreciate, there is an uncomfortable interface between search orders and an individual's privilege against self-incrimination, that is, the right to refuse to answer any questions, or produce any document or thing, if to do so would expose that person to criminal sanctions.[15] Although in one sense rather damning to assert this privilege, the consequence of relying on it has been to thwart the execution of many a search order, given the types of cases in which such orders tend

14 E.g., order to produce or deliver up documents, order to inspect, etc. See generally list at CPR, r 25.1

15 See, e.g., wording of Civil Evidence Act 1968, s 14(1) which is declaratory of the common law: *Rio Tinto Zinc Corpn v Westinghouse Electric Corpn* [1978] AC 547, p. 636

to predominate.[16] As a result, the right to rely on the privilege was *removed by statute* in cases involving *intellectual property* and *passing off*, although any incriminating evidence obtained *cannot be used in any related criminal trial.*[17] In other sorts of cases, the threat or risk of self-incrimination can be successfully removed by the promise, in writing, not to use the evidence obtained in any criminal proceedings - a sort of contractual version of the statutory provision which can, as appropriate, be included in the order.[18]

There are some further points to note about *both* freezing and search orders:

(i) Secrecy

In both cases, the application is almost invariably made *without notice*, because *secrecy* is essential. Given that the claimant is effectively saying to the court "*If the defendant knows I am asking for this order he will hide his money or destroy the evidence,*" then giving notice of the application would defeat its purpose. The situation may also be urgent, but the key is secrecy (the court will sit in private). Usually applications are made *after issue* of proceedings, but *before* those proceedings have been *served* (because of the secrecy aspect). In urgent cases, the application can be made 'pre-action', that is before proceedings have even been commenced, although a draft claim form should be produced to the court.

(ii) Level of Judge

Historically, these applications could generally only be made to a *judge* in the *High Court*. Only rarely is the County Court or any interim judge empowered to grant freezing or search orders. Since April 2014, however, *nominated* Circuit Judges in the County Court can make freezing orders in any sort of case.[19] This is a logical adjunct to other increases in the County Court's jurisdiction and workload brought

16 The right at common law to rely on the privilege was upheld by the House of Lords in *Rank Film Distributors Ltd v Video Information Centre* [1982] AC 380

17 Senior Courts Act 1981, s 72

18 See, e.g., *AT and T Istel Ltd v Tully* [1993] AC 45, HL

19 County Court Remedies Regulations 2014 (SI 2014/982)

in at that time. Search orders, however, remain essentially the purview of High Court judges only.[20]

(iii) Full and frank disclosure

The claimant must make *full and frank disclosure* of any facts which militate against the order being given. This is the general rule where without notice applications are concerned, but is particularly important where such severe injunctions are at stake. Any failure to make full and frank disclosure will result in the order being discharged.

(iv) Affidavit evidence

Written evidence in support of such applications is made by way of *affidavit*, not witness statement. This is a rare example of where affidavits are mandated by the rules.[21]

(v) Draconian orders

These orders are both very draconian, and you want to be aware of the various principles and safeguards which protect defendants as far as appropriate. These are clearly set out in both the White Book and BCP. So far as freezing orders are concerned, be aware of the limitations and *various grounds of variation or discharge.* With search orders, be aware of the safeguards in *execution.*

(vi) Undertakings

The various undertakings that a claimant gives when such orders are granted are very important. The undertaking as to damages is even more crucial with these sorts of injunction than with a 'normal' interim injunction - the more harm the order may cause, the more assurance the court will need that the claimant's undertaking in damages has substance. The various undertakings that might be

20 A High Court judge (or above) can grant an order in the County Court, but this would be rare. See *ibid* and *Schmidt v Wong* [2006] 1 WLR 561

21 PD 25A, para 3.1

needed in any given case are set out in the sample orders appended to PD 25A.

Bear in mind that, however exciting these forms of injunction are, freezing and search orders are to be treated as *exceptional*. Most litigation is able to proceed without them. They are different from the average interim injunction, and different from each other, although they share some common features and both give litigation value to a claimant by preserving evidence for trial or assets for enforcement. The fact that one of these exceptional orders may be appropriate in a case, does not mean that the other will be - but it is not unheard of for both orders to be made against the same, very mad or very bad defendant.[22]

revision tips

- Even if freezing and search orders are not on your course syllabus, they are sometimes referenced in the WB commentary about interim injunctions generally, and so it does no harm to know what they are.
- If required, be sure you can distinguish between 'normal' interim injunctions and these exceptional forms of order (and that you can distinguish between freezing and search orders).
- Try 'grading' on a scale of 1 to 10 the strength of cause of action required for the various interim applications we have been discussing so far. Assuming 10 to be the highest, summary judgment applications would be right up at the top and *American Cyanamid* cases would be right down at the bottom. The rest are somewhere in between- freezing orders might be about a 5; search orders about an 8?

It is worth reading ...

Another Hoffmann (J as he then was) judgment in the case of *Lock International plc v Beswick* [1989] 1 WLR 1268. Well written as always. This was in the days when the search order was called an *Anton Piller* order, but what the judge had to say about the strength of case required and the draconian nature of the order still holds true.

22 See, e.g., *Columbia Pictures v Robinson*, op.cit.

PART TWO

on to trial

CHAPTER 8

Allocation and case management

Once it seems clear that a case will proceed towards a trial, it will have to be allocated to a case management track. At the time of writing, there are three: (i) the small claims track (this is essentially citizen's justice); (ii) the fast track (for basic, no-frills litigation) or (iii) the multi-track (for more complex or 'needy' cases and/or where the trial will clearly last more than one day). Many defended actions will be able to proceed along a predictable path, with directions in more or less standard form (fine-tuned for any particular need of a case) and given without the parties having to attend court. This leaves case management (and other) hearings for the more complex and important issues.

Once a defence is filed a court official will *provisionally* allocate the case to a suitable track (largely based on the value of the claim), and serve on each party a notice of *proposed allocation*.[1] This notice will require the parties to file a completed *directions questionnaire* and serve copies on each other by a specific date, which in fast track and multi-track cases will be no less than 28 days after service of the notice.[2] If a party is unrepresented, the court will send such person the appropriate directions questionnaire - otherwise the notice will simply 'inform' the parties how to obtain it (by downloading it off the internet, basically). Unless the case seems destined for the small claims track, the notice will also require that the parties *file proposed directions* by

1 CPR, r 26.3(1). If there is more than one defendant, then this will happen when the last defendant has filed his defence, or the time for doing so has expired: CPR, r 26.3(2). Most of these allocation rules do not apply to claims which arrive onto the small claims track via the new RTA Small Claims Protocol, as to which *see below*: CPR, r 26.5A.

2 In small claims track cases, the questionnaire is more truncated and the period for its return can be shorter. See CPR, r 26.3(1)(b) and 26.3(6)(b). You can find the forms on the gov.uk website.

a specified date. The notice may also require other tasks to be completed (in multi-track cases this might include the filing of costs budgets or a disclosure report[3]) and will give the appropriate court address for doing so.

If a party fails to file a completed directions questionnaire in time, then if the claim is an ordinary County Court money claim, then a reminder will be sent, but further non-compliance (having usually been given a further seven days) will result in the claim or defence (as the case may be, depending on who failed to comply) being automatically struck out.[4] For other sorts of cases, the court will make such order as it sees fit in the circumstances, which can range from simply giving further directions to striking out.[5] The defaulter normally picks up the tab.

Once the completed questionnaires have been filed, the court will, as a *judicial act*, allocate the case to a track. If, before this happens, the parties are before the court on a different matter (for example an application for summary judgment), it may take the opportunity to deal with allocation at that hearing and/or dispense with the need for directions questionnaires and/or give appropriate case management directions at that time. This is just common sense - if the parties are already there, it is an efficient use of court time to complete as many tasks on that occasion as possible.[6]

Not surprisingly, the information on the directions questionnaires is geared to making sure the case ends up on the right track. The parties should consult and cooperate on allocation issues, but it is the claimant who pays the allocation fee. Note that allocation will, quite logically, be deferred where a 'stay'[7] has been requested (by all parties) or ordered to allow for attempts to settle the action.[8] If the court thinks it necessary, it can hold an allocation hearing, but it will *often deal with track allocation and give directions without doing so*, in which case it will notify the parties in writing by means of a *notice of allocation.*[9]

The track to which a case is allocated should reflect both its financial value

3 *See below*

4 CPR, r 26.3(7A)

5 CPR, r 26.3(8). As to strike out, see Ch 13

6 See generally PD 26, para 2.4

7 A 'stay' is a halt to proceedings (apart from any steps allowed by the rules or the terms of the stay). Proceedings can continue only if the stay is lifted. See Ch 13

8 CPR, r 26.4 and 26.5(2). Some (but by no means all) claims headed for the small claims track may instead be referred to the small claims mediation service under CPR, r 26.4A

9 CPR, r 26.9. Where parties are dissatisfied with where the case has been allocated they can appeal (if allocation was made at a hearing) or apply to the court to re-allocate the claim. If circumstances change, then a court may (on its own initiative or on application)

and its case management needs (often the latter follows from the former). When assessing financial value, the court will disregard interest, costs, any contributory negligence, and any amount not in dispute. The financial value (and complexity) of any counterclaim (or other additional Part 20 claim) will be relevant, although where there is more than one claim being made in a case, the court will not generally aggregate the amounts of the various claims when determining financial value, but rather go with the largest of them. As to non-financial considerations, rational factors apply - for example, the nature of the remedy, the complexities (procedural or factual) of the case, the importance of the outcome to persons not directly involved, the number of parties, the extent of oral evidence required, the circumstances and views of the parties and so on. Note too that the court is entitled to allocate a claim to a track higher or *lower* than its financial value alone would indicate, having regard to such considerations.[10] Money isn't everything!

The overriding objective requires that cases are dealt with justly and at proportionate cost, and the track options are designed to facilitate this. A brief summary of the attributes of each is set out below.

1. THE SMALL CLAIMS TRACK

Broadly, the small claims track is designed to provide a proportionate procedure for the simplest and most basic of cases. It is intended to be navigated by litigants in person, and not require the (expensive) input of lawyers. The small claims track is thus the normal track for defended claims not exceeding £10,000.[11] There are, however, refinements or exceptions in certain kinds of cases, including claims raising allegations of dishonesty and certain landlord and tenant cases.

re-allocate: CPR, r 26.10 and PD 26, para 11

10 See CPR, r 26.7/8 and PD 26, para 7. Claims by tenants against landlords for unlawful eviction cannot be allocated to the small claims track: CPR, r 26.7(4)

11 CPR, r 26.6(3)

Personal injuries actions are another and important special category. Under previous rules, if the claim for pain, suffering and loss of amenity (PSLA) exceeded £1,000, then the normal track was the fast track, even if the total value of the claim did not exceed £10,000. The rationale for this is that as one gets into more serious injuries, even if the claim overall is not over £10,000, the case may require features of the fast track which are missing from the small claims track, in particular the need for more expensive medical evidence and costs for legal representation. Until quite recently, this applied to all personal injuries actions.

Over the years, however, concerns had been growing about 'nuisance' whiplash cases, that is to say the perceived tendency to claim for whiplash injuries in very minor 'fender bender' cases, hoping either that the defendant's insurance company will settle just to avoid the hassle or that the case, if contested, will be allocated to the fast track, where lawyer's costs can be claimed, which makes such cases viable for some solicitors. To dis-incentivise these lawyer-assisted whiplash claims, a combination of rules and regulations now apply to road traffic accidents arising from the use of a motor vehicle on a public road occurring on or after 31st May 2021. These include fixed (relatively low) amounts recoverable for whiplash injuries, restrictions on expert evidence, a new, highly prescriptive small claims road traffic pre-action protocol[12] making use of a dedicated on-line portal (which will check if the claimant is in the habit of making such claims!) and ensuring that claims which fall off of this new protocol (if or to the extent that the claim is contested) end up not on the fast track, but on the small claims track where procedure is tightly controlled and the recovery of costs is very limited. To achieve this last component, the associated allocation rules needed changing.

The rules now distinguish between road traffic accident cases (which can typically give rise to whiplash claims) and other personal injuries actions, so that

12 Pre-action Protocol for Personal Injury Claims below the Small Claims limit in Road Traffic accidents ('The RTA Small Claims Protocol'). Unsurprisingly, this is not on the Bar exam syllabus.

whether the normal track for a defended personal injuries action (not exceeding £10,000) is the small claims track or the fast track will now essentially depend on two things: firstly, whether the case arises from a car accident or not and secondly, when the accident happened (or the cause of action arose). In effect the £1,000 PSLA threshold figure referred to above has now been increased to £5,000 for most *road traffic* accident cases (occurring after 31st May 2021) and to £1,500 in all *non-*road traffic related personal injury claims (from 6th April 2022).[13] Thus:

(a) for *road traffic accident* cases occurring *on or after* 31st May 2021, then (unless the overall claim exceeds £10,000) if the claim for PSLA does not exceed £5,000, then the normal track will be the *small claims track*, unless the claimant is a child or protected party, or the claimant was not on a public road in a motor vehicle (e.g., if walking or on a bike or a motorcycle or on a horse even), or the defendant was driving a foreign car).[14] Given the much higher threshold for the PSLA element, a much larger number of these sorts of minor car accident cases will now be forced onto the small claims track.

(b) for *road traffic accident* cases occurring *on or after* 31st May 2021 where the claimant is a *child* (and there is *no* whiplash claim) or the claimant was *not travelling in a car* etc, then (unless the overall claim exceeds £10,000) the *small claims* track will be the normal track if the PSLA claim does not exceed £1,000. This is also the case if the road traffic accident occurred *before* 31st May 2021(so the £1,000 PSLA threshold lives on in some situations).[15]

(c) If the *road traffic accident* occurred *on or after* 31st May 2021, and the claimant is a *child* or protected party *and there is a claim for whiplash*

13 It's a pity that they managed to make two sets of changes at two separate junctures, resulting in two different before and after dates!

14 CPR, r 26.6(1)(a)(ii)(aa). There are a lot of exemptions from this new scheme. Basically it targets minor personal injuries arising from minor car accidents on public roads: CPR, r 26.6A

15 CPR, r 26(1)(a)(bb) and r 26.6A(a)

injuries, the normal track will be the *fast track*. Indeed, in such cases, the claim 'must not' be allocated to the small claims track.[16] This is because, despite the whiplash claim, vulnerable litigants should not to be left to their own (on-line) devices.

(d) And if the personal injuries action is *not* a road traffic case and if value of the PSLA claim exceeds £1,000 (for actions arising *before* 6th April 2022) or exceeds £1,500 (for actions arising *on or after* 6th April 2022) then the normal track will be the *fast track*, even if the total claim does not exceed £10,000.[17]

There may, of course, be reasons why a claim falling within the value range of the small claims track is not ultimately allocated there. These might include the complexity of the case, the nature of the allegations or the need to make use of the more standard features of litigation, which are missing from this most basic track. The hallmarks of the small claims track are as follows:

- On allocation, a date for a hearing (and its length) will be fixed and directions given, usually in standard form. Directions differ according to type of case, for example holiday cases, building disputes and so on, but common to all are standard directions about exchanging only the documents which each party will by 'relying on' in the action, bringing original documents to the hearing, and an obligation to inform the court if the case settles.[18] If necessary, special directions can be given and/or a preliminary appointment fixed.
- *Other common features of litigation are missing*, including wider orders for disclosure, most interim remedies (except interim injunctions and

16 See CPR, r 26.6B

17 CPR, r 26.6(1)(a)(cc) and WB para 26.6.2

18 See Appendices A and B to PD 27A. Disclosure orders are more limited on the small claims track than on the others (as to which see generally Ch 9).

special rules for interim payments for road traffic small claims), most case management directions, most evidential rules, Part 36 offers, and the traditional approach to the conduct of the proceedings. The hearing is conducted on an informal basis, usually in the District Judge's room. If the parties agree (or if space is at a premium), the hearing will be conducted in private. Evidence is not generally given on oath[19] and use of expert evidence is limited.[20]

- The small claims track is designed to be navigated by the lay person, and so the scope for recovering *costs is severely constrained*. They are essentially limited to disbursements (for example, court fees) and out-of-pocket expenses. In particular, the idea is to exclude lawyers (who are expensive), and so the cost allowed for legal assistance is almost non-existent (if the court felt it was important that a party be legally represented, this would be a good reason to allocate to the fast track). The restriction applies both to the original hearing and any subsequent appeal.[21]

2. THE FAST TRACK

The *fast track is the 'Easyjet'* of the system, providing a no-frills, value-for-money route to justice for relatively inexpensive, straightforward and predictable claims. It steers a middle course between the bare necessities on offer on the small claims track and the more complex handling of cases on the multi-track, although it resembles the latter more than the former. The fast track will be the normal track for most defended claims which are not appropriate for the small claims track, which fall

19 See generally CPR, r 27.8

20 For example, costs for expert evidence are fixed: CPR, r 27.14(2)(g). See also WB Para 27.0.2 for a summary of small claims track features.

21 *Conlon v Royal Sun Alliance plc* [2015] EWCA CIV 92

within the *£10,000 to £25,000* monetary band, and where the need for expert evidence is limited and the trial will likely take *no more than one day.*[22] The hallmarks of the fast track are:

- Few or no interim hearings
- Standard directions
- Speedy timetable with a virtually immutable trial date fixed by the court when the case is allocated
- Limited numbers of experts
- Single joint expert evidence (on any one issue) admitted by means of a written report is the norm
- One day trial
- Trial costs are 'fixed'; 'summary assessment' of other costs[23]

On the fast track, the case will be actively managed to a *tight timetable* usually lasting no longer than *thirty weeks.*[24] This usually allows enough time to get the essentials completed, but little scope for embellishment. Case management directions will generally only be given at *two* stages: when the case is *allocated* to the track and once the parties have filed *pre-trial checklists.*[25] As on all the tracks, many directions are predictable and so are given using a standard form,[26] but they are not given on a 'one size fits all' basis. The court will 'tweak' the form as necessary to produce directions which are able to meet the requirements of the case at hand.

Directions on allocation

This first set of directions, which follows the (official) track allocation of the case, will lay down the case management *timetable*, including setting the trial date or 'window'.[27]

22 See CPR, r 26.6(4) and (5). The fact that the trial might last longer than one day is not by itself a conclusive reason for the court to allocate to the multi-track. Having said that, if the case involves a counterclaim or other additional claim and as a result the trial will last more than one day, then the court must allocate it to the multi-track: See guidance in PD 26, para 9

23 See below at fn 36

24 CPR, r 28.2(4)

25 CPR, PD 28, para 2.1

26 Model standard form directions are set out in the Appendix to PD 28

27 CPR, r 28.2(2). The trial 'window' is a period not exceeding 3 weeks during which the trial will take place, the precise date to be determined closer to the time.

Typically the matters to be dealt with in this first instance will include the identification and exchange of various items of evidence: documentary evidence, witness statements, expert evidence.[28] The court will have looked at the parties' statements of case and considered the information included on the directions questionnaire (that is what it is for!). Its main concern at this point is to equip the parties with the means (by reference to exchanged evidence) to identify and narrow the issues.[29] It will hold a hearing only if necessary.

Pre-trial directions

The second stage for giving directions occurs after pre-trial checklists have been filed, or dispensed with.[30] Again standard form directions will be tailored to the circumstances of the individual case. At this point the focus is on checking compliance with previous directions which have been given, and on the impending trial. Typical issues and directions at this stage include how evidence is to be received at trial, agreeing and filing bundles of documents, confirming the trial date and so on. More complex cases may need more sophisticated directions about the time to be allowed for examination and cross-examination of witnesses and so forth - it is, after all, only meant to be a one day trial. The parties should seek to agree such directions between themselves, which the court can then endorse (or make a different order) if it sees fit. Not less than two days before the trial, both parties should file a statement of costs.

In fast track cases, the court will attempt to limit the giving of directions to these two occasions, and so will normally do so *without the need for a hearing*. A crucial feature of this track is that the trial date, or 'window', is practically set in stone, so applications must be sought *promptly* if different or other directions are required.[31] Adherence to the timetable is encouraged. Minor variations can be agreed (in

28 Usually to be exchanged in that order. See generally PD 28, para 3 (para 3.12 contains the typical timetable).

29 PD 28, para 3.3

30 As the name suggests, pre-trial checklists assist the court in determining readiness for and the needs of the upcoming trial. See PD 28, para 6

31 If a party does not complain within 14 days, the court will assume he was happy with the direction in the circumstances then existing. A party needing to ask for a variation appeals if the direction was granted following a hearing, but otherwise applies to the court to reconsider. See generally CPR PD 28, para 4

writing) without troubling the court, and the rules allow parties to agree a maximum 28 day extension to complete steps which otherwise carry their own sanction for non-compliance.[32] But *in either event* the following *three key dates* must *not be altered or adversely affected.*

(i) the date for returning the directions questionnaires;
(ii) the date for returning the pre-trial checklists; or
(iii) the trial date/window.

The date for these three case management events can only be changed (or 'varied' as the rules put it) with the court's *permission.*[33] In particular, the court will not allow a failure to comply with directions to lead to the postponement of the trial 'unless the circumstances of the case are exceptional'.[34]

A fast track trial should only last one day. Were it to run over, the judge will normally sit the next day to finish the case off. Remember, too, that the trial judge may depart from the procedural judge's directions as to the conduct of the case. No doubt most witness statements will stand as the evidence-in-chief[35] and, given that the natural or designated time for speeches and cross-examination will be limited, it will be necessary for advocates to be very focused in their questioning.

As regards costs, at the time of writing, the normal rule is that on the fast track these will be dealt with summarily at the end of the trial. This means the judge will decide there and then how much the loser will have to pay toward the winner's costs, assisted by the various statement of costs submitted by the parties before the trial. As to the trial costs themselves, these are fixed by reference to the value of the claim.[36]

32 CPR, r 3.8(3)/(4)
33 CPR, r 2.11, r 26.3(6A) and r 28.4
34 CPR, PD 28, para 5.4
35 See Ch 17
36 From Oct 2023 the plan is that *all* costs recoverable in fast track cases will be fixed: see below and Ch 18 on costs.

3. THE MULTI-TRACK

The multi-track is for the more expensive, complex and/or time-consuming cases. Part 8 claims and specialist proceedings (for example TCC cases) are usually treated as appropriate for the multi-track. Many of the same 'classic' directions given in fast track cases are also relevant in multi-track cases, but the time frame may need to be more generous, or additional and more focused directions given. Multi-track cases are particularly prone to rack up costs, which is why the Jackson reforms concentrated on these in the drive to ensure that they are managed efficiently. Hard choices may sometimes be required. The idea is that if a direction or order applied for is not considered proportionate to the case or relevant issue, it should not be given, however reasonable it might otherwise be.

As with the other tracks, once a case is allocated to the multi-track, the court will give directions (which might include a requirement that the parties consider ADR) and hold such procedural hearings as may be necessary.[37] On the multi-track the court is required to set a trial window/date 'as soon as practicable' - a usefully elastic description.[38] Directions should be case-sensitive on the multi-track, which must be capable of meeting the needs of claims in a wide range of cases. Thus some multi-track cases will proceed very predictably; others will require more robust intervention.

Effective case management means that the court will intervene only as, and to the extent necessary. The parties are encouraged to do their part by agreeing case management directions, and submitting these to the court for approval (thus avoiding the need for a hearing, and so reducing costs).[39] When giving or agreeing any case management directions, both the parties and the court should use the relevant standard direction template as a *starting* point. At the allocation stage, for

37 See PD 29, para 4 for the range of options for allocation directions on the multi-track.

38 CPR, r 29.2(2)

39 CPR, r 29.4

example, the court will only ratify agreed directions if they include the essentials as a minimum, namely by setting out a timetable by reference to calendar dates, including a proposed trial date (or window), and providing for the exchange of documentary, factual and expert evidence.[40] The procedural judge will consider proposed agreed directions carefully, and use them if appropriate, but at the end of the day it is the court which has ultimate responsibility for the management of the case.

Thus some case management on the multi-track can be done 'on the papers' (based on completed directions questionnaires, pre-trial checklists, proposed directions and so forth), but where this is not possible, then one or other of the following may be necessary:

A. CASE MANAGEMENT CONFERENCES (CMC)

This is the *principal device for keeping more complex litigation focused and on track*, and can be held immediately upon allocation and thereafter as necessary to monitor and further the progress of the case. The purpose of these hearings is to ensure that the real issues are identified and directions given so that each case is managed according to its needs.[41] Notice is given to both parties (at least three clear days), but in practice it should be possible to anticipate the need for such hearings.

Before the first CMC in multi-track cases, the parties must now file and serve:

(i) In non-personal injury cases, disclosure reports[42]
(ii) Proposed directions (agreed if possible)
(iii) Costs budgets (agreed if possible)

Those attending a CMC need to be well versed with the case, and all relevant documents should be brought to court (in a case management bundle). If legal

40 CPR, r 29.1(2) and see PD 29, para 4.6/7
41 See generally PD 29, para 5
42 See Ch 9

representatives are not adequately informed, prepared or capable, a wasted costs order will normally be made.[43] It may assist to provide the court with case summaries.

At a CMC, the court will review the statements of case, allocate the case to a track (if this has not already happened), check compliance with any previous orders or directions, review any costs budgets (and make any necessary revisions), record any relevant agreement on the conduct of the case, and make any directions needed to move the case along. It is always incumbent on the court to promote the use of ADR, and if appropriate a stay may be granted to allow the parties to engage in such a process, although the court will be careful that these do not become unproductive delays disguised as attempts to settle.

Typically, either by (court sanctioned) agreement or at a CMC, directions (with deadlines) will cover the usual sorts of management needs,[44] including:

- the scope of disclosure of documents required
- the nature of the expert evidence, and how it should be obtained; experts on both sides will be more common on the multi-track
- disclosure of witness statements
- filing of pre-trial checklists
- whether it is possible to fix a trial date

Directions in a multi-track case might also include things like amendment of statement of case, use of witness summaries, and orders for inspection of relevant property. Parties should always attempt to deal with all case management needs at a scheduled CMC. This clearly saves money! If something arises which is not necessarily dealt with as part of case management (for example, an application for an interim payment), and it is clear that the application is opposed, the claimant should serve notice in time

43 PD 29, para 5.2(3)
44 PD 29, para 5.3

for it to be heard at the scheduled CMC. The more unusual the application, the more notice should be given, so the opposing party can made effective representations.[45]

B. LISTING HEARING

These are essentially a species of CMC and are not all that common. Again, each party must file, as directed, a completed pre-trial checklist, which is intended to assist the court as the trial date approaches. If outstanding matters remain at this point (for example because insufficient information was given), a listing hearing may be necessary. These hearings concentrate on matters affecting the trial date and are useful where it is proving difficult getting a case ready for trial. The main focus will be preparing and listing the case for trial.[46]

C. PRE-TRIAL REVIEW

If needed, a pre-trial review will typically take place about eight to ten weeks before the trial. This gives the court the opportunity to check compliance with earlier orders, explore settlement, and make any necessary directions as to the conduct of the trial - in particular, how the evidence is to be adduced and what time limits will be placed on cross-examination, speeches and so forth.[47]

D. COSTS MANAGEMENT

Costs management was an innovation of the *Jackson* reforms. These rules have been amended a few times since first implemented in April 2013, so the scheme continues to evolve. *Most Part 7 multi-track cases* are governed by the costs management regime set out in CPR, r 3.12-3.18 (and Practice Direction 3D). Exempted from the scheme are (a) claims made by or on behalf of a child, (b) claims which are for or worth an amount in excess of £10 million; (c) cases (rare on the multi-track) which are subject

45 See, e.g., ***Norbrook Laboratories Ltd v Carr*** [2010] EWCA Civ 1108

46 See CPR, r 29.6 and PD 29, para 8. Pre-trial checklists used to be called 'listing questionnaires' and so these hearings became known as listing hearings.

47 CPR, r 29.7/8 and PD 29, para 9

to scaled or fixed costs, and (d) litigants in person (since costs management is all about controlling lawyer's costs). Note also that it is always possible for the court to decide to apply costs management to any case (which would otherwise be ineligible), or to disapply it in any case, if it so chooses.[48]

The idea behind costs management is that, in appropriate cases, this will go hand in hand with case management so as to further the overriding objective. Because costs at the end of the day are usually awarded to the party who succeeds, there has been a tendency for litigants (or their lawyers) to 'throw money' at cases, thinking this will help them win and thus recover from the loser at the end of the day whatever they have spent in so doing. This, not surprisingly, drives up costs overall. The point about managing costs is to set an overall *forward-looking* budget, proportionate for the needs of a case, and then make case management decisions based on that budget. Thus projected costs budgets are prepared by the parties' legal advisors and either agreed or approved by the court. These budgets are then used as a basis for making case management decisions, and parties can clearly see their likely costs exposure if they lose. It's a little like putting in a new kitchen - you need to keep your requirements and financial outlay in balance. Costs management can itself generate costs, so will not always be appropriate - possibly not if the case is very complex or unpredictable. The idea is to impose budgetary restraint on those cases where (using a light touch) this would be both feasible and effective to keep costs proportionate. Cases subject to a fixed costs regime don't need it and exceptionally expensive cases won't benefit.

It is important in this context to *distinguish* between '*incurred*' costs (those which have already been spent), and estimated future costs, which are known as '*budgeted*' costs. The court can comment upon past costs and take them into account when making cost and case management decisions, but can only 'approve' budgeted costs. Cost management is all about setting a proportionate budget for the *future conduct*

48 CPR, r 3.12(1) and (1A). The exemption regarding children continues if and when the child reaches the age of 18, unless the court orders otherwise.

of the case - and keeping to it.[49] Where costs management applies, what essentially happens is this:

(i) The parties *prepare costs budgets*. There is a standard form (Precedent H) for this purpose on which is set out both incurred costs and budgeted costs for various stages of the litigation. The budgets must be verified with a statement of truth, signed by a 'senior legal representative of the party' (so not a para-legal!).[50] This requirement makes sense as it is really only the lawyers in charge of the case who know precisely what they are proposing to charge, and for what. It is principally lawyer's costs which need controlling.

(ii) The parties *file and exchange* their budgets. Although a litigant in person is not required to prepare a budget, parties who are so required must serve a copy of their budget on any litigant in person. As you might expect, the court can order parties to file and exchange budgets even if not otherwise required to by the rules, and it should do so if such parties actually want to do so (unless the circumstances are exceptional). If a case is a substantial one, the court may direct that budgets are initially to be limited to part of the proceedings (to be later extended as necessary to cover the entirety). It is worth noting that unless the circumstances are exceptional, the recoverable costs of both completing the budget form itself and the costs management process generally are set very low by the rules themselves. This is an attempt to keep the costs of costs management proportionate.[51]

(iii) Unless the court orders otherwise, any party who fails to file a costs budget *as and when* ordered or required, will be treated as having filed

49 See WB para 3.12.5. The usual point in time for making this distinction between past and budgeted costs is the first case/costs management conference.

50 CPR, r 3.13(5) and see PD, 3D, for details of budget format.

51 See CPR, 3.13 and 3.15(5).

a budget comprising *only the applicable court fees.* This is a draconian sanction,[52] no doubt intended to keep solicitors on their case management toes (litigants in person do not have to file costs budgets). The idea is that when this happens, the lawyers race back to court to be excused from this punishment, and with a proper budget, so that cost effective case management can at least be achieved from this point.[53]

(iv) Costs budgets should ideally be *agreed by the parties* (one of whom will probably have to pay those costs at the end of the day, so both should be on their guard). To that end, parties who have filed and exchanged budgets must then file an *agreed budget discussion report* no later than 7 days before the first CMC. This report should set out, for each phase of the litigation, which figures are agreed, which are not agreed, and briefly, reasons for any disagreement.[54]

(v) A court may make a *costs management order* at any time. It '*will*' do so where budgets have been filed and exchanged, *unless* it is satisfied that the litigation can be conducted justly and at proportionate cost without doing so. In a costs management order, the court will 'record' the extent to which both incurred and budgeted costs are agreed. Where there is disagreement on the budgeted costs, the court will 'approve' figures (having made revisions as appropriate) which appear to fall within the range of what seems reasonable and proportionate.[55] Remember that the court does *not* retrospectively approve costs which have already been spent; it only approves future *budgeted* costs. But (whether or not it makes a costs management order) the court can 'record' on the face of any case management order any comments it has about incurred costs which are to be taken into account in any

52 CPR, r 3.14 and see, e.g., the *Mitchell* case, discussed in Ch 13. The normal sanction is adjusted to 50% of the defaulter's costs if that party made a successful Part 36 offer: CPR, r 36.23

53 As to 'relief from sanctions' see Ch 13

54 CPR, r 3.13(2) and PD 3D, para 11

55 CPR, r 3.15(2) and PD 3D, para 7. In doing this the court will be looking at total budget figures for each phase of the litigation. The fine detail of how this number is arrived at may help explain the calculation, but the court is not in the business of fixing or approving rates of pay and so forth: CPR, r 3.15(8). After budgeted costs have been agreed or approved, the parties should re-file and re-serve budgets to reflect this: CPR, r 3.15(7)

subsequent costs assessment. Once a costs management order is made then, as the name implies, the court will thereafter control the parties' budgets in respect of recoverable costs.[56]

(vi) When making any case management decision the court *will have regard* to any available budgets of the parties and take into account the costs of any procedural step. This is so whether or not a costs management order was made. It's a bit of a cost/benefit analysis, which could lead the court to substitute a more proportionate direction than that proposed. The judge may well see why a party might want or need to take a particular step, but not permit it because of how much it would cost. Again, the court cannot retrospectively approve unbudgeted costs already incurred up to the date of any case management hearing, but it can record its views and take such costs into account when considering the reasonableness or proportionality of costs *going forward*.[57] This is why parties are required, for example, to give an estimate of the cost of any disclosure directions sought in a disclosure report[58] (which may lead to a more limited disclosure order if the budget requires), and when seeking permission to rely on expert evidence[59] (which may lead to some restrictions on the number of experts to be called).

(vii) If *significant developments* in a case warrant it, then a party must 'revise' its budgeted costs. This applies whether or not the revision is upwards or downwards, although it is usually only revisions upwards which cause problems. A 'significant' development will essentially be one which goes beyond the matters which could or should have been accounted for in the previous budget, for example, an unexpected need for additional expert evidence or an unpredictable increase of

56 CPR, r 3.15(3) and (4). 'Recoverable' costs refers to litigation costs which at the end of the day one party may be able to recover from another. See generally Ch 18

57 See CPR, r 3.17

58 See Ch 9

59 CPR r 35.4(2) and see Ch 17

the number of days needed for trial. The procedure here 'mirrors' the original filing and approval of budgets: revised budgets should be submitted promptly to other parties for agreement and subsequently to the court. A different form is used for this. Particulars of variation are only required for *additional* costs (which were not included on any previous budget). The revising party should submit the proposed variations along with the last agreed or approved budget, and an explanation of points of difference if other parties are not in agreement. As you might expect, the court may approve, vary or disallow proposed variations, or list a further costs management hearing which (in order to keep costs down) can be dealt with in writing or by telephone.[60]

(viii) At the end of the litigation, the recoverable costs of the winning party are assessed[61] by reference to the costs budgets. Here one needs to *distinguish between* cases where a costs management order was made and those where it was not. In both situations, when assessing costs on the standard basis, the court will have regard to the receiving party's *last* agreed or approved budget. If a costs management order *was* made, then the court will *not depart* from the figures in that budget *unless* satisfied there is a *good* reason to do so (and will take into account any comments about incurred costs made on the face of any court order).[62] If a costs management order was *not* made, then that budget is merely one factor in the court's assessment, but any bill of costs which exceeds the figures in that budget by 20% may be taken as evidence that the amount of costs now claimed is unreasonable or disproportionate (in which case they will be disallowed or reduced). In particular, if the

60 See CPR, rr 3.15A and 3.16. Costs management conferences are those which are solely for costs management. Where a conference is to covers both case and costs management it is sometimes called a Case and Costs Management Conference (CCMC).

61 As to costs orders and assessment of costs following trial, see Ch 18. The 'receiving' party is the party benefitting from having his costs paid for by another party (known as the paying party).

62 CPR, r 3.18

party paying costs reasonably *relied on* the figures in the other party's last budget (for example when agreeing to settle the case), the court may restrict the recoverable costs to that amount (or whatever sum is reasonable in light of that reliance), even if that amount is less than what would otherwise be considered reasonable and proportionate.[63]

Variation of Directions

Finally, on the multi-track, a party who wishes to ask the court to vary a case management direction should do so as soon as possible.[64] And as with the fast track, there is some scope for parties on the multi-track to agree to vary the case management timetable, and where the sanction for non-compliance is built into the rules, parties can in effect give themselves a maximum 28 day extension. But, again, the parties may *only* agree to vary a timetable direction on the multi-track if doing so does *not* affect or necessitate a change to the date of any of the following five *key* case management events, namely the date set for:

(i) return of directions questionnaires
(ii) any case/cost management conference
(iii) return of pre-trial checklists
(iv) any pre-trial review,

and

(v) the trial date/window.[65]

If any of these dates would be affected, the permission of the court must be sought.[66] As you might expect, the court will be very reluctant to vacate these dates, especially if the only excuse is a dilatory litigant!

63 CPR, r 44.4(3)(h) and PD 44 paras 3.5-3.7

64 See PD 29, para 6

65 On the fast track it is three case management events which may not be varied without the court's permission; the multi-track rule includes these same three, but adds two more common multi-track features, making five altogether.

66 CPR, r 29.5

4. PROPOSALS FOR THE FUTURE: A NEW INTERMEDIATE TRACK

Note that from Oct 2023, there are plans to introduce a new 'intermediate track' in the County Court to cater for simpler cases valued up to £100,000 (which are not appropriate for the fast track). It will have its own standard directions. This new intermediate track is intended to capture cases which can be tried in three days or less, with no more than two expert witnesses giving oral evidence on each side (so in effect, carving out a bit from the 'lower end' of the multi-track). In addition, and more controversially, all costs on both the fast and intermediate tracks will be covered by a fixed costs regime, so such costs will neither need to be managed nor assessed, thus saving money (which is the point). So keep alert and watch out for consequential rule changes.[67]

67 See Preface to WB 2023, and until new rules are created see draft proposals in *Extending Fixed Recoverable Costs in Civil Cases* on the gov.uk website.

revision tips

- In mainstream litigation, provisional allocation by a court official is followed by completion of directions questionnaires and then *formal track* allocation by a procedural judge. Note that the allocation procedure essentially applies to cases where liability is contested.
- Be aware of the basic hallmarks of the litigation tracks and check what detail is to be assessed by your exam syllabus. Remember that other aspects of a case beyond its value can affect where it will be allocated. Cases can be allocated to a track below as well as above that indicated by their value. Where possible (even on the multi-track) directions will be given without a hearing.
- Cost Management applies to most Pt 7 multi-track cases, so be aware how it works and what its purpose is. Remember that budgets refer to *future* costs. You might find PD 3D in the White Book has a strangely inaccurate numbering system in the right-hand margin (right-hand side in hard back version). To identify relevant paragraph numbers look on the left-hand side of the page, at the actual paragraph numbers.
- Be aware of the case management events which may not be affected or changed *without the court's permission*.

It is worth reading …

The content of the Directions Questionnaire, Form N181. It is not long, and will tell you a lot about what issues the court needs to deal with as, and after, it allocates a case.

The very useful outline of Costs Management at WD, Vol 1, para 3.12.2

CIP Properties (AIPT) Ltd v Galliford Try Infrastructure Ltd [2015] EWHC 481. Another readable judgment by Coulson J (as he then was) who was not convinced by the claimant's costs budget. The rules have been 'tweaked' a bit since this case, but the lessons learned are still valuable. It is a good example of how cost management works in practice, particularly how the court might deal with future costs when early costs have already used up what would have been reasonable and proportionate for the entire case.

CHAPTER 9

Documents and things:
disclosure/inspection/further information

Once a case has been allocated to a track, it is into the second half of the litigation process, which is dominated by disclosure of documents and related processes by which the parties - to the extent that they have not done so already - acquire relevant information about the nature of the case against them. This 'cards on the table approach' furthers the overriding objective; it allows parties to assess (or re-assess) the true strengths and weaknesses of their respective cases and so helps to narrow the issues and encourage settlement. Much of this exchange of evidence should in fact now happen during the pre-action phase.

An order for disclosure of *documents* heads the list of the (often standard) case management directions given on all of the tracks (unless it is thought to be unnecessary),[1] although on the small claims track disclosure will generally be much more limited than on the other tracks.[2] It is hard to think of a case which would not involve at least some documentary evidence (invoices, receipts, letters, records, wage slips and so on). So, these come first - but documents are not the only items with evidential value. Parties also acquire relevant information by means of requests or orders that relevant *things* be

1 Because, for example, disclosure has already taken place. See CPR PD 28, para 3.2/PD 29, para 4.2. In this context, the term 'document' is not limited to paper records. *See below*.

2 *See below* and PD 27, Appendix B

preserved, inspected, and examined for the purposes of litigation. It might be the car, whose brakes failed and caused an accident; or the equipment an employee was using when she was injured at work. If it is appropriate for an expert to look at these things and give an opinion on what went wrong, the expert will need access to them.

Parties can also request straight out *information* from their opponents, if the circumstances warrant it. These used to go by the somewhat sinister name of 'interrogatories' and could stop a case in its tracks by the sheer volume of (often feigned) curiosity; but the CPR now ensures that only legitimate requests will be sanctioned. If used properly, they can be very effective in ferreting out a weak case.

One thing to notice in the discussion which follows is that each of these types of orders is a typical (and usually uneventful) part of the normal litigation process. There are times, however, when disclosure orders are made even when there is no relevant litigation going on (yet), or against people not involved in ongoing litigation. In such cases, special rules apply.

1. DISCLOSURE OF DOCUMENTS

Disclosure of documents is the longest standing, and one of the most important ways in which relevant evidence is exchanged in litigation. When he took on the task of re-wiring the country's civil procedure system in the 1990s, Lord Woolf recognised the essential value of what then went under the rather nautical term of 'discovery'. But he put much of the blame for the length and costs of litigation on a process which at the time required a very wide range of documents to be disclosed.

Typically, this was the stage where cases 'went to sleep' under the old rules (which were open to tactical exploitation of various kinds). Lord Woolf referred in particular to the 'curse' of the photocopier (now we have the curse of the internet). Not surprisingly, it was felt that excessive disclosure led to an expensive, unwieldy and time-consuming process, often to little evidential purpose. For this reason, the CPR rules (on what was re-branded 'disclosure') are aimed at keeping this aspect of litigation *focused and proportionate* - and under court control. Further refinements were added in April 2013.

Orders for disclosure of documents form part of the normal litigation process. They can also, exceptionally, be ordered against parties who are not (at that moment anyway) being sued. It is important to distinguish between these two situations.

A. IN THE NORMAL COURSE OF LITIGATION

(i) Fast Track and Multi-Track Disclosure

The idea behind the disclosure rules is to ensure that the process is effective, yet proportionate, and able to adapt to the variety of cases which can come before the courts. To this end, disclosure in fast track and multi-track cases can take one of two pathways:

(a) in fast track claims, multi-track personal injury claims,[3] and other multi-track claims where the court so directs, disclosure is governed by CPR, r 31.5(1), which starts from the premise that parties should give '*standard disclosure*';

(b) all other multi-track cases (for example, complex commercial cases and such like) are governed by the so-called '*menu option*' procedure laid down in CPR, r 31.5(3)-(8), unless the court orders otherwise. These provisions were added by the Jackson reforms.

3 CPR, r 31.5(2). The litigation needs of personal injuries actions are pretty predictable whatever their value/track, and so standard disclosure is usually all that is required. These rules will need to be adapted for any new intermediate track, which is likely to resemble the fast track more than the multi-track.

(a) Standard Disclosure

Procedurally, under Part 31, a party 'discloses' documents by revealing their *existence.* This is usually accomplished by *exchange of disclosure lists.*[4] The person to whom such documents have been disclosed is then entitled to see, or 'inspect', any of the documents on the list which are still in the discloser's possession *and* which are not privileged or otherwise protected from scrutiny. Once *written notice* of the desire to see some or all of such documents has been given, inspection must be permitted within seven days.[5]

It is important to appreciate that this is actually a two-stage process - *disclosure* comes first, followed by *inspection,* although sometimes the word 'disclosure' is used loosely to refer globally to both aspects. Orders for disclosure are generally made on allocation or at a case management conference. Compliance is usually straightforward, so applications to the court will not often be necessary. Inspection can take place either by giving a party the opportunity to come and look at the requested documents, or (more commonly) by sending them photocopies. There is a right to request the latter, if reasonable copying costs are paid.[6] Inspection can even take place by electronic means. What is sensible varies from case to case and essentially depends on how many documents there are and what form they take.

Thus unless the court orders otherwise, the usual order for disclosure in cases governed by rule 31.5(1) is an order to *give standard disclosure.*[7] This requires[8] a party to disclose *only*:

(i) the documents on which he *relies*; *and*

(ii) the documents which:

- *adversely affect his own case*;
- *adversely affect another party's case*;
- *support another party's case*; *and*

4 CPR, r 31.2 and r 31.10(2). The parties can agree in writing to disclose without making a list. Such agreement must be lodged with the court. PD31A, para 1.4

5 CPR, r 31.3 and 31.15. There is a right to inspect documents which are not protected by privilege and so on (see Ch 17), and so if a party, for no good reason, forces another to apply to the court for an order to inspect, then that party will no doubt pay for their intransigence in the form of the costs of the application.

6 CPR, r 31.15(c)

7 CPR, r 31.5(1)(a)

8 CPR, r 31.6

9 Practitioners sometimes have to explain the purpose of these rules to their clients (who may baulk at 'helping' the other side) usually by pointing out that it is a two-way street.

(iii) the documents which he is required to disclose by a relevant practice direction.

In a nutshell, (i) and (ii) amount to all documents which either help or hurt[9] your own case, or help or hurt another party's case. This is usually determined by reference to the material allegations in the statements of case. They come close to, but do not exactly equate to all documents which are 'relevant' (so don't be fooled by this in an exam question) - for example, it has been held that standard disclosure does not cover documents which relate *purely* to cross-examination as to credit and to *no other issue* in a case.[10] If a document contains information, only some of which is disclosable, then the material which need not be disclosed can be redacted.[11]

As regards (iii), an example of a relevant practice direction would be PD 31B on electronic documents, which seeks to ensure effective disclosure without parties getting hopeless mired in cyberspace.[12]

So-called 'train of inquiry' documents (those on the 'far end of the spectrum of materiality' which are not themselves relevant, but which could contain information which may lead to such documents) were the bane of the old system, and it is important to note that they are *very intentionally not part of standard disclosure.* It is possible to ask the court for such an extended order, but it would take some very compelling advocacy (and a case with allegations of dishonesty or deceit at its heart) to persuade it to do so. The whole point of the CPR was to get away from requiring the disclosure of such documents.[13]

Remember too that standard disclosure can be *limited or dispensed with*, either by the written agreement of the parties or by court order.[14] This would happen, typically, where disclosure has effectively taken place already, usually in the pre-action phase. It is very important to realise, however, that parties *may not agree* between themselves

10 If a document casts doubt on the credibility of a party whose own evidence is important to the case, this could be seen as adversely affecting that party's case and is thus disclosable. See discussion at WB, para 31.6.2

11 WB, para 31.6.8

12 PD 31B gives detailed guidance on the maintenance, preservation and exchange of disclosable e-documents. At the time of writing this is not on the Bar examination syllabus.

13 See, e.g., discussion at BCP at 50.16, referring to Coleman J's comments in *O Co. v M Co.* [1992] 2 Lloyd's Rep at pp 350-351 and WB, para 31.6.3 and 31.6.4 (sub-para 4). Even if given, such an enhanced order should not be made until standard disclosure has been attempted.

14 CPR, r 31.5(1),(b),(c)

to *widen* the ambit of disclosure. Only the *court* can order this,[15] which it will only do if proportionate and necessary to achieve the overriding objective. This will be rare, even on the multi-track.

(b) Menu Option Disclosure

Standard disclosure was an improvement over the old rules, and it works well to keep the process within bounds, up to a point. Some multi-track cases, however, are so complex and document-driven, that even standard disclosure can be overwhelming. It was thus felt necessary to create more scope for making proportionate and bespoke orders, on a case-by-case basis. Hence the introduction of what have become known as 'menu option' disclosure orders.

In *non-personal injury multi-track* claims, the menu option system applies, unless the court orders otherwise.[16] Menu option disclosure breaks down into three stages, which is focused around the first case management conference ('CMC'):

> *Disclosure report*
>
> Not less than 14 days before the first CMC, each party must file and serve a disclosure report, verified by a statement of truth, which should describe relevant documents which exist (or may exist), where they are (including details of storage of electronic documents, and completed electronic questionnaires if appropriate) and the estimated costs of giving disclosure (which should tally with the party's costs budget[17]). It should also set out what disclosure directions are sought. The disclosure report is a way of getting the parties (as well as the court) to think carefully about this part of the process, knowing that time is money and costs are budgeted.[18]

15 CPR, r 31.5(1)(a)
16 CPR, r 31.5(2)
17 As to costs budgets, see Ch 8

Agreed 'proposal' for directions

Not less than seven days before the first CMC, the parties must seek to agree between themselves a proposal to put to the court about disclosure, which is in keeping with the overriding objective of dealing with cases justly and at proportionate cost. The parties can meet in person or by telephone. Any proposal must be filed with the court, which *may* approve the proposal and give the proposed directions without a hearing.[19] If it does, this is a bit like DIY disclosure orders. It could save a lot of court time and expense!

CMC disclosure direction (from the menu)

If the court does not give disclosure directions without a hearing, it will do so at the first (and any subsequent) CMC, *choosing from the menu of options*. Standard disclosure is one of the options; so too is a form of 'train of inquiry' disclosure. Other options include (i) that a party disclose the documents on which it relies, and at the same time request any specific disclosure it requires from another party and (ii) that, where practicable, disclosure be given by each party on an issue by issue basis. Not surprisingly, the court can also make any other order it thinks appropriate or dispense with (further) disclosure altogether.[20] The point here is that the court should make an order having regard to the overriding objective, the available costs budgets, and the need to act proportionately and limit disclosure only to what is really necessary to deal justly with the case before it.

Note also that the court may at any point give directions as to *how* disclosure is to be given, including what searches are to be undertaken,

18 CPR, r 31.5(3). And see Form N263

19 CPR, r 31.5 (5) and (6)

20 The menu is set out at CPR, r 31.5(7)

whether lists are required, whether disclosure should take place in stages and so forth.[21]

Whatever pathway a case is on, and whatever the extent of disclosure ordered, it is important to remember some key points:

(a) Not just paper

The first point is that 'documents' *are not limited to paper*, and include 'anything in which information of any description is recorded'[22] - for example discs, audio tapes, video cassettes, computer programmes, electronic data bases and so forth. Only one copy need be disclosed, although copies with *significant* modifications will be treated as *separate* documents.

(b) Possession or control

Secondly, a party's duty to disclose documents is limited to documents which are or have been in that party's *control*, that is, if -

- it is or was in his physical possession;
- he has or has had a *right* to possession of it (just as, for example, UK patients are entitled to their heath records by virtue of the Access to Health Act 1990);

or

- he has or has had a right to inspect or take copies of it.[23]

(c) Reasonable search (for documents needing to be disclosed)

Note also that although parties are now generally required to disclose a narrower, more focused range of documents than once was the case, the disclosing party is

21 CPR, r 31.5(8). After a long pilot period, a specifically bespoke disclosure scheme applies in the Business and Property Courts: CPR Part 57A. These rules are not, at the time of writing, on the BSB examination syllabus.

22 CPR, r 31.4

23 CPR, r 31.8

obliged to make a *'reasonable search' for all such disclosable documents* (or at least the ones which need searching for. The duty does not apply to documents the disclosing party 'relies on', since presumably these do not need to be found!). What is reasonable will depend on the circumstances of the case, and in particular common sense factors (including the number and significance of documents involved, the nature of the proceedings, the ease and expense of retrieval), as well as the overriding principle of *proportionality*, which may justify limiting searches by time, space or category.[24]

(d) Disclosure statement

The exchanged list *must* include a *disclosure statement*, confirming an understanding of and compliance with the duty to disclose, as well as making clear, where relevant, when and why it has not been reasonable to search for a document. These statements must normally be signed by the *parties personally* (since they have the primary responsibility to make full disclosure,) *not* their solicitors (who nevertheless should have explained early on to their client about the need to preserve documents for disclosure).[25]

(e) List in three sections

The exchanged list sets out disclosable documents in three discrete sections, which effectively tells the other side: (i) these are the documents I still have and which you may see; (ii) these are documents which I have but you are not entitled to see and (iii) these are disclosable documents I used to have but do not have them any more (and this is where they are).[26] The second section typically includes *privileged* documents. They go in the list because their existence needs to be disclosed, but the other side is not, at this stage anyway,[27] entitled to see them.

24 CPR, r 31.7(1) and PD 31A, para 2

25 There are exceptions, for example where the party is not an individual (in which case a human representative will sign the statement). See CPR, r 31.10(5)-(9), PD 31A, para 4 and see example at Annex A to PD 31A.

26 See Form N 265

27 An expert's report, for example, may be privileged from inspection at this stage, but will ultimately have to be exchanged if it is to be relied on at trial. *See below* Ch 17

(f) Continuing duty

The duty to disclose is a continuing one, and lasts until proceedings have finished. So if, after lists have been served and so forth, a party comes across or becomes aware of a document which should be disclosed, then every other party must be informed immediately.[28]

Finally, note the following points about disclosure in the normal course of litigation:

(g) Objecting to disclosure or inspection

Objecting to inspection and objecting to disclosure are two *very different* situations, which again require a clear understanding of the distinction between these two parts of the process. Both are covered in CPR, r 31.19. *Objecting to inspection* is something that routinely happens, typically when a party asserts privilege over certain disclosed documents. A party objects to inspection *not* by making any applications to the court, but by describing those documents in the second part of their disclosure list (usually very vaguely, for example 'documents created for the purposes of the litigation' or 'counsel's advice'). The reason for objecting to inspection must also be given; the most common is legal professional privilege. A party in receipt of the disclosure list who believes that the objection to inspection is unfounded is the one who may make an application to the court, supported by evidence, for a decision as to whether the claim to withhold inspection should be upheld.[29]

Objecting to disclosure is much more controversial, and very rare. A party who objects to disclosure of a document is basically saying that the other side should not even know about its existence, never mind being able to look at it! The only basis for claiming this would be so-called 'public interest immunity'- in effect a claim that revealing the document's existence would damage the public interest. This is a

28 CPR, r 31.11
29 CPR, r 31.19(3)-(7)

specialist area, and all you need to appreciate here is that if objecting to disclosure on this basis, a party *does* need to apply to the court, *without notice*, for an order permitting the withholding of disclosure. It makes sense that the application is made without notice - if the other side were given notice, they would then know about the document's existence, which would defeat the entire purpose of the exercise! Such applications and orders are very unusual, since if a public interest immunity claim over a document is upheld, the other side may well have no idea at all about it or anything that has gone on in respect of it, which is very antithetical to the 'cards on the table' approach under the CPR.[30]

(h) Possible limitations on inspection

The court can also impose limitations on the ambit of inspection (for example, limiting inspection of confidential documents to a party's medical and legal advisors) or agree that permitting inspection of a category or class of documents may be *disproportionate* to the issues involved and so need not take place. In *Webster v Ridgeway Foundation School Governors*,[31] for example, it was said that allowing inspection of a redacted version of the school's entire data base recording the behaviour of pupils would be such a huge task for the school, relative to its evidential value to the claimants, that it would be regarded as disproportionate. It is for the party who wants to limit inspection, on the grounds that it would be disproportionate, to flag up the matter in his disclosure list. The other side contests this by making an application for 'specific inspection'.[32]

(i) Immediate right to inspect certain documents

A party may *at any time* inspect a document which has been '*mentioned*' in a statement of case, witness statement/summary or an affidavit.[33] This is just a practical rule. Obviously, if the document in question has been referred to in one of these other

30 CPR, r 31.19 (1)-(2)

31 [2009] EWHC 1140 (QB)

32 CPR, r 31.3(2). Again, the ability to claim that inspection of a class or category of document would be disproportionate does not apply to documents on which the disclosing parties relies, no doubt because that party should actively want the other side to see such documents. Specific disclosure and inspection is considered below.

33 CPR, r 31.14. A document is mentioned if specifically or directly alluded to. *Rubin v Expandable Ltd* [2008] 1 WLR 1099

documents, its existence is then known and so there is no need to wait for the exchange of disclosure lists. The inspection process can follow immediately.[34]

As regards a document mentioned in an expert's report, assuming it has not already been disclosed, and if an informal request is refused, an *application* to the court will be necessary for an order to inspect.[35] How burdensome the request is will be key to the court's decision.

(j) Specific disclosure or inspection

What happens if a party thinks their opponent still has documents it should disclose, but has not? Or if a party wants to contest an opponent's assertion that it was unreasonable to search for (and thus disclose) a category or class of documents? This is where an application for '*specific* disclosure' comes in. A classic scenario is where a litigant fails to list all pertinent documents in their disclosure list. By the time the parties exchange lists it should be pretty clear what the issues in dispute are and each side (having produced their own lists) will have some expectations of what they expect to find in their opponent's list. Something obvious might be missing. Or a disclosed document may make reference to another document which was omitted from the disclosing party's list. In such circumstances, an application can be made for an order that the specific document or class of documents be disclosed.[36]

Similarly, if an opponent states in his disclosure statement that he has not searched for a class or category of documents (and so not disclosed them) on the grounds that it would be unreasonable to do so, this too can be challenged by making an application for specific disclosure. In this case, a party would seek an order that a search be made and that any documents located as a result be disclosed.[37] In either scenario, if the order for specific disclosure is made, and complied with, the inspection process will follow in the normal way.

34 CPR, r 31.14(1). The right to inspect is stated in very unqualified terms in this rule, but it has been held that a party's rights to object to, or the court's ability to restrict, inspection, apply (not that the need to do so is very apt to arise). See WB, para 31.14.1

35 CPR, r 31.14(2) and PD 31A para 7

36 CPR, r 31.12(2)(a)

37 CPR, r 31.12(2)(b)/(c)

Applications for 'specific inspection' are slightly different. As explained above, these are used to challenge a party who asserts (in his disclosure statement) that he is not required to permit *inspection* of a category or class of documents (whose existence is disclosed) because to do so would be disproportionate.[38]

As a matter of common sense, parties should attempt to resolve these issues between themselves, but if this is not possible then an application to the court will be necessary. Such is made in writing, on notice, supported by written evidence, and should specify the order sought and the reasons the applicant believes the document(s) in question (which must be described with reasonable precision) should be disclosed (and/or searched for) or inspection permitted. In deciding whether and to what extent to grant the order sought, the court will take into account *all the circumstances of the case and the overriding objective* (no surprises there!). In essence the court will be looking to ensure that the disclosure obligations required of the parties (or the nature of the case) have been carried out. How important or relevant is the document? Is it still in the other party's control? Is the order sought proportionate? Is the disclosure necessary for the just disposal of the case?[39]

In particular, where the document sought should have been, but was not, disclosed under an existing direction for standard disclosure, then specific disclosure will almost always be given (and vice versa).[40] But such orders are not limited to inadequate disclosure lists; they can come in handy at various stages of the litigation process. The court has a discretion to make such orders at any time, regardless of whether exchange of lists has already taken place. So, for example, the court can make an order for specific disclosure against a claimant before service of the defence has even taken place, where to do so would assist that defendant to plead a full defence (rather than a bare, and pretty uninformative, denial).[41] It is also worth noting that specific disclosure is one of the possible menu option directions.

38 CPR, r 31.12(3). This is a very specific application and is different from one challenging a claim that the disclosing party has a right to withhold inspection on grounds, for example, of legal professional privilege.

39 See WB, para 31.12.2

40 See PD 31A, para 5.4

41 As in ***Dayman v Canyon Holdings Ltd*** 11/1/2006 and see WB, para 31.12.2

Typically applications for specific disclosure or inspection are dealt with at classic case management junctures. But such applications can be made at any time and should be made as soon as the need arises. Indeed, a delay in seeking an order could well undermine any argument that the order sought is needed for the 'just disposal' of the case.[42]

(k) Use of disclosed documents

There is a long-standing and important principle, now given expression in the CPR, that a party inspects documents on the understanding that they (and their contents) will *only* be used for the purposes of the litigation in which they are disclosed, and not for a 'collateral purpose' (for example, to show to the media or share with a competitor, although the party who disclosed the document can consent to a collateral use). However, once the documents have found their way into the public domain, for example by being read in open court, this restriction ceases to be of effect, *unless* the court orders otherwise. Further, even if a document has not been made public, the court has power (although it would use it sparingly) to sanction its use for a collateral purpose.[43]

(l) Penalties for non-disclosure

Failure to make proper disclosure or to permit inspection of documents as required can result in very real and serious penalties. The principle sanction is built into the rules themselves, which explicitly say that the defaulting party may not rely on such document(s) , unless the court gives permission.[44] But this is just the in-built sanction - in an extreme case, the court might strike out the defaulting party's statement of case, which would end that party's case at a stroke.[45]

Finally, you will remember that the party himself must sign the disclosure statement -

42 See WB, para 31.12.1.1

43 See generally CPR, r 31.22. This is a complex area, but the rules attempt to tread a middle ground between ensuring disclosed documents are only used for the immediate litigation purpose, thus limiting their negative impact on the disclosing party; and, recognising that, when documents (and the information in them) have become public, it is hard to justify stopping the one party who may most need to use the document from doing so.

44 CPR, r 31.21

45 Unless relief from the sanction is given under r 3.9. See generally Ch 13

someone who dishonestly makes a false disclosure statement can be held in contempt of court.[46] This could, in a worst case scenario, result in a prison sentence!

(ii) Small claims track disclosure

In small claims track cases, different rules apply. Parties there are only required to disclose those documents on which they intend to *rely* at trial, such documents to be exchanged by the parties no later than 14 days before trial.[47]

B. EXCEPTIONAL DISCLOSURE ORDERS (AGAINST NON-PARTIES)

Disclosure of documents is a litigation tool and so an *important general rule* has been that it is *only* available against a party to on-going litigation. You cannot go wandering up and down your street seeking disclosure of documents from people you are not suing! Of course, nowadays, as pre-action disclosure is seen as a way of achieving fair settlement of claims without the need to litigate, so the exceptions to this rule have increased. In many ways the exceptions are close to becoming the rule. Nevertheless, it is still helpful to look at them from this perspective.

In one sense, disclosure under the pre-action procedure rules is clearly an exception to this general rule, since no action will have been officially commenced at that point. Indeed, the whole point of the pre-action protocols/PD is to avoid the need for proceedings. But it is part of a formal pre-action procedural process, so might be viewed as widening the rule (or the notion of litigation) to include not only the act, but also the foreplay.

In addition, there are some important, and more long-standing, exceptions to the rule that disclosure is only available against a party to the litigation to which it relates. It is important not to confuse them - examinations often test the novice's ability to distinguish between them.

46 CPR, r 31.23
47 CPR, r 27.4(3)

(i) The rule in *Norwich Pharmacal*

This is a common law exception,[48] which provides a procedure for getting disclosure of the *identity of wrongdoers*, so that a claim can be made against them.

To paraphrase Lord Reid in the leading case of *Norwich Pharmacal Co v Commissioners of Custom & Excise*:

> If, whether through any *fault of his own or not*, a person gets mixed up in the transactions of others so as to facilitate their wrongdoing, he comes under a duty to assist the person who has been wronged by giving him full information and disclosing the identity of the wrongdoers.[49]

The key component of the test is that the person who may be required to disclose the information must have *facilitated*, whether unwittingly or not, the *wrongdoing* of others, and be able to provide their identity.[50] It is very important to understand that *mere witnesses* or bystanders to an event come under no such duty and *cannot be made* to disclose what they saw *before* an action has even been commenced (they can of course be compelled to come to court to give evidence at trial). It does not take much involvement to be a facilitator, but being a mere witness is not enough.[51] In addition, the information sought must not be privileged or otherwise protected from disclosure.[52]

Remember, too, that facilitators need not *necessarily* have done something wrong themselves - in the *Norwich Pharmacal* case itself, the defendants were so-called 'innocent facilitators'. In lots of cases, however, facilitators have committed their own wrongs. Further, the applicant must have a 'legitimate interest' in the information, and not merely wish to satisfy their curiosity - this means that the order must be necessary in order to pursue a legal claim or otherwise hold the wrongdoer to account. If the applicant has no interest in seeking redress or already

48 Preserved, but not modified by CPR, r 31.18

49 [1974] AC 133, at 175, HL (my emphasis) and see WB para 31.18.2

50 The applicant does not need to prove the wrong, but must show some reasonable basis for saying a wrong was or was arguably carried out by the ultimate wrongdoer. See ***Mitsui & Co Ltd v Nexen Petroleum UK Ltd*** [2005], cited at WB para 31.18.3/4. This may explain the somewhat generous result in ***Murphy v Murphy*** [1999] 1 WLR 282 where the person who created a discretionary trust was required to disclose the name of the trustees to a potential beneficiary. There was no evidence that the trustees had in fact done anything wrong, but without the information the potential beneficiary could not actually ascertain whether the trustees had acted properly.

has the information or can get it some other (easier) way, then a *Norwich Pharmacal* order will not be made.[53]

Norwich Pharmacal orders are only available from the High Court because they derive from its inherent jurisdiction. They are not limited to disclosure of documents, and can include answering questions or providing a 'narration of facts'. However, the remedy, being equitable, is ultimately a matter of discretion and so even if all the other requirements have been satisfied, the court may still refuse the order if, for example, there is some public interest in doing so.[54]

Norwich Pharmacal is a kind of pre-action disclosure, because until the name of the wrongdoer is known, no action can be brought against that person. But it is known only by the name of the leading case, so be *very careful* not to confuse it with the procedure discussed below. In a nutshell, a *Norwich Pharmacal* application is appropriate when *the applicant knows he has a good claim against someone, but does not know who that someone is.* It will be for the 'facilitator' to supply that information. There have been cases extending the ambit of this form of disclosure to include, additionally, information to help the applicant assess the strength of and even the nature of the case against the wrongdoer. If this trend continues, there may be an eventual merging between this form of pre-action disclosure and that discussed in (ii) below. *But it is important to be able to distinguish between them. Examiners like to test this difference.*

The procedure for making the application is a little involved since it derives from the common law, and varies depending on whether the facilitator is innocent or not. If the former, the applicant issues a (Part 8) claim form against the 'facilitator', seeking disclosure of the identity of the wrongdoer. An interim application is then made *on notice* (to a Master in the KBD, a judge in the ChD), unless urgency or secrecy justifies not doing so - for example where the order is to be annexed to a freezing or search order.[55] Once the identity of the wrongdoer

51 See, e.g., ***Harrington v Polytechnic of North London*** [1984] 1 WLR 1293 and WB, para 31.8.6

52 For example, to protect journalistic sources. See WB. Para 31.18.7

53 It is not a requirement that the applicant will bring court proceedings, but the information must be needed to protect himself or assert his rights in some way, for example by a dismissal from employment or deprivation of pension rights. And see WB, para 31.18.4/5

54 This residual discretion is very broad. See ***Rugby Football Union v Viagogo Ltd*** [2012] 1 WLR 3333 at [17], cited and encapsulated at WB, para 31.18.8

55 See Ch 7

is disclosed, the proceedings against the facilitator have achieved their objective and so come to a natural end - a fresh claim can now be brought against the newly identified wrongdoer. Remember: if you already know the identity of your wrongdoer, you do not need a *Norwich Pharmacal* order!

If the claimant is also suing the 'facilitator' for his own wrongdoing, as is commonly the case, the *Norwich Pharmacal* application is made as an interim application in that action. Once the (other) wrongdoers are identified, then they can be joined to the claim or new proceedings brought against them.

It is the applicant who pays the costs of these applications, but these may be recovered from the wrongdoer at the end of the day.[56]

(ii) Statutory pre-action disclosure (from a 'likely' future defendant)

This form of pre-action disclosure is governed by statute and is available in both the High Court and County Court.[57] Somewhat confusingly for beginners, it is known as 'pre-action disclosure', as if it were the only one, so be sure you are able to distinguish it from the *Norwich Pharmacal* order. Statutory pre-action disclosure is appropriate where the applicant *knows who the defendant would be, but does not know whether the case is strong enough to make it worthwhile pursuing the claim.*

Over the years this kind of pre-action disclosure has evolved from being very limited in its scope[58] to being generally available in any sort of case, but not often necessary. Before the days of pre-action protocols and patient access to their medical records, a typical situation where such an order was sought might be one where the applicant went into hospital with a minor complaint and came out with a serious medical condition. Until the patient (and/or his advisors) got a look at his notes to find out what went on in the hospital, it was difficult to gauge whether the suspicion that the doctors had been negligent, and so could be successfully sued, was supported

56 Assuming the wrongdoer loses. See generally Ch 18

57 Senior Courts Act 1981 ('SCA 1981), s 33 and County Courts Act 1984 ('CCA 1984'), s 52

58 For many years it was only available in personal injuries and fatal accident cases.

by the evidence. This is what statutory pre-action disclosure allowed him to do. Pre-action protocols now generally serve this purpose, but of course the application may still be necessary if, for example, additional disclosure is required or a hospital does not comply with a request under the Access to Health Records legislation. Most cases nowadays involve commercial transactions, although even here such pre-action disclosure orders would be considered, if not exceptional, then unusual.[59]

CPR, r 31.16(3)(a)-(d) sets out the essential conditions for the making of such orders. Thus, the courts have power to make an order for statutory pre-action disclosure of documents against the respondent where both *that* person and the applicant are 'likely' to be parties to any 'subsequent' proceedings brought as a result. It is thus an order available against a *future* defendant whose identity is known and who is likely to be in *possession* or control of *material* documents, but *only* in respect of those documents which would (more probably than not) be disclosable in the anticipated litigation. This makes sense: an applicant should not be able to achieve a greater amount of disclosure pre-action than would be ordered once proceedings were actually commenced.[60] Moreover, in order to make the pre-action disclosure order, the court must be of the view that ordering early disclosure is *'desirable' to fairly dispose of* the anticipated proceedings, *save costs or encourage settlement*, for example by narrowing the issues or helping to avoid litigation altogether. If pre-action disclosure would not achieve one of these stated aims then it will not be ordered. In a sense, what the applicant must do is show not only that the *documents* in question would be disclosable in the normal course of litigation, but also that disclosing them *at this early stage* would further one of those specific objectives.

There has been much judicial consideration of what 'likely' means in the context of the rule (the wording of which has changed somewhat over the years), and in particular how strong the applicant's future case against the respondent must

59 *Carillion plc v KPMG LLP* [2020] 1416 (Comm) referenced at WB, para 31.16.4

60 In the case of a class of documents, it is for the applicant to show that the entire class would be covered by standard disclosure. It is not the respondent's job in this context to figure out which of a particular class would be covered and which would not.

appear to be at this early stage.[61] There must be some real basis for the anticipated claim, but if the applicant were required to show too strong a case at this point, it would defeat the purpose of the remedy, and so it now seems clear from cases upholding *Black v Sumitomo Corporation*[62] that there is no need to show that the claim is of a certain strength or even that it is likely to be brought, as such; just that if the claim were brought, the applicant and the respondent will be the likely parties (and in this context 'likely' means 'may well', not 'more probably than not'). Generally, therefore, the court will not look deeply into the merits at this stage, although if the case is weak on its face, this would strongly militate against an order being made. In any event, such disclosure should not be used as a 'fishing expedition' (or a 'speculative punt' as we now say) or to force disclosure of a document, the need for which is not made out.[63]

Because of the way CPR, r 31.16 is worded ('the court 'may' make an order'), it is said nowadays that decisions regarding orders for such pre-action disclosure require a two-stage approach. Stage one is about determining if the requirements set out above have been met. But even if the court decides that the *jurisdictional* criteria are made out, thus giving it the ability to make an order, the court has an overarching and unfettered *discretion* to refuse to do so, for example if it would be oppressive or otherwise not in the public interest. This has come to be known as the second - discretionary - stage.[64] At this second stage the court should take a step back and look at the application in the round, and in particular consider whether making the order sought would further the overriding objective.[65]

Procedurally, such applications are interim applications in the anticipated litigation (that sounds weird, I know), setting out the basis of the claim in the supporting written evidence. Any order made must specify the documents or class of documents to be disclosed by the respondent, who should provide information

61 Before the CPR, the wording included reference to whether a claim was 'likely to be made', but this was dropped from the current rule. There are still lots of 'likely's in CPR, r 31.16, but they refer to parties, not claims. So the pre-CPR cases are not binding, as such, but still give useful guidance. After all, you cannot have parties if you do not have a claim. See ***Smith v Sec of State for Energy and Climate Change*** [2014] 1WLR 2283.

62 [2002] WLR 1562

63 See WB, para 31.16.4. A court will not order pre-action disclosure where to do so would frustrate an agreement that the matter should go to arbitration and not litigation.

64 There is of course some element of discretion involved in determining jurisdiction at stage one (e.g., as to whether the disclosure

about such documents as would appear in a normal disclosure list.[66]

So this form of pre-action disclosure *differs* from the *Norwich Pharmacal* order in several respects, namely:

- It derives from statute, and is available in both the High Court and Country Court.
- It is *limited to disclosure of documents* which would be subject to *standard disclosure* in due course.
- It caters for the situation where a (prospective) claimant knows who his defendant would be, but he does not know, until he sees the documents, whether the case is worth pursuing.

The costs of applying for this type of pre-action disclosure order are usually borne by the person seeking the order, although if the court takes the view that the respondent forced an application unnecessarily (because it was obvious the court would make the order), it may award costs to the applicant.

(iii) Non-party disclosure: orders against 'strangers' to on-going litigation

Once a case has commenced, a party may be able to get an order for disclosure of documents against a 'stranger' to that litigation, in other words, someone who is *not* one of the *parties* to it. This may be allowed where the non-party has control over documents which are 'likely' to assist the applicant's case (by supporting his case or adversely affecting another party's case) *and* disclosure is '*necessary*' to fairly dispose of the action or save costs. And again, even if these essential criteria are met, the court still retains a discretion whether to make the order or not.[67]

This is not a form of pre-action disclosure, but it is very much an exception

would be 'desirable' to save costs etc). So the distinction between stage one and two is not a stark one. The important point is that even if the court concludes that all of the requirements of r 31.16(3) are made out, it retains a residual discretion to refuse to make the order.

65 *Hands v Morrison Construction Services Ltd* [2006] EWHC 2018 (Ch) and *Carillion* case, cited at WB, para 31.16.4

66 CPR, r 31.16(4)

67 CPR, r 31.17 (3). Note here the use of the word 'necessary' (at r 31.17(3)(b) instead of the word 'desirable' (as applies under r 31.16(3)(d)). And see discussion at WB, para 31.17.2.1

to the general rule we started with because the person against whom the disclosure is sought is not a party to the proceedings to which the disclosure relates. If the court did not have this power, the only way a party to litigation could get access to important documents in the hands of non-parties (if they were not willing to disclose voluntarily) would be to require them to attend as a witness at trial, along with the document.[68] Not only would this be a very roundabout and expensive way to achieve disclosure, but it would happen far too late for the desired purpose. Typical situations where such orders might be made are where organisations (for example, the police or a bank) hold documented information which is key to the applicant's case.

Having said that, imposing disclosure obligations on a non-party to on-going litigation (who, after all, has nothing whatever to do with the case or any harm done to the applicant) is considered a *very intrusive* order, and so the court's jurisdiction to make such orders should be exercised *with caution.* Often the decision involves balancing the applicant's right to a fair trial against the respondent's Article 8 right to privacy or indeed the public interest in confidentiality. If an order is made, it can be limited as appropriate.[69] And again, if there are other ways a litigant can get the information, this will render such an application (or order) unnecessary.[70]

Like pre-action disclosure orders against future defendants (discussed above), this exceptional form of disclosure also derives from statute and is available in both the High and County Courts.[71] The procedural requirements are set out in CPR, r 31.17. The application is made by way of interim application in the on-going proceedings, on notice and supported by written evidence. Any order made must specify what documents are to be disclosed and may ask the respondent to indicate where such documents are, if they are no longer in his possession or control.[72]

68 A person can be required, by means of a witness summons, to attend court to give oral evidence and/or to produce documents. See CPR, rr 32.2-32.7

69 See, e.g., ***Re Howglen Ltd*** [2001] 1 All ER 376 where an application sought in very general terms for disclosure against a non-party bank for records and interview notes resulted in a very precise order limited to three specific interviews identified in the written evidence accompanying the application. For the exceptional nature of this sort of order see WB para 31.17.4

70 E.g., under Data Protection legislation.

71 See SCA 1981, s 34/CCA 1984, s 53. 'Likely' is also taken to mean 'may well'.

72 See CPR, r 31.17(4) for what *must* be in the order and r 31.17(5) for what *may* be in the order.

2. INSPECTION OF RELEVANT PROPERTY AND MEDICAL EXAMINATIONS

Like documents (usually, of course, it is what is contained in the document which matters), objects can provide useful evidential information. In the rules, such things come under the general description of 'relevant property'. To get evidential value from such things, one might need to look at them or take samples from them, perform tests on them and so on. To do that, it may be necessary to preserve the property for one or other of these purposes. To that end the courts have power to make orders giving one party (or his advisors) access to relevant property in the possession of another party. Again, the general rule applies - such are normally available only against parties to the litigation in question. But, as ever, there are exceptions.

A. IN THE NORMAL COURSE OF LITIGATION

Preserving relevant property for inspection, testing and so forth is commonplace in litigation, and unexceptional. Parties are usually able to arrange this between themselves. If, for example, a claimant sues her employers because she was injured by a machine she was required to operate at work, it may be important to allow those who are qualified to pass judgment on the state of the offending machine a chance to inspect it while in the same condition it was in when the claimant was injured (or near enough). The machine is the 'relevant property' and an order, where necessary, would typically allow for the 'preservation' of the machine,[73] and access[74] to it so that it can be examined and so forth by a person who knows how such machines are supposed to work (an expert, in other words).[75]

An *analogous, but different* situation arises when seeking orders relating to the medical examination of a claimant to be conducted by the defendant's doctor in

73 The idea is that the machine is examined before any defects have been put right or repairs carried out.

74 It may well be at the defendant's premises.

75 See CPR, r 25.1(c)(i)-(iv). R 25.1(2) defines 'relevant property' as meaning any property which is the subject of the claim *or* as to which any questions may arise on a claim.

a personal injuries case. This can happen in the more complex cases where both sides are given permission to call competing medical evidence, but the claimant does not consent to being examined by the defendant's expert.[76] As the claimant is a human being and not a machine, the court *cannot* force the claimant to be examined - this would be an infringement of personal liberty. However, the court can achieve much the same result by the indirect method of ordering a halt to proceedings if the claimant *unreasonably* refuses such a medical examination. Whether or not a stay is granted is entirely within the discretion of the court - the facts of the individual case and a party's reasons for seeking, or resisting, the proposed medical examination, are all matters to be taken into account. There is a balance to be struck between the claimant's human rights and the defendant's litigation rights. A medical examination which might harm the claimant's health would, of course, pose special difficulties, which would need to be weighed in the balance. The court will order the stay if it would be 'just and reasonable'.[77]

Sometimes claimants are only willing to submit to a medical examination on conditions. Those which are personal to the claimant (for example, payment of fares getting to the examination, the presence of a friend,[78] an assurance the doctor will not discuss the case with the claimant except insofar as medically necessary, a request for a doctor of a particular gender for understandable reasons) will usually be uncontroversial. However, conditions which in effect amount to attempts to choose the defendant's expert for him (unless there are doubts about the competence or honesty of the choice of doctor) or interfere with the purpose of the examination will be more apt to be considered unreasonable.[79]

Applications for such orders (whether to gain access to inspect things or regarding the medical examination of claimants) are made on notice,[80] supported by written evidence which speaks to the need and relevance of the order. They are,

76 This sort of problem thus tends to arise on the multi-track. A defendant is entitled to test the severity of a claimant's injuries etc, but this is now often done on a joint basis, either by virtue of the relevant Pre-Action Protocol or a direction for a single joint expert.

77 An analogous problem arises if a claimant refuses to permit inspection of relevant but otherwise confidential medical records. The court would be more apt to order a stay than to order that a claimant permit inspection of such documents, since the latter would infringe the claimant's right to retain control over confidential material: See WB para 31.12.2 (sub-para 5).

78 But see ***Whitehead v Avon County Council***, the Times, 3 May 1995, CA, where the Court of Appeal upheld a decision that the claimant's action be stayed unless she

however, often rendered unnecessary by the other party's willingness to give access, because it is so obvious that this is precisely what the court would order.

B. EXCEPTIONAL ORDERS

The exceptions to the general rule that orders for the inspection, experimentation and so on of relevant property are available only against *parties* to the relevant litigation, mirror those statutory exceptions discussed above relating to disclosure of documents. Indeed, they too are statutory.[81] Thus it is possible, where the object in question may become relevant to the subject matter of *subsequent* proceedings, to get an order for inspection and so on *before* those proceedings have been started. Similarly, it is also possible to get such orders against a 'stranger' to on-going litigation, where that non-party is in possession or control of property which is relevant to the subject matter of that litigation.

When such an order is necessary, the application is again generally made on notice, supported by written evidence identifying the property in question and the need for the order. If the order is, *exceptionally*, made not only pre-action,[82] but also (doubly exceptionally) without notice, it is called a search order.[83] Thus it is that a 'search order' is really just a dramatic and surprising version of something which can otherwise be quite ordinary.

3. REQUESTS FOR FURTHER INFORMATION

In certain prescribed circumstances, a party can also get specific information by requesting it. Not surprisingly, perhaps, these are called 'requests for further information'. Sometimes a party might be vague about aspects of his case or

submitted to a psychiatric examination without a friend or relation being present.

79 See also ***Starr v National Coal Board*** [1977] 1 WLR 63, CA

80 CPR, r 25.3

81 See SCA 1981, ss 33 and 34/CCA 1984, ss 52 and 53

82 Or pre-service of proceedings.

83 See Ch 7

something might be mentioned in a witness statement which requires clarification. Before the CPR, the former situation was dealt with by something called 'Further and Better Particulars' (which was limited to asking parties to be more specific about the allegations made in their statements of case); and the latter was dealt with by 'Interrogatories' (a request for answers to questions where these would help 'fairly dispose of the action or save costs'). These two old procedures were rolled into one, so that a 'request' for further information under CPR, Part 18 can be used to seek clarification of any matter in dispute, or get additional information about any such matter, whether or not it is contained, or referred to, in a statement of case.

This litigation tool (and it is only a litigation tool - no exceptions here) can be very useful in exposing weaknesses in the case against you. It can reveal an inability to make, much less prove a specific allegation. Having said that, requests should be concise and will only be ordered where (and to the extent that) they are 'reasonably necessary and proportionate'; they should not be used as a delaying tactic, nor as a hit and miss expedition 'fishing' for factual ammunition. Their function is to enable the requesting party to 'prepare his own case or to understand the case he has to meet'.[84]

So, if a party looks at an allegation and thinks *"Well, like what?"*, or *"In what way?"* or *"How exactly?"*, this may indicate that an early request for further information about that allegation may well be appropriate.[85] Or the need for clarification may happen further down the litigation road, for example after evidence has been exchanged. The court can also use the procedure on its own initiative, for example to help narrow the issues or for case management purposes.[86]

Part 18 requests should be made as soon as practicable after the need arises. A party seeking further information should first serve a written request[87] on the party from whom it is sought, leaving a reasonable time for responding. The request should,

84 CPR, PD 18, para 1.2 and see WB, para 18.0.1 and 18.1.3

85 It is also a good way of testing your own drafting skills to ensure you have been as specific as possible in drafting the statement of case before it is served

86 CPR, r 18.1

87 PD 18, para 1.1

88 PD 18, para 1.7. The format of such requests is very precisely set out in PD 18, 1.6

89 PD 18, paras 2 and 3. The request itself is just a series of questions and is thus incapable of being true or false. So it does not need to be verified by a statement of truth, unlike other documents

where possible, be made in a single document (and not piecemeal) and (unless very brief) should be made in a separate document (and not in a letter). Such requests are very formal documents, and where practicable should be served by e-mail.[88]

Replies should mirror the format in which the request was made and must be verified by a statement of truth.[89] A party who objects to responding to a Part 18 request should inform the requesting party, with reasons, within the time given in the request.[90]

It is only in the absence of a proper response (or if the respondent objects to the request) that an application to the court for an order will have to be made. Where there has been no response at all to a written request within the time given (and at least 14 days have passed), no notice of application need be served on the other party and the court can deal with the application without a hearing. Otherwise, notice of application must be served on *all* parties to the claim (and not merely the one who objected to the request). The same is true of any order made under Part 18.[91]

Not surprisingly, such applications will be determined by reference to the principles of proportionality and in accordance with the overriding objective.[92]

containing answers, allegations and so on.

90 PD 18, para 4

91 PD 18, para 5.5/6/7. Whether the information is given voluntarily or not, the court may also direct that it may only be used for the proceedings in which it was given: CPR r 18.2.

92 If the issue is the adequacy of a reply to a Part 18 request, any order the court makes should be worded specifically enough that it will be clear whether the order has been complied with: ***HRH Prince Khaled Bin Abdulaziz Al Saud v Gibbs*** [2022], cited at WB, para 18.0.1 and see WB, para 18.1.10

revision tips

- Be clear that *standard* disclosure is the *normal* direction in fast track cases and personal injuries actions on the multi-track (small claims have their own, much narrower form of order).
- Other multi-track cases (think big commercial cases) are governed by the new *menu option* procedure, which allows for more focused and tailor-made orders. This will no doubt also be on the menu of options for exam questions, so make sure you understand it!
- Watch out for adaptations to the rules with the creation of a new intermediate track.
- Review what is meant by standard disclosure and how it unfolds - BCP's procedural checklist 25 is a useful summary. Know the key words in the rules (e.g., 'reasonable' search, 'specific' disclosure). And remember that in this context there is a distinction to be made between 'disclosure' and 'inspection'.
- Be clear about how disclosure orders against non-parties *differ* from those made in the normal course of litigation.
- Be clear about the distinction between ***Norwich Pharmacal*** orders and statutory pre-action disclosure of documents. This is typical fodder for examinations.

It is worth reading ...

The judgment in ***Smith v Secretary of State for Energy and Climate Change*** [2014] 1 WLR 2283. This was the last in a long line of appellate cases (you can sense Longmore LJ's frustration) about the court's approach to statutory pre-action disclosure. It is easy to follow and makes clear the distinction between the jurisdictional requirements of such applications and the exercise of the court's discretion. It would be interesting to know whether the claim was ever actually brought.

Practical Law (accessible via Westlaw) has two useful Practice Notes overviews: one on the Disclosure process generally and one on ***Norwich Pharmacal*** orders (a 'practical guide'). They are useful summaries and so good for revision (although take care in the section on 'form' of NP application since there is a slight misdescription of when these are made under CPR Pt 23. It is when the 'facilitator' is also a wrongdoer and proceedings have been issued against *them* that the NP application notice is made in those proceedings under Pt 23).

PART THREE

efficiency and control

CHAPTER 10

Limitation

The courts have never been sympathetic towards dilatory claimants - even less so are they under the CPR. The ethos of our procedural system is that litigation is to be avoided where possible, through well-informed pre-action conduct, ADR, and costs disincentives. If, however, litigation becomes necessary, claims should be commenced promptly, and in any event within a specified amount of time, known as the 'limitation period'. Once the claim form has been issued, it should be served in good time - negotiations can follow or continue once those two straightforward procedural steps have been taken. Amendments made late in the day can be problematic, and will only exceptionally be allowed once a relevant limitation period has expired. Finally, tight case management by the court will force the pace of litigation, so that once started, cases get to trial efficiently and speedily.

Limitation is the subject of this chapter; the other aspects of court control referred to above will be considered in those immediately following.

The general rule is that a claim must be brought within the relevant limitation period or face (or risk facing) the impregnable defence that it is 'time-barred'. The latter is a *procedural* defence and it is for the *defendant* to raise it - it must be specifically set out in the defence.[1] It will not be raised by the court on its own initiative, nor should the claimant anticipate it in the particulars of claim.[2] If a claimant does not

1 PD 16, para 13.1

2 The claimant, or his legal advisors, may well anticipate the 'risk' that a defendant might raise limitation, and might even make an application to the court about it, but no pre-emptive strikes of a *'just in case you mention limitation in your defence'* kind are ever made in the particulars of claim.

discontinue proceedings which are time-barred, the defendant can apply to have the case struck out as an abuse of process.

It would be very hard on defendants if they were perpetually at risk of being sued - memories fade and evidence can degrade over time. And so the purpose of limitation periods is to put a reasonable but finite limit on the time during which causes of action can successfully be pursued, and to stop unduly stale claims (that is, claims a defendant did not expect to have to meet) being litigated.

Fixed limitation periods have been laid down for different types of cases,[3] but a certain amount of flexibility has been built into the system over the years, in particular to help people who may for some considerable time be unaware that they have suffered actionable harm.

The result of a claim being time-barred is to extinguish the claimant's remedy.[4] In the case of adverse possession of land and conversion, expiry of the limitation period has the additional effect of extinguishing the claimant's title.[5] Proceedings must be 'brought' in time to avoid limitation problems. The date entered on the claim form by the court when it issues it will tell us when the case was commenced, but if the claimant has done all he needs to do in time (by delivering all the relevant documents and fee to the relevant court office), then he will have 'brought' the claim before limitation expired even if the court did not actually issue the claim form until after the time had lapsed.[6] If things are getting that close to the wire, however, it is a good idea for the claimant (or his representative) to ensure that the claim form is issued in time.

The important thing to remember is that what must happen during the limitation period is that the claim is *brought* (and, subject to the point made above, this is usually when the claim form was *issued*); service of the claim form can come later (but not much later). Third party claims are deemed to be commenced on the date the Third Party/Additional claim form is issued.[7] Counterclaims and set-offs are deemed to

3 Most are set out in the Limitation Act 1980 ('LA 1980'). The periods vary because different types of cases bring with them greater or lesser degrees of urgency, depending on things like how ephemeral the evidence is likely to be, what can be expected of claimants in such cases and/or the nature of the conduct alleged. For example, breach of trust claims brought by beneficiaries against trustees alleging fraud or conversion of trust property have no limitation period at all: LA 1980, s 21(1). This is partly because what is being alleged might well amount to a criminal offence.

4 Strictly speaking the cause of action still exists, but cannot effectively be pursued.

5 LA 1980, ss 3 and 4

6 Even if, for example, the incorrect fee was paid. See *Dixon v Radley House*

have been commenced on the same date as the original claim - they are, as it were, 'back-dated' to that date.[8]

1. KNOWING WHETHER A CLAIM IS TIME-BARRED

Determining whether the relevant limitation period has expired in any given situation is basically *a two-stage process.* It involves asking yourself two questions: how long is the limitation period in this case, and when did it start to run? Once these questions are answered, in most cases it can easily be determined whether a claim has been, or can be, brought in time.

As to the first question, most time periods are laid down in the Limitation Act 1980, as amended. The important ones are conveniently set out at BCP, table 10.1. Remember that personal injury claims can arise in contract as well as in negligence actions; generally speaking 'personal injuries' describes the nature of the damage caused by a breach, not the cause of action.[9]

As to the second question, time ordinarily runs from the (first full day after the) date the cause of action 'accrues', as it is called,[10] although statute has provided alternatives in some cases. The *nature* of the cause of action will normally dictate when it accrues and time starts to run.

A. LIMITATION PERIODS

Thus, looking at both questions together, as they relate to the general run of cases:

(i) Non-personal injuries claim founded on simple contract

The limitation period is six years. Time runs from date of breach. This can vary

Partnership (A firm) [2016] EWHC 2511 (TCC) and WB, Vol 2, para 8-3.2

7 LA 1980, s 35(1)(a). As to Third Parties generally, see Ch 3

8 As are new claims added by amendment: LA 1980, s 35(1)(b) and s 35(2). Amendments are dealt with in more detail in Ch 11

9 See wording of LA 1980, s 11(1)

10 The law ignores 'part days' when counting the time after a cause of action has arisen, and so the clock starts ticking from the start of the following (full) day. This gives the claimant the maximum amount of time to bring the claim, and no-one has to worry about what time of day the cause of action accrued. But when it accrues on the stroke of midnight (which is rare, but happens in so-called 'midnight deadline' cases), then there is in

depending on the nature of the contractual obligation which has been breached. For example, claims for breach of implied terms about satisfactory quality of purchased goods will normally run from the date the (unsatisfactory) goods were delivered. In claims for late delivery of goods, time would run from the contracted date of delivery.

(ii) Non-personal injuries claim founded on common law tort (not including defamation)

The limitation period is six years. Where the tort is actionable per se (that is, without having to prove damage, as with trespass), time runs from the date the tort is *committed*. Most tort actions, however, are only actionable on *proof of damage* (as is the case with negligence, nuisance and so on) and in those cases time runs from the date of *damage*,[11] unless the Latent Damage Act 1986 provides an alternative (*see below*).

(iii) Personal injuries and fatal accident cases

Here several special rules apply. First, the limitation period is shorter - it is *three* years. Time runs from the date the cause of action accrues (for example, the date of damage, if a negligence action) or, to deal with those cases where the claimant does not realise he has been injured until much later, from the so-called 'date of knowledge'. Analogous provisions apply to fatal accident cases (fatal accidents being the ultimate personal injury), although one needs to distinguish between claims brought on behalf of the deceased's estate (for the deceased's own injuries) and those brought by or on behalf of the deceased's dependents (for their loss of a breadwinner etc).[12] Further, even if time has expired, the court has a further discretionary power under s 33 to allow such cases to continue, nevertheless.[13]

effect no fraction of a day to ignore and the clock can commence at the same time as the cause of action (at midnight). In a sense, if the offending act or omission occurs part way through a day (as is usual), the law lets the claimant get to the beginning of the next day before starting the clock. But if the act or omission occurs at midnight, then the claimant is already at that point and needs no assistance getting there from the part-day rule. See *Matthews v Sedman* [2021] UKSC 19 and WB, Vol 2, para 8-3.1

11 Sometimes easier to describe than identify. See, e.g., *Khan v R M Falvery & Co* [2002] and related cases cited at BCP para 10.9 and WB, Vol 2, para 8-5

12 If the injured person dies before bringing a claim, but before limitation in his claim has expired, that

Date of knowledge

This is specifically defined in the Limitation Act 1980. It is important to remember that the requirements are *conjunctive.* There are three (sometimes four) components. In a nutshell, the date of knowledge is the first date when the claimant knew *all* of the following:

- that the injury is significant (in other words, worth suing over, assuming a defendant who admits liability and could satisfy a judgment),

and

- that the injury was caused by the act or omission which is alleged to be actionable,

and

- the identity of the defendant.[14]

In essence, if you were to date stamp each individual part of this knowledge puzzle, the date the last piece fell into place (or the latest date recorded) is the date of knowledge. Limitation would expire three years after this date.

Note too that date of knowledge is all about the date certain *facts* became known. Knowledge of law, or the legal implications of those facts, is irrelevant.[15] In addition, claimants will be expected to act reasonably (given their situation) in acquiring knowledge for these purposes, for example by making such inquiries and seeking such expert advice as the circumstances warrant.[16]

The date of knowledge provisions were first introduced in the 1960's to assist miners who had suffered damage to their lungs while down the pits, but were unaware of any injury until their disease (pneumoconiosis) manifested itself many years, often decades later. However, there were still some litigants who failed to bring a claim

action will vest in his estate, in which case time for bringing the claim (on the deceased's behalf in effect) will be three years from the date of death or, if later, the date of the personal representative's knowledge: LA 1980 s 11(5). Claims brought by or on behalf of the deceased's dependents, for their own loss, is a separate action brought under the Fatal Accidents Act 1976 (FA 1976). Here time runs from the date of death or, if later, the date of knowledge of the relevant dependent: LA 1980, s 12(2). Note, however, that no dependency claim can be brought under the FAA 1976 if the deceased's own cause of action was statute barred (or otherwise could not be pursued) when he died: LA 1980, s 12(1)

13 Although s 33 cannot be used to 'revive' a deceased's own claim which

in time even once they had the requisite knowledge - some had taken poor advice from the employers who had caused the harm! As a result, further provision was passed, now s 33(1) Limitation Act 1980, giving the court a *discretion*, where it thinks it *equitable*, to let a personal injuries claim proceed notwithstanding that it is out of time. In exercising the discretion the court does *not extend* the limitation period, but, rather, overlooks the fact that it has expired, and lets proceedings carry on regardless. For this reason it is inelegantly known as 'disapplying' the limitation period.

Section 33 Discretion

Section 33(3) of the Limitation Act 1980 says that the court should have regard to '*all of the circumstances*' of the case when deciding whether to exercise its discretion, and 'in particular' those factors contained in a relatively long list at s 33(3)(a)-(f). These are largely a matter of common sense and include things like the length and reason for the claimant's delay in bringing proceedings,[17] the effect of the delay on the cogency of the evidence, the behaviour of the defendant after the cause of action arose, how promptly the claimant acted once time (as extended by the date of knowledge provisions) began to run and so on. It is worth having a look at this list yourself - but remember it is *not* exhaustive. The specific matters mentioned there are 'exemplary, not definitive'. The discretion is unfettered.[18]

What the court must do is *balance* the prejudice to the claimant in not being able to pursue the personal injuries case on the one hand, against the prejudice to the defendant in having to meet an old claim. 'Forensic' prejudice (the state of the relevant evidence) is an important part of this equation - the loss of the ability to meet the claimant's claim on its merits will weigh more heavily than the loss of a procedural defence, as such (and what that might mean financially to the defendant). The overriding question is one of justice: would it be fair, in the circumstances, to let the case continue?

---

had become statute barred before his death, thus precluding a dependency claim under the FAA 1976: LA 1980, s 12(1)

14 If the act or omission of someone other than the defendant is relevant, as is common in vicarious liability cases, then the identity of that person also needs to be known: LA 1980, s 14(1)(d)

15 LA 1980, s 14(1)

16 LA 1980, s 14(3) and ***Adams v Bracknell Forest Borough Council*** [2005] 1 AC 76, and see generally relevant commentary in BCP or WB, especially para 8-38 of Vol 2 of the WB.

17 Ss 33(3)(a) and (b). The relevant delay for these purposes is that between the end of the limitation period and commencing the action. See e.g., ***Long v Tolchard*** [2001] PIQR P2, CA. Delay during the limitation period would be material to other of the factors.

It is for the claimant to convince the court that it is equitable to disapply the limitation period - how difficult or easy that will be will very much depend on the facts of the particular case.[19] Factors not specified in the s 33(3) list which might also be relevant include how long the defendant has known about the claimant's claim (the earlier the notification the better for the claimant), the reason for not pursuing the claim from the outset, and whether the claimant has an alternative claim in professional negligence against his or her legal advisors. Note, however, that the latter, while obviously pertinent, is not necessarily decisive. There are several drawbacks to suing your own solicitors (not least of which is that you might like them!), so it should not be viewed as an easy option. Indeed, if there can still be a fair trial against the original defendants, there is a lot to be said for allowing the case to proceed against them, as the ones who (allegedly) caused the damage in the first place! As it was put in *Cain v Francis*, a tortfeasor only deserves to have his obligation to pay damages removed if the passage of time has significantly compromised his ability to defend the claim.[20]

Applications under s 33 are made to a High Court or Circuit judge (although in the Country Court application may be made to the District Judge if the case is within his or her trial jurisdiction), usually as an interim application, but sometimes as a preliminary issue to be determined before trial. The court may need to hear oral evidence in order to exercise its discretion properly, as for example where there are allegations of child abuse or psychological damage.[21]

At one time it was held that if a claim had been commenced within the limitation period, but the claim had not progressed to trial because of a 'self-inflicted' wound resulting, for example, in the case being struck out,[22] s 33 could not be used to start a second, identical claim.[23] These were known as 'second action cases'. However, this (rather artificial) restriction was removed by *Horton v Sadler*,[24] and such

18 *Nash v Eli Lilly & Co* [1993] 4 All ER 383, at 402 (CA). And see discussion in WB, Vol 2, para 8-94.1

19 See *Sayers v Hunt* [2013], I WLR 1695

20 [2009] 3 WLR 551, para 69, per Smith LJ

21 See *R v Nugent Care Society* (Practice Note) [2010] WLR 516, CA.

22 See Ch 13

23 *Walkley v Precision Forgings* [1979] I WLR 606

24 [2007] 1 AC 307

cases will be determined like any other, although why the first claim was 'lost' may well be relevant to the court's decision.

(iv) Claims under the Latent Damage Act 1986 (LDA 1986)

Just as with injuries to people, sometimes other sorts of damage (for example, to buildings from poor construction) happen before it is noticeable. Thus, where damage (*other than* for personal injuries) is latent, not patent, a claim in the *tort* of negligence may be brought under the LDA 1986, which inserted ss 14A and 14B into the Limitation Act. S 14A offers two alternative limitation periods: six years from the date of damage or a shorter period of *three years*, to run from the earliest date when the claimant *knew*, in effect, that damage worth suing over was caused by an identifiable defendant. This is known as the 'start date', and these provisions are clearly analogous to the 'date of knowledge' in personal injuries and fatal accident cases.[25] You might think of them as applying to injured buildings, rather than injured people, but bear in mind that the LDA 1986 can also apply, for example, to tort-based claims against professional advisors for negligent misstatement.

There are, however, three *important* aspects in which such cases of latent damage *differ* from those involving personal injuries: one is that s 14A applies *only* to claims in tort, and does not extend to contractual negligence. It thus cannot be used where liability in contract and tort is concurrent - it is limited to claims for negligence where the duty of care arises solely in tort.[26] Secondly, there is a so-called 'long-stop' preventing LDA 1986 cases being brought after 15 years from the negligent act or omission.[27] No such statutory long-stop applies to personal injuries. And thirdly, there is no discretion to 'disapply' the relevant limitation period as there is in personal injury cases. Examiners may well want to test you on these differences!

---

25 Discussed above. Compare the very similar wording in s 14 and s 14A LA 1980. Note that any action already statute-barred before the LDA 1986 came into force cannot be saved by its provisions: WB, Vol 2, para 8-43

26 *Société Commerciale de Réassurance v ERAS (International) Limited* [1992] 2 All ER 82. Some judges have wondered aloud why the legislation should be limited in this way, but have always concluded that to decide otherwise would usurp the function of Parliament. See WB, Vol 2, para 8-43

27 LA 1980, s 14B

B. Further instances of common limitation periods

(v) Contribution claims

The limitation period here is *two* years, but time only begins to run from the *date of judgment, arbitration award or settlement* of the main claim (as regards both liability and quantum.)[28] Most contribution claims are made by way of an additional claim (for example, third party claim) under Part 20 and are dealt with at the same time as the main action.[29] But if this has not happened, then a defendant has a further two years after liability and *quantum is established* (by award or settlement agreement) to bring his contribution claim.

(vi) Recovery of land cases

The limitation period here is twelve years. There are detailed provisions set out in Schedule 1 of the Limitation Act 1980, but (very) broadly, time runs from the date of dispossession or, if later, from the date when the claimant's interest in the land vested.

(vii) Enforcing judgments

The limitation period is six years, and time runs from the date on which the judgment became enforceable. As to arrears of interest on any judgment debt, limitation expires six years after the date on which the interest became due.[30]

(viii) Judicial review

This time period is more analogous to lodging appeals.[31] Such claims must be made *promptly* and in any case within three *months* after the grounds for making the application arose.[32] The time for making the application can be extended by the court if there are good reasons.

28 LA 1980 s 10 and *Aer Lingus Plc v Gildacroft Ltd* [2006] EWCA Civ 4. See WB, Vol 2, para 8-22

29 Third party proceedings are discussed in Ch 3

30 LA 1980, s 24. For enforcement procedure see Ch 19)

31 Judicial Review is not an appeal mechanism as such, but rather a challenge to and review of public law functions. It is a very complex area. See Ch 19

32 CPR, r 54.5(1)

This is a very basic summary of some of the most common limitation periods (the detail in Schedule 1 of the Limitation Act 1980 goes on for four pages!); the ability to understand and apply this sort of essential knowledge is what an unseen assessment will test. If and when a limitation problem arises in practice (or in an open book exam), then clearly you will need to check the detail in the relevant statute and/or case law to identify and advise on the issue and answer any questions asked.[33]

C. Factors which delay or prevent time starting to run

Be aware, too, of the various circumstances which can stop the limitation period from *beginning* to run when it otherwise would. They include:

(i) Children and protected persons

This is a common situation. Where the claimant is a 'child' when the cause of action accrues, the limitation period will *not start to run* until that child becomes 18 years old.[34] As we saw in Chapter 3, a person who has not yet attained the age of majority is said to be acting under a legal 'disability'. So too is a 'protected person' who lacks the mental capacity[35] to conduct proceedings. Like the litigant who has not yet turned 18 years of age, if at the time the cause of action would otherwise have arisen, the claimant is of unsound mind (possibly because of the injury suffered), then time will not begin to run until the mental incapacity has ended. Be aware, however, that once time has started to run, *later* mental incapacity *cannot* stop it again.[36] It's a bit like a horserace - a legal disability can keep the starting gates from opening; but once they have opened and the horses have got out, there is no stopping them until the race is over. With children it is very easy to identify the exact moment that their legal disability ends; mental incapacity can be more complicated.

Note too that, notwithstanding that a mental incapacity may still be on-going,

33 And always check your examination syllabus for examinable detail

34 LA 1980, s 28

35 Within the meaning of the Mental Capacity Act 2005. See LA 1980, ss 28 and 38(2)

36 It would be very awkward for a defendant if it could, since he would have to keep checking up on the claimant's mental health to know if limitation was running or not. It is easier with the claimant's age, since once you become 18 there is no going back. This is not necessarily true for mental health.

s 28(4) provides that there is a 'long-stop' period of 30 years from the date of accrual for claims for the recovery of land. Other claims, such as personal injuries actions, are not limited in this way.[37]

(ii) Misconduct

Misconduct on the part of the defendant can have a similar effect. If, for example, the claim is founded on an act of *fraud* by the defendant, or if the defendant has *deliberately concealed* a fact relevant to the right of action, time will not start to run until the claimant has, or could with reasonable diligence have discovered the fraud or concealment.[38]

Note that ss 14A and 14B of the Limitation Act 1980 (the Latent Damage Act provisions discussed above) expressly do *not* apply to acts of deliberate concealment of damage by a tortfeasor. In such cases, the normal six year limitation period would apply, but time would not start to run until the claimant has (or could with reasonable diligence have) discovered the concealment.[39]

(iii) Mistake

Similarly, where the claimant's claim is for relief from the consequences of a mistake,[40] time will not start to run until the mistake is (or could with reasonable diligence have been) discovered. A good example of this is *Peco Arts Inc v Hazlett Gallery Ltd.*[41] In that case, the claimant had, on advice of a specialist, bought a drawing from the defendants. It was an express term that the drawing was an original, signed by the artist. Six years later, the drawing was re-valued, and no doubts were cast on its authenticity at that time. Five years after that, it was found to be a reproduction (obviously a very good one). The claimant sued for return of the purchase price as the money had been paid under a mutual mistake of fact. It was held that 'reasonable

37 LA 1980, s 28(4)

38 LA 1980, s 32(1)a and (b). Re the latter, see example in *Cave v Robinson Jarvis and Rolf* [2002] UKHL 18, [2003] 1 AC 384. Unlike the situation with the mentally incapable claimant, a deliberate concealment by the defendant after time has started to run can operate to 're-set' the clock, as it were: *Sheldon v R.H. Outhwaite (Underwriting Agencies) Ltd* [1996] AC 102 - in such cases the defendant has control over his own behaviour!

39 LA 1980, s 32(5)

40 In the legal sense.

41 [1983] 1 WLR 1315

diligence' is a matter of fact in any given case, and here it meant acting like a prudent buyer of valuable art, which is what the claimant had done. He was thus able to recover.

Two final points to note generally about limitation. The first is to remember that limitation time periods do not, as such, apply in respect of claims for *equitable* relief.[42] These will, of course, be defeated by 'delay' and 'acquiescence',[43] in deciding which the court has a wide discretion - as is in the nature of equity!

Finally, a note of caution: the relationship between the pre-action phase and problems of limitation must be watched closely. As regards personal injuries claims, to an extent the s 33 discretion is an arguable fallback if proceedings are brought out of time. Having said that, it is a matter of simple common sense that a limitation period should never knowingly be allowed to expire. Paragraph 17 of the pre-action PD also specifically warns against this. So if a claimant is in the midst of a protocol or the pre-action PD, and the relevant limitation period is about to expire, 'protective proceedings' should be issued and served, giving the other parties as much notice of the intention and need to do so as is practicable. The parties could then invite the court to extend time for service of the statements of case, or allow a stay in proceedings while the recommended pre-action steps are completed.[44] This must be of general application.

42 LA 1980, s 36(1). Sometimes ordinary time limits can assist the court by analogy.

43 Specifically preserved by LA 1980, s 36(2)

44 Pre-action PD, para 17

revision tips

- Make yourself a table of the mainstream limitations periods: when time starts and how long it lasts. Be clear about the different permutations so that you can *recognise a limitation scenario when you see one* in an exam. Watch out especially for personal injuries claims involving children - there may be quite a few variables to consider.
- Remember that the discretion under s 33(3) LA 1980 to disapply the limitation period in personal injuries claims is *unfettered*, and not limited to the factors in the statute. The case law tells us this. What are sometimes referred to as non-statutory considerations (although the statute does say 'all the circumstances'!) include the possibility of a fair trial, early notification and possible alternative claims open to the claimant. But every application must be judged *on its own merits*. There is nothing 'off-the-peg' about the s 33 discretion.
- With limitation questions in the examination, always check what is being asked: do they want to know when time *started* to run or are they asking when the limitation period *ended*. It is easy to get wrong-footed if you aren't careful.

It is worth reading ...

The judgment of ***Jackson LJ in Sayers v Chelwood (Deceased)*** (also known as *Sayers v Hunter*) [2013] 1 WLR 1695. Easy to follow and (after a review of the 'tangle of case law') clearly demonstrates how the s 33 discretion is exercised. Note what he says about the costs so far, and the 'glitzy' ads which united the claimant with his (less than effective) legal team.

Amendment of statement of case

In the course of litigation, a party may wish to amend the wording of a statement of case[1] after it has been filed or served. This is a common occurrence, which often happens after disclosure of documents or other evidential information comes to light. Amendments can range from the correction of minor 'slips' or changes to how the claim is pleaded to more significant adjustments to the presentation of a case. A claimant who wants to add a new defendant, for example, will have to amend the claim form as well as the particulars of claim. A defendant may want to amend the defence or add a counterclaim.

As a general proposition, the overriding objective of dealing with cases justly and at proportionate cost means that if made in good time, and for sensible reasons, amendments of this kind are often uncontroversial and allowed almost as of right (if not by agreement). It is important that the real issues in any given case are litigated and it would be very harsh if a mistake or omission in a statement of case could not be put right, so long as the other parties are not prejudiced or court time wasted. However, problems can arise if a party seeks to amend very late in the day and it poses real difficulties if a relevant limitation period has expired.

1 'Statement of case' is a generic description for the typical documents setting out a party's case in any litigation, i.e. a claim form, particulars of claim (if not on a claim form), defence, reply, additional claim form and any further information given in relation to any of these: CPR r 2.3.

CHAPTER 11

As you will see by the way this chapter is set out, it is important to *distinguish between* amendments sought *before* limitation has expired and *after* it has expired. It is much more difficult for a claimant seeking to amend in the latter situation. It is also necessary to distinguish between amendments which involve a change in parties and those which do not. This is especially so if limitation has expired. But even if it has not, there are some subtle differences to note. Somewhat confusingly you might think, although CPR Part 17 deals with amendments to statements of case generally, where the proposed amendment involves a change of parties, this is covered by CPR Part 19.

1. AMENDMENT *BEFORE* EXPIRY OF A RELEVANT LIMITATION PERIOD

The following points provide a summary of the position.

A. AMENDMENT *BEFORE* SERVICE

A party is allowed to amend a statement of case at any time *before* it has been served on any other party.[2] *No permission of the court is required*, but a court could later disallow the amendment.[3] Such amendments are obviously made quite early on,[4] given that the exchange of statements of case is one of the first things that happens in any litigation. It makes sense to say that if the other party has not even seen it yet, it is no big deal to make changes to the document before they do.

B. AMENDMENT AFTER SERVICE

However, if the statement of case has *already been served*, as often happens, it can only

2 CPR r 17.1(1). Remember that the claim form is a statement of case, and a claimant seeking to make a change in the party/parties suing or being sued would have to amend the claim form, as well as any separate particulars of claim: r 19.4(1)

3 CPR, r 17.2. An application to disallow such an amendment should be made within 14 days of service of the amended document.

4 The claim form must be served within 4 months of being issued, with the other statements of case usually following within a fairly short period of time.

5 Note that permission is required of all other parties, not merely the one affected by the amendment: CPR, r 17.1(2)

6 CPR, rr 17.1(3) and 19.4(1)

7 Substitution is essentially a combination of a removal and an addition.

be amended either with the *written consent* of all of the other parties or t*he permission of the court,*[5] *unless* the amendment involves a *change of party*, in which case the court's *permission is always required* after the claim form has been served.[6] This special requirement about amendments involving a change in party is sensible when you think about it - the court is happy enough for the named parties to sort out the nature of the allegations between themselves, but if new or different parties are to become involved, the court would like to know about it. Otherwise it might go a long time thinking the case is *Bob v Alice*, when in fact it has become *Bob and Carol v Ted and Alice* (I am showing my age here). Like any host, the court wants to know who is invited to the party! More to the point, it wants to have a say about the guest list.

C. GENERAL PRINCIPLES FOR GRANT OF PERMISSION TO AMEND

Under CPR, r 19.2, the court has a broad power to order a party to be added, removed or substituted[7] to existing proceedings. The main consideration in any court decision whether to permit a change of *parties* (where there is no limitation problem) is whether the amendment is '*desirable*'. This is the expression used in the rules. In the case of an application to add a new party, the court may permit this if it is desirable 'so that the court can resolve all matters in dispute in the proceedings'.[8] What is or is not desirable is ultimately for the court, in its discretion, to decide.[9] The court may also order a party to be removed if this is desirable, and where an existing party's interest or liability has passed to another (e.g., where a party dies), the court may order the latter party to be substituted for the former, again where this is desirable to resolve the matters in dispute (which it usually is).[10]

Insofar as permission to make other amendments to a party's statement of case (not involving a change of party and with no limitation issues), the guiding principles are set out in the case law, which (like the rules) has evolved over the

8 There are actually two versions of this desirability test for adding parties, the second of which is where there is an issue between an existing party and the proposed new party which is connected to the matters in dispute in the proceedings and it is desirable to add the new party to resolve that connected issue: See CPR r 19.2(2)(a) and (b). See also ***Molavi v Hibbert*** [2020] EWHC 121 (Ch) where permission was not granted on either basis and it was emphasised that a party seeking to add a party under r 19.2(2) should identify which of the two limbs is being relied upon.

9 CPR, r 19.2 is expressed in terms of what the court 'may' do. Decisions here are essentially case management decisions.

10 CPR, r 19.2(3) and (4). Procedure implications

years. CPR, r 17.3 gives the courts a very broad discretion, and central to any decision is the *overriding objective*, and the need to deal with the case 'justly and at proportionate cost.' In the bad old days, before the CPR and effective case management, the courts were not very interested in why the need to amend arose or how late an amendment application was made, or indeed what effect the amendment might have on the needs or progress of the litigation; it was assumed that any injustice could be compensated by an order of costs against the amending party.[11] The situation is very different now.

These days we are a lot more sophisticated (and less tolerant of bad habits and laziness), and the courts are very clear that not all amendments can be 'paid for' in this way. In the modern era, applications will always involve the court striking a *balance* between injustice to the applicant if the amendment is refused, and injustice to the opposing party and other litigants in general, if the amendment is permitted. Both the *reason* for the need to amend and its *timing* will be relevant, as will the *effect* of the amendment on court time and resources and the other parties.[12]

Many amendments will be uncontroversial, especially if sought early on and for sound reasons (in which case the other party should consent to it and not force a court application). But late amendments[13] can be particularly problematic, especially if so late that the trial date is threatened. Litigants have a legitimate expectation that trial dates will be kept and not adjourned without good reason, and so a heavy burden lies on a party seeking a very late amendment to convince the court that the reason for the delay is a good one[14] and that the prejudice to the other parties and the court is outweighed by the justice in allowing the amendment. It is still a balancing act, but the odds are stacked against applicants in this situation unless they have very strong arguments in their favour. Amendments sought once the trial is underway may invite the greatest degree of scepticism, since by that time it may be apparent

of the death of parties is discussed in Ch 3

11 Brett MR, in the very old case of ***Clarapede v Commercial Union Association*** (1883) 32 WR 262 put it like this: 'However negligent or careless may have been the first omission, and however late the proposed amendment, the amendment should be allowed if it can be made without injustice to the other side. There is no injustice if the other side can be compensated by costs.' Those days are long gone.

12 See ***Pearce v East & North Herts NHS Trust*** [2020] EWHC 1504 QB for a useful summary of the court's approach to the exercise of its discretionary under CPR r 17.3, and WB para 17.3.5

13 'Late' is a relative term but an amendment will be late if it could have been advanced earlier or involves duplication or repetition

that a claim or defence is without merit or that the amendment will serve no useful purpose or that it represents such a departure from the pleaded case that it comes across simply as an act of desperation.[15] It also helps, as Lloyd LJ wryly observed, if a very late amendment is to be sought, that the amended text should at the very least satisfy the basic 'requirements of proper pleading'.[16]

It perhaps goes without saying that an application to amend to add a new claim will be refused if the proposed new claim has no real prospect of success. You will no doubt recognise this as the summary judgment test, which applies equally to proposed amendments as it does to stand-alone claims. Any proposed amendment must carry a degree of conviction, be coherent and supported by evidence establishing a factual basis for the allegation.[17] Indeed, it is important to remember that applications to amend come in all shapes and sizes, and the court has to balance the various factors by reference to the explanations and circumstances in the specific case in front of it. So a late amendment might be allowed if the explanation for it is a good one or it is only a formality; but an earlier amendment might be refused if the matters raised are considered minor or peripheral. Every case is different.

D. THE COSTS OF AMENDING

The *usual order* for costs is that the party *making the amendment* must pay the *'costs of and arising from' the amendment.*[18] Having said that, there may be reasons to justify a departure or adaptation of the general rule. In particular, if a party could have but unreasonably refused to consent to an amendment and in effect forced an unnecessary or contested application to the court, it might be ordered that the amending party pay the costs occasioned by the amendment (since these arise either way), but leaving the recalcitrant party to pay the costs of seeking court permission.[19]

of procedural steps which have already been completed. An amendment is considered 'very late' if it jeopardises the trial date. See generally WB para 17.3.8

14 An amendment suggested by new counsel or a 'fresh pair of eyes' is not considered a particularly good excuse: *Quah Su-Ling v Goldman Sachs International* [2015] EWHC 759 (Comm)

15 But if appropriate, they can be allowed even then, and indeed even after judgment has been given but before the judgment has been drawn up and sealed (which would be highly exceptional!). See WB para 17.3.9

16 *Swain-Mason v Mills & Reeve LLP* [2011] EWCA Civ 14 at [73]. And see WB para 17.3.8 for a series of examples illustrating some outcomes of late applications.

E. PROCEDURE FOR SEEKING PERMISSION

Permission to amend is sought by application notice. Applications to add or substitute a new party can be made by an existing party or a person who wants to become a party, and written evidence should be included setting out the new party's interest or connection with the claim.[20] No person can be added or substituted as a *claimant* unless written consent of that person is given and filed with the court.[21] Notice of application and evidence in support should be served on existing parties (and any other person who would be affected by the order) and the application can be determined without a hearing if all existing and proposed new parties agree. If the application is disputed and alleged to have serious knock-on effects to case management, then a case management conference should generally be convened.[22]

As regards other sorts of amendments to a party's statement of case, evidence in support may not be necessary if the purpose of any changes is clear from the proposed amended statement of case, which must be filed with the application. Traditionally *both* the original text (struck through in red) and the amended text (also in red) is shown - otherwise it is difficult for the court to know what is being proposed! Multiple further amendments will result in a very artistic display, since with each change a different colour is used. An amended statement of case should be verified by a statement of truth, unless the court orders otherwise.[23]

Amendment applications are normally dealt with by a Master or District Judge, as part of the court's case management function, although applications may if necessary be made to the trial judge.

So amendments are not often controversial because, most of the time, they are sought early, are not tactical and payment of costs can compensate for the time and trouble they cause. Late, burdensome or indulgent amendments will be harder to justify. There is, in addition, one especially important situation where no costs order

17 See WB para 17.3.6
18 CPR, PD 17 and r 19.4(10). As to what this means see PD 44, para 4.2
19 *La Chemise Lacoste SA v Sketchers USA Ltd* [2006] EWHC 3624 (Ch) and see WB para 17.3.10
20 CPR, r 19.4(2)
21 CPR, r 19.4 and see discussion in Ch 3
22 The court can of course also make an order under r 19.4 on its own initiative: CPR, r 19.4(7),(11)
23 See generally CPR, PD 17, and WB Vol 1, para 17.1.2
24 LA 1980, s 35(1). This is sometimes referred to as 'relate-back.' Note that it does not apply to third party claims.
25 An amendment is 'made' when the statement of case is actually amended, which would be after permission to amend was given, if this was required. If there is a dispute as to whether or not the new claim

could ever compensate for the injustice caused by a proposed amendment, and that is where a relevant limitation period has expired. Thus, if an amendment would deprive a party of the defence that the action is statute-barred, it will *not* ordinarily be allowed.

2. AMENDMENT *AFTER* EXPIRY OF RELEVANT LIMITATION PERIOD

For the purposes of limitation, any new claim made in proceedings (by amending to add or substitute a new party or a new cause of action) will be *deemed* to be a separate action and to have been commenced on the *same date as the original claim.*[24] This is a purely practical provision, designed to achieve predictability and uniformity. You can see, however, that if the original claim was brought *within* the relevant limitation period, but the amendment is made *after* it has expired,[25] the effect of this deeming provision would be to deprive the new defendant (or the original defendant defending the new cause of action) of a limitation defence. No amount of money by way of costs can make up for that. In this situation, therefore, the *general rule* is that a claimant may *not* amend *once a relevant limitation period has expired.* The idea is that once limitation has expired, a party should not be able to achieve something by way of amendment, which could not be achieved by actually bringing a separate claim.

As always, there are *exceptions*, which essentially fall into *three* types of amendment, discussed below.

A. AMENDMENTS HAVING THE EFFECT OF ADDING A NEW CLAIM

As an exception to the general rule, the court *may*[26] allow an amendment, even after the expiry of the limitation period:

which the claimant seeks to raise by amendment is statute-barred at the time of the application to amend, the onus is on the claimant to prove that the defendant's limitation defence is not reasonably arguable or that in any case the amendment falls under the limited exceptions discussed below: ***Cameron Taylor Consulting Ltd v BDW Trading Ltd*** [2022] EWCA Civ 3 and see WB, para 17.4.2 (although the passage quoted there is not that enlightening).

26 Note that it says 'may' not 'must'. There is still a discretion to say 'no' if justice requires it.

27 Not all proposed amendments do this necessarily. Some may just simply resolve obvious mistakes. See e.g., ***Evans v CIG Mon Cymru*** [2008] EWCA Civ 390, where the claimant considered

(i) To add or substitute a new claim/cause of action[27] if it arises out of the *same or substantially the same facts* as are already in issue on any claim previously made in the original action.[28] An obvious example might be a claim for breach of statutory duty being added, after limitation had expired, to an existing claim in negligence, relating to the same facts and accident. Assuming the proposed amendment has the effect of raising a new claim which would otherwise be statute-barred, the court will then consider it by reference to the 'essential facts' already in dispute, including those set out in the defence. But whether it decides that the new claim arises out of the 'same or substantially the same' facts as those already in issue will always, to some extent, be a matter of fact, degree, and motivation. Again, every case is different.[29]

(ii) To add or substitute a new *personal injuries/fatal accidents* claim when the limitation period has been *disapplied* under LA 1980, s 33.[30] Obviously it would be a bit strange if the court had discretion to allow a personal injuries action to continue alone, but not in addition to some other existing claim.

(iii) To allow a party to an existing action to raise a *counterclaim* or *set-off* for the *first* time. This exception is statutory. Counterclaims are deemed to have been commenced on the same date as the original claim, so it makes sense to allow an amendment to plead a counterclaim which, were it not for this deeming provision, would be out of time.[31] The logic behind this exception is to prevent the injustice which could occur if a claimant, by timing his claim very strategically, were able to deprive the defendant of a defence.[32] But note that the counterclaim must be an 'original' counterclaim (we are *not* talking about amending an existing counterclaim!). So long as the party proposing the amendment has not previously counterclaimed,[33] and the counterclaim was not statute barred when the claim form in the action was issued, then this exception will apply.[34]

suing her employers both for an 'accident at work' and 'abuse at work'. She decided not to pursue the bullying allegation. The particulars of claim sought remedies for an 'accident at work' but because of a typing error, the claim form referred to remedies for 'abuse at work'. After limitation had expired, the defendants attempted to get the particulars struck out because they were irrelevant to the claim form. The claimant applied to amend the claim form so as to substitute 'accident at work' for 'abuse at work'. The Court of Appeal (no doubt sensing that there really were bullies at work here) held that the amendment should be allowed and the particulars not struck out. It said that whether a proposed amendment has the effect of raising a new claim had to be determined

B. AMENDMENTS HAVING THE EFFECT OF ADDING A NEW PARTY

As an *exception* to the general rule, an amendment to add or substitute a new party, once the relevant limitation period has expired, *may*[35] be allowed where:

(i) The court has exercised its *discretion* under s 33 to *disapply* the relevant limitation period in a *personal injuries/fatal accident* claim.[36] Exercising this discretion can result in the addition of a new party, as much as a new claim (or both simultaneously).

(ii) The amendment merely alters the (legal) '*capacity* in which a party *claims*, so long as that new capacity is one which that party had when the proceedings started or has since acquired'.[37] A typical example would be where a person has sued in a personal capacity, and wants to amend to carry on (the same claim) in a representative capacity (or vice versa). In a sense the claimant does not change, so much as their legal status. If such an amendment were to have the effect of adding or substituting a claimant (in addition to changing the capacity of the existing claimant), then one or other of the exceptions set out in this section would have to apply.[38]

(iii) The claim against the new party was not statute-barred when proceedings first began and the amendment is 'necessary'.[39] An amendment to add or substitute a party, once the relevant limitation period has expired, will *only be necessary* where:

(a) the original party has died, or been declared bankrupt, and his interest or liability has passed to the new party. This is just a common sense provision.[40]
(b) the amendment is *legally* necessary to maintain the action, that is to say where the claim cannot be 'properly carried out' by or against the original party unless the new party is added or substituted for

by looking at the entire claim as pleaded up to that point, not the claim form alone. What was involved in that case was not the raising of a new claim, but a clerical error.

28 LA 1980, s 35(5)(a) and CPR, r 17.4(2). So if a defendant makes claims or allegations, these become 'facts in issue' in the claim: *Mullaley & Co Ltd v Martlet Homes Ltd* [2022] EWCA Civ 32

29 Various examples are set out at WB, para 17.4.4.3 and BCP, para 31.28. The *Mullaley* case, op. cit., is a useful example and encapsulation of how the court decides what constitutes 'the same or similar' facts.

30 See generally Ch 10

31 See LA 1980, s 35(1),(2) and (3)

32 A set-off defence, for example, as to which see Ch 5

the existing claimant or defendant'.[41] This exception corrects highly technical defects in a fairly narrow range of circumstances. It covers things like needing to join the Attorney-General before the case can continue because the proceedings should have been brought as a relator action; or needing to add a co-claimant to maintain an action vested jointly in two people. If the action is technically sustainable in law without the addition or substitution of the new party, then it will not be permitted under this provision (but it might qualify under the next).[42]

(c) there has been a *mistake in naming a party* to the original claim.[43] This is a rather vexed, and vexing, area of procedure, not least because aspects of the relevant legislation and the pre-CPR rule have been sprinkled about in two different places in the current rules: Part 17 which deals with 'Amendments to Statements of Case' and Part 19 which deals with 'Parties'. As the subject matter at hand is the addition or substitution of parties by amendment, it is perhaps not surprising that this 'division of labour' might have happened, but the relationship between the provisions in CPR, r 17.4(3),[44] and those in CPR, r 19.6(3)[45] has caused no end of judicial headache.

Mistake in name

The main problem is that both sets of rules contain different aspects of the one previous rule, which was stated to allow an amendment to 'correct the name' of a party (even if, in one sense, this resulted in the 'substitution' of a new party) if the court was satisfied that the mistake was a 'genuine mistake' and was not 'misleading or such as to cause reasonable doubt as to the identity of the person intending to sue or, as the case may be, intended to be sued'.[46] For some reason, the notion of 'correcting'

33 And is on the opposite side of the record to the defendant to the (proposed) counterclaim.

34 *Al-Rawas v Hassan Khan and Co (A Firm)* [2017] EWCA Civ 42

35 Again this is a 'may' not a 'must'. See CPR, r 19.6(2), and WB, para 19.6.1. Note that in 2023, some renumbering of these rules took place and *so what was CPR, r 19.5 is now r 19.6.* All the case law to date will be referring to the previous rule number. But the principles are unchanged.

36 LA 1980. S 35(3) and CPR, r 19.6(4)

37 CPR, r 17.4(4) My emphasis

38 *Roberts v Gill* [2009] 1 WLR 531

39 CPR, r 19.6(2)

40 CPR, r 19.6(3)(c)

41 CPR, r 19.6(3)(b)

42 *The Insight Group Ltd v Kingston Smith* [2013] ALL ER 518, and see examples in WB, para 19.6.5

a mistake but only if it was 'genuine' and caused 'no reasonable doubt' about the 'identity' of the party in question only made it into CPR, r 17.4(3), but the idea of the actual 'substitution' of one party for another who was 'named in the claim form in mistake' is really all that appears in CPR, r 19.6(3)(a). So where does that leave us?

Trial and appeal judges have been grappling with the relationship between these two provisions for some years now, and have eventually come to a fairly settled view. Inevitably there is some overlap between the two rules: the statutory authority for both is s 35 of the Limitation Act 1980 and both are about mistakes in naming parties which can be cured by amendment after limitation has expired. In addition, both are about mistakes *not in identifying the correct party to sue or be sued, but in getting that party's name right.* In the pre-CPR case law it had been said that where a party is named 'by reference to a description' which is 'specific to the particular case', then any mistake in that name is likely to be one which can be corrected without injustice. So, for example, if in suing a defendant, the claimant gets the right *description* (for example, his employer, his landlord), but the wrong name, there is 'unlikely to be any doubt as to the identity of the person intended to be sued. But if he gets the wrong description, it will be otherwise.' This is known as the *Sardinia Sulcis* test.[47]

But the two modern rules differ in the situations and solutions they cater for. Rule 17.4(3) is for more superficial mistakes which can be cured by '*correcting*' the error - for example spelling mistakes or clerical errors, as where the names of the claimant and defendant were accidentally transposed.[48] So long as the mistake is genuine and no one has been misled as to the identity of the party in question, it can be corrected under r 17.4(3). The simplest examples are cases where the name given for the defendant is incomplete or incorrect and the defendant files an acknowledgment of service, giving their full or correct name. If limitation has expired, the claimant will have to apply to correct the mistake under r 17.4(3), but this in unlikely to be

43 CPR, r 19.6(3)(a)

44 The title to CPR, r 17.4 is 'Amendments to statements of case after the end of a relevant limitation period': r 17.4(3) allows an amendment to 'correct' a mistake as to the name of a party.

45 The title to CPR, r 19.6 is 'Special provisions about adding or substituting parties after the end of a relevant limitation period.'

46 RSC Ord 20, r 5

47 *The Sardinia Sulcis* [1991] 1 Lloyd's rep 201

48 As in *Teltscher Brothers Ltd v London & India Dock Investments Ltd* [1989] 1 WLR 770, cited at WB, para 17.4.5

opposed and the claim form etc will *not* need to be re-served.[49] The party has not changed, but it now has its proper and accurate name.

Rule 19.6 is for more fundamental mistakes which can only be cured by '*substituting*' a new party for the incorrectly named party. It rather pre-supposes that both the existing party and the party to be substituted exist (or did exist) as separate entities. If the court permits a new party to be substituted as a defendant under this rule, the claimant will have to start from scratch with them (by serving the claim form on them and so on), and the defendant which was replaced will cease to be a party.[50]

The leading case is *Adelson and another v Associated Newspapers Ltd*,[51] which approved this division of labour between the two rules and set out the following principles about applications under CPR, r 19.6(3)(a):

- Rule 19.6(3)(a) goes beyond mere corrections of mistakes in the naming of a party, but allows the *substitution* of a new party for the original named party.
- The court must be satisfied that the person who made the mistake, directly or through an agent, was the person responsible for issuing the claim form;
- The applicant must show that had the mistake not been made, the new party would have been named in the claim form;
- The mistake must be as to the name, *not the identity* of the party, thus endorsing the *Sardinia Sulcis* test. A typical example these days might be where a claimant brings a claim for negligent advice against his former accountants, who were a partnership when the advice was given but have since become an LLP. If the claim form and other documents indicate that the claimant named the LLP as defendant thinking it

49 An acknowledgment of service making such a correction does not relieve the claimant of the need to amend the claim form

50 The similarities and distinctions between the two rules is discussed at WB, para 19.6.3. These are not always stark, but applicants in any doubt about which is the applicable rule in their case can try both (in the alternative).

51 [2008] 1 WLR 585

had given the advice when in fact the practice was a firm at the time the advice was given, then this will be a mistake as to name and not identity. But because both the firm and the LLP exist (or have existed) as separate entities, then the mistake can only be cured by removing the LLP and substituting instead the partnership as defendant.[52] Other cases may be more difficult and how lenient or harsh a court will be in deciding the matter can also depend on other factors in a case, which can sometimes be rather quirky. Some, including *Adelson* itself (where the application to amend was refused), were applications by claimants to change their own names (when you might think they would know who they were from the outset!), and in those cases the court is more apt to think there has been a change of mind about who should sue, rather than a mistake in naming that party. This distinction between mistakes as to name and not identity is key to the operation of r 19.6(3)(a).[53]

- No injustice should be caused if the application is granted. This is how the court can factor in questions about the genuineness of the mistake and whether anyone has been misled, despite this not being a stated requirement in r 19.6(3)(a), as it is in r 17.4(3). If there are concerns, especially if the party to be substituted would be completely taken by surprise by the amendment, then the court can exercise its discretion (remember the rule says 'may', not 'must') to refuse to allow it.[54]

Finally, *note carefully* that *pure additions are not allowed* by operation of either CPR, r 17.4(3) or CPR, r 19.6(3)(a). The former merely allows for the correction of an existing party's name: the wording of the latter, is explicitly limited to *substituting one party for another.* You cannot use r 19.6(3)(a) to start out with one defendant and end up with two![55]

52 As in *The Insight Group Ltd v Kingston Smith* [2012] EWHC 3644 (QB), cited at WB, para 19.6.4. In these sorts of cases there is often a corporate connection between the named party and the one to be substituted (or a change in legal status).

53 See the useful examples set out in WB, para 19.6.4

54 See *Adelson* case, op. cit., and WB, Vol 1, para 19.6.1/2

55 *Broadhurst v Broadhurst* [2007] EWCA 1828

C. AMENDMENTS HAVING THE EFFECT OF ADDING A NEW DEFENCE[56]

Here the *emphasis is different* because limitation periods basically concern claimants, not defendants. Thus, amending a defence after the action's limitation period has expired is not usually a problem.

So here, the general rule is that the court *will* allow a *defendant* to amend the defence, *even after the limitation period has expired, unless* the claimant can show that he or she would be *prejudiced by it in a way which cannot be compensated in costs.* This would be the case, for example, where a defendant suddenly blames another person whom the claimant cannot now sue because the action against that person is statute-barred. In *Cluley v RL Dix Heating, (a firm)*[57] for example, the claimant sued the defendants for breach of contract. The original defence admitted the contract but denied breach. After the limitation period for the contract action had expired, the defendants sought to amend their defence to deny the contract, and allege that the claimant should have sued other people. The amendment was not allowed, because it was now no longer possible for the claimant to sue any other parties, because limitation had expired, and the defendants must have known much earlier whether they had a contract with the claimant or not.

In this sort of situation, the position can be summarised in this way: a defendant will be allowed to amend his pleadings to raise a new defence allegation, even after the relevant limitation period has expired, *unless*:

- the effect of the amendment is to blame another party whom the claimant cannot now sue,

and

- it is the defendant's fault in not seeking to amend earlier.[58]

However, if on a closer look, it turns out that the claimant knew all along of the facts giving rise to the defence amendment, that amendment may be allowed.[59]

56 This is sometimes called amendments affecting accrued rights (i.e. the right of defendants to plead a limitation defence).

57 [2003] EWCA Civ 1597, referred to at WB para 17.3.5 (final para). This also runs up against the notion of withdrawing admissions (CPR Part 14), which at the time of writing is not on the Bar Exam Syllabus

58 *Weait v Jayanbee Joinery Ltd* [1963] 1 QB 239

59 As in *Turner v Ford Motor Co* [1965] 2 All ER 583. There is a short, useful exposition of these cases at BCP, para 31.29

revision tips

- Be confident in differentiating between:

  (i) amendments sought before *versus* after the limitation period has expired, and

  (ii) amendments which require a change of party *versus* those which do not - both before and after limitation has expired.

- Check the facts of any question carefully so you know what is being asked (for example, is the limitation period still current? Is it a change of party or to the cause of action which is needed?). Examiners love to test you on these differences.
- In 2023, CPR, r 19.5 was redesignated r 19.6 (this sort of thing happens from time to time). Up to that point, of course, the case law referred to the original rule number, so don't let that confuse you.

It is worth reading ...

If you like family feuds, you might enjoy ***Hague Plant v Hague*** *[*2014] EWCA Civ 1609. The Hagues make the Vandervells look jolly! You don't need to read beyond para 43, but this was an early example of the modern approach to applications to amend (within the limitation period). A more recent, and less convoluted illustration is found in ***Pearce v East and North Hertfordshire NHS Trust*** [2020] EWHC 1504 (QB). Very easy to follow, and contains a useful summary of the relevant principles at [10].

American Leisure Group Ltd v Olswang LLP [2015] EWHC 629 (Ch). A classic example of a case where, after limitation has expired, the court may give permission to substitute one party for another, where the latter was named in mistake for the former. The negligent advice had been given before the firm of solicitors became an LLP. But the judgement is also a good reminder that the power is discretionary, and appeal courts will not interfere if the discretion has, as here, been properly exercised.

CHAPTER 12

Renewal of claim form: extending time for service

In Chapter 10 we looked at the prescribed time periods for bringing proceedings, after which, with certain exceptions, a defendant will have an unanswerable limitation defence. To avoid a case being time-barred, therefore, a claimant should bring the action before the relevant limitation period has expired. As discussed in Chapter 3, an action is commenced when the claim form is issued by the court. Once this happens, the next step is to *serve* it on the defendant while the claim form is still valid for service.[1]

The claim form is valid for service for *four months* if it is to be served within the jurisdiction.[2] Note that service does not need to have actually occurred during the period of validity. What the claimant must do (and examiners love to test you on this) is to *complete the step required* by the rules to effect the chosen method of service.[3] The claimant has until midnight on the last day of the 4 month period of validity to do this.[4] Thus it is the date the *act of* service is completed that matters here, not the deemed date of service.[5]

A claim form must be served while it is valid. If a claimant has a reason for not being able to do this, an extension may be sought by agreement with the party to be served[6] or by court order. Extending the period of validity by court order is sometimes referred to as 'renewal' (like a library book), and as we shall see, the rules are very strict (like some librarians). If the limitation period in the action has not yet expired, there

1 CPR, r 7.5

2 Unless the period is extended by the court, *see below*. Where the claim form is to be served outside the jurisdiction, which can be more time-consuming, the period of validity under the rules is six months: CPR, r 7.5(2).

3 See generally Ch 4 on service.

4 CPR, r 7.5(1)

5 The deemed date of service of the claim form is still important as it tells us when the next step in the litigation process should happen.

6 Only *written* consent will be effective in these circumstances: CPR, r 2.11 and *Thomas v Home Office* [2007] 1 WLR 230

is no huge reason to panic since an alternative would be to issue fresh proceedings.[7] *It is where the relevant limitation period has expired (or will do so soon) that serious problems arise.*

When the court serves the claim form, applications to extend validity should not often be necessary. But where claimants choose to serve the claim form themselves, there is scope for trouble. The key to understanding renewal is to see the *relationship* between the limitation period in the action and the period during which the claim form is valid for service - *but not to confuse the two.*

It is also crucial to *distinguish between* applications to extend made while the claim form is still valid for service and applications made after the claim form has expired. It is much more difficult to get an extension in the latter situation than the former (which itself is not that easy).

1. APPLICATIONS TO EXTEND *DURING* THE PERIOD OF VALIDITY: CPR, r 7.6(2)

Renewal is typically sought when a claimant is having difficulties serving a defendant. The general rule is that an application for an extension of the claim form's validity for service should be made *before* the claim form expires.[8] In such cases, sometimes referred to as 'prospective applications', the court has a *general discretion* to renew. The case law tells us that the court will exercise this discretion in accordance with the overriding objective; allowing the extension if it can do so justly, but mindful of the importance of ensuring that cases progress expeditiously. In particular, the court will look closely at the attempts made to serve (both when and how) and the reason for the need to renew - the better the reason, the more likely they are to allow the extension: *Hashtroodi v Hancock*.[9] If there is a *'good reason'*, it has been said that

7 There would be a cost, because you would have to pay to start fresh proceedings, but all would not be lost.

8 Or as specified by court order: CPR, r 7.6(2)

9 [2004] 1WLR 3206. There is no explicit requirement to show that attempts to serve have been made (as there is when applying after the claim form has expired, *see below*), but the application is apt to be more successful if reasonable attempts to serve have been made. See WB, para 7.6.2, sub-paras 1-3

10 See, e.g., ***Hoddinott v Persimmon Homes (Wessex) Ltd*** [2007] EWCA Civ 1203 where this was one factor among many.

11 Compare ***Cecil v Bayat*** [2011] 1 WLR 3086 (extension denied) and ***The Khan Partnership LLP v Infinity Distribution Ltd*** [2016] EWHC 1390 (Ch)

the courts should also consider the *balance of hardship* between the parties in either granting or refusing the extension of time. It would be relevant, for example, to consider the implications of the claimant's merely issuing fresh proceedings were the application to be refused.[10] In particular, if limitation in the action has (by this time) expired, this will be an important consideration. In this context, it is a serious matter effectively to deprive the defendant of a limitation defence, and so granting an extension in such circumstances would require significant countervailing factors [11] The main thrust of the court's approach to renewal has always been that a claimant should issue *and* serve proceedings promptly. Usually, this is neither expensive (in the scheme of things), nor difficult. If any hiatus in proceedings is desired, it can occur *after* service of the claim form, not before.

So what amounts to a good reason? Not much, is the short answer. Historically, under the old rules, reasons which were *not* thought to be good reasons included: negotiations in progress, a strong case, an honest mistake, an oversight, difficulty in obtaining evidence.

Reasons which *were* considered to be good reasons under the old rules included a defendant evading service, or otherwise being obstructive, a defendant explicitly asking not to be served, or saving a defendant costs. Note the theme here: either the defendant is behaving badly and/or making service difficult, or the claimant is doing the defendant a favour. The cases under the CPR have continued in this vein.[12]

Remember that decisions in individual cases are merely a *guide* to the outcome of any given renewal application which has been made prospectively, although the reasoning can be enlightening. Every case is different and courts have a complete discretion. Having said that, the cases confirm a generally *restrictive* approach even in these cases. The overriding objective is, of course, overriding in such situations.

(extension partly allowed). And see ***ST v BAI (SA) (t/a Britany Ferries)*** [2022] EWCA Civ 1037, where the principles governing applications under r 7.6(2) are usefully summarised at [62], cited at WB, Vol 1, para 7.6.2

12 Compare, for example, the ***Hoddinott*** case (delay in receiving the expert's report on quantum was not a good reason; the claimant should have served the claim form and sought an extension of time for serving the particulars of claim instead) with ***Imperial Cancer Research Fund v Ove Arup & Partners Ltd*** [2009] EWHC 1453 (TCC), June 23, 2009 (the claimant's need to evacuate the premises, investigate a water leak and obtain an expert's report on the liability of the defendant, and possibly others, was a good reason, especially as

2. APPLICATIONS TO EXTEND MADE *AFTER* EXPIRY OF THE CLAIM FORM: CPR, r 7.6(3)

This is a much more difficult scenario. Where the application to renew is made *after* the claim form has already *expired* (sometimes called a 'retrospective' application), the court's *discretion is severely constrained* by the fact that it *may only* make an order to extend time *if* (a) the claimant has taken 'all reasonable' steps, but failed (or the court was unable) to serve the claim form in time *and* (b) the application was made promptly.[13] Although not required by the rule, giving an explanation as to why the application was made after (rather than before) the claim form expired would not go amiss, either. In any event, this is an *exceedingly narrow* set of criteria, really focusing only on failed attempts to serve in time. If no attempt at all was made to serve in time, this is apt to be fatal to the applicant's case, no matter how apparent it is that the claimant's case is a strong one.[14]

Furthermore, there is virtually no escape from the confines of CPR, r 7.6(3). In a line of cases,[15] the Court of Appeal decided that CPR, r 7.6 constitutes a *complete code*, so that recourse may not be had to other powers[16] under the CPR, nor even it seems the overriding objective, to mitigate the severity of r 7.6(3) - except in *very exceptional* circumstances. The possibilities are:

(i) To apply retrospectively for an order for alternative service;[17]

(ii) To get an order dispensing with service under CPR, r 6.16. This will only be granted in exceptional circumstances, and only it seems if an attempt has been made by the claimant to serve;[18]

(iii) To remedy, under CPR, r 3.10, what is in effect a 'de minimis' or technical error in service.[19]

---

the defendants had been slow to disclose plans and documents when asked).

13 Albeit that the period of validity has already passed. See CPR, r 7.6(3). It is the steps taken to serve the claim form during its validity which matter: ***Drury v BBC & Carnegie*** [2007] EWCA Civ 497

14 As in ***Vinos v Marks & Spencer Plc*** [2001] 3 All ER 784, where the extension of time was refused (despite the defendant having admitted liability) because no reasonable attempt had been made to serve the claim form in time. An ineffective attempt to serve may not fare much better, especially if the mistake could have been corrected in time. The rule is very strict. See WB para 7.6.3

15 E.g., ***Kaur v CTP Coil Ltd*** [2000] LTL 10/7/2000: ***Vinos v Marks & Spencer plc*** [2001] 3 All ER 784: ***Godwin v Swindon***

Each of these is a possible circumvention, but the circumstances need to be truly exceptional. The long and the short of it is: the rule is strict, and is strictly enforced. Too many exceptions would dilute the message: serve the claim form in time!

An application to extend validity is made to an interim judge under Part 23, using an application notice supported by written evidence, setting out relevant time periods (for example, date of issue) and reasons why the extension has become necessary. Because at this point there is no defendant on record, the application is made without giving notice to the other side.[20] If renewal is granted, the first the defendant may know about it, therefore, is when the (extended) claim form is served. A defendant who wishes to dispute the extension should first acknowledge service in the normal way, stating an intention to defend, and *then* apply on notice within seven days of service to have the order extending the validity of the claim form set aside. The same would apply to a defendant who has been served with an invalid claim form, although in this case the claimant will likely cross-apply for an appropriate court order.[21] In either case, it is important for defendants to act promptly in these circumstances, since delay could be taken as acceptance of valid service.

The rules on extending the validity of the claim form essentially reflect the fact that, at the very least, the court must be satisfied that there was a compelling reason for a claimant not doing something as cheap and easy as 'popping' the claim form in the post (or letting the court serve it!). The ultimate no-no, of course, is to apply for renewal after both the limitation period and the claim form have expired, when the claim will effectively be lost. Not only is r 7.6(3) very strict in its own terms, but the courts will always be more reluctant to deprive a defendant of a limitation defence when the claimant issues proceedings at the very last minute. Do not forget, however, that so long as the limitation period in the action has *not* expired, it always

Borough Council [2002] 1 WLR 997

16 E.g., the general power to grant extensions of time, to grant relief from sanctions or remedy procedures in error, all found in Part 3. See generally, discussion of case management at Ch 13

17 Under CPR, r 6.15(2)

18 *Anderton v Clwyd County Council (No 2)* [2002] 1 WLR 3174

19 See e.g., *Steele v Mooney* [2005] 1 WLR 2819: *Phillips v Symes (no 3)* [2008] 1 WLR 180

20 See generally Ch 4. Note that a claimant who has been granted an extension without notice to the defendant needs to be aware that the order may subsequently be set aside on application by the defendant.

21 Unless it is simply easier and no more expensive (assuming limitation has not expired as well) to issue another claim form and start again.

remains the case that (unless the court has barred a claimant from re-litigating, and admittedly at some cost) a *fresh* action can be commenced. If limitation is about to expire, this might be the safer option.

revision tips

- Be clear about the interrelationship, but also the difference between the limitation period in an action and the period during which the claim form issued in the case is valid for service. Do not confuse the two.
- Be clear about how *very strict* the rule is if the application to extend time for service of the claim form is made *after* the claim form has expired. Even the overriding objective does not help much here!
- If the claim form has become invalid for service, but the limitation period in the action has not yet expired, starting again is a possibility which should always be considered. It might even be the cheaper option!

It is worth reading …

The judgment of Lady Justice Carr in ***ST v BAI (SA) (t/a Britany Ferries)*** [2022] EWCA Civ 1037. Don't worry or be distracted by the fact that this case involved service out of the jurisdiction and thus special service rules. Just focus on the aspects relevant to extending time for service of the claim form under CPR, r 7.6(2), especially paras 58-65. Note too how much less difficult it is to be allowed to extend time for service of the particulars of claim (as opposed to the claim form itself). And come back to this case when you have learned about appeals. The Court of Appeal makes clear that the proper exercise of discretion cannot be faulted just because the appellate court might have decided the matter differently.

Drury v BBC & Carnegie [2007] EWCA Civ 96. An interesting defamation case. Eady J (retired), whose decision was appealed against, became one of the foremost experts in the world on this complex subject. But even he was wrong-footed by the constraints of the court when faced with an application to renew after the claim form had expired!

CHAPTER 13

Case management:
powers and sanctions

Once a case has been provisionally allocated to a case management track and the directions questionnaires have been returned, the procedural judge will essentially need to consider three things:

- Whether the claim or defence (or part of it) should be *curtailed at this stage*, for example by means of striking out[1] or summary judgment.[2] If appropriate, the court will fix an early appointment to hear argument from both sides;
- Formal allocation to the appropriate track, either by confirming the provisional allocation or re-allocating the case to another track. We saw in Chapter 8 that several factors will be relevant to this, including complexity, evidential needs and predicted length of trial, but often the value of the claim will dictate which track it goes on;
- Case management. Directions upon allocation are generally given by reference to standard forms, adapted to the individual needs of the case at hand, and parties are encouraged to agree directions for the court to approve. Multi-track cases will tend to need more proactive management, and may require a case management conference before

1 Read on.
2 See Ch 5

> initial directions can be given. On all tracks, initial directions on allocation will usually, at the very least, cover disclosure of documents, exchange of witness statements, and expert evidence.[3]

Once allocated, a case then proceeds on its given track through its interim stages to trial or settlement. Effective (and indeed cost-effective) management of its progress by the courts is a crucial part of the ethos and effect of the CPR - without it, the overriding objective cannot be achieved. It had long been recognised that the system which the CPR replaced resulted in delay and expense which was often disproportionate to the issues or amount at stake in a case. The Woolf reforms' answer was to put the court firmly in the driving seat, giving it an array of powers and sanctions to control the conduct of litigation. But a decade on, it was still felt that some judges were too tolerant and forgiving of litigants (or often their legal representatives) who failed (for no good reason) to comply with directions and orders of the court. As Lewison LJ put it in 2012: ' ... courts at all levels ... have lost sight of the damage which the culture of delay and non-compliance is inflicting on the civil justice system'.[4] Jackson LJ's solution was to put a whip in the court's hand.

CPR, r 1.4(1) thus places a *duty* on the court to further the overriding objective by *actively managing cases*, which includes: encouraging a co-operative approach to the conduct of litigation; identifying the real issues at an early stage and disposing summarily of others; encouraging the parties to use ADR where appropriate; controlling the pace and progress of cases, considering whether the 'likely benefits' of taking a particular step will 'justify the cost' of taking it; dealing efficiently with cases (for example by using technology or dealing with cases without a hearing); giving directions which ensure that if the case goes to trial, it proceeds 'quickly and efficiently,' and so on.[5] If any of the parties is a litigant in person, the court must

3 These are all discussed in other chapters. Directions on the small claims track will be more truncated than on the others. Directions in cases requiring the filing of pre-trial checklists will focus on preparations for and conduct of the upcoming trial: see relevant practice direction and focus on the detail required by your examination syllabus.

4 *Perry v Brands Plaza Trading* [2012] EWCA Civ 224

5 CPR, r 1.4(2). It is worth reading and digesting this rule in its entirety.

exercise its case management powers with such adaptations as may be warranted to achieve the overriding objective.[6]

The *ammunition* given to the court for this purpose is found in CPR, Part 3, which gives the court an exceedingly wide range of powers and punishments. These include making orders on its own initiative (without being asked, and with or without a hearing)[7]; making orders with conditions (for example, paying money into court) and built-in punishments (so-called 'unless orders'[8]); contacting the parties in order to monitor compliance (which requires a 'prompt response'); imposing (and, where warranted, giving relief from) sanctions for non-compliance with court directions and orders; extending or refusing to extend time; controlling the nature and extent of evidence to be adduced at trial and so on.[9] In a nutshell, the court can do nearly anything it likes. Part carrot, but a lot of stick! Let's look at some of these powers and sanctions in turn.

1. STRIKING OUT

This is an attack on a party's statement of case or conduct of that case. Strictly speaking, causes of action are not struck out as such, but the term is used rather loosely. Of course if, say, a claimant's particulars of claim are struck out in their entirety, it follows that the claim will end up being stayed or dismissed.[10] If a whole defence is struck out, there is no longer an answer to that claim. If only part of a case is struck out,[11] then the rest of a viable claim or defence can continue. Striking out is the *most severe sanction the court can impose, and should be used sparingly*. The court *may* strike out all or part of a statement of case if it appears:

(i) that it discloses *no reasonable grounds* for bringing or defending the claim;

6 By being as helpful as possible while remaining (and appearing to remain) impartial: CPR, r 3.1A and WB, para 3.1A.1

7 Any party who is unhappy with such an order can apply to have it varied or set aside. See generally CPR, r 3.3

8 A typical 'unless' order might sound like this: '*Unless* by (date/time) the defendant do file and serve a list of documents giving standard disclosure, the Defence will be struck out and judgment entered.'

9 See CPR, r 3.1, which sets out the extensive powers of the court and is worth close scrutiny.

10 Usually with costs to be paid to the defendant. If the claimant seeks to start again before paying these, the court will stay the second claim until he does: CPR r 3.4(4)

11 See wording of CPR, r 3.4(1)

12 CPR, r 3.4(2), which does

(ii) that it is an *abuse* of the court's process *or* is otherwise likely *to obstruct the just disposal* of the proceedings; *or*

(iii) that there has been a *failure to comply* with a rule, practice direction or court order.[12]

Ground (i) and (ii) cover statements of case which do not amount to a legally recognisable claim or defence[13] or which are unreasonably vague, incoherent, vexatious, scurrilous, obviously ill-founded or otherwise amount to an abuse of process.[14] It is important to note that, where relevant, the court can and should exercise this power at an early stage (for example, when a claim is issued or a defence is filed), thus saving a party the expense of making an application. A court official, for example, who receives a claim form that fails to meet the standards required, will issue it, but may then consult the judge who in turn may, on his or her own initiative, make an appropriate order in the circumstances. Possibilities include staying proceedings pending the filing of a 'proper' statement of case, requesting the filing of relevant further information, or, in the worst cases, striking out the offending statement of case (and entering such judgment as the other party may be entitled to).[15] The court may order a hearing to canvass the options.

Ground (iii) covers cases where the problem lies not in the statement of case itself, but in *the way* the claim or defence has been conducted. Sanctions for non-compliance are discussed below, but striking out on this basis (which is a little like a procedural death penalty) should normally be a *last*, not a first resort. Note the following.

(i) Built-in strike out sanction

Occasionally the strike out sanction is *built into* the rules themselves (for example, where there has been non-payment of fees payable at the track allocation and listing

not limit any other power of the court to strike out a statement of case: r 3.4(5)

13 See examples in PD 3A, para 1. Ground 3.4(2)(a) should be made out on its face and so evidence in support of the application will not usually be necessary: PD 3A, para 5.2. And see discussion at WB, para 3.4.2

14 Abuse of process etc., (ground 3.4(2)(b)) covers claims where a malicious intent is manifested (e.g., pursuing a vendetta) but it can also include situations where there is no ill will, but the claim is 'improper.' For example proceedings brought which are time-barred can be struck out for abuse of process. Other examples include attempting to re-litigate decided issues ('res judicata') or starting proceedings as a way of mounting a 'collateral

stages, the court will send a notice stating the date by which these must be paid, failing which, according to the rules, the claim will be struck out[16]) or, more commonly, it is built into a court order (an 'unless order'). In both such cases, the sanction follows *automatically* if default occurs (unless an extension of time had been, or a reprieve is given[17]). To obtain judgment (with costs) after an automatic strike out of this kind, the innocent party need only file a request.[18]

(ii) Strike out versus summary judgment

Striking out and summary judgment may be viewed as something of a twin-set, in the sense that many cases falling within CPR, r 3.4(2) may also fall within Part 24, which provides for summary disposal of claims or defences which have no reasonable prospect of success. The overlap is not complete (summary judgment is not about non-compliance, and various procedural requirements relevant to Part 24 do not apply to CPR, r 3.4) but both possibilities should be considered in relevant cases.[19]

(iii) Deadly weapon

When dealing with non-compliance, strike out is the court's *most draconian sanction*, and should be reserved for the most *obvious* and *serious* cases. In *Biguzzi v Rank Leisure plc*,[20] the Court of Appeal drew attention to the fact that there are several alternatives to a strike out to be considered in any given situation before deploying the weapon of last resort. A court asked to make a strike out order should first consider whether a lesser sanction might be more proportionate, especially given the effect striking out would have on a party's right of access to the courts, which has particular importance under Art 6 of the European Convention on Human Rights. It is *common*, at the very least, to make an 'unless order' instead of jumping straight to a strike out (in effect giving the non-compliant party one last chance), but there is *no requirement* that the

attack' on a final decision against the claimant which has already been made in another (usually criminal) court. See discussion at WB, paras 3.4.5 and 3.4.9

15 PD 3A, paras 2-4

16 CPR, r 3.7(2)-(4)

17 CPR, PD3A, para 1.6. Relief from sanctions is discussed below. Note that the parties can agree to extend time for compliance in such cases for up to 28 days, so long as no hearing date is imperilled: CPR, r 3.8(4).

18 CPR, r 3.5. Unless orders can also be worded to include the consequence of the strike out. *See below.*

19 CPR, PD 3A, para 1.5. Summary judgment is discussed in Ch 5

20 [1999] 1 WLR 1926

court do this.[21] In the case of *Raja v van Hoogstraten*,[22] for example, the defendant had apparently arranged for the claimant to be killed in order to prevent him giving evidence - he did not need any second chances!

(iv) Conditional and consequential orders

CPR, r 3.4(3) gives the court power to make appropriate orders consequential on ordering a strike-out. These could range from entering such judgment as might follow to making suitable case management directions. Similarly, an 'unless order' can be worded to encompass not only the striking out of the defaulter's statement of case as a consequence of non-compliance but also the effect which would follow from this (e.g., judgment or dismissal). Again such consequences would automatically ensue, without the need for any further court order.[23]

2. STRIKING OUT IS NOT THE ONLY FRUIT! RANGE OF SANCTIONS FOR NON-COMPLIANCE

The court has various weapons which it can use to actively manage cases and give effect to the overriding objective. The power to impose sanctions for non-compliance is critically important for maintaining control of the conduct of litigation. Generally speaking, the philosophy behind the CPR will not work if the court's bark is always worse than its bite. The Jackson reforms were particularly predicated on the notion that if the court's bite were fiercer, this will prove a better deterrent, thus reducing the need for it to bark. The court now has a much greater range of sanctions at its disposal than before the CPR,[24] which should assist in ensuring that in any given case the punishment 'fits the crime'. Again, note the following:

21 *Bot v Barnick* [2019] EWHC 3704 (QB)

22 [2006] EWHC 1315 (Ch)

23 See discussion at WB, para 3.4.19. Note however, that the reference to ***Workman v Forrester*** there contains an error. In that case the defendant's appeal was dismissed, not upheld (it was the District Judge's order which was upheld!).

24 As set out in CPR, Part 3

(i) Timetable directions

Not all acts of non-compliance are of the most serious kind. An example of a minor default might be a failure to comply with timetable directions.[25] So long as the key case management events in a case remain unaffected, the parties should seek to resolve such problems between themselves by agreeing a new date for compliance or some other solution.[26] Furthermore, an 'innocent' party faced with an opponent who has not complied with a timetable *direction* should neither let sleeping dogs lie (by sitting back and letting the default get worse by the passage of time) nor immediately rush to the court. Instead, the middle ground of a *written warning* should first be given.[27] This should warn the defaulting party of the intention to make an application to the court if the direction is not complied with by a reasonable (stated) time. If this does not do the trick, an application to the court may be made for an order to enforce compliance or for a sanction to be imposed, or both. If a sanction is imposed, this could range from a minor one (e.g., a costs sanction) to a more severe one (e.g., an 'unless' order), depending on the circumstances, but should be proportionate and effective.

(ii) Pre-action default

Another type of default is non-compliance with pre-action protocols or the pre-action PD. Minor breaches will not cause much concern and certainly should not be viewed as an excuse itself for non-compliance by the other party, but where a failure to comply with appropriate pre-action conduct results in unnecessary litigation and/or costs, sanctions can follow. These would focus on adverse costs and/or interest orders as a punishment for not trying hard enough to avoid litigation (ignoring an offer of ADR, for example, could be construed as not giving it any serious consideration). The directions questionnaire specifically asks whether the parties have completed

25 Directions tend to be more impersonal than orders. It is a bit like the difference between, *"I want you children to play quietly in there"* (a direction) and *"Tommy! Put down that vase!"* (an order). Breach of the latter is often considered (other things being equal) more serious than breach of the former.

26 See Ch 8

27 PD 28, para 5.2 (fast track) and PD 29, para 7.2 (multi-track)

protocol steps,[28] so lack of compliance should come as no surprise at the end of a trial (and may even be punished earlier).

(iii) Built-in sanctions other than strike out

We saw that the strike out sanction is contained within certain provisions of the CPR, or can be built into a court order (an 'unless order') in cases of non-compliance. This applies to other sorts of sanctions as well, and again if the default occurs the sanction will automatically follow. So, for example, CPR, r 35.13 says that if a party fails to disclose expert evidence as required,[29] that party will not be allowed to rely on that expert evidence at trial, unless the court gives permission.[30] This is a common sense, tailor-made sanction which is intended, and usually does, encourage compliance! Similar sorts of rule-based sanctions tripped up defaulters in the cases of *Mitchell v News Group Newspapers Ltd* ('*Mitchell*')[31] (failure to file/serve costs budget in time) and *Durrant v Chief Constable of Avon and Somerset*[32] (failure to file/serve witness statements in time).

3. RELIEF FROM SANCTIONS

Where a sanction for non-compliance has been ordered or mandated by a rule or practice direction, it will *automatically* take effect unless the defaulting party applies for (and is granted) 'relief from the sanction' under CPR, r 3.9.[33] The text of this rule was amended following the Jackson review to support a policy of low, or no, tolerance to non-compliance. The old rule (which required the court to consider 'all of the circumstances' and then set out a list of obvious factors which might be of particular relevance) was thought to give judges too much scope for lenience. The current rule now requires the court to consider all the circumstances of the case, *so*

28 See Form N181, Part C
29 See generally below at Ch 17
30 Some rule-based sanctions are more discretionary, allowing the court to make some other order if appropriate.
31 [2013] EWCA Civ 1537
32 [2013] EWCA Civ 1624
33 'Relief from sanctions' under CPR, r 3.9 is a very specific application, and is different from appeals or applications to vary or set aside (orders made by the court on its own initiative, for example). But if judgment is entered following a strike out sanction, then the application to set aside that judgment is determined by reference to r 3.9

as to enable it to deal *justly* with the application, including the need for litigation to be conducted *efficiently and at proportionate costs*; and to *enforce compliance* with rules, practice directions and orders.

The application must be supported by written evidence, and the reason for the default had better be good! In *Mitchell*,[34] the Court of Appeal made clear that the courts were on a mission. In that case, they said that the court, in applying r 3.9, must apply the overriding objective and perform a balancing exercise, taking into account all relevant factors. But it stressed that the *two most important factors* were those listed in the rule, namely the need for litigation to be conducted efficiently and at proportionate costs, and the need to enforce compliance with rules, practice directions and orders. It also made clear that in exercising its discretion, the courts should take a holistic approach to justice. There was to be a 'shift away', as it was put, 'from exclusively focusing on doing justice in an individual case ... a tougher, more robust approach to non-compliance and relief from sanctions is intended to ensure that justice can be done in the majority of cases'.[35]

The relevant principles were restated in *Denton v TH White Ltd*, which set out a three-stage approach. The court will first look at the *nature* of the default in question,[36] and how significant or serious it is - if it is trivial or insignificant (more of form than substance, or a narrowly missed deadline with no case management repercussions), then the court will usually grant relief from the sanction. Where the non-compliance is serious or significant, then the court will look at *why* it occurred. In this context, inefficiency or incompetence of a party's solicitors (for example, overlooking a deadline, pressures of work, lack of cover for ill staff) is unlikely be a good reason; circumstances *outside the control* of the defaulting party/solicitors might be. The better the reason for the breach the more likely relief will be granted, even if the default was a serious one.[37]

34 Op. cit.

35 Per Jackson LJ, quoted in *ibid*, [38]

36 At this stage the court is focused on the significance of the default in respect of which relief from sanction is sought, although if the sanction arose from non-compliance with an 'unless' order, then it will be necessary to look at the default underlying that unless order. See generally WB, para 3.9.4 on this first stage.

37 See discussion at WB, para 3.9.5

Thirdly, the court will look at *all the circumstances* of the case, giving *priority* to the factors set out in CPR r 3.9(1)(a) and (b).[38] This is so even if the default is both serious and the reason for it poor. This third stage is an important part of the process since it should help ensure that, despite its low tolerance to non-compliance, the court responds to an application for relief in a way which is rational as well as proportionate.[39] Some sanctions impact more on a litigant's legal advisors (to keep them on their toes) than on the litgant directly, which can affect how forgiving (or not) a court will be.

It was not the aim of the Jackson reforms to 'turn ... compliance into 'trip wires', nor into 'the mistress rather than the handmaiden of justice.' The point is to enable the cost-effective progress of litigation (and the administration of justice) by means of compliance with rules and court orders, not to 'render compliance an end unto itself'. The court should not lose sight of the fairness of the proceedings and the wider interests of justice. It will be particularly keen to discourage opportunism by the non-defaulting party.[40]

Three further points. One is that an application for relief from sanctions presupposes that the sanction was in principle properly imposed. If a party wishes to contend that it was wrong to make the order, the appropriate procedural route is to appeal (or exceptionally, to ask the court which imposed it to vary or revoke it).[41] Secondly, if a party feels it needs more time to comply with an unless order, then where possible the parties should agree an extension under CPR, r 3.8(4). This latter provides that where a rule/order requires a party to do something within a specified time *and* an automatic sanction for non-compliance is built into the rule/order, then (unless the court orders otherwise) the time for compliance can (by prior written agreement of the parties) be extended by up to a maximum of 28 days, so long as no hearing date is affected.[42] This avoids an application to the court. And where an application to the court is necessary, one which is made before time has expired will (as you might expect)

38 These two factors are not of paramount importance, but because they are highlighted in the rule the majority in *Denton* felt they were of particular importance.

39 It is at this stage that it can become relevant if the defaulter has a history of defaulting. See generally WB, para 3.9.6

40 See e.g., *Summit Navigation Ltd v Generali Ramania Asigurare Reasihurae SA* [2014] EWHC 298 (Comm) at [49]. In that case the one who was wasting money and delaying progress of the case was not the defaulting claimant but rather the defendants who thought they would get a 'fortuitous' dismissal of the case against them because of a 24 hour delay in the claimants giving security for costs. See discussion at WB, para 3.9.7 and compare outcomes in the

be looked upon more favourably than applications for *relief* from sanctions after the event. Finally, the principles governing relief from sanctions also apply to applications seeking the imposition of a particular sanction, but as adapted to that task.[43]

Worst case scenarios

Only in *exceptional* circumstances will the court let a failure to comply with a direction or 'unless order' lead to the postponement of the trial.[44] Where (in the worst case scenario) an action has been struck out following a failure to comply with an 'unless order' (or other contemptuous behaviour), a second claim brought on the same basis (even if not statute-barred) would normally also be struck out (as an abuse of process).[45]

Punishment to fit the crime

The cases on sanctions since the inception of the CPR show that each case must be decided on its own merits, and pre-CPR cases will be irrelevant and unappreciated in court unless they speak to the overriding objective. Cases decided before the Jackson reforms may not fare much better. A noticeable theme of these cases is that the courts should be fair and flexible in exercising their wide and varied powers, ensuring that any penalty is commensurate with the nature of the default. The post-Jackson era ushered in a more robust approach, in the interest of serving the wider public interest in efficient and proportionate civil justice.[46] Even so, there are many procedural penalties available to the court to deter and punish delay and inefficiency. A sanction which deprives a party of fair access to the courts (for example, striking out) should still be seen as a sanction of last resort.[47]

Viridor and *Diriye* cases mentioned there.

41 *Mitchell*, op. cit. [44]

42 CPR, r 3.8(3) and (4). This provision was added to avoid an avalanche of applications to the court for extensions of time for compliance. It's a little bit of self-help for the parties (but it does require cooperation).

43 *Walsham Chalet Park Ltd v Tallington Lakes Ltd* [2014] EWCA Civ 1607 cited at WB, para 3.4.1

44 See, e.g., *Woodward v Finch* [1999] CPLR 699

45 *Johnson v Gore Wood and Co* [2002] 2 AC 1

46 *Mitchell*, op. cit.

47 It was noted in *Mitchell* that the costs sanction imposed in that case caused no prejudice to the claimant himself.

4. OTHER CASE MANAGEMENT POWERS

Extension of time and correcting irregularities

The court has general power to extend or shorten the time period for compliance with any rule, practice direction or court order (even if applied for after that time has expired)[48] and the power to take steps itself to remedy procedural errors.[49] These powers will be used in keeping with the overriding objective and in such a way as not to prejudice other parties. As always, applications made in good time will fare best. Remember, however, that (as we have seen) these powers may not be used in respect of applications to renew invalid claim forms which have expired.[50]

Applications to revoke or vary

The court's powers to make case management orders include the power to revoke or vary an order. It will do so sparingly, to ensure that applicants do not get 'two bites at the cherry', and so as not to undermine the appeal process. The discretion to revoke or vary will normally be limited to cases where (i) there has been a 'material change in circumstances' or (ii) where the facts on which the original order was based were misstated, or (iii) where there was a manifest mistake on the part of the judge who made the order. In addition, the application must be made promptly.[51]

Stays

This is a bit like the dog command. A 'stay' is an order producing a temporary halt to proceedings which can effectively become a permanent state of affairs.[52] While a stay is in effect, no other steps may be taken to progress the claim (except as set out in the order).[53] The power arises and is applicable in all sorts of situations. Some examples are:

48 CPR, r 3.1(2)(a). Applications are 'made' when the application notice is received, not when the hearing takes place: r 23.5

49 CPR, r 3.10

50 Note that CPR, r 3.1(2) begins: 'Except where these Rules provide otherwise.' *And see* Ch 12 for extending time for serving claim forms.

51 *Tibbles v SIG plc* [2012] 1 WLR 2591, cited in ***Mitchell***, op cit. And see CPR, r 3.1(7)

52 It is not, however, the same thing as discontinuing an action or getting judgment.

53 But it does not stop time running for other purposes.

(a) A stay of proceedings in a personal injuries case so long as the claimant unreasonably refuses to undergo a medical examination.
(b) A stay of proceedings while a preliminary point is argued which may have the result that the action will proceed no further.
(c) If a claimant accepts an offer of settlement,[54] the proceedings will be stayed, effectively ending the case.
(d) The *Tomlin* order, which is a special form of consent order, stays any further proceedings in the claim which have been compromised, except for the purpose of putting into effect the terms set out in the schedule to the order.[55]
(e) A stay of execution pending an appeal.
(f) A stay in proceedings for a month to attempt a settlement. This can be requested in the directions questionnaire. The court can of course order a stay of whatever length for these purposes at any appropriate time.

Discontinuance

This is something a claimant (or a person in position of a claimant) does if he or she, having commenced proceedings, decides that the wiser course is to abandon the whole or part of a claim against the defendant. The claimant merely serves a notice of discontinuance on the defendant (agreeing, in the process, to pay the defendant's costs). The claimant does not require the permission of the court unless an interim order has been made (for example, an interim payment has been made) or there is some aspect of the case which might need 'unraveling' (for example, an undertaking has been given to the court or there is another claimant involved, who might be left in the lurch).[56]

If permission is required, the claimant will usually be given it, subject to appropriate orders as to costs and any corrective orders which might be needed (for example, to repay an interim payment). The court is usually only too delighted to be

54 See Ch 15
55 See Ch 19
56 See CPR, r 38.2(2). If the claimant is acting under a disability (e.g., a child), then the court's approval must be sought. See Ch 3

relieved of cases, although very occasionally it may feel that a case has progressed so far that the claimant ought to lose openly and publicly.[57]

If discontinuance follows the filing of a defence, then a second claim brought on the same (or substantially the same) facts would not be allowed, unless the court gave permission.[58]

revision tip

- Read CPR 3.1-3.11 and PD 3A (without commentary) - or at least those rules which are on your syllabus. The rules are clearly set out. You need little else to remind you of the court's powers!

It is worth reading ...

Leggat J's terse judgment in ***Tchenguiz v Grant Thornton UK LLP*** [2015] EWHC 405 (Comm). A short instructive example of a striking out case and a reminder of how (or how not) to draft Particulars of Claim, whether you are in the Commercial Court or not!

For an unsettling but readily understandable case, see ***Oliver v Shaikh*** [2020] EWHC 2658 (QB) where, in an unusual 'hat trick', the Defence was struck out on all three grounds set out at CPR, r 3.4(2).

Lord Neuberger's judgment in ***Prince Abdulaziz v Apex Global Manangement Ltd*** [2014] UKSC 64, a Supreme Court decision which discusses both the granting of and relief from sanctions in the interesting context of a Saudi royal who, having invoked the English jurisdiction, refused to abide by its rules because of a princely objection to signing court documents. There are other procedural goodies as well: a reminder that appeal courts should not lightly interfere with lower court case management decisions and a very memorable example of the importance of litigants *personally* signing disclosure statements!

57 *Fox v Star Newspaper* [1900] AC 19, HL. Similarly, and for the same sorts of reasons, a defendant can apply to set aside a notice of discontinuance: CPR, r 38.4

58 CPR, r 38.7

PART FOUR

typical defendant's initiatives

CHAPTER 14

Security for costs

In the past, claimants made much of the running in litigation; the claimant, after all, is the party who sets the ball rolling and historically, it was the claimant who (generally speaking) set the pace of the proceedings. With the introduction of the CPR, that all changed of course - it is the court which now controls and sets the agenda.

Even so, defendants (if all they are doing is defending) will still of necessity spend much of the time reacting either to something the claimant has done (not least of all bringing the claim) or to the court's management of the case. Defendants may respond with deadly effect, of course, but nevertheless they are often prodded into action by something or someone else. It is also worth remembering that a claimant with a weak case does not have to bring proceedings (and would be well advised not to do so). Unless and until a claimant sees reason, however, a defendant with a meritorious defence[1] really has little choice but to defend. A claimant chooses to be a claimant; the same is not true of defendants.[2]

That being the case, and despite the fact that there are obviously many requests or applications which either party to litigation can make if necessary,[3] there are three important procedural initiatives *commonly (sometimes only) taken by defendants*. One of these is bringing in third parties. We looked at this in the context of parties and additional claims in Chapter 3. The other two are applications for security for

1 Not so strong as to succeed in striking out the claim, perhaps, but still good enough to win at the end of the day.

2 See WB para 25.13.1, referencing Nugee LJ's observations in *Axiom Stone (London) Ltd v Heathfield International LLC* [2021] EWCA

3 For example, a request for further information, an application for specific disclosure, seeking summary judgment, and so on.

costs, discussed in this chapter and offers of settlement, discussed in the next. Unlike the first two of these, which only defendants do, the CPR has made it possible for claimants also to make offers to settle.

Occasionally a claimant brings proceedings against the defendant simply for its nuisance value. The case may have a limited prospect of success,[4] but it has every ability to cost the defendant time, inconvenience, and expense. More mundanely, and much more commonly, a defendant may feel confident that there is a good chance of defeating a claim brought against him, but at the same time be concerned that the claimant, as loser, will be unable to meet any order for costs made against him.[5] In this context an impecunious claimant can be as much of a problem as an impecunious defendant.

Some, *but by no means all*, defendants are able to get protection in this kind of situation, in the form of an order for security for costs. If granted, the order must specify how much, how and when security must be given.[6] Security can be given in various ways, but the most common is by making a payment into court. The usual order in the King's Bench Division requires the claimant to pay a specific amount of money into court as security for the payment of any costs order which may eventually be made in favour of the defendant, and stays the proceedings until that security is given.[7] The money is held as a secure fund out of which the successful defendant's costs can be paid.[8]

Thus, the court has a *discretion* to order a *claimant* (or *party in the position of claimant*[9]) to give security for his opponent's *costs* in fairly limited circumstances. There are essentially *two hurdles* to be surmounted. The defendant must *first* establish that the claimant is one of those kinds of claimants against whom an order for security is *possible*. This is a very *narrow class* of what might be thought of as qualifying *claimants*[10] who are described by reference to situations which might make payment under, or enforcement of, a costs order, difficult. In a nutshell, the possibilities[11] are where:

4 If it is completely and obviously without merit, of course, the claim could be struck out or the defendant might get summary judgment.

5 As to costs, see generally Ch 18

6 CPR, r 25.12(3)

7 See form of order PF44. In the Commercial Court, claimants are usually given a reasonable time to comply (during which time the case progresses) failing which the action is stayed or struck out.

8 The money paid into court thus remains available for the payment of costs to the defendant, even if the claimant becomes insolvent. Any balance (or if no costs are payable to the defendant) will go back to the claimant.

9 Note that this would include, for example, a counterclaiming defendant, who for the purposes of the counterclaim is a

(i) The claimant is ordinarily resident outside the (domestic or EU/Hague Convention) jurisdiction;
(ii) The claimant is an 'impecunious'[12] company ;
(iii) The claimant has changed his address so as to evade service;
(iv) The claimant failed to give a correct address in the claim form;
(v) The claimant is an 'impecunious', nominal[13] claimant;
(vi) The claimant has taken steps in relation to his assets which would make it difficult to enforce an order for costs against him.

This first hurdle, which must be established as a matter of *fact*, has been usefully described as a gateway or pre-condition to getting an order.[14] If a defendant cannot surmount it, that is the end of the story - there would be no scope for an order for security for costs. Note, too, that impecuniosity is not, by itself, a ground for ordering security. It is part of the equation for pre-conditions (ii) and (v), above, and may be relevant if the court is in a position to *exercise its discretion*, but impecuniosity alone is not enough to get the defendant over this first hurdle.

A few of these gateways are pretty straightforward or speak for themselves, but two merit some closer scrutiny:

The impecunious company

'Impecunious company' is used as shorthand for this pre-condition, which requires that it be shown that the claimant is a company or other incorporated body (whether British or foreign) and there is reason to believe that it will be unable to pay the defendant's costs if ordered to do so (see CPR r 25.13(2)(c)). There are two aspects to this. The first is simple: the claimant must be a company or incorporated body. There is no provision for getting an order for security against an unincorporated association. In addition,

claimant (unless the same is a purely defensive set-off as explained in WB para 25.13.2). See CPR, r 25.12(1) which refers to applications made by 'a defendant to any claim.' For the sake of clarity, I will merely refer in this chapter to 'claimants' and 'defendants'.

10 This is my expression, not the CPR's.

11 See CPR, r 25.13(2) for exact wording.

12 'Impecunious' is used here as shorthand. *See below*.

13 'Nominal' essentially means that the claimant is just a frontman. Claimants suing in a representative capacity are specifically excluded from the description.

14 *Infinity Distribution (In Administration) v Khan Partnership LLP* [2021] EWCA Civ 565, cited in WB, para 25.13.1

it must also be shown that there is 'reason to believe that the claimant will be unable to pay costs if so ordered'. The defendant does not need to prove on the balance of probabilities that the claimant company won't be able to pay (that is asking too much of the defendant), but equally it is insufficient merely to believe or speculate that for one reason or another the claimant company 'might' or 'may' be unable to pay (that asks too little of the defendant). The test falls somewhere in between: the defendant must provide objective evidence (not merely his own reasonably held belief) so as to give *the court* reason to believe that the claimant company *will be* unable to pay such costs. Typical ways of doing this would be to establish that the company is in liquidation or where its turnover is less than its debts or where its assets are not easily converted into cash. Obviously, questions about ability to pay must be decided at the time of the application, but the court is entitled to look into the future as to what assets may be available to the company at the *relevant time* (when costs might become payable). But every case is different and will turn on its own facts.[15]

Taking steps which hinder enforcement

Under r 25.13(2)(g) security for costs may be ordered against a claimant who has taken steps in relation to their assets (e.g., dissipating assets or transferring assets abroad or to family members) which could make it difficult to enforce an order for costs against them. It is important to remember that for the purposes of passing this gateway, the court is not concerned with when the steps were taken nor with the claimant's motivation at the time, but only with *the fact* that the steps in relation to his assets were taken and the effect that would have on enforcing costs orders. Having said that, motive, intention or the time when the steps were taken *could well be* relevant to the exercise of the court's discretion (discussed below).[16] The test is an objective one, but where, for example, a claimant denies having any assets to

15 See generally WB, para 25.13.12

16 *Aoun v Bahri* [2002] EWHC 29 (Comm), cited at WB para 25.13.16

deal with but nevertheless has a very lavish lifestyle (allegedly funded by family and friends), the court may infer both the existence of assets and the taking of steps to hinder enforcement.[17]

Second hurdle

It is important to remember that even if this first hurdle is surmounted, it does not necessarily follow that the defendant will get the order for security. There is a second hurdle. Such orders *are discretionary* and to make the order the court must be satisfied that having regard to 'all the circumstances' it is 'just' to do so. This is all the rule says.[18]

Older cases[19] attempted to list the sorts of factors which the court might look at in order to do this. For example: are there any special difficulties in enforcing a costs order? Is it obvious (without conducting a mini-trial, which would waste time and money[20]) that the merits clearly favour one side over the other? How clear is it that the defendant will win and not get his costs from the claimant? Could the defendant recover costs from someone other than the claimant? What impact would the order have on the claimant? These are really just common sense considerations focused on the purpose behind the application - the risk that the defendant, if successful, will not recover their costs.

In the post-CPR case of *Nasser v United Bank of Kuwait*,[21] the court said that its discretion was to be exercised by applying the overriding objective (no surprises there) so as to afford 'proportionate protection' against the 'difficulty identified' by the pre-condition relied upon in making the application for security for costs. So, for example, if the claimant is resident outside the jurisdiction, how easy or hard it would be to enforce a costs order will be especially relevant. Are there capital assets in the jurisdiction? If the claimant is an impecunious company, the court might be more focused on how to protect the defendant without stifling a genuine claim. Is the defendant being a bully?

17 As in ***Dubai Islamic Bank PJSC v PSI Energy Holding Co BSC*** [2011] EWCA Civ 761 referenced at WB para 25.13.16

18 CPR, r 25.13(1)(a) and see WB, para 25.13.1

19 For example, ***Sir Lindsay Parkinson & Co v Triplan*** [1973] QB 609

20 An investigation into who is likely to win the substantive action is strongly discouraged. The merits are only relevant to such applications where it can easily and clearly be demonstrated (by the party raising the issue) that there is a very high probability of success or failure: ***Chernukhin v Danilina*** [2018] EWCA Civ 1802 and see WB, para 25.13.1.2

21 [2002] 1 WLR 1868

Did the defendant contribute to the company's financial difficulties? Should the need to protect the defendant yield to the claimant's right of access to the courts?

This question of whether an order for security would prevent the claimant from continuing the claim is an important one. A court should not make an order which would, as it is put, 'stifle' a genuine claim. But it will not be assumed that an order for security would necessarily have this effect. There is effectively *a burden of proof on the claimant to establish this* on the balance of probabilities, and in order to do so a claimant would have to show, on the evidence, that it is unable to give security, either from its own resources or by way of raising the amount needed from others who could assist, such as relatives and friends.[22]

Delay in making the application might also be relevant. Every case, and every application, will be determined on the basis of its individual facts.

An application for security for costs is made on notice to a Master or District Judge (as the case may be), using the normal Part 23 procedure. The application notice must be served on the claimant at least three clear days before the hearing and be supported by written evidence, setting out the basis for the application and factors relevant to the exercise of the court's discretion. It should also include an estimate of the likely costs of defending the claim. Such applications will normally be made at the first case management conference - orders for security for costs are not appropriate in small claims track cases because of the restrictions on recovering costs in such claims, but they can be made in respect of the costs of an appeal[23] .

If the court is minded to make an order for security, the next question is: for how much? The first point to make is that the amount of security to be ordered (and how it is to be given) is entirely within the court's discretion.[24] Having said that, the amount chosen should 'be neither illusory nor oppressive.'[25] A conventional approach has been to fix the amount of security at about two-thirds of the estimated costs up to

22 *Goldtrail Travel Ltd v Aydin* [2017] UKSC 57 and see WB para 25.13.1.1

23 CPR, r 25.15

24 *Infinity* op cit, cited at WB para 25.13.1

25 *Hart Investments Ltd v Larchpark Ltd* [2008] 1 BCLC 589

the stage of proceedings for which security is ordered (so past as well as future costs can be included in the figure). It is common to order security in convenient stages, rather than one huge amount right up to end of trial (the case might settle, after all), but there is no hard and fast rule. Orders should be case-specific, and geared to the specific risks revealed by the evidence.

Do not lose sight of the fact that this is an order about security *for costs*. It is nothing to do with damages. Winning defendants do not, of course, get damages; they avoid paying them. But (other things being equal) they would normally be entitled to some costs from the losing claimant.[26]

Joint claimants can complicate matters, especially if one, say, is resident outside the jurisdiction, but the other is not. Assuming no other pre-condition is relevant, it is clear that an order cannot be made against the claimant who lives in this country, since that person is not what we are calling a qualifying claimant. But would the court make an order against the other claimant who does come within CPR, r 25.13(2)(a)? The courts get edgy about claimants who reside beyond the reach of the jurisdiction, concerned that it is too easy for them to scurry away without meeting their litigation obligations, including payment of costs if they have lost or abandoned the case.

This may be why they are head of the list of qualifying claimants! But does the fact that there is another claimant within the jurisdiction make it more or less likely that the order will be made against the one who is not? As you might expect the answer is that it depends on the circumstances, and in particular how confident the court is that the defendant will be able recover his costs from the resident claimant.

Thus, it may be possible to get an order against the foreign claimant if the two claimants are not relying on the same cause of action or each claimant will be solely responsible for his own share of the defendant's costs (or it is impossible to predict the liability on costs). Conversely, it may not be appropriate to grant the order against

26 See comment of Bingham LJ cited at WB para 25.13.1

the foreign claimant where both claimants are relying on identical causes of action and will be jointly responsible for costs, and there are sufficient funds to enforce against - if, in effect, the defendant could recover all of his costs from the claimant who is inside the jurisdiction.[27] In essence, the court has to balance the protection afforded the defendant by the claimant within the jurisdiction against concerns about allowing foreign claimants to bring actions here without giving security.

revision tips

- Remember that it is only *defendants* who apply for and get orders for security for costs *against* claimants (or those in the position of a claimant). Watch out for counterclaims, when roles are reversed! When dealing with an exam question, take time to note who is doing what to whom. It is easy to get confused in the heat of the moment.
- Remember the two hurdles! The first is a question of fact; the second is a matter of the court's discretion. The defendant needs to get over both.
- Concentrate on the topics examinable on your course syllabus. The most common pre-conditions for seeking security for costs (both in practice and in assessments) are that the claimant resides outside the jurisdiction, is a company in financial difficulties or one who has dealt with its assets in a way which hinders enforcement of any costs order. At the time of writing, the BSB WB commentary paragraphs focus on the last two of these. But note that the final five principles summarised in ***Ackerman v Ackerman*** set out at WB, para 25.13.16 are of general application to the exercise of the court's discretion (and are not exclusive to pre-condition r 25.13(2)(g)). This could have been made clearer.

It is worth reading ...

Al-Kornky v Time Life Entertainment Group Ltd [2005] EWHC 1688 (QB). The subject matter is troubling but the judgment of Eady J is easy to follow and instructive as to how applications for security for costs work. The claimants (who by this time were resident out of the jurisdiction) sued the author and publishers of a memoir about modern slavery for defamation. The case is a little old, but it is still a good example of the sorts of matters that arise in the exercise of the court's discretion in this context. The book (plus a sequel) is still available on Amazon.

27 See discussion in *Slazengers Ltd v Seaspeed Ferries International Ltd* [1988] 1 WLR 221, cited at WB, para 25.13.9

CHAPTER 15

Part 36 and offers of settlement

A formal offer of settlement is something defendants have been more apt to do than claimants, but claimants can, and increasingly do, make such offers as well. Part 36 of the CPR, described as a 'self-contained procedural code' and very prescriptive in nature, now deals with a whole range of situations where a formal offer to settle a case might be made:[1] by a claimant or by a defendant; before or after a claim has been commenced; where the relief sought is money and where it is not - even in respect of appeals. These are all known globally as 'Part 36 offers'.

As we have seen, much of the CPR is focused on getting parties to avoid unnecessarily resorting to, or prolonging litigation to resolve their differences. They are, for example, asked to consider alternative solutions, to focus on the real issues in dispute, to be open and cooperative in the conduct of litigation. Part 36 offers perform a vital part of this process by encouraging parties to settle their dispute at the earliest possible stage, rather than fighting it out to the bitter end. A party who receives a realistic offer of settlement should always give serious thought to accepting it because the risk is that the person making the offer ('offeror') will be awarded the costs incurred of continuing the litigation, if the person to whom the offer was made ('offeree') fails to achieve a better outcome at trial. This can be a very heavy price indeed.[2]

1 CPR, r 36.1. Part 36 offers can arise in many contexts - claims, counterclaims, third party claims etc: CPR, r 36.2. Part 36 does not, however, apply to small claims: CPR, r 27.2(1)(g). Offers made in the context of the low value RTA and similar protocols are covered by specially adapted rules set out in Part II of Part 36. These latter provisions are *not* on the BSB syllabus at the time of writing.

2 Note that a Part 36 offer made in respect of a claim which goes to trial has effect only in respect of the costs of those first instance proceedings. If an issue in that case is then appealed, a separate Part 36 offer must be made in order to get costs protection for the appeal proceedings: CPR, r 36.4

Advising on the terms of an offer of settlement, and whether to accept or reject such offers, requires considerable professional skill and experience. At this point, what is important is to understand how the Part 36 scheme works in practical terms, which is what this chapter aims to help you to do.

It is useful to distinguish between offers made by defendants and offers made by claimants.

1. PART 36 OFFERS BY *DEFENDANTS*

The principle behind the Part 36 procedure in this context is that a claimant should accept an 'acceptable' offer by the defendant to settle the case rather than proceed to trial regardless, thereby increasing the costs the defendant would have to pay when the claimant only wins at the end of the day what was earlier on offer. Claimants who fail to accept offers which it turns out should have been accepted, will (almost invariably) find that they will pay the costs of having unnecessarily continued to trial.

For many years, in money claims, defendants actually parted with their money when putting formal offers on the table. These were known as 'payments into court' and were abolished in 2007. Now *only the offer* goes on the table, whatever the nature of the claim.[3] Defendants thus make formal Part 36 offers to settle, which must be in *writing*,[4] and which must normally remain on the table for a stated period of *at least* 21 days (or up to the end of trial if the offer is made less than 21 days before the trial starts[5]) - for the claimant to accept or not. This initial period is known in the rules as the 'relevant period.' For the discussion which follows I will assume this to be the *minimum* 21 days (which is typical), although it *can be longer.*[6]

In a nutshell this is how it works: if the claimant accepts the offer during

3 Non-money claims were never susceptible to payments into court, so these always involved a formal written offer known as a '*Calderbank* letter', as to which see the discussion at the end of this chapter. Special cases still requiring a payment into court are now covered by Part 37

4 CPR, r 36.5(1)(a). Form N242A is usually, but need not necessarily be used for this purpose. Having said that, the courts have observed, with some exasperation, that using this form avoids a lot of difficulties which can otherwise arise. See PD 36, para 1.1. It is worth having a look at Form N242A.

5 CPR, rr 36.5(2) and 36.3(g)(ii), and see, WB para 36.5.1.7

6 CPR, r 36.5(1)(c). The parties can agree to extend the 'relevant period' specified in the offer, but the court has no power to do

this initial 21 day period, then all proceedings are stayed. The defendant will be required to pay the claimant's costs up to that point. If the claimant never accepts the offer, and the case goes to trial, the trial judge will not normally know anything about the offer. If at the end of the trial, the outcome for the claimant is better than what was on offer,[7] then costs would be apt to 'follow the event' in the normal way, which means that the losing defendant pays the winning claimant's costs.[8] If, however, the outcome for the claimant is no better or is worse than what was on offer, the costs incurred *after* the expiry of the 21 days after the offer was made will be awarded *against* the otherwise successful claimant. So from that point, the claimant will (almost always) have to pay the defendant's costs - and, of course, bear his own.

Strategically, the amount of a defendant's Part 36 offer should tempt the claimant into compromising the case, without offering too much!

Here are some important points to note generally:

(i) A Part 36 offer can be made at *any stage* of proceedings (even during the pre-action phase and even during trial) and *the amount increased (or the offer otherwise improved)* at *any* time. An offer is made when it is *served* on the other party; if the latter is legally represented, then service *must* be on the legal representative.[9]

(ii) A Part 36 offer is *treated as including all interest* (up to the end of the 21 day/relevant period, although provision in the offer can be made for interest payable after this date).[10]

(iii) The claimant should be able to determine to what the offer relates and can seek clarification where required - *in the first instance from the offeror*, but by application to the court if necessary.[11] It is a formal and explicit requirement that it be made clear whether the offer is in full

this: ***Begum v Barts Health NHS Trust*** [2022] EWHC 1668 (QB) at [10]

7 Where the claim is for money, this can usually be determined by comparing the amount on offer with the amount awarded (comparing like with like so far as interest on the sum is concerned). Comparing offer with outcome can be a lot more tricky with non-money claims.

8 There is discretion under Part 44 to deviate from the general rule. See Ch 18 on costs generally.

9 CPR, r 36.7(2) and PD 36, para 1.2 (which also applies to notices of acceptance or withdrawal of offers).

10 CPR, r 36.5(4), (5) and WB para 36.5.1.6

11 CPR, r 36.8(1)

and final settlement of the whole of the claim, or just some part of it (and if so, which part or issue), and whether it takes into account any counterclaim. The offer must also make clear that it is made pursuant to Part 36. It does not have to (but can) state that the offer is 'without prejudice except as to costs', since this goes without saying.[12]

(iv) A defendant's offer to pay money should *normally* be an offer to pay this as a *single* sum, payable within *14 days* of acceptance, although there are special rules in personal injuries actions about how to deal with claims for future pecuniary loss, provisional damages and recovery of State benefits. An offer to pay the sum on offer *later* than 14 days after acceptance will not be treated as a valid Part 36 offer (unless the offer is in fact accepted).[13]

(v) Usually, a defendant wants to offer the whole amount appropriate before the heaviest costs are incurred so as to take advantage of the costs protection. The earlier the realistic offer is made, the fuller the protection for the defendant. Having said that, it would be silly to make an offer without a fair degree of evidential information so as to have a good idea of the strengths and weaknesses of the claim etc.

(vi) Normally offers are made and accepted under Part 36 *without the intervention of the court.* It is the *exception, not the rule* for the claimant to need permission to accept a Part 36 offer. Examples of when, exceptionally, permission is required include where the claimant is a child or otherwise acting under a legal disability,[14] where the trial has already started,[15] and sometimes where there are multiple defendants and the Part 36 offer is made by some but not all of them.[16]

(vii) A claimant not wanting to accept a Part 36 offer need not do anything. Such offers are not formally 'rejected', as such (even if that expression

12 CPR, r 36.5(1) and r 36.16(1)

13 CPR, r 36.5(3) and r 36.6(2)

14 So the court can ensure that the interests of the vulnerable claimant are being served: CPR, r 21.10

15 CPR, r 36.11(3)(d). Some revelation may have occurred at trial which puts the claim (and hence the offer) in a new light.

16 Essentially, permission is required where the status of the claims against any remaining defendants may be unclear. So if the claimant sues two defendants jointly or in the alternative (so both not necessarily liable), he will not need permission to accept the Part 36 offer made by one of them so long as he discontinues the claim against the other, who also gives written consent to the acceptance. Similarly, if Defendants are sued as severally liable (where one can remain liable even after

is sometimes used), but simply not accepted. *In contrast to the making, accepting and withdrawing of Part 36 offers, all of which require notices in writing, there is no procedure for rejecting such offers.* Even a counter-offer does not operate to extinguish an earlier offer. A Part 36 offer can be *worded to expire automatically* after the relevant period has elapsed. *Otherwise* only a *formal withdrawal* will take an unaccepted offer off the table. As odd as it may seem, it is thus possible to have several offers on the table at once![17]

(viii) The fact of a Part 36 offer should not normally be revealed to the trial judge until issues of both liability and quantum have been finally determined. The risk of prejudice is obvious, so this is an important principle. The exceptions are very limited.[18]

Both the White Book (Vol 2, Section A1) and BCP (Checklist 29) include a useful resumé of the procedural detail. What follows is an overview, looking at four different possible scenarios. Let's assume the defendant makes a Part 36 offer in a money claim, well before the trial date and which complies with all necessary formalities. The relevant period is the usual 21 days:

A. THE FIRST 21 DAYS

During this initial period, the claimant may accept the offer and *be assured of getting costs* - this amounts to something like a 'package deal.' The claimant must notify the defendant in writing[19] that the offer is being accepted. It will follow that the claimant is entitled to 100% of his costs up to the date of serving the notice of acceptance - these would include, typically, the cost of getting advice on whether to accept the offer or not. The amount of such costs, if not agreed, will be assessed on the standard basis if they are not fixed.[20] The court has *no power* (in this specific

judgment has been obtained against others), a claimant is free to accept a Part 36 offer from one and continue against the other. Otherwise, claimants need the court's permission to accept a Part 36 offer made by some of a number of defendants. CPR, r 36.15

17 CPR, r 36.9(3) and (4)(b) and *Gibbon v Manchester City Council* [2010] EWCA 726

18 See CPR, r 36.16(2)/(3)

19 If the defendant is legally represented then the notice must be served on his legal representative: PD 36, para 1.2. There is no particular format for written notice of acceptance - a letter will do, although Form 242A, if used, has a notice of acceptance form which accompanies it. Notice must also be filed with the court. PD 36, para 3.1

20 Only costs (including recoverable pre-action costs) of the claim to which

scenario) to make any other order as to the costs to be paid.[21]

It is important to remember that *during this initial period, the defendant may not withdraw the offer (or alter its terms to be less advantageous), unless the court gives permission* which it would only do if there had been a 'change of circumstances' since the offer was made, rendering it unjust to hold the defendant to it.[22] This would be rare. A key feature of the rules is that once a Part 36 offer is made, it should normally remain on the table for the taking for the *whole* of this initial relevant period.

B. AFTER THE 21 DAYS (BUT BEFORE TRIAL)

After the initial 21 days has expired, assuming the offer was not time-limited or withdrawn, the claimant may still accept it, subject to the parties agreeing costs. The claimant will not usually get costs incurred after the end of the initial 21 day period; quite the reverse in fact. The usual outcome would be that the claimant gets costs up to that point, but the defendant would be entitled to costs from the end of the initial 21 day period until the date of (the delayed) acceptance. If the parties cannot agree, the court will, unless it is unjust to do so, make just such an order (to include the costs of having to ask the court to make the order as to costs!)[23]

Equally, if a defendant's Part 36 offer has not been accepted by the end of the initial 21 day period, the defendant may formally withdraw it or make it less generous. This is done by serving written notice; no permission of the court is required at this point.[24] A defendant wanting to now make a *less* advantageous offer, should take care to ensure that the previous offer is formally withdrawn, so that the latter can no longer be capable of acceptance. *Improved* offers, of course, do not present such a problem. They can be made at any time.

Note that a withdrawn offer (or one which does not comply with the formalities sufficiently to be considered a proper Part 36 offer) cannot give rise to an 'official' costs

the Part 36 offer relates are automatically recoverable: CPR, r 36.13(1)-(3)

21 See WB, para 36.13.1. Some discretion can come into the equation where the offer, which is accepted during the relevant period, was made only in respect of part of the claim. If the claimant then abandons the rest of his claim, he will (logically) only be entitled to the costs relating to that part of the claim which was settled, 'unless the court orders otherwise': CPR, r 36.13(2) and WB para 36.13.2

22 CPR, r 36.10(3). If, during this 21 day period, the defendant were to serve a notice to withdraw (or make less attractive) his Part 36 offer, then this notice will be deemed to take effect *only after* the relevant period has expired without the offer being accepted. If a notice of acceptance were also

sanction under Part 36, but it can (and will) still be 'put into the mix' and taken into account by the court (as can any offer to settle) in deciding final costs orders. What importance it might have on the order as to costs is entirely up to the wide discretion of the court under Part 44. In a suitable case, the court can even treat a withdrawn Part 36 offer as having the same consequences as if it had not been withdrawn.[25]

C. DURING TRIAL

If a claimant wants to accept a Part 36 offer once the trial of the action has started, this brings into play two conflicting propositions. The first is that the claimant requires the court's *permission* to accept the offer *once the trial has started.* Maybe the claimant's case is not going so well, and it would be unfair to let him take advantage of an offer which he has spurned for so long. But the rules also require that in the normal course of events the trial judge must not know about any Part 36 offers which have been made, until the case is over. So how does a claimant ask for permission from the court without the court finding out that the offer has been made?

Ask another judge, is the short answer. Of course, if (as is commonly the case) the defendant does not object to the claimant accepting the Part 36 offer even at this late stage, then it is unlikely to cause a problem because the only remaining issue will be the question of costs. The defendant might object, however, if the trial has revealed unanticipated weaknesses in the claimant's case. This happened in the old case of *Gaskins v British Aluminium Co.*[26] After failing in his application to the trial judge for permission to accept a 'payment in' (as it was then called), the claimant then made a second application to the judge for a re-trial because he (the judge) now knew about the fact of the payment in. The Court of Appeal was not enamoured with this argument, especially as the only reason the trial judge found out about the payment into court was because the claimant had told him! They

served before the end of the 21 day period, then it will 'trump' any notice served by the defendant during this period, unless (on the latter's application) the court gives permission for the initial offer to be withdrawn or reduced, which it will only do in very limited circumstances. See CPR, r 36.10

23 CPR, r 36.13(4)(b) and (5). The same idea applies in the other circumstances set out in r 36.13(4), which includes where the offer is made very close to (less than 21 days before) the trial.

24 CPR, r 36.9. Again if the claimant is legally represented, then the notice should be served on his legal representatives.

25 CPR, r 44.2(4) and see WB, para 36.2.1

26 [1976] 1 All ER 208

also pointed out that it would be strange if a claimant whose case is going badly at trial could get a new trial simply by seeking permission to accept the amount on offer, and when this is refused, necessarily getting an order for a re-trial. It was up to the judge to decide whether, all things considered, carrying on with the trial in such circumstances created an injustice.

This essentially remains the case, especially for an inadvertent disclosure of the fact of a Part 36 offer.[27] Even after an inappropriate disclosure at trial, the judge should think long and hard before ordering a new trial, and in particular about the expense and proportionality of such a course.[28] But where a claimant seeks permission to accept the defendant's offer after the trial has begun, the rules now suggest a simple solution - unless the parties are happy for the trial judge to deal with the matter, the claimant should simply apply to another judge.[29]

In the majority of cases, permission to accept even at this late stage will be granted, although the court's discretion is unfettered and if the circumstances (and in particular a *change* in circumstances) warrant it, as in the *Gaskins* case, then permission will be denied.[30] If acceptance is allowed, either by consent or with the court's permission, the usual rule is that the claimant recovers costs up to the end of the initial 21 day period, but the defendant recovers his costs thereafter - a claimant who has left it this long to accept the offer will end up paying a lot of money in costs!

D. THE CLAIMANT NEVER ACCEPTS THE OFFER

A claimant must obtain a judgment which is '*more advantageous*' than the defendant's Part 36 offer in order to avoid the cost penalty of failing to accept it. For money claims, all that is required is that the claimant recovers more in money terms than the amount on offer, *however small the difference*.[31] So even if the claimant recovers only one penny more than the amount on offer, he will normally be entitled to his costs in

27 *Garratt v Saxby* [2004] EWCA Civ 341

28 If the disclosure was intentional or clearly the fault of one party, and a new trial ordered, no doubt that party (or possibly his legal advisors) would be asked to pay (a considerable amount) for the wasted costs. Junior Counsel beware!

29 The same idea would apply where permission is needed to withdraw a Part 36 offer under CPR, r 36.10 (i.e. before the end of the relevant period) if the trial judge has already been allocated to the case. See PD 36, paras 2.2 and 3.2

30 For a current case on this, see ***Capital Bank plc v Stickland*** [2004] EWCA Civ 1677

31 CPR, r 36.17(2). It is important to compare like with like, especially as regards the interest element. Note that where a defendant's Part 36 offer is followed

the usual way.[32] But if the claimant falls short of this mark, the sanction kicks in: the court *must* order that the claimant gets his costs up to the end of the relevant period, but *thereafter* the claimant will have to pay the defendant's costs (*and of course bear his own*), unless such an order is unjust. This is sometimes referred to as a 'split order', since the defendant pays the claimant's costs up to a *certain stage*, after which the roles are reversed. It is easy to see how serious this consequence can be - it can take a very large bite out of a damage award, or consume it altogether. And there can be some very hard cases, given the difference a penny can make.[33]

The costs consequences of 'not beating' (as the saying used to be) a defendant's Part 36 offer in respect of a money claim should be predictable, and so will not be departed from lightly. Having said that, there are circumstances when the specific sanctions set out in Part 36 will not apply, namely:[34]

(i) where the offer had been formally withdrawn (or made less advantageous and the less advantageous offer has been beaten),

(ii) where the offer was not a properly formulated Part 36 offer. If an offer does not comply with the prerequisites of Part 36, then these rules do not apply. In deciding whether an offer is compliant, a court may overlook a very minor or technical error, but will otherwise expect strict compliance with the Part 36 requirements,[35]

(iii) where the offer was made less than 21 days before trial (unless the court overlooks this fact),

or (as indicated above)

(iv) where the court considers it would be *unjust* to make the mandated order. In deciding this question, the rules say that the court will take *all the circumstances* into account, including the terms of the offer, when it was

by a formal admission or interim payment, the amount admitted or paid is not to be notionally added to the amount offered in the Part 36 offer when deciding whether that offer is as or more advantageous than the judgment: see WB, para 36.17.2

32 Assuming there was no other reason to deviate from the general rule that the winner gets his costs. See e.g., ***Allison v Brighton & Hove City Council*** [2005] EWCA Civ 548 (where the claimant exaggerated the claim and so got only 25% of costs in the pre-offer period). And see Ch 18

33 Unless these are fixed, costs orders against claimants under CPR, r 36.17(3), are normally assessed on the standard basis, although if the claimant's conduct was so poor as to take it 'outside the norm' (beyond the mere fact of not 'beating'

made, what the parties knew at the time the offer was made, the relevant conduct of the parties and whether the offer was a genuine attempt to settle the proceedings. Note that it is a '*formidable obstacle*' to persuade the court that the usual costs order would be unjust in any given case. Were it otherwise, the entire purpose of the rules in promoting sensible compromise and avoiding unnecessary costs would be undermined.[36]

Finally, remember that defendants can also make Part 36 offers in non-money claims. The process is just the same as for money claims, but when one is not dealing with hard cash, it can be more challenging to determine, in any given case, whether a judgment at the end of a trial is more 'advantageous' than an offer which was made, but never accepted. In such cases, the court simply has to look at the case in the round, taking all of the circumstances into account.

2. PART 36 OFFERS BY *CLAIMANTS*

Claimants can, and are very much encouraged to, make Part 36 offers themselves. In other words they can offer to settle the action on stated terms in exchange for not pursuing the case to trial. Indeed, a defendant's Part 36 offer which is not accepted may well be met with a claimant's own Part 36 offer (a formal counter-offer in effect).[37] A claimant's Part 36 offer will be made and accepted just as one made by a defendant. *So most of the matters and formalities applicable to the latter, as discussed above, apply equally to the former, with appropriate adaptation.* The main difference is the nature of the consequence to a defendant of not accepting an acceptable offer by the claimant. If the claimant's offer is made and never accepted, and the outcome

a defendant's offer), then a court, in its general discretion under r 44.3, might order such a claimant to pay costs on (the more punitive) indemnity basis. See WB, para 36.17.3 and Ch 18

34 CPR, r 36.17(7). The costs protection afforded claimants in personal injuries claims can prevent such costs orders being enforced. See Ch 18

35 See WB, para 36.2.4.1

36 See CPR, r 36.17(5) and WB, para 36.17.5. See also r 36.17(7)

37 But remember that such a counter-offer does not operate as any formal rejection of the defendant's Part 36 offer, as discussed above.

at trial is *as or more* advantageous to the claimant than his own offer, the defendant will suffer *various costs and interest 'penalties'* - in effect because the defendant forced the claimant to litigate to the bitter end to get justice. Thus, unless it thinks it *unjust*, the court *must* order that the defendant pay:

(i) a punitive rate of interest on the damage award (not to exceed 10% above base rate) *for some or all of the period* starting with the date on which the 21 day/relevant period expired;
(ii) costs (including recoverable pre-action costs) at the indemnity (rather than standard) rate for the period after the 21 day/relevant period expired; *and*
(iii) interest on those costs (not exceeding 10% above base rate).

In addition,

(iv) a further 'reward' for claimants making successful Part 36 offers was introduced on 1 April 2013, as part of the Jackson reforms. This effectively amounts to a bonus to the damage award (or other remedy), and is described as an *'additional amount'* (not exceeding £75,000) calculated on a sliding scale depending on the size of the judgment. *Thus*:
(a) In *money* claims, the additional amount is 10% of the first £500,000 of the amount of *damages* awarded, plus 5% of any amount above £500,000, up to a maximum of £1,000,000 (using these figures, this is where the £75,000 maximum figure comes from).
(b) In *non*-money claims, one works off of the *costs* figures, so the additional amount is calculated at 10% of the first £500,000, plus 5% of the next £500,000 of costs awarded to the successful claimant.[38]

38 As with defendant's offers, the Part 36 consequences do not apply to claimants' offers which have been formally withdrawn, are not properly constituted offers under Part 36 etc. Note too that only one 'additional amount' can be awarded, once the entire case has 'been decided', even if several successful claimant's Part 36 offers, relevant to different issues, have been made in the one case. CPR, r 36.17(4)(d) and see WB, para 36.17.4.4

This additional reward both encourages claimants to make sensible Part 36 offers and gives defendants more incentive to accept such offers. Note that the additional amount is an 'all or nothing' award. It seems that there is no jurisdiction to order a reduced amount; either the claimant gets the additional amount or (if the court considers it unjust) he does not.[39]

In one of the earliest cases involving a claimant's Part 36 offer, a chemist, Mr Garfoot, sued a former colleague at Boots (the chemists), Ms Walker, for libel after she had accused him of rape. He was never charged, but following an investigation his employers had moved him to another branch. The claimant said the allegation was completely false and had caused severe damage to his reputation. He made a claimant's Part 36 offer to settle for £25,000 in damages. The defendant did not accept the offer and at trial Mr Garfoot was awarded £400,000.[40] The defendant was ordered to pay considerable costs (it was a jury trial) on an indemnity basis and interest at a punitive rate, and nowadays Mr Garfoot would also have got an additional amount of £40,000.

Bear in mind, however, that a claimant only needs to win a case on the balance of probabilities. *Garfoot v Walker* was a very dramatic loss - there may be times when a defendant comes close to winning, and so may have been more justified in not accepting a claimant's offer.

One particular problem that can arise is when a claimant makes an 'offer' for all of the relief sought in the claim, and then succeeds in full. This is sometimes referred to as a '100% offer' and could be an easy way of getting a 10% uplift in damages and so forth when nothing much was really on offer by way of compromise. Claimants do not have to 'beat' their own offer, and so unless the claimant's case is very strong, this might (in theory at any rate) seem an unfair result. It was for this reason that one of the factors for the court to take into account when deciding

39 WB para 36.17.4.4. But *JLE v Warrington* [2019], cited there, is an obiter observation in a High Court case, so watch this space.

40 *Garfoot v Walker*, the Independent, 8 February 2000

whether it is 'unjust' to order the mandated consequences under Part 36 is whether the offer was a 'genuine attempt to settle' the proceedings. 100% offers by claimants do not meet this description.

So there must be an element of compromise in what the claimant is offering for the court to be able to conclude that it is a genuine offer to settle, as opposed to (as one judge put it) a demand for 'total capitulation'. How much of a concession is required will depend on the circumstances of the case, and in particular the court's view of the strength of the claimant's claim. In an open and shut case, a 95% offer was said to be a genuine attempt to settle.[41]

3. PART 36 OFFERS v '*CALDERBANK*' OFFERS

Part 36 offers are the most common way in which civil claims are compromised, but they are not the only way. Indeed, CPR r 36.2 explicitly says that nothing in the Part 36 rules prevents parties making an offer to settle in whatever way they choose. A typical alternative to a Part 36 offer is the so-called *Calderbank* offer (named after the case of *Calderbank v Calderbank*), which was first used in the family law courts, but which has general application.

Like a Part 36 offer, a Calderbank offer is an offer to settle, and is made in writing. Provided it is made in a genuine attempt to settle a dispute, such an offer will also be protected from disclosure to the court without joint consent of both parties until all matters of liability and quantum have been decided. Assuming it is made clear in the *Calderbank* letter that the offer is made 'without prejudice save as to costs', then it can have costs consequences, and these could resemble those under Part 36. But this is where the similarities with Part 36 end.

41 In this context, a claimant's Part 36 offers are often made in percentage terms (e.g., to accept, say, 90% of damages to be agreed or assessed in due course). This means the issue of costs can be dealt with after liability is determined but before damages have been assessed. See WB para 36.17.6 and cases mentioned there.

It is especially important to note that a *Calderbank* offer is *not* a Part 36 offer and so does not attract the automatic costs consequences *mandated* by Part 36. Only offers made in accordance with the formal requirements set out in Part 36 can do so. With a *Calderbank* offer, the court will consider the fact and terms of the offer, but only as part of the general exercise of its *discretion* on costs orders under r 44.2. This could produce the same or similar result as with a Part 36 offer, but will not necessarily do so. The court's discretion under r 44.2 is very wide.

A *Calderbank* offer will therefore be apt to give less (or less predictable) costs protection. And it certainly cannot result in a claimant being awarded the 'additional amount' under Part 36, since r 44.2 is only about orders as to costs. So if there is a choice, a party (and especially a claimant) will usually make a Part 36 offer. But on occasions a *Calderbank* offer can offer greater flexibility than a Part 36 offer - for example, where a defendant seeks enhanced costs in respect of aspects of the claimant's claims (which the defendant alleges are false and dishonest) as part of his offer to settle the genuine parts of the claimant's claim. Part 36 is not nuanced enough for this sort of settlement offer.[42]

42 See WB, para 36.2.1

revision tips

- Look at Form N242A. Note the formalities, required to trigger the Part 36 consequences. Technical defects may be overlooked but not fundamental omissions.
- To understand the implications of making and accepting (or not) Part 36 and other settlement offers, it is important to distinguish between:

  - Part 36 **vs** *Calderbank* offers

  - The costs implications of accepting a Part 36 offer within vs after the expiry of the 'relevant period'

  - The formalities of making, accepting and withdrawing Part 36 offers vs the lack of formality in 'rejecting' them.

  - The costs implications after trial of 'successful' Part 36 offers made by claimants **vs** those made by defendants.
- Watch out for adaptations to these rules as the fixed costs regime expands.
- Get a confident grasp of the basics. This will make it easier to understand the more nuanced detail. Part 36 is fertile examination territory.

It is worth reading ...

The judgments in ***SG v Hewitt*** [2012] EWCA Civ 1053, about acceptance of a Part 36 offer well after the relevant period, and when the court might depart from the usual order in such circumstances. The facts are straightforward and as the claimant was a child, you can revise that aspect of procedure too!

Foskett J's judgment in *JMX v Norfolk & Norwich Hospital NHS Foundation Trust* [2018] EWHC 185 (QB), which is mainly focused on what amounts to a 'genuine attempt to settle' in the context of a claimant's offer. It is easy to follow, sets out a bit of history and focuses on the notion of what may or may not be a 'token discount' from full liability in an offer by the claimant. Notice that the judge did not appreciate being bombarded with the 'without prejudice' correspondence, and that this case is a good example of the fact that the '10% above base rate' interest referred to in r 35.17(4) is a maximum, not a starting point!

continues ...

continued ...

The case of ***Smith v Trafford Housing Trust*** [2012] EWHC 3320 (Ch). Do not be put off by the fact that some aspects of the Part 36 rules (and rule numbers!) were different a decade ago. Just focus on what Briggs J had to say about its being a 'formidable obstacle' for a party to show that the costs consequences mandated by Part 36 would be 'unjust' (despite his finding that it would be unjust in the circumstances of this case!). In fact, the judge did decide in Mr Smith's favour (because his reputation was at stake and the Defendant's Part 36 offer did not deal with that aspect), but he made clear this was very much the exception to the strict provisions of the rule.

PART FIVE

trial matters

CHAPTER 16

Preparations for trial

Civil cases do not often go all the way to trial. Some are put down early by the court; most are compromised by the parties. Trials vary in their complexity, but one thing they all have in common is that they are very expensive. The cost of many trials will far exceed the expense of all the interim proceedings in the case put together!

If, however, the parties cannot agree a settlement, the dispute will have to be determined by the court. In such cases, there may be a number of pre-trial matters or preparations to bear in mind. These can include:

A. NOTICES

'Notices to admit' and 'notices to prove' further the overriding objective by helping to narrow the issues in a case in a cost-effective way. This shorthand is not very descriptive. To make it clearer, I will supply the missing element (in brackets).

(i) Notice to admit (facts)

A notice to admit is an invitation to another party to admit certain facts or part of a case. Thus one party may serve on another a notice requiring that other party to admit such facts or part of the serving party's case as is set out in the notice. These tend to focus on what are *essentially uncontroversial matters.*

No application to the court is required. A party just serves the notice on his opponent (no later than 21 days before trial), setting out the facts to be admitted.[1]

To the extent that the facts are admitted, they cease to be an issue at trial. Any admissions made can be used against the party making the admission but *only* in the proceedings in which the notice was served and *only* by the party who served the notice (and not any other party).[2] To the extent the facts in the notice are not admitted, there is no sanction built into this specific provision, but the CPR cost rules are wide enough to produce the result (as existed under the previous rules) that the party refusing to admit the facts in the notice may have to pay the costs of proving those facts at trial, regardless of the ultimate outcome of the case.

The cost rules require the court to have regard to the *conduct* of the parties when making an order for costs, including whether it was 'reasonable for a party to ... contest a particular issue'.[3] Much will depend, therefore, on how silly or sensible it was not to admit the fact or facts in question. The procedure must not be used oppressively, or indeed unreasonably. In other words, parties should not ask their opponents to admit what is clearly a real issue in dispute. No costs consequences would follow when an opponent predictably refuses to make such an admission.

Suppose, for example, a claim in negligence following a car accident, the outcome of which will depend on how well those in control of the cars were driving at the time. To ask the defendant to admit his negligence would be ridiculous - that is the main issue in dispute. But if the defendant had failed to admit the fact of the accident itself or where it happened, then (assuming it clearly happened when and where alleged, and nothing turns on these facts), serving on him a notice to admit would be appropriate. If he does not admit them, the claimant will still have to prove them, but the defendant will likely be ordered to pay the costs of doing so, unless he can come up with a good reason for making the claimant do so.

1 CPR, r 32.18 and see Form N226. Do not confuse a notice to admit facts with a request for further information under Part 18 (see Ch 9). The latter seeks clarification or information from an opponent in order to better understand the case to be met, while the former invites admissions from an opponent of (what should be) uncontroversial matters.

2 CPR, r 32.18(3). The court may allow a party to amend or withdraw any such admissions on such terms as it thinks just: r 32.18(4)

3 CPR, r 44.5(3). And see generally Ch 18

(ii) Notices to prove (the authenticity of documents)

The gist of this is that it is assumed, and a party is *deemed* to admit, that documents *inspected by him on disclosure* have not been tampered with or otherwise fabricated, in other words that they are authentic. This is because, generally speaking, it is not the authenticity of a document which is at issue in any given case, but rather the document's evidential or legal effect. If, however, authenticity is *disputed*, a 'notice to prove' its authenticity must be sent to the disclosing party. This puts the disclosing party on notice that authenticity of those documents is in issue.[4]

B. HUMAN RIGHTS QUESTIONS[5]

The effect of the Human Rights Act 1998 ('HRA 1998') is to make rights under the European Convention for the Protection of Human Rights and Freedoms ('Human Rights Convention') 'directly enforceable' against 'public authorities', thus obviating the need for individuals to apply to the European Court of Human Rights.[6] 'Public authorities' include, but are by no means limited to, the courts, which under s 3 must minimise interference with the Human Rights Convention, and interpret legislation so as to be compatible with it. Where a court is satisfied that a provision in primary legislation is not compatible with a Convention right, it may make a 'declaration of incompatibility.'

Lay clients are apt to find breaches of their human rights around every corner. But parties must be cautious to raise points only when appropriate.[7] The rights which are most likely to figure in civil litigation are Art 6 (right to fair trial), Art 8 (right to respect for private life), and Art 10 (freedom of expression).

4 The notice must be served by the latest date for serving witness statements or within 7 days of disclosure of the document, whichever is later: See CPR, r 32.19

5 BCP devotes an entire chapter to this subject (Ch 91).

6 The European Court of Human Rights (which sits in Strasbourg, France) is an entirely different entity and jurisdiction to the European Court of Justice (which sits in Luxembourg). Many people do not realise this.

7 See e.g., *Williams v Cowell* [2000] 1 WLR 187

Procedurally, note the following:

- Details of any human rights point raised must be set out in the statement of case (or appeal notice).[8]
- Claims for declarations of incompatibility may not be heard by a judge below the status of High Court Judge.[9]
- If there is a real prospect of a declaration of incompatibility being made, this is obviously a factor in deciding whether to transfer a case from the County Court to the High Court.[10]
- Declarations of incompatibility strike at Acts of Parliament, so the government has an interest which is protected by allowing the relevant minister to 'intervene'.[11] Appropriate notice must be given.[12]

It used to be important to remind students *not to confuse* these rules designed to ensure that sufficient safeguards are in place when arguing a human rights point in the domestic courts, with the procedure required when making a reference to the European Court of Justice regarding a point of European Union law. The UK has of course now left the EU and there is no longer any scope for such references and the relevant procedure has been revoked. At the time of writing, the Human Rights Act 1998 remains on the statute books.

C. TRIAL ARRANGEMENTS AND TIMETABLE

Trials normally take place at the court where the case is being managed (multi-track cases are usually heard at a Civil Trial Centre), but they can be held elsewhere if the circumstances demand it.[13] When a case is listed for, or is approaching trial, the court may have to make decisions (in consultation with the parties) about

8 PD 16, para 14.1
9 CPR, PD 2B, para 7A
10 CPR, r 30.3(2)(g)
11 Another means by which parties are sometimes added to proceedings. CPR, r 19.5(4)
12 CPR, r 19.5(1)
13 See, e.g., PD 28, para 8.1 (fast track) and PD 29, para 10.1 (multi-track).

any number of things, such as whether there are any preliminary issues to be dealt with (for example, if a disputed point of law is particularly relevant to the outcome); whether there is any reason why the trial (or some aspect of it) should not be conducted in public, as is the general rule;[14] and how the trial itself should 'play out'. This latter is called the trial 'timetable' and involves considerations of how long should be spent conducting various aspects of the trial, including speeches, reception of expert evidence and allocating time limits on questioning (especially cross-examination). Decisions may need to be made about the reception of certain evidence.[15] The parties can express views on these in the pre-trial checklist; in multi-track cases, such decisions will usually be made on a pre-trial review. Remember that the rules give the courts a great deal of flexibility regarding how they will deal with trials. Have a quick look at BCP 's procedural checklist 28.

D. TRIAL BUNDLES

Unless the court orders otherwise, all documents likely to be referred to in a trial must be put into a paginated file known as a 'trial bundle'. The claimant is responsible for preparing this, and so it is the claimant who should file the bundle not more than seven days and not less than three days before the start of the trial (not too early, not too late!).[16] The parties should agree the contents, so far as this is possible. Identical bundles should be made available for each party, the judge and a further set for use by the witnesses while giving evidence. Rival bundles are never lodged (although disagreements between the parties can be noted in the bundle itself). Unless there is some ruling or order to the contrary, all the documents in the bundle are admissible as evidence of their contents. Have a look at PD 32, para 27 which sets out the requirements for trial bundles, including what should be included in them and their presentation. The idea is that all participants have easy access to the relevant documents in the case

14 CPR, r 39.2. See Ch 17 for exceptions.
15 See generally BCP, para 61.16
16 CPR, r 39.5(2)

(statements of case, witness statements, expert's report and so on). In High Court cases (in the KBD and ChD), reading lists must also be lodged with the trial bundle, so that during what is often referred to as a 'reading day' the judge can easily get up to speed with the case. An agreed case summary often helps with that process.

E. SKELETON ARGUMENTS

We have seen that these are used for the more complex interim applications. They are also compulsory for High Court trials and are often a good idea for (or required by direction in) the County Court. These should *concisely* summarise the submissions to be made in relation to any substantive or controversial issues raised, and cite authorities to be relied upon (which should be in the reading list!). They should be filed two days before trial (KBD) or with the trial bundle (ChD). It is often a good idea to provide a short chronology of the important events.

Skeleton arguments allow the judge to do effective pre-reading and focus the mind of the advocate who prepares it. They are not, however, a substitute for effective questioning and oral advocacy.

F. TRIAL RUNNING ORDER

The trial will follow the timetable previously laid down (or that laid down by the trial judge at the beginning of the trial)[17] - generally trials follow a fairly predictable sequence of events:

Opening speech (if required)

It is usually the claimant who begins, as it is his case. An opening speech should put the case into context, but it can be dispensed with. A judge, having read the papers in the trial bundle, may feel it is unnecessary.[18]

17 The trial judge may confirm or vary any timetable given previously, or if none has been given set his own: see, e.g., PD 29, para 10.3

18 See, e.g., PD 29, para 10.2

Claimant's case

The claimant presents his case. This includes real and documentary evidence, and of course the evidence-in-chief, cross examination (and, if necessary re-examination) of witnesses. This is discussed in more detail in Chapter 17.

Submission of no case to answer

This is rare in civil cases. If the defendant is going to make such a submission, then the time to do this is at the end of the claimant's case, although usually the defendant will first be asked whether he wants to call any evidence (you might think he would not, if the claimant's case is weak enough to give rise to a submission of no case), because it is considered rather compromising to ask the single judge who in a civil case (usually) sits alone and is the trier of both fact and law, to rule on the merits of the claim if the evidence is incomplete. If the defendant, having been given the opportunity, decides to call no evidence, then the submission of no case will be determined on the balance of probabilities (this is really rather like hastening the end of the trial, and judgment will be entered for whichever party succeeds on the submission).

If (unusually) the defendant were not given the choice, the submission should be determined by reference to whether the claimant has no real prospect of success. In this situation, were the submission to fail, then the defendant would be allowed to carry on and call his evidence in the usual way.[19]

Defence case

After the claimant, it is the turn of the defence. If the defence is to call evidence, it may (but usually does not) make an opening speech. It then calls its evidence in the same way as the claimant. Where there is more than one defendant, they present their evidence in the order in which they appear on the record (for example, on the statements of case).

19 See generally BCP, para 61.45

Closing speeches

Where the defendant has called evidence, the defence closing speech goes before that given by the claimant. Closing speeches should be focused on inferences to be drawn from the evidence and any legal points that have arisen. They should be germane and persuasive. Remember, most civil trials are in front of a single, professional judge - this is a very different audience than most criminal trials, where speeches are more commonly directed at lay people (magistrates or juries).

Judgment

After the trial, the judge must decide the case and give judgment.[20] This often happens immediately, but in complex cases judgment can be reserved. Once all the evidence has been heard (for example, after speeches), the parties are not usually allowed to adduce more evidence, but a judge may accede to a request to reopen if judgment has not yet been given, if to do so would be in keeping with the overriding objective. Once judgment is given (but before it has been recorded), the test is much more as it would be if the case went on appeal (and if the Court of Appeal would give permission to hear new evidence,[21] then it would probably be sensible for the judge to do so at this point).

On the rare occasions where a civil trial is heard by judge and jury (for example, defamation) then the procedure and conduct of the trial will much more mimic that in Crown Court cases.[22]

G. NON-ATTENDANCE AT TRIAL

What happens if a party fails to attend trial? Under CPR r 39.3(1) the court may proceed with a trial despite the non-attendance of a party, and may strike out the claim or defence (and any counterclaim or defence to counterclaim) of the absent party. As you might expect, this discretion should be exercised with great care. In

20 And deal with costs, as to which see Ch 18
21 For appeals, see Ch 19
22 See generally *It's Criminal!*

deciding whether to grant an adjournment or proceed under r 39.3, the judge should have regard to all the circumstances of the case (e.g., reasons for non-attendance, disadvantage to the other side, length of probable delay, effect of delay on memories of witnesses, risk of wrong decision being made and so on).[23]

Note that parties can be considered to be 'present' if their lawyer attends, even if they themselves are not there, *unless* the court has ordered a party to attend *in person*, in which case they cannot be present by representation, or even by videolink![24]

Where it is the claimant who does not attend the trial, then it is open to the court immediately to dismiss the case (since the burden of proof is on the claimant) or to strike out the claim under r 39.3(1)(b). The defendant need not do anything, unless a counterclaim has been made. The court may also strike out the absent claimant's defence to the counterclaim, but will still require the defendant to prove its counterclaim in order to get judgment. For the same reason, if it is the defendant who has failed to attend, the court may strike out the defence, but will also require the claimant to prove its case. This is logical since the burden of proof is always on the party asserting its claim. But in both these latter situations the court will be proportionate about what it expects of the attending party - often only requiring reference to the statements of case and witness statements, both of which should contain statements of truth.[25]

And if no party attends (how bad is that!), the court may strike out 'the whole of the proceedings'.[26]

Not surprisingly, the court has power both to restore any proceedings which were struck out due to non-attendance,[27] and to set aside any judgment entered as a result.[28] Applications to restore or set-aside are made under Part 23 and must be supported by evidence.[29]

It is important to note that the court's discretion to restore and/or set-aside is not a broad one. The court may grant such an application but *only if* three conditions are *all*

23 *General Medical Council v Adeogba* [2016] EWCA Civ 162

24 *Falmouth House Ltd v Abou-Hamdan* [2017] EWHC 779 (Ch), cited at WB, para 39.3.4. I can easily imagine a tricky exam question on this point!

25 See WB paras 39.3.4 and 39.3.5

26 CPR, r 39.3(1)(a)

27 CPR, r 39.3(2)

28 CPR, r 39.3(3)

29 CPR, r 39.3(4)

met, namely (i) the applicant acted *promptly* once becoming aware of the need to make the application, (ii) there was a *good reason* for not attending the trial, *and* (iii) the applicant has a *reasonable* prospect of success at trial.[30] If these three requirements are satisfied, the court then has a discretion whether to restore proceedings and/or set aside, but it would be a very exceptional case where the court would not grant the application once this 'strict trio' of conditions has been met. Further, such cases are fact-specific, and the discretion is subject to the overriding objective. In particular, when deciding whether the three conditions have been met, the court should not be overly rigorous or judgmental, either about the applicant's case or conduct.[31] The right to a fair trial is an important one.

revision tips

- Have a look at what is on a pre-trial checklist. This is Form N170 and can be found on the WB online service via Westlaw.
- Have a quick look at BCP's procedural checklist 28.

It is worth reading ...

The judgments in ***Williams v Cowell*** [2000] 1 WLR 187, an interesting case about a bi-lingual Welshman who refused to speak English in court (even though it was his second language). He claimed that being forced to do so violated his human rights. There is a heartfelt plea from the judges (one of whose surnames is Judge!) about not turning trials into 'human rights seminars'.

Mohun-Smith v TBO Investments Ltd [2016] EWCA Civ 403. This was a case of the very strict requirements of CPR r 39.3(5) running up against a very strict trial judge, who was unimpressed with the sick note and lack of alacrity of the defendant, who by this time had no legal representation. The Court of Appeal makes clear that judges in these circumstances should be rather more generous spirited and open minded in deciding these matters than the trial judge in this case had been.

30 See CPR r 39.3(5), which assumes there is no other procedural defect rendering any judgment irregular or a nullity. See WB para 39.3.7

31 See comments of Master of the Rolls in ***Bank of Scotland v Pereira*** [2011] EWCA Civ 241 and also ***Mohun-Smith v TBO Investments*** [2016] EWCA Civ 403, cited in WB, para 39.3.7

CHAPTER 17

Evidential matters in civil cases

By and large whether a claim succeeds or fails at trial will depend on the facts of the case. What view the court takes on these will, in turn, depend on the quality of the evidence before it. It is therefore very important to have a firm grasp of the rules and principles about the admissibility and reception of evidence in civil cases, not only for any examination you will be required to pass (that goes without saying) but also as a foundation for embarking on practice with confidence.

Of necessity this is an overview of a vast subject. Because the strict rules of evidence do not apply to small claims track cases,[1] the focus here will be on the other tracks. For more depth and detail, consult the text of your choice.[2] If the truth be told, criminal evidence is the more entertaining branch of the family, and most evidence textbooks will concentrate on it. It is also the focus of the evidence chapters in the companion to this book, *It's Criminal! A Guide to Learning Criminal Litigation, Evidence and Sentencing* ('It's Criminal!').[3] BCP usefully has an entire chapter devoted to civil evidence, written by Adrian Keane, who, with Paul McKeown, is the author of the excellent *Modern Law of Evidence* ('Modern Law').[4]

Before reading on, you should ensure you have a grasp of the basic concepts

1 CPR r 27.8/PD 27, para 4.3

2 If you have a choice. Textbooks differ in their approach, and you may find that one works better for you than another. It is like cars - take a test drive before committing yourself to a major purchase!

3 *It's Criminal!* by the author (Worth Publishing, latest edition).

4 Oxford University Press. Any refs here are to the 14th edition (2022). Unless you are provided with a specific book, always use the latest edition of any text you rely on.

(especially relevance, admissibility and weight, and the difference between these) and terminology (for example how different 'types' of evidence are described) of the law of evidence. It is especially important to understand the *distinction between facts in issue and collateral facts.* The latter are those that relate to a subsidiary matter which, while not among the facts in issue in a case, can nevertheless affect whether a fact in issue has been proved or not. Examples are matters going to the *competence* of a witness to testify, and facts relevant to some other *pre-condition to the admissibility* of an item of evidence (these are matters which need to be determined before the evidence is admitted, and so they are also known as 'preliminary' facts or issues). The most common example of collateral facts, however, are those which affect the *credibility* of the evidence, although it is important to note that there are times when evidence relevant to credibility merges with evidence directly relevant to a fact in issue, and indeed an item of evidence can be relevant to *both* of these.

In addition, there are two important principles to bear in mind when considering the evidential issues in this chapter.

(i) Whether an item of evidence is admissible will depend in the first instance on the law of evidence. Evidence must be *relevant*, but it will only be admissible if, in addition, it is *not excluded* by any of the rules of evidence.[5] These are considered below.

(ii) The CPR gives the court *in civil cases* an *overarching discretion to exclude* otherwise admissible evidence, if this is in keeping with the overriding objective. It is important always to bear this in mind. The rules specifically provide that the court may control the evidence in a case by giving directions as to *what evidence it wants to hear, on what issues and in what form.*[6]

5 Historically, the common law rules of evidence tended to focus on what could not be admitted at trial, not what could. Modern statutes are often more positively expressed.

6 CPR, r 32.1, and r 32.2(3). See precise wording.

This chapter covers a lot of territory. For the sake of convenience, I have divided it into three sections: (1) pre-trial evidential considerations; (2) admissibility and reception of special categories of evidence; and (3) witnesses and the course of testimony at trial.

1. PRE-TRIAL EVIDENTIAL CONSIDERATIONS

A. BURDEN AND STANDARD OF PROOF IN CIVIL CASES[7]

Burden of proof

The burden of proof is the obligation imposed on a party to *prove* a fact in issue. A party who fails to discharge this burden will lose on the issue in question. This is often referred to as the 'legal burden' and should be *clearly distinguished* from the so-called 'evidential burden', which is not a burden of proof at all.

In civil cases, the pleadings will initially tell us what facts are in issue - they will consist of all of the matters (not admitted by the defendant) which a claimant must prove in order to win his case, plus any matters raised by the defendant (not admitted by the claimant) which must be proved in order for that aspect of the defence (and/or any counterclaim) to succeed. The facts in issue are thus partly determined by the *substantive law* (for example, the constituent elements of a breach of contract claim), and partly by the *statements of case.*[8]

It is important to understand that only *one* party bears a burden of *proof* on any given fact in issue.

In civil cases the incidence of the legal burden of proof may sometimes be pre-determined by agreement between the parties concerned, as in some standard form contracts of insurance.[9] Sometimes, it is allotted by statute.[10] But generally

7 At the time of writing, this topic has been removed from the Bar Exam syllabus

8 If you put statements of case side by side, and contrast and compare, it should be clear what the issues in dispute are. Later concessions may narrow the issues.

9 See BCP, para 49.38

10 See *ibid*, para 49.39

speaking the legal burden of proof is determined by reference to various, sometimes competing, common law principles. The first general principle is: 'he who asserts must prove (not he who denies)'. So if, for example, the claimant sues in negligence, it will be for him to assert in the particulars of claim, and thus prove (except as admitted by the defendant) the nature of the duty of care owed by the defendant; breach of that duty by the defendant; and the recoverable damage suffered as a result. And, if, for example, the defendant alleges contributory negligence, the burden is on him to prove this. In 99% of cases, the principle 'he who asserts must prove'[11] tells us in a civil case where the burden of proof lies.

But sometimes, especially when dealing with contractual clauses which limit or exclude liability, it can be difficult to know who is asserting what. There may also be a particular outcome which the court, in the circumstances, thinks is fair. In such cases, other principles come into play, including: 'it is more difficult to prove a negative than a positive' and 'when in doubt place the burden on the party who can more easily discharge it'.

In the case of *Constantine (Joseph) SS Line Ltd v Imperial Smelting Corp Ltd*[12] a ship, which had been hired out on charter, was destroyed by an explosion. The charterers claimed damages from the ship owners for breach of contract (because the ship was no longer able to carry its contracted load). The ship owners' defence was frustration. The charterers argued that the owners could not rely on frustration unless they proved that the explosion was not their fault (or the fault of their on-board crew). Because the cause of the explosion was unknown, the allocation of the burden of proof on this issue (was it caused by negligence or not?) became decisive, as is the way with these sorts of cases.[13] The House of Lords, concerned to arrive at a just result, held that, once the owners had proved the frustrating event (the explosion), the charterers bore the burden of proving fault on the part of the ship

11 Or should have been asserted in the case of a poorly drafted statement of case: see ***BHB Billiton Petroleum Ltd v Dalmone SpA*** [2003] EWCA Civ 179 which said that the pleadings are a guide to what is being asserted, but not necessarily definitive.

12 [1945] AC 154

13 Although courts should resolve cases in this way only as a last resort and not as an excuse for indecision: ***Stephens v Cannon*** [2005] EWCA Civ 222

owners because it was difficult, if not impossible, for the latter to prove a negative, in other words, that they had not been negligent. As Viscount Simon LC put it:[14]

> Does the application of the doctrine require that the owners should affirmatively prove that those on board were keeping a good lookout, were obscuring lights, were steering as directed and so forth?

Ease of proof is the principle which unites the *Constantine* case with that of *Levison v Patent Steam Carpet Cleaning Co*,[15] but the result was different. The difference is sometimes explained by the fact that the latter is a bailment case, but in reality this was a device to achieve justice in the case. The claimants had sent an expensive Chinese carpet to the defendants for cleaning. The defendants failed to return it and concluded that it had been stolen. They relied on a clause in their contract with the claimants limiting their liability for loss, the effect of which was to make them liable for £44 rather than the £900 the carpet was worth. Lord Denning MR hated exclusion clauses on the best of days, and they were only operative if the party relying on them had not been in 'fundamental breach' of contract. The question then arose: was it for the Levisons to prove the defendant's breach or for the defendants to disprove it? The Court of Appeal held that it was for the defendants to prove that they had not been guilty of a fundamental breach, because they could more easily discharge the burden. The Levisons did not know what went on at the cleaner's premises; the defendants were the ones who knew what had happened to the carpet once they took possession of it and so were better placed to show that they had handled the carpet properly (or not, as it turned out).

In civil cases, then, the approach to such quandaries is largely pragmatic and guided by fairness in different circumstances. Thus, on those rare occasions (and they are rare) when 'he who asserts must prove' does not provide the answer to the

14 Op. cit. at pp.161-2
15 [1978] 1 QB 69

question (or seems to answer it in the wrong way, perhaps), the court will be apt to find it by asking which party would find it easier to discharge the burden of proof on the issue in question, even if that involves proving a negative.

Standard of proof

Unless in a special category of case,[16] the standard of proof in civil cases is the 'balance of probabilities'.[17] This is so even where the allegation is so serious as to amount to the commission of a criminal offence (for example, fraud or assault). The courts wrestled for some time with how to deal with such allegations in a civil context, but it is now clear (if it was not before) that the *standard stays the same*, however serious the allegation. Previous attempts, including that of Lord Nichols in *Re H and others*[18] to distinguish between the standard of proof (which is immutable) and the strength of evidence which might be required to meet that standard, were frowned upon (perhaps a bit unfairly) in *Re B (Children) FC*,[19] another child abuse case where nobody's evidence could be believed on some key issues of fact. The court was at pains to say, in slightly exasperated tones,[20] that:

> Once and for all, there is only one civil standard and that is proof that a fact in issue more probably occurred than not … Inherent probabilities are simply something to be taken into account, where relevant, in deciding where the truth lies … [and] neither the seriousness of the allegation nor the seriousness of the consequences should make any difference to the standard of proof to be applied in determining the facts.

16 Committal proceedings, for example (see Ch 19) or where required by statute, such as applications for Sexual Offender Orders under the Crime and Disorder Act 1998, s 2. See BCP, para 49.41

17 This translates into proving that it is 'more probable' or 'more likely' than not that something happened.

18 [1996] AC 563 (a gruesome child abuse case).

19 [2008] 2 FLR 141 (UKHL 35), [2009] 1 AC 11

20 Lord Hoffmann quoted here, at *ibid* [13]. In an earlier case he had given a useful example by saying that as a matter of common sense it would take more compelling evidence to satisfy the court that *"the creature walking in Regent's Park was, more likely than not, to be a lioness, than to be satisfied to the same standard that is was an Alsatian."* ***Secretary of State for the Home***

'Evidential burden'

The evidential burden is *not* a burden of *proof.* It is an obligation to put forward enough evidence on a particular issue to allow the question to go before the fact finder for a decision; the burden is discharged when there is sufficient evidence to justify, as a possibility, a favourable finding. The evidential burden is a low threshold - certainly discharging it does not by any stretch mean the legal burden of proof will be discharged. A party bearing a legal burden of proof on an issue, who cannot even discharge the evidential burden on that same issue, will lose, without the other side having to say anything.[21]

By and large the party with the legal burden on an issue also bears the evidential burden, so they tend to go together as a twin-set. There are several exceptions in criminal cases where a defendant has an obligation, when raising certain defences,[22] to put forward sufficient evidence to make the issue a live one; but the burden of proof remains squarely on the prosecution to disprove that defence beyond reasonable doubt. The only situation in a civil case where the legal burden of proof and an evidential burden might be 'split' between parties in a similar way is by virtue of the operation of a rebuttable presumption 'of the evidential variety',[23] where adducing some evidence to the contrary is all it takes to rebut the presumption operating in favour of the person with the legal burden of proof. This is discussed in the next section.

Presumptions[24]

So-called 'presumptions' can have an effect on the burden and standard of proof. They operate, to a greater or lesser degree, by allowing fact finders to draw certain conclusions ('the presumed fact') from other facts ('the primary facts'). One tends to refer to three 'types' of presumption, although only one is a 'real' presumption.

Department v Rehman [2001] 1 AC 153, at [55].

21 Except, *"I win!"* Submissions of no case to answer are much more prevalent in criminal cases than in civil, where such actions would likely be struck out or summarily determined well before trial.

22 For example, self-defence, duress. See generally, *It's Criminal!* Ch 15

23 *See below*

24 This is a short summary. Check your syllabus for required detail. Not all include presumptions, as such, for examination purposes.

(a) 'Presumption of fact'

This is not a presumption so much as an inference to be drawn, as a matter of common sense, from certain facts. Such presumptions are really just examples of commonly recurring circumstantial evidence. The way these operate is that if the primary fact is proved, the presumed fact *may* be presumed. There is no *compulsion*.

Examples from the criminal law include notions like the 'doctrine of recent possession', which is an inference to be drawn from the fact that a person is in possession of recently stolen goods. An example more germane to civil cases is the so-called 'continuance of life' which allows a fact-finder to conclude that if a person was alive on a certain date then, unless there is evidence to suggest otherwise, that person was still alive on a later date. This depends, of course, on how long the period is and how well the person was in the first place.

This presumption can also work in individual cases: as in the case of the missing canoeist who 'came back from the grave'?[25] He was presumed dead on the basis of the alleged circumstances of his disappearance (parts of a broken canoe, clothes found washed up on the beach and so forth) and the fact that he had seemingly not reappeared, which made it a logical inference.[26] The coroner had been under no compulsion to agree, however, because less than seven years had passed.[27]

(b) Irrebuttable (or conclusive) presumption of law

This is not a presumption so much as a rule of substantive law. It works like this: if the primary fact is proved, the presumed fact *must* be presumed. It is compulsory. This kind of presumption is incapable of being rebutted.

One good example of this in civil cases is the deeming provision regarding service (for example, service of the claim form),[28] which effectively creates an irrebuttable presumption of the date of service. Another is s 13 Civil Evidence Act

25 The case of John Darwin and his wife has been documented on several occasions, most recently in 2022 along with a TV dramatisation.

26 As it happened, he hid in the house next door while his wife waited to claim the life insurance money, then they both fled to Panama.

27 At which point the 'presumption of death' could have been relied upon. *See below*.

28 See generally Ch 4

1968, which says that in the context of defamation proceedings, a person convicted of an offence shall be *conclusively* taken to have committed that offence. This is a rule to avoid re-running criminal cases in the context of the civil claim.[29]

(c) Rebuttable presumptions of law

These are true presumptions, of which there are many examples.[30] Their purpose is two-fold: firstly, to *save time and effort* when in 99 cases out of 100 the presumed fact follows from the primary fact (for example, the 'presumption of legitimacy') or, to *resolve a dilemma* (for example, the 'presumption of death'). As to the latter, these are only applicable when there really is a dilemma. If the court will make the inference you want from the facts at hand, you do not need to resort to a dilemma-resolving presumption!

Rebuttable presumptions operate as follows: if the primary fact is proved, the presumed fact *must* be presumed, *unless* there is evidence to the contrary.

A rebuttable presumption thus casts a burden on the party against whom it operates. How onerous this burden is (that is to say, how much evidence is needed to rebut the presumption) varies from presumption to presumption. In some cases, the presumption can be displaced if *some evidence* to the contrary is produced (a so-called 'evidential presumption'); in others, it can only be displaced on the balance of probabilities (a so-called 'persuasive presumption'). As a broad generality, the greater the social interest in the state of affairs to which the presumption is directed, the harder it is to rebut. For example, the presumption of legitimacy is harder to rebut than the presumption of proper working order, since the law is reluctant to brand people bastards!

As one example, the presumption of death works like this: if there is no acceptable evidence that a person was alive at some time during a continuous period

29 Civil Evidence Act 1968, s 13(1)

30 See generally discussion at BCP para 49.11ff

of seven years or more, that person will be presumed to have died at some time during that period if it can be proved that:

- people exist who would be likely to have heard from them during that period;

and

- they have not heard from them during that period;

and

- all appropriate enquiries have been made[31]

Note that the presumption is merely that death occurred at the latest by the end of the seven years. It says *nothing about the date of death.* It would seem that, in civil cases anyway, this is an 'evidential presumption',[32] which would be consistent with the law being reluctant to declare dead, people who may be alive! But there is no clear authority, perhaps because any substantial evidence that the person was alive would stop the presumption from operating in the first place.

Presumptions of this kind may conflict. If they are of equal strength (for example both 'evidential presumptions'), they are thought to cancel each other out, so that the case is determined on the basis of the ordinary rules regarding the burden of proof, although again the court will have regard to policy considerations.

B. PRIVILEGE AND RELATED CONCEPTS

Many of the common law rules of evidence developed out of a desire to ensure a fair trial. For the same reason, openness underpins much of the conduct of civil litigation. The rationale for the principles relating to privilege and public interest immunity, however, has less to do with these motivations, important though they are,

31 *Chard v Chard* [1956] P 259

32 See *Prudential Assurance Co v Edmunds* (1877) 2 App Cas 487

and more with another competing idea which is given priority, namely that there are some occasions when the benefit in withholding evidence from inspection by the court or an opponent should prevail over the public interest in openness and putting all of one's 'cards on the table'. For this reason, it particularly impinges on the rules about disclosure of evidence.[33] Occasionally secrecy will trump transparency.

It is important to distinguish between the various forms of privilege, between privilege and public interest immunity, and between privilege and the without prejudice protection. There are essentially two types of privilege: the privilege against self-incrimination, and legal professional privilege (which itself takes two forms). These privileges are personal - they can only be waived by *the person* they protect. There is also the protection of 'without prejudice' communications (often referred to as a privilege, but perhaps more accurately described as a protection), which (if applicable) must be waived by *all* parties whom it protects.[34]

Public interest immunity ('PII') is not a privilege as such - it imposes a *duty*, not a right to withhold disclosure and obliges the court to exclude evidence on the grounds that its disclosure would damage the public interest. Such an obligation cannot be waived by anyone. PII can and should be distinguished from legal professional privilege.

The litigation context in which these issues usually arise in the first instance is during disclosure of documents and other evidence. The basic principles are as follows:

(i) Privilege against self-incrimination

The privilege against self-incrimination is as old as the rule of law. It is designed to protect a person from being compelled by the State to give incriminating evidence against himself. The classic formulation was given by Lord Goddard LJ when he said that 'the rule is that no-one is bound to answer questions if the answer would, in the

33 See generally Ch 9

34 For special rules about the protection (or not as the case may be) of journalist's sources, see Contempt of Court Act 1981, s 10

opinion of the judge, have a *tendency to expose* [him] to any *criminal* charge, penalty or forfeiture which the judge regards as reasonably likely to be preferred or sued for'.[35] The privilege is of particular importance, of course, in criminal cases; less so in civil cases, where some judges have considered its invocation archaic and unjustified.[36] Indeed, over time statute has whittled away at the privilege in some specialist civil contexts where the public interest in obtaining the information is thought to outweigh the 'right to silence.' There are now various legislative provisions which require specified persons in specific circumstances to answer questions or produce documents or information, notwithstanding that to do so may tend to incriminate them.

A prime example in civil cases relates to search orders,[37] where the right to rely on the privilege to avoid compliance was removed by s 72 Senior Courts Act 1981 in cases involving intellectual property and passing off. Although the privilege against self-incrimination may not be relied upon in such cases to avoid complying with the order, there is a protective quid pro quo: namely that the answer and information supplied as a result of complying with the order may not be used in evidence in any resulting prosecution. The latter charge would have to be made out using other evidence.

In other cases, the threat or risk of self-incrimination may be removed by the promise that the disclosed evidence or information will not be used in any criminal proceedings. Such safeguards and trade-offs keep these specific inroads into the privilege against self-incrimination from interfering with the Art 6 right to a fair trial.[38]

(ii) Legal professional privilege

Legal professional privilege is a long-standing fundamental right which is central to the administration of justice. It is the right of the *client* (and survives their death), and not their lawyers.

35 *Blunt v Park Lane Hotel* [1942] 2 KB 253, at 257, CA

36 See e.g., *Lord Templeman in AT&T Istel v Tully*, as cited in *Modern Law*, p. 728

37 See Ch 7

38 See generally *Modern Law*, p.733ff and WB 31.3.31

There are two 'heads' of legal professional privilege. It is important to distinguish between them:

Head 1: 'Legal advice privilege'

Confidential communications (whether written or oral) between a *professional legal representative and client* made in connection with the giving or receiving of *legal* advice to that client are protected by legal advice privilege. *This is so whether or not litigation is contemplated or underway at the time*, and includes documents which evidence or reveal the substance of any such communications, as well as documents intended as such, even if in fact they were not communicated.

It is important to note that the giving or receiving of legal advice must be the '*dominant purpose*' behind the communication in order to be protected by this privilege.[39] Documents do not magically become privileged by the fact that at some time they managed to find their way into the hands of a solicitor.[40]

Here the communication is a two-way street and can be thought of in the form of a straight line, with the client at one end and the legal advisor at the other. The client gives the legal advisor information (orally and/or in documents), wanting to get legal advice; the legal advisor communicates that legal advice to the client or seeks more information in order to do so (orally and/or in documents). This can be an on-going, oft-repeated process.

Thus, legal advice privilege is not confined simply to the act of telling a client about the law; conversely, not all advice (and certainly not every communication) is privileged. Communications in furtherance of a crime or fraud are a well-recognised (and sensible) exception to the principle - it is no business of lawyers to be hatching criminal plots! The purpose of the communication is to be broadly construed, but in essence to be protected the advice must be sought or given in a relevant *legal* context.

39 *R (Jet2.Com Ltd) v Civil Aviation Authority* [2020] EWCA Civ at [95], which borrowed the notion of a 'dominant purpose' test from litigation privilege (although the purpose is different. The legal advice sought or received need have nothing to do with litigation under this head of legal professional privilege).

40 See WB para 31.3.11

In complex cases, issues can arise about who is a client (if not an individual) and what is legal (as opposed, say, to financial) advice.[41] But the essential idea is straightforward enough. The reason for this privilege, of course, is that it is in the public interest that people should be able to get legal advice in complete confidence. Other parties are therefore not entitled to know of the content of such communications, unless the privilege is waived (by the client).

Head 2: 'Litigation privilege'

This brings a third person into the equation. *Confidential communications* between a professional legal advisor and/or his client and a *third party*[42] are privileged where the '*dominant purpose*' in creating the document (or making the communication) is to use it or its contents for the purpose of adversarial *litigation* which at that time was pending or 'reasonably in prospect'.[43] Proceedings are 'reasonably in prospect' if they are a real likelihood, rather than a mere possibility. This privilege includes obtaining and collecting evidence to be used in litigation as well as getting information which may lead to the obtaining of such evidence.

The typical example of a document covered by litigation privilege is an expert's report. So long as the right person (that is, the person *commissioning* the document) has the right motivation (*litigation*), then it is immaterial whether the litigation actually takes place. Indeed the purpose of the communication can be to head off, avoid or settle litigation.

The 'dominant purpose' part of the test is important. Where there is a second, non-litigation purpose in the creation of the document, then to be protected it must be shown (by the party asserting the privilege) that the litigation purpose was clearly paramount at the time the document was *created*. In *Lask v Gloucester Health Authority*, for example, it was held that an accident report which was required by NHS rules

41 See instructive list of examples where the privilege attached in BCP, para 50.108. And see generally WB, para 31.3.6

42 Not in the Part 20 sense of course. Here the lines of communication can be seen as forming a triangle so as to involve three people instead of two.

43 *Waugh v British Railway Board* [1980] AC 521

to help prevent such accidents in future was not privileged, since the ability of the health authority's solicitors to make use of the report if a claim were made was at best only an equal function of the report. That was not good enough - the litigation purpose must be *the* dominant purpose for the creation of the document.[44]

The rationale behind litigation privilege is that parties should be free to prepare for and make decisions about litigation confidentially. A party thus need not produce such documents for inspection at the disclosure of documents stage. This can be useful when, for example, litigants receive an unfavourable report from their own expert. As we shall see, however, such evidence as one proposes to *rely* on must be *exchanged* pre-trial[45] in the interests of openness.[46] In effect, the party seeking to adduce the evidence must waive his privilege in the information before (not merely as) the evidence is adduced. This is so no-one is taken by surprise, and everyone can respond sensibly to the evidence at trial. But a party who does not want to rely on such a privileged document, can (usually) bin it.[47]

Waiver of legal professional privilege

Legal professional privilege belongs to, and can *only* be waived by, the client. Waiver can be expressed, implied or even unintentional. Often the purpose and degree of the waiver is clear - a typical example was referred to in the previous paragraph when discussing the exchange of expert evidence pre-trial. Sometimes the content of certain legal advice may be important to explain relevant behaviour on the part of the client (or the advisor), and the question may arise as to the *extent* to which the privilege has been waived. The answer will depend upon what has been disclosed, why and in what circumstances. There is a public interest in upholding legal professional privilege, but a court may decide there has been a waiver if (and to the extent that) it would be misleading or unfair for one party to benefit from a partial

44 (1991) 2 Med LR 379. And see WB, para 31.3.9

45 Exchange of expert evidence comes after disclosure of documents in the typical timetable. See e.g., PD 28, para 3.11

46 If the evidence is to be adduced in open court, its confidentiality no longer really needs protecting.

47 Although it might well provoke a re-evaluation of the case. And sometimes the price of permission to rely on one expert is showing your opponent the report you now want to bin. *See below*. An obviously privileged document mistakenly shown to an opposing party may only be used by that party with court permission: CPR, r 31.20

disclosure without also being required to disclose more. Decisions on waiver (and its extent) should be fact-sensitive; the underlying principle is that of fairness.[48]

In *Re D (a child),*[49] for example, the mother of the child in question needed to explain away two diametrically opposed accounts of the father's involvement (or not) in the child's injuries. In one witness statement she said the father was blameless; in a second, she said it was the father who had injured the child. She explained the change of heart by reference to various meetings with her solicitor and barrister and set out parts of what was discussed in those meetings. It was held that she had waived legal professional privilege in all the meetings with her legal advisors over the five week period leading up to the change of story which was set out in the second witness statement. This was so despite the fact that (1) her witness statements had been drafted by her solicitor and (2) the waiver was unintentional (neither she nor her solicitor realised that the material in her second witness statement would amount to a waiver of privilege).

(iii) 'Without Prejudice' communications

In a sense this can be viewed as something of a 'mirror image' of litigation privilege, because it also involves the solicitor or client and another person - specifically the other party to the dispute. The 'without prejudice' rule works like this: private communications, whether oral or written, made in a *genuine attempt to settle* an existing dispute may not be given in evidence or otherwise disclosed to the court at any subsequent trial of the matter (the other side, of course, knows all about it). Not all communications are protected, just those directed at attempting to settle the claim. The purpose of this rule, which protects both sides jointly and can only be waived if *both* sides agree,[50] is to encourage willing, open and effective negotiation by removing the fear that any admissions apparently made during the exchange will be used at

48 *AG v VD* [2020] EWHC 1947 (Fam), and see discussion at WB, para 31.3.24

49 [2011] 4 All ER 434

50 No negative inference can be drawn if one party is unwilling to waive the protection. See Jackson, para 5.20

trial against the party who made them, the attempts to settle having (rather obviously) failed. If such communications were not so protected, most ADR processes would be significantly undermined.[51] There is thus a focus on protection from the revelation of *concessions or admissions*, although most attempts to by-pass the rule by cutting and pasting around such admissions in otherwise protected correspondence have failed.[52]

The 'without prejudice' status of a communication should be made clear, often by writing those words at the top of the correspondence. It is possible to exclude the protection for specific purposes. In particular, it is common to make offers of settlement 'without prejudice except as to costs', which means that the protection lasts until the time (after liability and quantum have been determined) when the court needs to make a costs order, at which point reference can be made to the correspondence. This is the usual means by which a court can factor into their order as to costs the attempts made by the parties (if any) to settle the matter by other means. It is important to remember that in order to be able to refer to an offer of settlement in this way the magic words 'except as to cost' must follow the words 'without prejudice'. [53]

Bear in mind too that the court will look at the substance, rather than the form of the communication, so that the over-enthusiastic use the words 'without prejudice' (usually written in bold letters by amateurs) does not necessarily afford protection to the document (and vice versa - a document may be protected even if those words are not used). Most legal advisors properly label their correspondence as required, but it is the context (existing dispute) and *purpose* behind the communication (genuine attempt to settle that dispute) which matters.[54]

Note too that, in effect, the protection extends to attempts at settlement which *fail*. If or to the extent that they *succeed and the case settles*, the protection has served its purpose and is no longer needed because there will be no litigation of that dispute. So if, for example, it later became necessary to prove the fact or terms of *the settlement*

51 It does not really matter if no litigation has yet started so long as the main purpose of the communication is to settle the dispute and it is foreseeable that in the absence of a settlement litigation would ensure: ***Barnetson v Framlington Group Ltd*** [2007] EWCA Civ 502, cited in WB, para 31.3.39

52 See, e.g., ***Re New Gadget Shop Ltd*** [2005] EWHC 1606 (CH)

53 Sometimes the (old fashioned) wording is used: 'without prejudice save as to costs'. See Jackson, para 5.21

54 Communications which do not meet these criteria will not be protected by the without prejudice rule. See *ibid*, para 5.23 for some examples.

agreement itself, the previously protected communications leading up to that settlement would now become admissible for this limited purpose.[55]

(iv) Public Interest Immunity ('PII')

This is a very different concept to those discussed above. Certain documents must be withheld from disclosure and/or inspection if it is found that revealing their existence or contents (or both) would be injurious to the public interest. Typical examples in a civil litigation context might be Cabinet minutes, social work records, and the design of military or police equipment. Public interest immunity is thus a *duty, not a privilege* and such claims can fall into two types: class claims (a claim that all documents of a certain class, for example diplomatic dispatches relating to national security, need to be protected) and individual claims (a claim that a specific document needs protection because of its contents). The former are regarded more sceptically than once was the case.

Typically, a relevant minister provides a certificate stating the grounds for objecting to disclosure and/or inspection. The certificate is not conclusive and it is for the *court* in each instance to determine where the public interest lies.[56] To this end the court must *balance* the public interest in concealment against the public interest in the fair and open administration of justice.

It is for the party seeking inspection to show why the public interest lies in openness. This can be made difficult by CPR, r 31.19(1), which says a PII claim may be made *without notice*, and any order made on such application must *not*, unless the court orders otherwise, be served on any other person. Thus under Part 31, it strikes both at disclosure *and* inspection, unlike legal professional privilege which prevents inspection but not disclosure as such.[57] With a PII claim, the other side may have no idea what is going on, which can have obvious human rights implications.

55 See *ibid*, para 5.25. If the without prejudice principle was being abused, justice might also demand disclosure of otherwise protected communications, but this would be exceptional: ***Unilever plc v Proctor & Gamble Co*** [2000] 1 WLR 2436.

56 *Conway v Rimmer* [1968] AC 910

57 Since a privileged document's existence appears, however obliquely described, on the disclosure list. See generally Ch 9

2. ADMISSIBILITY AND RECEPTION OF DIFFERENT CATEGORIES OF EVIDENCE

A. OPINION EVIDENCE

As a general rule, opinion evidence is not admissible at trial. Witnesses must normally confine themselves to telling the court about the facts, and not express opinions about those facts. To do so would either be considered an irrelevance (unless the state of mind of the holder of the opinion is pertinent) or an intrusion on the role of the judge[58] deciding the case, whose opinion is really the only one that matters. There are, however, some *important exceptions* to this general rule. The main ones are: (i) opinions of other courts allowed by statute, (ii) the perceptions of witnesses of fact, and most importantly (iii) the opinions of experts.

(i) Previous judgments

Judgments of a court are a form of opinion evidence, since a finding of guilt or a finding of negligence, for example, is really nothing more than the opinion of the tribunal trying the case. Before statutory intervention, there was a blanket rule that the judgments of previous tribunals are not admissible in subsequent cases as evidence of the facts on which they were based. This is known as the rule in *Hollington v Hewthorn*.[59] The logic of that decision is that the opinion of a previous court on facts which were not rehearsed in front of the present tribunal are irrelevant. It is the latter's opinion that counts.

This decision had its obvious drawbacks and so was reversed regarding use of subsisting convictions in civil cases by the Civil Evidence Act 1968, s 11-13. Section 11 creates a rebuttable presumption that a convicted person (whether convicted on a guilty plea or not) *committed the offence(s)* in question, 'unless the contrary is proved'.

58 Most civil cases are decided by a single judge, but there are juries in rare cases, most notably some libel actions. There is no longer a 'right' to jury trial in a defamation case: Defamation Act 2013, s 11 and *Yeo v Times Newspapers* [2014] EWHC 2853 (QB).

59 *Hollington v Hewthorn and Co Ltd* [1943] which dealt specifically with admissions of previous convictions in a civil trial.

A very typical example of the use of s 11 would be in a personal injuries action arising out of a car accident. If the defendant driver had, in respect of the same accident, been convicted of dangerous driving, this would be cogent evidence of his negligence, since the criminal standard of proof is higher than the civil standard.[60]

For precisely this reason, it is very difficult, but not impossible, to discharge the burden of rebutting this presumption. According to Lord Diplock in *Hunter v Chief Constable of West Midlands Police*, although the standard to be met in proving the contrary was the 'balance of probabilities', in the face of a conviction after a full hearing this is 'likely to be an uphill task'.[61]

The conviction must be pleaded *in the particulars of claim.* Details of the date and type of conviction, and a statement of its effect, including the issue in the case to which it relates, must be included.[62]

It is important to remember that s 11 is about the admissibility of subsisting *convictions. Acquittals* do not say nearly as much about a person's innocence as a conviction says about guilt. For that reason, evidence of an acquittal remains inadmissible in a subsequent trial, unless there are exceptional features.[63]

(ii) Non-experts: perception evidence of witnesses of fact

To an extent, we see the things we think we see, and so there is always some element of opinion in statements like *"It was dark"* or *"I saw her"*. But it would be very time-consuming (and tedious) to over-analyse such observations. Therefore, an ordinary witness will be allowed to express this sort of opinion as a 'shorthand' way of describing things personally perceived, where attempting to differentiate between fact and inference would be difficult, if not impossible. It is useful to think of this as *'perception' evidence.* Examples include: *"He was drunk"*, *"The car was very old"*, *"The weather was stormy"*. How much easier to let a witness estimate a person's age, than

60 S 12 performs a similar function insofar as previous findings of adultery and paternity are concerned, and s 13 creates an irrebuttable presumption insofar as the evidential value of convictions in defamations cases.

61 [1982] AC 529, at 544

62 CPR, PD 16, para 8.1

63 And see BCP, para 49.96

to have to delineate all the various features of his or her demeanour. Where the 'opinion' best conveys the facts perceived, it will be admissible (and of course can be challenged).[64] This is a common sense exception, which is about ordinary witnesses describing ordinary things. It is very different from the next exception.

(iii) Expert witnesses

Often aspects of civil cases require a level of knowledge which ordinary people (including judges) do not possess, unless they have special training. For example, if the claim were against a surgeon for carrying out an operation negligently, it would be difficult for the judge to know what a specialist, carrying out such an operation, would (or should) have done in the circumstances, which will be important in deciding liability. The judge is a judge, not a doctor. This is where the important role of the expert witness comes into play.

A party's ability to reply on expert evidence at trial depends in part on whether it is *admissible* under the laws of evidence, and (if so) on whether the court is willing to receive it under the CPR *procedural* rules.[65]

Admissibility

As an exception to the general rule, therefore, *relevant expert opinion* evidence is admissible where required to help the judge decide the case. It is important to appreciate the conditions for admissibility and to note the following:

> *The issue in question must call for expertise*
>
> The first requirement for admissibility is that the tribunal of fact (who in most civil cases is the judge) *needs* the assistance of the expert to do its job properly, because the matter at issue is beyond its ordinary

64 Civil Evidence Act 1972, s 3(2)

65 See observations of the Privy Council in ***Bergen v Evans*** [2019] UKPC 33 at WB, para 35.0.1.1 and those of Deputy Master Henderson in ***Declan Colgan Music Ltd v UMG Recordings, Inc*** [2023] EWHC 4(Ch), at WB para 35.0.1

knowledge. Typical examples in civil cases include medical evidence on the cause and extent of personal injuries, surveyor's evidence on the state of allegedly defective buildings, handwriting experts where authorship of signed documents is disputed. If the matter in question is within the everyday experience of the tribunal of fact, then an expert's opinion is inadmissible. A good example is found in *Larby v Thurgood*, where it was held that the claimant's motivation to find higher paid work was a matter within ordinary experience, but the *likelihood* of his finding such work (given the job market, the claimant's qualifications and so on) was not. Thus the opinion evidence of an employment consultant was admissible on this latter issue, but not on the former.[66]

Expert must be qualified in a recognised field

The second requirement is that, if such evidence is needed, it should come from a *suitably qualified* expert competent in a *relevant and recognised area of expertise*. How experts gain their expertise is not usually important, so long as it has been acquired, although these days most experts will be 'professionally' qualified. Usually the more letters the better after the expert's name.

Expert must be independent and impartial

Thirdly, the expert should be (and be seen to be) independent and impartial. This requirement goes to the admissibility of the evidence, but is also reinforced by the overriding duty of the expert to the court set out in CPR r 35.3.[67]

66 [1993] ICR 66. See also *Liddell v Middleton* [1996] PIQR (CA) on when accident reconstruction experts would and would not be necessary.

67 And see WB, para 35.3.2

Experts must keep to their subject.

It is important to remember that experts may only give expert opinion evidence on matters within their expertise. So in our example, a doctor is a good start, but not good enough. The appropriate expert would be a surgeon (usually a consultant) with recognised expertise in the specific type of operation carried out on the claimant - in effect, the sort of person the claimant may, with hindsight, have wished operated on him.

The quirky expert

Some areas of expertise are more experimental or quirky than others, and the question can arise as to whether, and if so when, the court should refuse to entertain opinions of doubtful reliability. A witness's area of expertise must be one the court is prepared to *recognise*. But science is constantly evolving and creating new areas of expertise. The English Courts have tended to be rather open-minded about these things, so that by and large unorthodox approaches are more likely to affect the weight than the admissibility of an expert's evidence. Even so, where the expert's opinion is pushing at scientific boundaries, or where medical knowledge is incomplete, courts should exercise caution.

Primary vs secondary facts

Remember that expert witnesses are expressing opinions on certain facts in the case at hand (such as, in our example, what actually happened during the operation in question). It is important to appreciate that those underlying facts must themselves be proved by admissible evidence. These are called the 'primary facts' and this is known as 'laying the proper groundwork'. Having said that, the research or reports or other materials ('secondary facts') which experts use or rely upon in forming and expressing their opinions need not themselves be admissible, but will be made available for the court and the other parties to examine.

Judge ultimately decides the issues

Cases often turn on the nature and quality of the expert evidence. Expert evidence tends to trump non-expert evidence (if the issue calls for expertise), but this is not inevitable.[68] But where a judge prefers the evidence of a witness of fact to that of an expert, *reasons* justifying the preference should be given. If each side has an expert, whose evidence conflicts, it is fairly obvious that a judge will have to choose whose is to be preferred. And again, sufficient reasons for preferring one expert to another must be given. But bear in mind that although an expert can express a view on an issue in dispute, it is ultimately the judge, not the expert who must decide the case.[69] The role of the expert is to assist, *not usurp* the role of the judge. Assessing the expert evidence is not a 'rubber stamping' operation. Expert evidence can be rejected if there are sensible reasons for doing so. What a judge *cannot* do is assume the role of the expert - a judge who happens to have special expertise is not entitled to apply it when acting judicially.[70]

Reception of expert evidence at trial

One of the most significant procedural changes wrought by the CPR occurred in the area of expert evidence; parties seeking to rely on expert evidence must comply with the relevant rules under Part 35.

68 See, e.g., *Fuller v Strum* [2002] 1 WLR 1097, where the evidence of attesting witnesses to a (contested) Will was preferred over a handwriting expert.

69 There was a time when experts were not allowed to express views on the 'ultimate issues' in dispute. This restriction was abolished in civil cases by the CEA 1972, s 3(3). And see WB, para 35.0.4

70 See generally WB, para 35.0.3

In the old days, parties brought along their own experts (who may have had varying degrees of interest in the overall justice of the case) to slug it out in court against each other - the court exercised little control over the process. The situation is completely different today. As we have discussed, not only does the court manage the pace of litigation, but it also controls the evidence to be adduced at trial (which may involve excluding otherwise admissible evidence) by making directions about the amount of, and manner in which any evidence is received. This power is to be exercised in accordance with the overriding objective and is *particularly important when dealing with the evidence of experts*, which can be both time-consuming and expensive.

This dramatic reversal of the former freedom of litigants to conduct their cases as they wished was brought about by the very strong feeling that the 'bonfire of the vanities' arising from the widespread, adversarial use of experts had become a lengthy and costly exercise in bias.[71] So, for most straightforward, lower value claims, out goes the 'tame' expert witness for both sides; in comes the 'single joint expert', which is defined by CPR, r 35.2(2) as 'an expert instructed to prepare a report for the court on behalf of two or more of the parties (including the claimant) to the proceedings'.

Expert evidence is often limited and/or governed by bespoke rules in small claims track cases, so the discussion below concentrates on trials on the other tracks.[72] As we have seen, directions concerning expert evidence will usually be made when allocating a case, or at a case management conference.

There are several important points to note generally regarding the reception of expert evidence at trial. The first is that, by CPR, r 35.4(1), 'no party may call an expert or put in evidence an expert's report without the *permission* of the court'. If there is no permission, a party cannot adduce the evidence at trial. Note that the rule is focused on a party being able to rely on evidence from an expert *instructed by*

71 Experts have always owed a duty to the court in expressing their views, but the pre-CPR rules did little to reinforce this requirement

72 We are focused here on relying on expert evidence at trial. Written evidence in support of *interim* applications can include a reference to expert evidence without having to comply with the requirements of Part 35

them for use in the proceedings in question; it does not stop a party making evidential use of expert evidence which, say, had been adduced in previous proceedings.[73]

When seeking permission, a party must provide *an estimate of the costs* of procuring such evidence (because experts can be very expensive), identify the proposed expert's *field of expertise* and the *issues* which the expert evidence will address, and (where practicable) give the court the expert's name.[74] This information allows the court to do a cost-benefit analysis and assess whether the expense of the expert is justified (and indeed whether the issue in question requires expert evidence). If permission is granted it shall only be in relation to the expert or field named in the application, and the court may specify the issues which the expert should address.[75]

Secondly, the court is under a duty to *restrict* evidence to 'that which is *reasonably required* to resolve the proceedings'. The burden will lie on the party seeking to rely on expert evidence to justify doing so and the principle of *proportionality* will be an important consideration. The idea is to reduce the inappropriate use of experts to bolster a case, and the court will have to balance the desire to save time and costs against the requirement to do justice. The question of whether the expert evidence is reasonably required is, as you might expect, fact sensitive and should be determined by reference to the overriding objective.[76]

In larger, more complex claims, *competing experts* on an issue (and sometimes more than one issue) may be reasonably required and so permitted. This is most likely to happen in multi-track cases. But in smaller, more straightforward claims, the value of two opposing experts will not ordinarily justify the expense, particularly where they are merely being used to lend 'authority' to facts which can be proved in other, more straightforward ways - for example, by admitting certain readily understandable statistics. In many cases where the question, '*What is good practice?*' is capable of being answered by one knowledgeable person in the relevant field, the court will not need

73 Such evidence would have to be adduced as hearsay evidence, as to which *see below*. The court could still disallow the admission of the hearsay evidence, but as part of its general discretion to control the evidence, not by virtue of r 35.4. See WB, para 35.4.2.1

74 CPR, r 35.4(2)

75 CPR, r 35.4(3)

76 CPR, r 35.1. The more necessary the evidence is for the court to do its job, then the more apt the evidence is to be reasonably required. See e.g., the ***Colgan*** case op.cit., and WB para 35.4.2.2 and examples at 35.1.2ff

or want to sample from a buffet of experts' opinions - the fixed price menu will do.

Indeed the single joint expert is the *norm* on the fast track. The court always has the power in any case to direct that expert evidence be given by a single joint expert,[77] but if a claim has been allocated to the small claims or *fast track*, the rules *specifically provide* that if permission for expert evidence is given, the court will *normally direct* that such evidence is given by *one expert* on a particular issue.[78] In such cases, the court essentially asks itself, 'Is evidence from an expert really required on this issue?', and if so, 'Is there any reason why such evidence should not come from a single joint expert?', looking at all the circumstances of the case.[79]

The single joint expert

Pre-trial

On the fast track, the court will (a) usually limit expert evidence to no more than two expert fields (if more is required this may indicate a need to allocate to the multi-track), and (b) direct that such evidence be given by a single joint expert (unless there is a good reason not to do so). The parties may already have agreed to a single joint expert, which the court can sanction, or the court can make a direction on its own initiative, even if the parties do not want it![80]

The single joint expert in this context is 'jointly instructed' and so receives instructions from both sides. Instructions should be clear, setting out the expert's role, relevant background information and purpose of his or her evidence.[81] If possible, the parties should try and agree a single set of instructions for the one expert, but if this is not possible, they should disclose to each other the (different) instructions they have given.[82]

Experts express their opinions in the form of a *report*, which must comply with certain requirements, to include details of the expert's qualifications, the substance

77 Even when the parties ask to instruct their own experts: CPR, r 35.7

78 CPR, r 35.4(3A). Analogous provisions are likely to apply to a new intermediate track to be created for County Court claims not exceeding £100,000. The aim is to restrict all costs in these (and fast track) cases by a fixed costs regime. See Chs 8 and 18

79 See the common sense factors highlighted at PD 35, para 7 which the court will be taking account of when considering whether or not to direct that expert evidence should come from a single joint expert.

80 See CPR, r 26.6(5)(b) and para PD 28, para 3.7(4) and 3.9(4)

81 See para 20 of Guidance for the Instruction of Experts in Civil Claims 2014, referenced in (and set out immediately after) PD 35 in the WB.

82 See WB, para 35.8.2

of the instructions the expert was given, an indication as to whether opinions other than that expressed by the expert are possible, give reasons for the expert's own opinion (or inability to express an opinion, if that is the case), and so on. Such reports should be written as clearly and concisely as the nature of the case allows, be addressed to the court, and make clear that the expert understands that his or her overriding duty is to the court (and not to any party who may be paying their fees). The report should be verified by a statement of truth.[83]

Where both parties instruct (and so share the cost of) a single joint expert, then of course both are entitled to a copy of that expert's report. In a sense, this sort of witness belongs to both parties, and to neither party, because there is only one and because an expert's principle allegiance is always to the court.[84] There is scope for seeking *clarification* of the expert's report (*see below*), but what if a party is really unhappy with the evidence of the single joint expert? Would the court ever permit that party to call their own expert to challenge the single joint expert's evidence? The court has a discretion to allow this but would only do so if fairness and the overriding objective really demanded it. There must be a rational ('not fanciful') reason for objecting to the joint expert's evidence, and the court must be satisfied that the *only way* to achieve justice to *both sides* in the *specific* circumstances of the case is to let one party effectively abandon the joint expert and adduce their own evidence.[85]

At trial

The way in which expert evidence is received at trial is also controlled by the court. The default position is that expert evidence is to be given in the form of a written report, unless the court directs otherwise. The court is not likely to order otherwise in a fast track case; indeed the rules provide that on the *fast track* the court will *not* direct an expert to attend in person to give oral evidence *unless* it is 'necessary to do

83 CPR, r 35.10 and PD 35, para 3

84 CPR, r 35.3

85 *Hinson v Hare Realizations Ltd* [2020] EWHC 2386 (QB) and see discussion at WB, para 35.7.4

so in the interests of justice'.[86] Remember that fast track cases should only last one day and the trial costs are fixed. To be allowed to have the expert there at the trial, the court would have to be satisfied that oral evidence from him or her has probative value which would outweigh the attendant time and costs.

In any event, the report prepared by the single joint expert would usually 'represent' *the only* expert evidence in the case on the issue to which it relates, and so there would not often be any point in hearing the same evidence given orally. But if a single joint expert is called to give oral evidence, then all parties may ask questions.

Separate experts in complex cases

Pre-trial

In complex cases, or where the expert evidence is very technical or controversial, the court will more likely allow the parties to have their own expert (at least on the issues which are controversial[87]). This is more usual on the multi-track. In such cases, the rules about how instructions should be given, and the form reports should take (discussed above), still apply. As does, with even greater purpose, the requirement that the expert's primary duty is to the court, and not to the party instructing him.[88]

We saw that where the expert evidence is given by a single joint expert, both parties will get a copy of the (one) report and will both know from the outset what that evidence is. But the situation is different when the court allows parties to rely on their own experts, whom they instruct and pay for separately. As we saw earlier, an expert's report created for the purposes of litigation is the quintessential example of a privileged document, which protects it from inspection by an opponent at the disclosure of documents stage. However, a party who is given permission and seeks to *rely* on such evidence at trial will be required to serve a copy of the report on the other side before trial. Usually such disclosure is directed to be mutual

86 CPR, r 35.5

87 It is possible to direct a single joint expert on some issues and allowing the parties to call their own experts on others: see e.g., *Peet v Mid-Kent Healthcare Trust* [2002] 1 WLR 210

(or simultaneous, so one has not seen the other's beforehand), but in some cases it may be appropriate to allow sequential exchange (for example, where there is a prospect that a claimant's report might be agreed by the defendant, which would save costs). In effect, the privilege in the document must be waived if a party wants to make use of the evidence at trial. This rule ensures that both sides can know the nature and strength of the case against them, and so make informed decisions about compromising the action. It is very important, and sanctions for non-compliance are severe. A party who fails to disclose an expert's report as directed, may not use it at trial or call the expert to give evidence orally unless the court gives permission.[89]

Where the defendant has participated in the selection of the claimant's expert during the pre-action phase, but the claimant chooses not to rely on that expert at trial but seeks to instruct another, the court may require the claimant to show the defendant (and thus waive privilege in) the first expert's evidence as the price of being allowed to rely on the new expert. Such conditional orders, sometimes known as *Edwards-Tubb* orders, are intended to discourage 'expert shopping', and so much would depend on the apparent motive for the need to change expert.[90]

The rules allow a party to put a set of *written* questions to another party's expert about the evidence in their disclosed report. This is a useful bit of procedure to ensure that everyone is clear about the real issues in dispute. Questions must be *proportionate*, may only be put *once*, must be put within *28 days* of service of that expert's report on the party asking the questions, and must be for the purpose *only of clarification*, *unless* the court gives permission or the other party agrees. Any answers given to such questions will be treated as *part* of that expert's report. Where such questions have been put to another party's expert, and that expert does not answer them, the court may sanction the party instructing that expert, either by ordering that they are unable to rely on (some or all of) the evidence of that expert and/or

88 The expert's duties and responsibilities are in part dictated by the common law of evidence and the procedural rules which reinforce them. See WB, para 35.3.2

89 CPR, r 35.13. To give permission the court must give relief from the sanction, applying the ***Denton*** test (see Ch 13). Note also that in Part 35 (and unlike disclosure of documents under CPR Part 31) the reference to 'disclosure' refers to letting the other side see the expert's report. The typical direction refers to the 'exchange' of this evidence.

90 Such orders were named for ***Edwards-Tubb v JD Wetherspoon plc [2011] 1 WLR 1373***. The same power exists where the court has given a party permission to rely on one expert and that

unable to recover from any other party the costs of instructing that expert.[91]

Note too the court's ability to order without prejudice *discussions between opposing experts* if this would help identify where they agree and where they do not.[92] The point of such discussions is not to try and settle the case but to identify the extent of agreement between the experts and thus help to narrow the issues. This is really a private meeting between the experts, and so *neither* the parties (who are not impartial!) nor their lawyers (who might be tempted to interfere) may attend, *unless* the parties *and* the experts agree or the court orders otherwise.[93] An agenda might be helpful and the experts must prepare a statement for the court setting out the issues on which they agree and the issues on which they disagree (and in summary, why). Not surprisingly, the contents of such discussions cannot be referred to at trial unless the parties consent.[94]

At trial

Where the court has allowed the parties to instruct their own experts, it follows that there is a greater likelihood that the experts will give their evidence orally, where they may be asked to explain aspects or technicalities in their report (which will be put into evidence before evidence-in-chief) or to respond to other evidence which has been heard, and then be tendered to have their views tested and cross-examined in the usual way.

It is important that those instructing experts ensure the availability of their expert for trial or as otherwise required by the court. The unavailability of a party's chosen expert will only very rarely be sufficient grounds to vary the case timetable or delay the trial.[95]

If there are a lot of experts in a complex case, this can take some considerable time as each expert goes into the witness box individually and sequentially. To make

party later seeks to change expert. See discussion at WB, para 35.4.4

91 CPR, r 35.6 and see PD 35, para 6. Written questions can also be put to a single joint expert appointed under r 35.7

92 CPR, r 35.12

93 See generally PD 35, para 9. If legal representatives do attend such discussions, they should not normally intervene except to answer questions put to them, and the experts can still choose to exclude them from part of their discussions: para 9.5

94 And where experts reach agreement on an issue during their discussions, such will not bind the parties unless they expressly agreed to be bound by such agreement: CPR, r 35.12(5)

95 See WB, para 35.0.2

this part of the process more efficient and effective, the court can direct (typically at the first case management conference) that contested expert evidence ('of like disciplines') be heard 'concurrently'. This has become known colloquially as 'hot tubbing'. Under this procedure, instead of being examined and cross-examined in turn, the experts in a discipline all give evidence together (in a controlled way and round a table, perhaps, rather than in a tub!), and at the same time.[96]

Finally, it is important to note that where a party has disclosed an expert's report, *any* party may 'use' that report as evidence at the trial, without needing to ask the court for permission do so.[97] This can come in handy when a report has been exchanged but is not relied upon at trial by the disclosing party because it does not assist their case[98] or the disclosing party is no longer involved in the proceedings. This does not happen very often, but if other parties can make use of the evidence then they may do so.

B. WITNESSES OF FACT

Just as with opposing expert's reports, the rules also provide for the *early exchange* of the evidence of the *witnesses of fact to be adduced* at trial. This is done by exchanging witness statements.[99] We saw that these are used as the means of putting evidence before the court when making interim applications. They are also the format in which the evidence to be given by a witness at trial is disclosed to the other side, although the court may, exceptionally,[100] give permission for such evidence to be disclosed by exchange of a witness summary (which are never used in interim applications).

Witness statements, like experts' reports, must comply with certain requirements, including the formal title of the proceedings, information in the top-right hand corner about when, by whom and on whose behalf the statement was made, identifying any exhibits, and whether it is a first or subsequent statement in

96 See CPR, PD 35, para 11

97 CPR, r 35.11. Strictly speaking, the court still retains its overall discretion under r 32.1 regarding what evidence it wants to hear, but would be unlikely to exclude this sort of evidence (unless the intention was to impugn it). The important point is that the party wanting to make use of the disclosed report need not first seek the court's permission to do so.

98 As in the ***Edwards-Tubb*** case referred to above. And see WB, para 35.11.1

99 CPR, r 32.4

100 For example, when some practical problem arises in completing the formalities of the witness statement. See CPR, r 32.9(1) and WB, para 32.4.3

the case. It should be made clear in its opening paragraphs, who the witness is, and why the statement is being made. The statement should, if practicable, be in the maker of the statement's own words and should be expressed in the first person. It should make clear what information is not within the witness's own knowledge, and be verified by a statement of truth. Documents referred to in the statement must be *formally exhibited.* Witness statements should be only as long as necessary to cover effectively and efficiently, the issues in dispute.[101]

The point of the pre-trial exchange of the evidence of the witnesses of fact is to promote openness and efficiency in the conduct of litigation, and encourage early settlement of cases. Note the other procedural similarities with expert evidence:

(i) Directions for the exchange of witness statements are usually made upon allocation, or at a case management conference. They may be made on other occasions, as necessary. Witness statements are not usually exchanged in small claims track cases.

(ii) The evidence of witnesses of fact is as capable of control by the court as is expert evidence. The court can give directions limiting the amount and extent of such evidence, whether by identifying who can be called and whose evidence may be read and/or limiting the length and format of witness statements and/or limiting the issues to which factual evidence may be directed.[102] Again, the idea is to ensure that witnesses only give evidence as required and that time and costs are not wasted on marginal issues and the production of wordy and irrelevant content.

(iii) Normally *mutual* exchange between the parties is ordered so that one side's evidence is not tainted by having read the other side's version of events, although occasionally there may be some benefit in sequential exchange.

101 See generally CPR, PD32, para 17ff and WB, para 32.4.5

102 CPR, r 32.2(3)

(iv) Normally, this mutual exchange of witness statements is directed to take place some weeks *after* disclosure of documents (but before exchange of expert evidence). This allows witnesses time to consider and comment on some of the documentation, if relevant to do so.

(v) Privilege in the witness statements is *waived on exchange.*

(vi) If the evidence of fact is *not exchanged as directed*, the witness may not be called to give oral evidence, *unless* the court gives permission (and, again, to give permission the court must give relief from the sanction, applying the *Denton* principles).[103]

(vii) Statements that need to be exchanged are those containing the evidence of the witnesses a party *intends to rely on* at trial. There is no need to disclose a statement from someone who will not be called as a witness at trial.

(viii) In addition (fairly obviously) witness statement should only include matters capable of being adduced at trial. They should not include inadmissible evidence.

Use of witness statements at trial

By the party calling the evidence:

A witness statement is not evidence in itself. Rather it is a means of disclosing what the evidence of the witness will be. It is a longstanding and important principle that where a party intends to rely on the evidence of a witness whose statement has been served on the other party/ies, then (unless the court orders otherwise or the statement is admitted as a hearsay statement) that witness should be called at trial to give their evidence orally.[104]

Having said that, the rules invoke a useful time-saving device: where a witness

103 CPR, r 32.10. And see Ch 13

104 CPR, r 32.5(1) and *see below* regarding admission of hearsay.

105 CPR, r 32.5(2)

106 The court might exercise its discretion to hear some or all of the evidence-in-chief orally if, for example, the evidence is very complex or there are doubts about the credibility of the witness or if there is a conflict in the evidence on a crucial issue.

is called to give evidence, his witness statement shall *stand* as his *evidence-in-chief*,[105] *unless the court orders otherwise*.[106] However the evidence-in-chief is given, it will start off in the same way (the witness will be called, identify herself, be sworn and so on) and end up in the same way, when the witness is tendered for cross-examination. To the extent that the statement stands as the witness's evidence-in-chief, the gap between those two will be very short.[107]

And what if a witness giving evidence has something to say or add that was not contained in the witness statement? There are provisions in the rules for a witness to be allowed, *with the court's permission*, to 'amplify' their witness statement and give oral evidence on new matters which have arisen since the statement is made. But there must be a 'good reason' not to 'confine' witnesses to their statements, since the other side may be taken by surprise by new material, which is precisely what the rules about exchanging witness statements are intended to avoid. It can be a tricky line to tread; if the court is too strict about amplification then witness statements will tend to be long and unfocused on the 'just in case' principle. But if amplification is too readily granted, then witness statements might go to the other extreme and be overly superficial or otherwise omit important evidence, of which the other side might be unaware until trial. And one cannot assume that any injustice to the other side caused by the need to amplify can be remedied by a costs order. An uncontroversial 'clarification' may not cause problems, but sometimes seeking to serve a 'supplemental' witness statement will be the better approach where there has been a significant correction or alteration to the witness's evidence. But every case is different, and the overriding objective will be key to the trial judge's decision on whether or not to allow amplification.[108]

107 In effect the court treats the witness as having given the evidence in the witness statement. As a result, quite logically, the witness statement is available for inspection (by members of the public who would otherwise have heard the evidence-in-chief given orally), unless for some reason the court orders otherwise (e.g., in the public interest or to protect confidential information): CPR, r 32.13

108 CPR, r 32.5(3) and (4) and see WB, para 32.5.2.

By the other side:

Where the witness is called to give evidence

The other party or parties may *cross-examine* the witness on any aspect of the disclosed witness statement, regardless of how much of the evidence in the statement might have been referred to in any oral examination-in-chief.[109]

Where the witness is not called to give evidence

If a party who has served a witness statement does not either call the witness to give oral evidence, or put the statement in as hearsay evidence, then any other party may themselves put the (entire) disclosed statement in as hearsay evidence. No permission need be sought to do this.[110] Further, the rules expressly provide that a witness statement can only be used for the purposes of the proceedings in which it was disclosed, unless the witness consents in writing or the court gives permission or the witness statement has been put in evidence at a hearing in public.[111]

Evidence of fact in the form of photographs, models or plans

If a party intends to admit factual evidence in the form of a photograph, model or plan (which is not contained in a witness statement or expert's report, to be dealt with orally at trial, or covered by the hearsay notice rules[112]) then such evidence will *not be received* at trial unless prior notice under CPR, r 33.6 has been given and the other parties given the *opportunity to inspect* the item of evidence and agree to its admission into evidence without further proof of its accuracy. The idea behind this provision is to give the other parties the opportunity, if necessary, to object to the accuracy of the photograph (or whatever) and seek orders as necessary for gathering and presenting their own version of the evidence in question. For example, in *Orford v Rasmi Electronics Ltd*,[113] one of the reasons for ordering a retrial (in a case stemming from the claimant's

109 CPR, r 32.11

110 CPR, r 32.5(5). This is analogous to the position with disclosed experts reports. Again, the court retains its overall discretion under r 32.1, but the party seeking to rely on the witness statement is not required to seek the court's permission first. Note however that r 32.5(5) permits a party to put into evidence the *whole* of the witness statement; it does not allow a party merely to put into evidence some of it. See WB, para 32.5.3

111 CPR, r 32.12

112 *See below.*

113 [2002] EWCA Civ 1672, at WB, vol 1, para 33.6.1

unhappy employment with the defendant) was that a plan of the factory premises, including the claimant's office within it, was not shown to the claimant until the morning of the trial, even though it had been in existence for five months.

The amount of notice required will depend on the context and the other evidence in the case. Commonly notice is given when witness statements are exchanged. And where the other party (having been given proper notice etc) agrees that the item of evidence accurately shows what it purports to show, then there will be no need for proving this at trial.

C. HEARSAY EVIDENCE IN CIVIL TRIALS

Admissibility

The rule against hearsay is a venerable, if not always venerated, rule of evidence. Hearsay evidence can be defined as an assertion which is *not made by a person while giving testimony* in court, but which is nevertheless relied upon (in those same proceedings) to establish the truth of what was asserted. Very broadly, the rule excludes evidence of the *"Mary told me the car she saw was red"* variety, which cannot be easily tested under cross-examination. If the colour of the car is pertinent, let's have Mary tell the court what she saw.

To understand whether an out-of-court statement is or is not hearsay, one must focus on the *purpose* to which the evidence is being put. In relation to any such item of evidence one must ask: What job of proof is this statement being asked to do? Is the tribunal of fact being asked to believe that what was said in the statement is true?[114] Or is it relevant for some other purpose - for example, to show that the statement was made at all, or the tone of voice in which it was made?[115] If the former, the assertion is hearsay; if the latter, it is not.[116] There are now many exceptions to the rule against hearsay. The common law rule was abolished in civil cases many years ago,[117] principally because juries are rare in civil trials. Evidence is thus not

114 Often referred to as 'truth of contents'.

115 The person who heard the statement can give direct evidence of these facts.

116 See e.g., *Subramanian v Public Prosecutor* [1956] 1 WLR 965

117 By the Civil Evidence Act 1995 ('CEA 1995')

excluded in civil trials *solely* on the grounds of its being hearsay (it may be excluded on some other basis). It is still important, however, to know whether or not an item of evidence is hearsay because of the need to give advance notice to the other side of the intention to adduce such evidence. If the evidence is not hearsay, these special procedural rules do not apply.

Reception at trial

Thus, in civil proceedings, no hearsay - of whatever degree[118] - may be excluded merely by virtue of its being hearsay, except where the live witness, as it were, would not have been competent to testify when the statement was made.[119] But there are requirements to tell the other side of the intention to adduce hearsay evidence, and other safeguards.[120]

The only issue for the judge, when considering hearsay evidence adduced at trial, is what *weight* to ascribe to it. This depends in part on common sense considerations affecting the *reliability* of the evidence, including how easy it would have been to call the witness to give direct oral evidence, how close in time the statement is to the event it describes, whether it involves multiple hearsay, whether there is any ulterior motive in keeping the witness away. It can also depend on the extent to which the party relying on the hearsay evidence has complied with the notice rules (and if they have not, why not). It is also worth noting that the parties can agree to waive or forego the notice rules.[121]

Hearsay comes in different shapes and sizes - oral, written, first and second-hand and so on. How proper notice is given of the intention to adduce hearsay evidence, depends in part on what form it takes. Thus:

(a) Where the hearsay evidence takes the form of the *witness statement* of a person who is *not* being called to give oral evidence, then the party intending to adduce that evidence must, when serving the statement on

118 CEA 1995, s 1(2)(b)

119 E.g., because of unsound mind.

120 These notice rules relate to adducing hearsay evidence at trial. They do not apply to interim hearings: CPR, r 33.3/CEA 1995, s 2(4)(b)

121 CEA, 1995, ss 4 and 2(3)

122 CPR, r 33.2(2)

123 Permission should be sought within 14 days of receiving notice of the intention to rely on the witness statement and not call the witness. CEA 1995, s 3(2) and CPR, r 33.4. Surprisingly, you might think, this is even possible where a party has made

the other parties, 'inform' them of that intention and explain why the witness is not being called.[122] That is all that is required to give notice in these circumstances. It is *important to appreciate* that in this situation, parties on the other side may, *with the court's permission*, require that the 'live' witness attend to be cross-examined on their statement[123] - if indeed he or she is alive (a dead witness is a particularly compelling reason for wanting to adduce the statement as hearsay!). The purpose of the general admissibility of hearsay evidence is not, after all, to keep witnesses who can give evidence away from a party's opponents. Similarly, it is also possible for other parties to call evidence impeaching the credibility of the maker of the witness statement (for example evidence of bias) if this would have been possible had the witness given evidence in the witness box. Notice must be given of the intention to adduce such undermining evidence in these circumstances.[124]

(b) If the hearsay is merely contained *within* the evidence of a witness who *is* being called to give oral evidence, then beyond the exchange of the relevant witness statement nothing further need be done.[125] That is sufficient notice. The other side, by reading the witness statement, can instantly see the nature and source of the hearsay contained within it, and can cross-examine the witness on it, or otherwise deal with it.

(c) But if the hearsay takes some *other* form (for example, an invoice from a shop or a diary entry), then the party wanting to adduce the evidence complies with the rules by serving *formal notice* to the other side, clearly identifying the hearsay evidence, stating the intention to adduce it and again giving reasons for not calling the maker of the statement (here the person who wrote up the invoice or made the diary entry). If the

use of r 32.5(5) to put an opponent's unused witness statement into evidence, even though (in effect) that would amount to the opponent cross-examining what (at one time anyway) was their own witness, as in ***Douglas v Hello! Ltd*** [2003] EWCA Civ 332, cited at WB, para 32.5.3

124 S 5(2) CEA 1995 and CPR, r 33.5. Notice should be given within 14 days of receiving notice of the intention to rely on the witness statement and not call the witness. This provision respects the rule against rebuttal, and its exceptions, explained below. See BCP, 53.14

125 CPR, r 33.2(1)

> evidence is in the form of a document, a copy should be supplied if a party requests it. Such a notice must be served no later than the time for exchanging witness statements.[126]

It is important to note that a failure to comply with the notice rules does not render the hearsay evidence inadmissible as such, but it can affect the *weight* attributed to it and/ or result in an adverse costs order.[127] And, of course, it is always worth remembering that ultimately it is for the court to decide (applying the overriding objective) what evidence it wants to hear, on what issues and in what form.[128] Having said that, hearsay evidence is usually neither expensive nor time-consuming to receive into evidence at a civil trial. One reason for the relaxation of the hearsay rule is that sometimes such evidence is the best on offer or the most cogent (for example, business records). But this is not always the case, so remember that the more crucial the evidence, the less a party will choose (assuming there is a choice) to rely on a second-hand account of an event which will carry less weight than evidence which can be tested by, and stands up to, cross-examination. In other words, just because you can do something, does not necessarily mean you should. Other alternatives may need to be considered, such as applying to take a witness's evidence by deposition pre-trial, or (preferably in many cases) seeking an order that evidence be given on the day by video link.[129]

D. CHARACTER EVIDENCE IN CIVIL CASES

The law of evidence has always been more lenient about the admissibility of bad character evidence in civil cases without juries - that is to say most civil cases. The assumption is that judges sitting alone are able to make the necessary distinctions between evidence which is relevant to culpability and evidence which is relevant to credibility - an important distinction in principle, but one which can sometimes

126 CPR, r 33.2(3) and (4)
127 CEA 1995, s 2(4)
128 CPR, r 32.1
129 An order that evidence be given by deposition is an expensive option, where effectively the evidence is given and cross-examined on in a formal setting before the trial. The evidence is reduced to writing and the resulting deposition may (not must) be given in evidence unless the court orders otherwise. A party intending to admit a deposition must give notice to all other parties at least 21 days before the hearing. The court may require the deponent to attend court to give evidence orally, but this would be highly unusual. Evidence by video-link, of course, is cheaper and more immediate and the judge can see the witness's demeanour. See CPR, r 34.8/9/11 and WB para 34.8.6

be difficult to maintain.

Character evidence can be relevant in one of three ways:

(i) It can be a fact in issue (as in defamation cases);
(ii) It can be relevant to a fact in issue if it demonstrates that it is more likely that the party is or is not capable of doing what is alleged. This is known as evidence of 'disposition' or 'propensity';
(iii) It can be relevant to the credibility (or 'credit') of a witness. If the witness is an habitual liar, perhaps their version of events is not to be believed.

It is useful to distinguish between good and bad character evidence.

Bad character relevant to credibility

People giving testimony in a civil case, including parties to proceedings, are open to attack on their credibility as witnesses by means of evidence of their bad character, subject to the restrictions set out in *Hobbs v CT Tinling and Co Ltd*[130] and the court's general discretion to control cross-examination.[131] According to the *Hobbs* case, such questions are only proper if the nature of the imputation would seriously affect the opinion of the court as to the credibility of the witness on a matter to which he had testified. If the evidence of bad character is very remote in time or nature, it will struggle to meet this test. Indeed an attempt to 'delve into a man's past ... to drag up such dirt as can be found'[132] might smack of desperation.

Bad character showing propensity

As regards evidence of *disposition or propensity* (to do something 'bad'), the test for admissibility in civil cases is essentially *one of relevance*. So long as the evidence is *'logically*

130 [1929] 2 KB 1
131 CPR, r 32.1(3)
132 See e.g., *R v Sweet-Escott* (1971) 55 CR App R 316 (per Lawton J, at p. 320). Criminal cases, of which this is one, are now governed by statue, as to which see *It's Criminal!*, Ch 19

probative' of the matter in issue, it will be admissable unless it would be oppressive or unfair,[133] and again its reception at trial will be subject to the civil court's discretion to exclude evidence if in keeping with the overriding objective to do so.

The leading case is *O'Brien v Chief Constable of South Wales*,[134] involving an allegation of malicious prosecution following a miscarriage of justice review. The House of Lords (as it then was) held that the test of admissibility in civil cases is different, and less strict, than in criminal cases. Lord Philips said that the test was that of relevance in that the evidence is admissible if it is 'potentially probative' of an issue in the claim. He went on to say that the policy considerations giving rise to the position in criminal cases (and in particular the Criminal Justice Act 2003) should be kept in mind by a civil court when giving effect to the overriding objective. Where the risk of prejudice was *'disproportionate' to its relevance*, the judge should 'manage' the case accordingly by excluding the evidence, but the civil courts are *not* bound to apply the criminal test to a civil suit.

Any arguments on whether evidence of bad character should be admitted, therefore, will turn on its probative value (which need not be huge) measured against its prejudicial effect, which should not be disproportionate to the persuasive value of the evidence. Criminal lawyers will recognise this balancing act - it is not very different from the general discretion to exclude prosecution evidence in criminal cases.[135] Bear in mind, however, that the implications of losing most civil actions are not generally so severe as to make it particularly easy to convince a judge that it would be disproportionate to allow in relevant evidence of this kind. But again, every case is different and claims alleging the most serious allegations will be those where this balancing act is most difficult to execute.

Good character evidence

Some of the older cases suggest that evidence of good character is never admissible

133 *Mood Music Publishing Co Ltd v D Wolfe Ltd* [1976] CH 119, CA

134 [2005] 2 AC 532

135 In criminal cases the court is concerned that the probative value 'outweighs' (or justifies) the prejudicial effect. 'Disproportionality' is a somewhat wider notion.

in civil cases, presumably because even very virtuous people can be careless once in a while. It must be doubted whether this could be so in a case involving very serious misconduct or allegations of a criminal nature. Perhaps a more modern approach is to say that admissibility depends on relevance and the probative value of the evidence, bearing in mind that none of us are perfect all of the time. See, for example, *Hatton v Cooper*,[136] a case arising out of a collision where there was little evidence of what had actually happened. The Court of Appeal held that the trial judge improperly relied on evidence from the claimant's employer to the effect that the claimant was an excellent driver. But in so doing, the court referred not to a blanket ban as such, but to its lack of probative value in the case - 'completely worthless', was how Jonathan Parker LJ bluntly put it.

3. WITNESSES AND THE COURSE OF TESTIMONY

A. COMPETENCE AND COMPELLABILITY

As you prepare for trial, it is important to know whether the witnesses you want to call are legally capable of giving evidence - and if so, whether they can be required to give evidence if they are unwilling to do so voluntarily. *Competence* refers to the first of these; *compellability*, to the second.

The general rule is that all persons are *both competent*[137] *and compellable.* Exceptions in criminal cases involve spouses and civil partners of the accused and defendants themselves. There are *no such exceptions in civil cases.* An important exception relating to children (and persons of unsound mind) applies in *both* criminal and civil cases. The tests differ, although they borrow from each other.

136 [2001] RTA 544

137 The basic test for competence for adults is whether the witness is capable of understanding the nature of the oath and able to give rationale testimony.

Children

Test for competence

The manner in which a child's[138] evidence is given is tied up with competence. The first question is whether the child is competent to give *sworn* evidence. The test is one which used to govern both the civil and criminal law, and is known as the test in the case of *R v Hayes*.[139] Does the child understand the *'solemnity of the occasion'* and the *special obligation* to tell the truth, 'over and above the ordinary social duty' to do so? In other words, are they aware that in telling their story in a court it is especially important to be truthful. This is sometimes referred to as being '*Hayes* appreciative'. The idea behind the *Hayes* test was to move away from the need for belief in the divine sanction against lying, and so secularise the test for the giving of sworn evidence.

If the child does not satisfy the *Hayes* test, the court can look to s 96 of the Children Act 1989, which applies to a child who is called as a witness, but who does not, in the court's opinion, understand the nature of the oath (in the *Hayes* sense). Such a child's evidence can be heard *unsworn*, if, in the court's opinion, the child understands that it is his duty to tell the truth and he has *sufficient understanding* to justify his evidence being heard.[140] This in essence is not only about intelligibility, but also about being able to distinguish between the truth and a lie. It seems to be a somewhat stricter test than in criminal cases.[141]

If the child does not pass the requirement for the giving of unsworn evidence either, then that child is *not competent* to give evidence.

Procedure for assessing competence

It will be for the court to form an opinion on these matters before hearing the child's evidence (obviously). The judge, if necessary, will do this (usually on an earlier occasion if the issue is controversial) simply by asking the child some questions,

138 A person is a child in the legal sense if under the age of 18

139 [1977] 1 WLR 23

140 Children Act 1996, s 96(2)

141 In criminal cases it is rather assumed that children who are 14 or over can give sworn evidence. See Youth Justice and Criminal Evidence Act 1999, ss 53-57

in part to determine intelligibility and in part to ensure the child understands the importance of telling the truth, especially in the context of a trial. Except in family law cases,[142] all such inquiries will be made in open court. Whether a child warrants such an examination is a matter for the judge - there is no fixed age for these things, but as a rule of thumb, inquiry would be made of a child under 14, although much would depend on the child in question. The 'watershed' which divides children who are normally thought to be able to give sworn evidence from those who are too young to do so tends to fall between about eight and ten years. But some quite young children have been thought capable of giving unsworn evidence. Following *Hayes*, questions will be secular in nature. It will be for the person tendering the child as a witness to prove the child is competent.

A child who is judged competent to give evidence (whether sworn or unsworn) will also be *compellable* to give that evidence. If this seems a little harsh, remember that arrangements can be put in place to assist the child in giving his or her evidence.

Special arrangements

Special arrangements can be made for any vulnerable or frightened witnesses, including children. The general rule that evidence is to be given orally and in open court is qualified by the court's ability to control the way in which evidence is received. For example, CPR, r 32.3 provides that a witness may provide evidence through a 'video link' or 'by other means'. In *Polanski v Conde Nast Publications Ltd*[143] it was said that videoconferencing orders are readily available to all litigants in civil proceedings. 'Special measures' as they are called in criminal cases,[144] include screens, videotaping examination-in-chief, giving evidence by video link and so on. In this technical day and age especially, there does not seem to be any reason why these cannot equally be employed as appropriate in civil cases: consideration and decisions about such

142 These are not covered by the CPR and will usually be heard in private.
143 [2005] 1 WLR 637
144 See generally *It's Criminal!* Ch 17

measures can be made at a pre-trial review, if not earlier. Special protocols for the conduct of cross-examination of children and vulnerable witnesses apply in criminal and family law cases, and there have been calls to extend these to all civil cases.[145]

Note too that interpreters, signers and so on can be used to help witnesses with special needs to give their evidence.

Persons with mental incapacity

In civil cases, persons with mental incapacity must be able to satisfy the *Hayes* test to be competent to give sworn evidence. It is important to remember that not all mental impairment leads to an inability to give evidence on oath. But if this is not possible, note that there is *no provision* (as there is for children) enabling such a person's evidence to be heard unsworn. Just as with children, the court will assess the competence of the witness before the evidence is heard. It may be necessary to hear expert evidence about the mental condition in question, and in particular how it would impact (or not, as the case may be) on the ability to give sworn evidence.

Again, if the witness is found to be competent, that witness is also compellable to give evidence. Special measures may be put in place as appropriate.

Witness summons

As we have seen, in civil cases, where a witness is competent to give evidence, he or she is also almost always compellable.[146] Most witnesses attend court voluntarily. A compellable witness who is reluctant to attend may be ordered to do so by the court. The mechanism by which a witness is ordered to attend is a witness summons (literally 'summonsing' that witness to court). This is a document, issued by the court, which requires one named witness to attend at a named court address on a named date and time, to give evidence *and/or* produce specific (relevant) documents in a named

145 If the witness statement stands as the evidence-in-chief, then the focus is really on the cross-examination. And see *Vulnerable Witnesses and Parties within Civil Proceedings*, Civil Justice Council, final report, February 2020 at judiciary.uk, and CPR, PD 1A.

146 Heads of foreign states are an exception.

case.[147] To facilitate compliance, travelling expenses will be offered or paid. This is logical, given the compulsory nature of the summons. The amount offered should also include an amount by way of compensation 'for loss of time' (e.g., at work).[148]

Issuing a witness summons in civil cases is usually purely administrative, although the court can set aside or vary the summons if appropriate (like entering judgment in default in most money claims[149]). It should be served at least seven days before, and will be binding until the conclusion of, the hearing to which it relates. Permission to issue a witness summons is only required where it is very close to trial (less than seven days) or where attendance is required to give evidence or produce documents at an interim hearing or some date *other than* the trial date.[150]

A witness summons is a court order and failure to comply (for example by not turning up at all or turning up and refusing to give evidence or answer legitimate questions as required) is a contempt of court, punishable by fine or imprisonment. The circumstances will dictate whether, and if so, what punishment should be given. In the County Court, if no travelling expenses were offered or paid at the time of serving the summons, then no fine can be imposed.[151]

Witness summonses obviously have their place (and can be helpful where a witness wants to be seen to have been compelled), but it is as well to remember that no order of the court can make a person give favourable evidence. One should always think twice about calling reluctant witnesses. There may be no sensible alternative, but unless you are prepared (and have a game plan in mind), they can sometimes do more harm than good.

B. WITNESS HANDLING/ADDUCING EVIDENCE AT TRIAL

There are some longstanding evidential principles relating to the giving of oral evidence at trial. Some of these rules can be confusing for beginners, so by way of

147 CPR, r 34.2(1)
148 CPR, r 34.7 and see Form N20
149 See Ch 5
150 CPR, r 34.3 and 34.5
151 County Court Act 1984, s55(3)

introduction, it may help you to bear in mind the following in order to make sense of what might seem a disparate set of rules.

The three stages of oral testimony are examination-in-chief, cross-examination and (if necessary) re-examination. Context is very important, and so you should be able to differentiate the rules which only pertain to evidence-in-chief, those which only pertain to cross-examination and those which apply across the board. This will help you to understand and remember them.

It is important to remember that a witness's credibility, or 'credit' as it is sometimes called, is a relevant fact in any given trial because it is something which makes that witness' version of events more or less likely to be true. Some of the witness handling rules require an appreciation of the difference between questions going *solely* to the credit of a witness and questions which are relevant (or also relevant) to a fact in issue in the case.

There is always a rationale behind each of the witness handling rules, which (even if rather outdated) can help you remember them. It is also the case that modern statutory and procedural rules have decreased the importance of some of these principles to civil trials. Check your exam syllabus for the extent (if any) to which the following rules are to be tested.

(i) Examination-in-Chief

First we begin with some rules about presenting one's own evidence and examining witnesses-in-chief. It is as well to remember that, although a judge may ask questions of a person giving evidence from time to time, it is essentially the advocate's job, not the judge's, to question witnesses. Moreover, the credibility of the witness is an important aspect of getting one's case across. There are, however, *limits* on what an advocate may do to *bolster* the quality of the evidence being presented.

The prevalence of letting a witness's statement stand as his or her evidence-in-chief, renders some (but not all) of these rules rather redundant in civil cases. Indeed examination-in-chief is something of a dying art in civil trials, but you need to be aware of these rules for those occasions when you need to re-examine a witness following cross-examination or indeed when (or to the extent that you may be) called upon to examine a witness-in-chief in the old-fashioned way - for example, if given permission to 'amplify' the witness statement.

The rule against asking leading questions in examination-in-chief

Leading questions are those which include or suggest a particular answer, thus 'leading' the witness from the one to the other.[152] An obvious example might be: *"You were driving slowly as you approached the bend, weren't you?"* which (assuming the driver's speed is at issue and controversial) invites the curt response *"Yes"*. The purpose of the general prohibition against asking leading questions in chief is obvious and really just a matter of common sense. The evidence is meant to come from the witness who directly perceived the event in question; not the advocate, who did not. The idea behind questioning your 'own' witness, who may well be inclined to want to give helpful evidence, is to *elicit* the evidence from them, not put words into their mouths. This is sometimes easier said than done. The rule, however, is not strictly applied where introductory or formal matters are concerned or where the subject matter of the question is not in dispute.

The so-called 'hostile witness'

In civil cases, this now will only arise to the extent that evidence-in-chief is conducted orally (for example to amplify or clarify matters in the witness statement).

Sometimes witnesses get muddled or say the wrong things. There is nothing an

152 Or assume facts not in evidence. An example might be (assuming it is not established that the traffic light was green), *"When the traffic light turned green, what did you do?"*

advocate can do about a witness who is 'unfavourable' in this sense, except soldier on as well as possible. This is because of the general common law rule *against impugning or contradicting your own witness*. You cannot on the one hand put a person forward as a truthful witness for your cause, and then turn around and suggest that the testimony is not to be believed when that witness does not say what you wanted or expected.[153]

However, if such a witness actively does not wish to tell the court, truthfully, what he knows, then that witness can, with the court's permission, be declared 'hostile.' This allows the advocate to cross-examine the witness to the extent of asking leading questions and, if necessary, putting to him any previous 'inconsistent' statement. These principles apply to both civil and criminal trials.[154]

Unless you are prepared, it is not ideal to have a hostile witness on your hands. After all, that witness is supposed to be on your side! The judge could well attach little if any credibility to the evidence.

Of course, if (as is the norm in civil trials) the witness statement stands completely as the evidence-in-chief of the witness, then the risks of this happening are almost nil.

The rule against previous consistent statements

A 'previous consistent statement' is a statement made by a witness on an occasion *before* the trial which is *consistent* with that witness's testimony *at* trial. The general rule, in both civil and criminal cases, is that such statements (also called self-serving statements) are not admissible to bolster the *credibility* of the witness's evidence *in court*. The rationale for the rule is that the evidence does not improve with repetition, and there is a risk that a witness may be tempted to manufacture evidence and so artificially increase the credibility of his story by merely repeating it several times before the trial takes place. Do not confuse this rule with the hearsay rules, or indeed with the fact that usually the witness statement stands in

153 Although other witnesses may be able to repair or counteract the damaging testimony.

154 Criminal Procedure Act 1865. For more detail, see BCP, para 49.59ff or, in a criminal context, ***It's Criminal!***

155 In this scenario the witness is using the memory refreshing document in the witness box to facilitate the giving of their evidence. The court can also permit a witness to take a break from the giving of evidence, refresh their memory from a document (created when

for a witness's evidence-in-chief in a civil trial (in which case the witness statement is *not a previous* consistent statement) - these aspects of one's evidence can interact with one another, but they need to be distinguished conceptually.

As ever, there are exceptions to this rule against self-serving statements. The two common law exceptions which apply to civil (as well as criminal) cases are (a) statements rebutting an allegation of recent fabrication and (b) memory refreshing documents. In addition, (c) such statements are admissible in civil trials with the *permission* of the court.

(a) Statements rebutting allegation of recent fabrication

This is a common sense exception. If, under cross-examination, a witness's version of events is challenged as being a 'recent' invention, it would be very unjust if the general rule prevented that witness rebutting that allegation by pointing to earlier statements which are consistent with their evidence-in-chief. Where applicable, this would be done in re-examination, but only to the extent relevant to, and necessary to rebut the allegation. Note, however, that if the allegation is that the story has been untrue from the outset, then the general rule would prevail.

(b) Refreshing memory

A witness giving oral evidence-in-chief who has difficulty remembering events to which their evidence relates may be permitted, while giving that evidence,[155] to 'refresh their memory' by reference to documents, such as a log book or diary entry or other written statement. Such documents must have been made 'contemporaneously'[156] and be produced for inspection by the court and other parties. The principle

the witness's recollection was significantly better, and which they had not read beforehand), and then return (without the document) to resume the giving of their evidence. The point about these common law rules is that the giving of evidence should be a test of veracity not a feat of memory. For further detail see generally BCP, para 49.52ff and (in a criminal context) *It's Criminal!*

156 This needn't be literally contemporaneously, but it should have been as soon after the events as possible and in any case while they were still 'fresh in the mind'. *R v Richardson* [1971] 2 QB 484

operates not only where such documents are used to 'jog' the memory, but also where the witness has no independent recollection of the events at all, but can give evidence of the accuracy of the document. In either case, the common law preserves the notion (some would say fiction) that it is the testimony of the witness, not the memory refreshing document, which constitutes the evidence in the case, unless the party cross-examining the witness goes beyond the parts of the document used in chief to refresh that witness's memory, in which case the document itself can be admitted into evidence.[157]

As with the hostile witness, the need and scope for refreshing the memory while giving evidence-in-chief has been much reduced as life and civil litigation has modernised. First, almost everyone who is called upon to give oral evidence will be sensible enough to re-read their witness statement so that they are well prepared for what can be a stressful occasion. Secondly, in most cases, the witness statement stands as the evidence-in-chief of the witness (so one can move swiftly on to cross-examination). If the evidence-in-chief is not in fact given orally, then there is no scope for the memory refreshing rules to apply.

And there is a third reason, and that is the ability of the court to give a party *permission* to put into evidence a previous statement made by a witness, who has been, or was to be called to testify.[158] So if, for example, a witness were giving oral evidence-in-chief and ran into problems remembering things, it would probably be easier for the court to allow the party who called the witness to admit the previous consistent statement of that witness instead of getting bogged down in the memory refreshing rules. Having said that, a court, when exercising

157 *Senat v Senat* [1965] 157 P 172, and CEA 1995, s 6(4)

158 CEA, s 6(2)(a)

this discretion, would be attentive to the general policy behind the rule against previous consistent statements and want to ensure that in such a case a party was not given the advantage of two pieces of evidence (on the stand and as a previous consistent statement) for the price of one.

Evidential status of admissible previous consistent statements

It is important to remember that the rule against previous consistent statements (and the exceptions to it) are all about earlier statements being admitted (or not) to show *consistency* with, and so bolster the *credibility* of the evidence given in court. *The rule makes no sense without evidence being given in chief*, which is capable of being bolstered in this way. There has to be something with which to show consistency! The rule thus collides with, but should not be confused with, the admissibility of hearsay in civil cases, which covers a wider range of out-of-court statements (including many when the maker of the statement is not present in court). As discussed above, hearsay evidence is generally admissible in civil cases, and so if evidence of a previous consistent statement is admissible as an exception to the general prohibition, then not only can it show *consistency* with the evidence of the testifying witness, it will also be admitted to show that the matters stated are *true*.

(ii) Cross-examination

Unlike examination-in-chief, cross-examination works on the assumption that the witness does *not* favour the case of the party on whose behalf it is conducted. So some of the limitations imposed on the former do not apply to the latter. For example, there is no general ban on leading questions since it is not thought that the witness will be very motivated to follow the cross-examiner's lead. Similarly, because the witness has not been called in support of the case of the party conducting the cross-examination, the latter is free (by all proper means) to discredit the witness.

In this context, there are two particularly important rules applicable to cross-examination in civil cases.[159]

(a) The rule against rebuttal on collateral issues

If parties were allowed to call evidence to rebut a witness every time an oppositional reply was given in cross-examination, trials might take a very long time indeed to complete. And if the time is not well spent, lengthy proceedings are not in the public interest. So, to keep trials efficient and focused, an important limitation is put on a party's ability to contradict a witness in this way. The rule, which is applicable at common law to both civil and criminal cases, is that answers given in cross-examination on *purely 'collateral'* matters (for example, questions merely going to the credibility of the witness but which are *otherwise irrelevant* to any of the issues in the case) may not be contradicted by rebuttal evidence. This is sometimes called the rule of 'finality of answer', which is a confusing description, because the rule does not mean that the judge must accept the truth of the answer given, nor does it mean that the questioner should not be given every reasonable opportunity to extract the admission in cross-examination which he or she seeks. What it does mean is that evidence may not be *adduced* by the party asking the questions to rebut the answer given by the witness. Hence, it might be better described as the rule *against rebuttal.*

The purpose of the rule is to prevent advocates getting off the point and proceedings getting bogged down on peripheral and essentially irrelevant issues.

There are two points to bear in mind when considering the rule against rebuttal. First, it can *only apply to matters which have been properly put* to a witness in

159 See also *It's Criminal*! where these rules are considered in more detail (they apply to criminal as well as civil cases).

cross-examination. If the question cannot be asked, then there will be no answer to rebut! It's worth remembering this: there are more restrictions on cross-examination in criminal trials, but the civil judge has a discretion to 'limit' cross-examination.[160]

Secondly, the difficulty with applying the rule is that it is not always easy to determine what matters are relevant to an issue in the case, and what are relevant only to credibility or some other purely collateral issue. It is important to appreciate (both in practice and for examination purposes) that the rule only precludes rebuttal evidence in respect of questions going *solely* to collateral matters. Even if a line of questioning speaks to a witness's credibility, if it also speaks to a fact in issue in the case, then the limitation does *not* apply. In addition, there are, as always, the inevitable *exceptions* to the rule. Thus, it is permissible to adduce evidence to rebut answers given in cross-examination by a witness on the following collateral issues:

- ***To prove previous convictions of the witness***
  If a witness is properly cross-examined about a previous conviction (in order solely to undermine their credibility), and denies it or refuses to answer, then the conviction may be proved against him.[161] Dishonesty offences are typically used in this way, but other offences may (depending on the circumstances) also speak to a witness's credibility.

- ***To prove the witness's general reputation for untruthfulness***
  Whether or not a witness has a relevant previous conviction, a witness's credibility may be impugned by others speaking to his or her general reputation for telling lies.[162] This is a long-standing, common law exception, but is not often invoked.

160 CPR, r 32.1(3) and see, e.g., *Watson v Chief Constable of Cleveland* [2001] EWCA Civ 1547

161 Criminal Procedure Act 1865, s 6

162 *R v Richardson* (1968) 52 Cr App R 317

- ***To prove the witness is biased***
  Evidence is admissible to contradict a witness's denial of partiality for or against one of the parties to proceedings, in order to show that he is prejudiced as to the outcome of the case. For example, in *R v Shaw*[163] it was held that the accused was permitted to call evidence to contradict a prosecution witness who, in cross-examination, denied having threatened to 'get even' with the accused after the two had argued. This is a sensible exception to the rule against rebuttal. If a witness has a vested interest in the outcome of a case, the fact finder ought to know about it. But there has to be some basis to the allegation of bias (which brings the exception into play) beyond a mere attack on the credibility of the evidence, and this can sometimes seem a fine distinction. For example, it has been said that a denial that a bribe was *offered* to a witness could not be contradicted, whereas a denial that a bribe had been *accepted* could, because it was only the latter fact which actually said something about the partiality of the witness.

- ***To prove a physical/mental disability affecting the reliability***
  If a witness has a mental or physical impairment affecting the reliability of his evidence, then this is something which those whose job it is to assess that evidence (the judge, in most civil cases) should know. Thus if, for example, an identifying witness denies in cross-examination that he suffers from night blindness or is prone to hallucinate, then evidence may be called to prove that he does suffer from such disabilities.[164] The evidence of disability can itself be rebutted, although only insofar as is necessary to meet a specific challenge to the witness's reliability

163 (1888) 16 Cox CC 503, Assizes.

164 See observations of Lord Pearce in *Toohey v Metropolitan Police Commissioner* [1965] AC 595

and should not extend beyond this in an attempt merely to bolster the credibility of that witness.[165]

Previous inconsistent statements

Clearly, one of the most effective ways of undermining a witness in cross-examination is to put to that witness a statement made by him or her on an earlier occasion which contradicts the evidence given at the trial. Unsurprisingly, these are known as previous *in*consistent statements and so long as the statement is relevant 'to the subject matter of the ... proceedings', then the witness may be cross-examined on it and, if necessary, the statement may be adduced to rebut the witness's testimony in court. This is by virtue of ss 4 and 5 of the Criminal Procedure Act 1865, which applies to both civil and criminal cases and sets out the manner in which such statements are to be put to a witness. The point is to protect witnesses from being unfairly surprised during cross-examination and to give them a chance to deal with the inconsistency. If a previous inconsistent statement is admitted into evidence (because the witness does not concede its accuracy), it will be admitted for the truth of its contents in a civil trial because there is no bar to hearsay evidence. However what weight is to be attached to it vis-à-vis the oral evidence of the witness is entirely up to the judge as fact-finder.

(iii) Re-examination

Witnessnes who have been cross-examined may be re-examined by the party who called them, within the *same constraints as apply to examination-in-chief.* This will not often be necessary. The point of re-examination is to repair any damage done in cross-examination, which may have left the witness's version of events ambiguous or incomplete. It is not permitted to ask questions which do not arise from the cross-examination, unless the court gives permission.

165 This used to be known as 'oath-helping'

revision tips

- Public interest immunity may not be on your exam syllabus, but if it is, make sure you can distinguish it from legal professional privilege (LPP).
- Distinguish also between

  a) legal advice privilege and litigation privilege, both 'heads' of legal professional privilege, *and*

  (b) legal professional privilege and the without prejudice protection.
- Regarding hearsay evidence, be aware of what *form* hearsay evidence takes, which can dictate how advance notice to the other side is given.
- Regarding expert evidence:

  - Use of the single joint expert on any given issue is the norm on the fast track, the evidence to be admitted in written form, unless the court orders otherwise. Analogous provision will be required when an intermediate track is introduced, likely October 2023.
  - Separately instructed experts, giving oral evidence, will be more acceptable and common in multi-track cases.
  - The expert's duty is to the court to express a true, complete and independent professional opinion, even if this is adverse to the case of the party calling them.

It is worth reading ...

CPR, r 32.1 (if you have not already).

The judgment in ***Rogerson v Eco Top Heat & Power Ltd [2021] EWHC 1807 (TCC)***. The facts are easy to follow and there is a good review of the case law in the area of ***Edwards-Tubb*** orders. Note the interface between privilege and disclosure of expert evidence, and what the cases say about when the court has jurisdiction to make such orders.

Rogers v Hoyle [2014] 3 WLR 148. This may put you off loop-the-loop, but there is lots to enjoy procedurally here: experts, the rule in ***Hollington v Hewthorn***, the admissibility of expert evidence not covered by Pt 35, hearsay. You could just read Leggat J's judgement, which was upheld on appeal.

AG v VD [2020] EWHC 1947 (Fam). This involves a different sort of war between nationalities, but is easy to follow and explains waiver of privilege in clear terms.

The judgment in ***Warner v Penningtons*** (***A Firm***) [2010] EWHC 1753 (Admin). This case is not long and it covers at least 5 aspects of litigation in addition to expert evidence, including summary judgment and third parties (of which there are several). A good one for a revision check!

PART SIX

last orders

CHAPTER 18

Paying the piper:
costs principles and orders

Costs are a highly significant aspect of civil procedure - they overshadow almost every aspect of the litigation process, from start to finish. At least four different parts of the CPR are devoted to the subject.[1] A related issue is how litigation is financed. Litigants are primarily responsible for paying their own legal fees, which will be incurred on their behalf from the moment they first engage solicitors, but there may be various funding options open to them, depending on the situation.[2] Where public funding is still available, it will be the Lord Chancellor, acting through the Legal Aid Agency ('LAA') who pays the lawyers, with or without contributions from the litigant himself. One way or another, costs can quickly add up.

There is, however, a generalised expectation that a losing litigant will usually be required to pay the winner's costs. This obviously helps the winner with his legal bills. But the extent to which this is what the court actually orders can depend on other factors, and in particular the conduct of the parties. The courts have become very adept at case-specific costs orders. Personal injuries actions now have special costs rules. The interplay between costs and public funding can also throw up specific considerations. The unifying theme is: who pays for the expense of litigation?

Much of this book, as indeed much of civil litigation, is devoted to what goes on

1 CPR, Parts 44-47ff. At the time of writing, the focus of the Bar examination is Part 44

2 Funding options are considered in more detail below.

before trial. There are a host of *interim* applications which might be made, at the end of which there will be an order for costs. Not surprisingly, these are known as interim costs orders. What order a judge makes on an interim application will depend on the situation. There may be a clear winner. Or success may be tempered by some aspect of failure or poor litigation behaviour, resulting in the court's 'docking' a percentage of that litigant's costs. Some applications are essentially managerial and/or otherwise to be treated as part of the general 'costs of the claim'. If the application arises only because one of the litigants failed to follow the rules, that party may have to pay the costs thus 'thrown away,' whatever the outcome.[3]

You need to be aware of the various possible interim costs orders, what they mean and in what circumstances they might be ordered - some of the more common are conveniently set out in the rules themselves.[4] Most are self-explanatory, although there are some interim costs orders which can confuse beginners. One is understanding the difference between 'costs in the case' and 'claimant's (or defendant's) cost in the case'. 'Costs in the case' means that whoever wins the substantive case at trial will recover (from the loser) the costs of that interim application. 'Claimant's (or defendant's) costs in the case' is a little more favourable to the named party: it means that if the named party wins at trial, he will recover from the loser the costs of the interim application, but if he loses, he will not be made to pay the other side's costs of that application (so the latter will have to bear his own costs of that interim application, no matter what happens at trial).

Where the court decides the parties should each bear their own costs, then the order can either be 'each party to pay its own costs' or 'no order as to costs.'[5] Such an order may be appropriate when there are no obvious winners and losers, or everyone both wins and loses, or it just seems fair in the circumstances. Interim costs orders should be capable of meeting any kind of situation.

---

3 For example, on a successful application to set aside default judgment which was properly entered, discussed in Ch 5

4 PD 44, para 4.2. BCP, Table 69.1 also has a useful list of the common costs orders, interim as well as final, and their meanings.

5 In most cases, the result is the same if the court really does make no order as to costs (that is to say, is silent on the matter). There are some exceptions (e.g., where the court has given leave to appeal, in which case the deemed order is applicant's costs in the case): see CPR, r 44.10

Although much of what follows also applies to interim costs orders, the focus of this chapter will be *final* orders, that is, costs orders made after final determination of the issues at trial. In particular it will review basic principles, and highlight some of the more complex issues that can arise in making such orders.

Let us start with *two important propositions*. The first is this: whether, when and in what amount costs are ordered to be paid by one party to another, are in the *discretion* of the court.[6] It is vital to remember this. Nevertheless, there are various principles, guidelines and indeed rules and statutes which inform, shape and sometimes constrain the exercise of this discretion, the most dominant of which is that the general rule is that *the loser should normally be ordered to pay the winner's costs*. But think of this as a *starting point* because the court is free to make a *different* order if the circumstances warrant it.[7]

Note too that only 'recoverable' costs may be the subject of a costs order. Not every expense incurred by a litigant will necessarily qualify. To be recoverable, the costs must be the 'costs of' or 'incidental to' the proceedings. Costs 'incidental to' is a rather wider concept than the costs 'of' the proceedings, and can include costs incurred prior to commencement which are linked to the dispute, but would not include a party's costs of seeking funding nor expenditure related to issues which never got beyond the pre-action phase and bear no relevance to the matters ultimately litigated.[8]

It is the advocate's responsibility to seek the appropriate order for costs, and this requires an understanding of what orders are possible as well as knowledge of how (or how quickly and accurately) costs will or should be quantified in any given case. In a nutshell, as regards final orders as to costs made by the judge at the end of proceedings, there are essentially two issues to think about: firstly, who pays, and secondly, how much?[9]

6 CPR, r 44.2(1)

7 CPR, r 44.2(2)

8 See discussion at WB, para 44.2.3

9 As to *when* costs are payable, the general rule is that a party must comply with a costs order within 14 days of a summary assessment, the issue of a certificate after a detailed assessment, or such other date as the court orders: CPR, r 44.7

1. WHO PAYS?

The *guiding principle*[10] is that, as a general rule, costs should (as it is sometimes quaintly put) 'follow the event'. Officially, this is described as meaning that the 'unsuccessful' party will be ordered to pay the costs of a 'successful' party.[11] It is sometimes also (less quaintly) referred to as 'costs shifting' (since the winner's burden of paying his own legal costs 'shifts' to the loser, who then would have two sets of costs to pay: the winner's and his own). The basic idea is to make litigation an unattractive alternative of last resort.

Nevertheless, the court can (and often does) make a different order. In deciding what order to make, *the court must have regard to all of the circumstances*,[12] such as the complexity of the case, the amount of money involved, and so on. In this context, CPR, r 44.2(4) particularly requires the court to have regard to the following:

(i) the *conduct* of all of the parties,
(ii) whether a party has been *partially*, even if *not totally* successful, and
(iii) *any admissible offer* of settlement made (which is not one to which Part 36 strictly applies[13]).

CPR, r 44.2(5) further sets out a (non-exhaustive) list of the sorts of conduct which might be relevant to the court's decision on costs. It can include pre-action behaviour as well as the manner in which the case was pursued or defended. So, for example, was the appropriate pre-action protocol or PD complied with? Did the claimant exaggerate his claim? Was it reasonable to pursue or defend a particular allegation? Did a party flout the rules? Or unreasonably (in the circumstances) reject a proposal to engage in ADR or an informal offer to settle?[14] The idea is to move away from

10 This principle, which is hardwired into the civil costs system, seems to have survived most of the Jackson reforms.
11 CPR, r 44.2(2)(a)
12 CPR, r 44.2(2)(b)
13 The costs consequences of Part 36 offers following judgment are entirely governed by Part 36, and not Part 44. It is offers of settlement which do not amount to Part 36 offers (e.g., *Calderbank* offers) which are relevant here. See Ch 15 and WB para 44.2.13, sub-para 2
14 See CPR, r 44.2(4) and (5) and discussion/examples at relevant paragraphs in the WB commentary.

'all or nothing' costs awards, and towards those which are more nuanced, case sensitive and so more accurately reflect the level of success achieved by the receiving party.[15] The court is thus given wide powers to achieve this, ranging from depriving an otherwise successful party of some of their costs to awarding different costs on different aspects of a case to different parties. The possibilities include courts ordering (either alone or in combination):[16]

(i) only a proportion of another party's costs (also called 'percentage orders');
(ii) a stated amount in respect of another party's costs;
(iii) costs from or until a certain date only (sometimes called 'time specific' orders);
(iv) costs incurred before proceedings have begun;
(v) costs relating to particular steps taken in the proceedings;
(vi) costs relating only to a distinct part of the proceedings (also known as issue-based orders)
(vii) interests on costs from or until a certain date, including a date before judgment.

An issue-based costs order might be made where a party has won overall, but was nevertheless unsuccessful on some identifiable issue or issues (raised by them), especially if a disproportionate amount of time and expense was spent in dealing with it. A typical issue-based order would *deprive* the otherwise successful party of their costs on that issue (leaving them to pay those costs themselves). However, the court's discretion is wide enough for it to go further and actually require the otherwise successful party to pay the otherwise unsuccessful party's costs on that issue, but

15 See WB, para 44.2.7, sub-para 2

16 CPR, r 44.2(6). There are some special situations which require additional considerations when deciding costs. These are discussed below.

this would be a very draconian order (clearly signalling the court's disapproval). Depriving the overall winner of some of their costs is one thing, but making them pay any costs to the overall loser is quite another.[17]

Because issue-based orders can get complicated and time-consuming to work out, other alternatives, and in particular the percentage order is both popular and encouraged by the Court of Appeal. Indeed, CPR r 44.2(7) specifically requires that before making an issue-based order, the court should consider making a percentage or time specific order instead. The percentage order is a broad-brush approach, which will not work in all cases, but its simple beauty is that it is often able to reflect not only the overall outcome of the case, but also the loss on a particular issue or other deduction for poor litigation conduct.[18]

It perhaps goes without saying, but it is also important when making costs orders, that judges clearly state their reasons. In *Straker v Tudor Rose*, the Court of Appeal said that the judge should first identify the successful party and then consider whether there were reasons for departing from the general rule and, if so, to make clear the factors justifying this.[19] And the courts can be very sophisticated about fine-tuning costs orders to be case-specific. In *Midland Packaging Ltd v HW Chartered Accountants,*[20] for example, the claimant had clearly won in money terms, having been awarded substantial damages, and beaten a Part 36 offer made by the defendants. But the judge decided that in other respects the success had only been partial. In particular the claimant had grossly exaggerated the amount of the claim and had been unsuccessful on points which occupied a significant amount of court time. They had made an 'unreasonable' counter-offer in response to the defendant's Part 36 offer. The judge concluded that the defendant had in fact been successful on six out of eight issues which the court had been required to determine and that there had been no real attempt to narrow the issues on the part of the claimant, who had

17 See WB, para 44.2.10

18 See WB, para 44.2.8 and examples set out there.

19 [2001] EWCA Civ 368. And see WB, para 44.2.4

20 [2011] Costs LR Online 39 (you can ignore the references to the *Carver* case, which has since been disapproved).

overplayed its hand and fought the case to the bitter end. He therefore awarded the defendant 75% of its costs from the date of the claimant's counter-offer, to be offset against the costs otherwise due from that defendant to the claimant.

2. HOW MUCH?

A. BASIS OF ASSESSMENT

Once the court decides which party should pay whose costs and what form the costs order should take, it will then go on to make clear the basis on which such costs should be assessed. Unless the figures are fixed by the rules,[21] in deciding how much one party will have to pay the other, there are two 'bases of assessment': the *standard* basis and the *indemnity* basis. Both of these only allow such costs as are 'reasonable in amount' and 'reasonably incurred', but *the* standard basis (and *only* the standard basis) has a *further requirement of proportionality*, which means that costs which are *disproportionate in amount may be disallowed or reduced, even if reasonably or necessarily incurred.*[22] In short, with the standard basis of assessment, proportionality trumps both necessity and reasonableness. Costs incurred will be proportionate if they bear a 'reasonable relationship' to such things as the value, complexity, or public importance of the litigation. The needs of vulnerable parties or witnesses will also be relevant as would whether any additional work was generated by the conduct of the party paying the costs.[23]

Furthermore, any doubts on these matters are resolved in favour of the pay*er* on the *standard* basis and in favour of the pay*ee* on the *indemnity* basis.[24] The indemnity basis of payment is therefore the more expensive for the payer and is only used in certain specified circumstances (e.g., to reward claimants making successful Part 36

21 *See below.*
22 CPR, r 44.3(1) and (2)
23 See CPR, r 44.3(5)
24 CPR, r 44.3(2)(b) and (3)

offers[25]) or to be punitive where a party's conduct has been sufficiently poor that it can be said to come 'outside the norm' of what is considered ordinary and reasonable litigation behaviour.[26] As the name implies, the normal basis of assessment is the standard basis. Unless specific reference to the indemnity basis is made, the presumption is that costs should be assessed on the standard basis.[27]

B. QUANTIFYING COSTS

If a case settles, the amounts payable by way of costs can be agreed between the parties; the terms of any settlement should cover the payment of costs. This can include any costs of a stand-alone ADR process, which are otherwise normally shared equally (or with each party paying their own costs of the process).[28]

If the court orders (or the CPR dictates) that a party is to pay costs to another party, this then needs to be turned into an actual amount in money to be paid. Where the amounts are not fixed, the basis of assessment tells us in principle what costs are included, but this then needs to be translated into hard cash.

Procedurally, there are essentially three ways in which costs orders are quantified. Costs, or aspects of costs, might be:

(i) *Fixed*, in which case set amounts will be used which are 'fixed', usually by reference to the value of the case (the greater the value, the greater the amount). In order to keep the expense of litigation down, fixed costs are becoming more and more prevalent. Such costs neither need to be 'managed' nor 'assessed'. They are especially aimed at reducing lawyer's fees. At the time of writing, fixed recoverable costs ('FRC') are used for the following:

- early disposal of simple cases (for example, money claims exceeding

25 See Ch 15
26 This is a pretty high bar, and includes things like bringing a dishonest claim or flagrant disregard of court orders. See WB, para 44.3.8
27 CPR, r 44.3(4)
28 If the case settles after proceedings have begun, claimants need to be careful about agreeing to discontinue the action, since the rules (CPR, r 38.6) require claimants who do this to pay the defendants costs. See Ch 19. Note that it is possible to ask the court to make a decision on costs alone where all other matters have been agreed between the parties (although this of course increases the costs so should be avoided if possible!). See Jackson, paras 10.01, 10.03 and 10.15

£25 where default judgment was obtained or summary judgment given), unless the court orders otherwise (which it would do if there were any complexity involved);

- small claims track cases, where no lawyer's fees are recoverable at all, and only certain fixed amounts for court costs (for example, costs of issuing proceedings) and expenses (for example, travel costs) can be recovered, unless warranted by a party's unreasonable behaviour.
- fast track *trial* costs (these are fixed rates to cover the advocate's fees, plus an bit extra if the solicitor's attendance was necessary). The amounts allowed depend on the value of the claim. The court can award a lower amount than the relevant fixed figure if the behaviour of a party warrants it. These costs are relatively small (and for straightforward cases), and so if a lower value case begins to look as if the trial may be more complicated than at first supposed, this might be a good reason to move it up to the multi-track.
- All costs in low value personal injury claims (road traffic, employer's or public liability claims). These are governed by dedicated pre-action protocols, and where such claims 'exit' off of these special procedures (because the parties cannot agree damages), then recoverable costs will continue to be fixed (the fees are fixed on the protocol as well). Effectively, therefore, most fast track personal injury actions are covered by a fixed costs regime.

From October 2023, FRC will be extended to *all* costs on the fast track, and on a new intermediate track for simpler cases valued up to £100,000.[29] So watch this space!

29 Until new rules are published, for information see *Extending Fixed Recoverable Costs* on the gov.uk website. At the time of writing, fixed costs, covered in CPR, part 45, are not on the Bar Examination syllabus, but this could change, so always check your syllabus.

(ii) *Summarily assessed*, that is to say, quantified on the spot after the trial or hearing and on a somewhat rough-and-ready basis. On a summary assessment parties to whom costs will be paid will typically ask for their costs to be assessed (where the amounts are not fixed) by reference to the figures in their statement of costs, which will have been filed beforehand. It will be for the paying party to argue that certain figures should not be allowed, either at all or in a reduced sum. The parties and their legal representatives are required to assist the judge in this process.[30]

As a general rule,[31] the court will make a summary assessment of any unfixed costs at the conclusion of:

- fast track trials
- interim hearings lasting no more than one day
- appeals lasting no more than one day
- 'unreasonable behaviour' assessments in small claims track cases

But whenever a court makes an order about costs, it should *always* consider whether to make a summary assessment of those costs (which are not fixed).[32] This is just common sense, since if it is appropriate to do so, it saves time and money.

(iii) The subject of a *detailed assessment*. This is a separate and expensive procedure used essentially for cases where costs are not fixed and/or cannot be summarily assessed, and is appropriate for lengthy and complex cases and where the receiving party is publicly funded or a child.[33] Because the time it can take to assess costs in this way can be

30 A party failing to do their part (e.g., by failing to file a statement of costs as required) may be ordered to pay the costs of any further hearing (including a detailed assessment hearing) caused by that failure. See CPR, PD 44, para 9.5 and 9.6

31 Unless there are good reasons not to do so. See CPR, PD 44, para 9.2

32 CPR, PD 44, para 9.1. These provisions will need adapting to the proposed extension of fixed costs. See FN 29

33 But a summary assessment can be used when the child is the *paying* party: PD 44, para 9.8 and 9.9

very protracted, it is important to note that where a detailed assessment is ordered, the court *will also* order the party who will be paying those costs to pay a 'reasonable sum' on account, unless there is a good reason not to do so. The party who will ultimately receive the costs may have limited resources and expenses to pay in the meantime (e.g., to their solicitors), and so this is just a sensible provision.[34]

Finally, where costs are assessed by the court, CPR, r 44.4 gives judges some guidance on how to go about deciding just what amounts in costs are reasonable, proportionate and so on. As usual the court should take account of 'all the circumstances' and also have regard to various common sense factors, such as the value of any money or property involved, the importance of the case to all of the parties, any complexities or specialised skill or knowledge involved, as well as the conduct of the parties before and after proceedings started and in terms of the efforts made, if any, to settle the dispute.[35]

Note that the court should, in particular, give effect to any orders which have already been made in the case, typically an interim costs order. And on the multi-track, a costs management order will likely have been made. Where such an order has been made, then when assessing costs on the standard basis the court will have regard to the last agreed or approved budget, and *will not depart* from the figures in that budget *except for good reason*. The court should also take into account any comments about incurred costs which have been recorded on the face of any court orders.[36]

Even where a costs management order has not been made, one of the *factors* the court should have regard to is the 'receiving party's last approved or agreed budget'.[37] If there is a difference of 20% or more between the costs claimed and the costs shown in the budget, this may be regarded as evidence that the costs claimed are unreasonable or disproportionate. Much would depend on the reasons given

34 CPR, r 44.2(8) and WB para 44.2.12

35 Notice that conduct is an important theme in these costs rules and can be relevant here as well as deciding what costs order to make and on what basis to assess them. This point is made in WB, para 44.2.20, sub-para 2

36 CPR, r 3.18

37 CPR, r 44.4(3)(h)

for the discrepancy. And where it appears that the paying party 'reasonably relied' on the figures in the receiving party's budget, the court may restrict the recoverable amount in costs to a sum which is reasonable 'in light of that reliance', even if that figure is less than the amount (being reasonable and proportionate) which was actually incurred.[38]

3. PAYING THE LEGAL TEAM/FUNDING LITIGATION

There are several ways in which litigants might be able to fund litigation. If money is no object, then there is always the traditional retainer. But private funding is expensive - a solicitor's bill typically includes the solicitor's remuneration for work done on a case (at an hourly 'charge-out' rate, plus 'unit' costs for letters and phone calls), together with counsel's fees (briefs and paperwork), plus 'disbursements' (court fees, travel costs, expert's fees). Often the client will be asked to make a payment on account, and could be paying out for some time before being awarded any costs from the other side at the end of the day (if successful).

There was a time when the main alternative to private funding was legal aid, but as the availability of the latter has disappeared, other forms of funding arrangements have attempted to fill the void. Other possibilities are:

(i) Trades union or other third party funding. Some trades unions pay for legal costs of claims made by their members arising from accidents at work. This of course would depend on union policy and the claimant being a member of the trades union. Other third party funding would normally take the form of big players effectively investing in the outcome of a high value case.

38 CPR, PD 44, para 3. And see Ch 8 for costs management.

(ii) *Before* the event legal expenses insurance ('BTE' insurance). This is commonly allied to a person's home or motor insurance, and covers a person against the risk of having to pay legal costs in litigation (sometime just one's own, sometimes also the risk of having to pay the other side's costs). It is called '*before* the event' insurance, because it is taken out before the need to pay for lawyers arises.

(iii) *After* the event litigation expenses insurance ('ATE' insurance). This is an insurance policy taken out *after* the need arises. It can cover one's own legal expense, but is commonly taken out, about the time a claim is made, to cover the *risk of an adverse costs order.* Not surprisingly, such insurance can be very expensive. ATE insurance is/was often taken out in conjunction with CFA agreements, discussed below.

(iv) Conditional Fee Agreement ('CFA'). A CFA is a form of 'no win, no fee' agreement with solicitors, which was originally intended to help fund personal injuries actions when legal aid was withdrawn from such cases. The lawyers work (and charge) as normal, but agree that if the client loses the case, he will not have to pay anything to the lawyers acting *for him*; but if he wins the case, his solicitors will be entitled to charge him at the usual rate for the usual things ('base costs'), plus a pre-arranged 'uplift' by way of a 'success fee'. ATE insurance is needed to protect against the risk of having to pay the other side's costs if the case is lost. The extent of the success fee is intended to reflect the risks involved in taking on the action, so that if the case is a sure winner, the success fee should reflect this, although sometimes if types of cases are viewed in the round, the success in one case can be viewed (by the solicitors, anyway) as financing failure in another. At one time, both the success fee and the costs of ATE insurance were recoverable from the unsuccessful party, but it soon became apparent that these were the 'principal drivers' of the high cost of litigation. As a result, *neither* the success fee *nor* the costs of ATE insurance (except ATE premiums for expert reports on liability and causation in clinical disputes[39]) *is any longer recoverable from the loser.* This, of course, would leave a successful litigant distinctly out of pocket, and as a result a different variant of the no-win, no-fee agreement was created: the 'DBA'.

(v) Damages-Based Agreement ('DBA').[40] These are available in *all* civil claims and are really a form of contingency fee agreement (which used to be banned). They are a form of 'no win, no fee' because the client pays nothing (except disbursements) while the litigation is running, and if the claim is lost, nothing more will be payable to her legal team (and so one still needs to guard or be protected against having to pay the other side's costs). But if the claim is successful, the client agrees to make a 'payment' (to include counsel's fees) out of the damages recovered. This typically is a percentage, which in *non-personal* injury claims *must not exceed 50%* of the sums ultimately recovered, and in *personal injuries* claims *must not exceed 25%* of the damages comprising PSLA and past pecuniary loss (not counting the sums recovered under a CRU, since these go not to the client, but to the State). So a DBA agreement *may not take bites out of damages payable on a personal injury claim for future pecuniary loss.* The DBA must be in proper form, in writing and with the terms and conditions carefully set out (to include the claim or action to which the DBA relates, what the payment includes and why it was set at the chosen rate and so forth).[41]

39 For this reason, CFAs are still common in such cases. See Legal Aid and Punishment of Offenders Act 2012 (LASPO 2012), s 46

40 LASPO 2012, s 45. DBAs have had some growing pains and get a mixed reception from law firms. In October 2019 proposals for revising the 2013 regulations (qmul.ac.uk/law/research/impact/dbarp) were published for consultation. See also ***Zuberi v Lexlaw Ltd*** [2021] EWCA Civ 16

41 See generally BCP, para 5.16ff.

> DBAs were conceived in 2013 as part of a *triumvirate* package intended to protect claimants and quell the market in *personal injuries claims*. They help a claimant fund their claim. In addition, and to help compensate successful personal injury claimants for no longer being able to recover their CFA 'success fee' and ATE insurance premium, a second part of the package was that PSLA damages were given a 10% uplift by virtue of the decision in *Simmons v Castle*.[42] Last (but not least), personal injury claimants also now benefit from costs protection in the form of QOCS, which are discussed below.

In general, a party's funding arrangements do not affect the order for costs which the court might make (although as you might expect, subject to special rules regarding pro bono representation, costs actually need to have been incurred to be the subject of a costs order[43]). Moreover, it is rare for the courts to be asked to interfere with (or make any determination in respect of) the fees owed by parties to their own legal team, but it can and will if there is a dispute. As regards the traditional retainer, as well as certain aspects of CFAs or DBAs, when there is a judicial assessment of how much a party owes its solicitors (known as 'solicitor and own client' costs), *the indemnity basis applies*, modified by various presumptions regarding client approval and so on - a basis, clearly, which is *more* 'expensive' than the standard basis, which is the usual basis of assessment of costs between the parties to litigation (known as 'inter-partes' or 'party and party' costs).

It is easy to see, therefore, that even if the case is won, what a party has to pay his own legal team (whether the solicitors' bill is disputed or not) will usually be more than what will be recovered from the unsuccessful opponent in litigation - and so there will almost always be some gap between outlay and what one, as

42 [2013] 1AER 334

43 This is known as the 'indemnity principle' (not to be confused with the indemnity basis of assessing costs!) which just means that one party cannot recover from another a sum in excess of what they are liable to pay their own lawyers.

winner, recovers in costs from the loser. This discrepancy, which may vary in its size, is one of the *risks of litigation.* Even if relatively small it represents 'nuisance value' and is relevant to any decision to litigate or settle. Lay clients should be much better informed these days about how much of a bill they are running up with their solicitors, and so should have a clear idea both before and throughout the litigation of what the costs-benefit risks are at any given time.[44]

4. PUBLIC FUNDING AND COSTS

Civil legal aid is not widely available. There are very strict eligibility requirements and many types of claims are *specifically barred* from its ambit, most notably *personal injury* (including now most clinical negligence), claims, defamation, conveyancing and matters relating to company or partnership law. One way or another many civil claims are simply ineligible - full stop (whatever the applicant's means). If available at all, legal aid is only offered to individuals.

The means testing is also very strict - so that (where available) only the very poorest can qualify. There is something of a sliding income scale under which litigants receiving public funding will be required to contribute some money of their own towards the cost of litigating.

In addition there are nine criteria for full representation, which include considerations of alternatives to litigation, whether the small claims track can deal with the claim, and whether alternative funding is a viable option. In money cases, a cost-benefit formula applies, which is a crude way of assessing value for money. Borderline cases will only be funded if the matter raises humans rights issues or is otherwise of public importance.[45]

44 Solicitors are under a professional duty to provide this information to clients.

45 For detail on getting legal aid funding, see BCP, Ch 7

46 There are administrative costs associated with public funding, which would not be recoverable litigation costs.

47 LASPO 2012, s 25

48 When an adverse costs order happens as a result of a defendant's Part 36 offer which a legally aided claimant did not accept and ultimately fails to beat, this can be devastating for that otherwise successful litigant. The defendant may be allowed to set off some of the amounts he owes the claimant (in damages as well as costs) against the costs he would otherwise expect to recover from the

The LAA pays civil legal aid lawyers in accordance with relevant provider contracts and rates of pay either negotiated or set by the relevant regulations. And if a legally aided party is successful, then the court will make an order for costs on exactly the same principles as apply in unassisted cases. But as with private funding, there is always apt to be a short fall between what has been paid out and what is recoverable in costs from the other side.[46] This shortfall is *not written off* by the state. A winning publicly funded claimant will be required to make up the difference out of his damages, or other award because the LAA has a 'first charge' on any 'property recovered or preserved' by a legally aided litigant to recoup their costs of funding that person's litigation.[47] This 'statutory charge' will bite whenever the state pays out more to finance the latter's litigation than it recovers from that person's contribution to their representation, plus any costs paid by the other side. In this context, if full costs are not payable by the losing defendant, this could result in a large proportion of any damage award being paid to the LAA. The underlying principle is that the publicly funded litigant should be in a similar position to a successful privately paying litigant.

And what if the legally aided party is the loser or is otherwise subject to an adverse costs order?[48] This brings s 26(1) of LASPO 2012 into play. This provision gives some costs protection to such litigants by limiting a publicly funded litigant's liability to pay costs to that amount, if any, which it is 'reasonable' for him to pay, having regard to all of the circumstances, including the resources of the party and their conduct.[49] Obviously, there is a correlation between a litigant's ability to quality for legal aid and his lack of resources, so a privately funded claimant succeeding against a legally aided defendant might find he will have to pay for his own victory.

But at least claimants can choose whether to litigate. This is not true of defendants.[50] What about the privately paying defendant who has no choice but to

claimant, and anything left over could be subject to the statutory charge: See, e.g., *Cook v Swinfen* [1967] 1 ALL ER 299. A variant of this principle is the so-called '*Lockley* Order' which allows interim costs payable by a publicly funded litigant to be offset against any eventual damage award: *Lockley v National Blood Transfusion Service* [1992] 1 WLR 492

49 Certain items are excluded when assessing the person's 'resources'. See Civil Legal Aid (Costs) Regulations 2013, reg 13(1)

50 Beware the defendant bringing a counterclaim. He becomes a claimant in respect of that action.

fight or settle, while the claimant is publicly funded? In this rare situation, help may be available from LASPO, s 26(6)(d) which allows the court to order the state to pay the costs of the successful defendant if certain conditions are met. These are very strict and such orders are uncommon.[51]

5. SPECIAL COSTS SITUATIONS

Finally, there are several situations to look out for which require a variation on or adaptation of the usual costs theme.

A. COST PROTECTION IN PERSONAL INJURY/FATAL ACCIDENT CASES: 'QOCS'

This is a form of costs protection, given *only to claimants* and *only* in respect of claims for damages *for personal injuries and fatal accidents*,[52] in part to compensate them for losing the ability to claim the costs of CFA success fees and ATE premiums from an unsuccessful defendant.[53] It works a little like s 26 of LASP0 2012 to protect claimants in such cases from adverse costs orders. It is just a pity it has such an unglamorous official title: qualified one-way costs shifting - or QOCS, for short.

This is basically how they work: claimants will recover their costs from the defendant if they win, but will not be required to pay the defendant's costs if they lose (thus obviating the need for ATE insurance). So the costs shifting only works one way, in the claimant's favour, but it is 'qualified' by (a very few) exceptions intended to weed out those who do not deserve (or qualify for) such protection: hence the name. Defendants thus need to be very aware of the operation of the QOCS rules, although more often than not they are big insurance companies, and not penniless individuals.

51 For further detail see BCP, para 68.61

52 'Claimant' extends to *claims* (for personal injuries) made by a defendant by way of a counterclaim or by means of a Part 20 claim (but not a claim for a contribution or indemnity): ***Wagenaar v Weekend Travel*** [2015] WLR 1968. Also specifically excluded are applications for pre-action disclosure against a prospective defendant: CPR, r 44.13

53 CFAs, discussed above, were devised as an alternative method of funding when personal injuries actions ceased to be eligible for public funding.

It is important to appreciate that QOCS protection does not prevent an order for costs being made against a claimant; what it does is severely constrain the extent to which such orders can be *enforced*. So, the court will make a costs order as normal, but any order against the claimant can *only* be enforced to the extent that the sum involved *does not exceed* any amount of damages (plus interest) which the claimant might have been *awarded by the court or agreed by way of settlement.* This is important when defendants make offers of settlement, and in particular Part 36 offers. So, where a claimant has won the case, but failed to 'beat' the offer, then the damages the claimant has won will be a fund out of which he can be asked to pay some or all of the costs he will almost certainly be ordered to pay in those circumstances (some of which can also be set off against any costs the defendant is ordered to pay the claimant). Similarly if a claimant accepts a defendant's Part 36 offer after the 'relevant period' - that sum will be a fund out of which costs payable to the defendant (agreed or court ordered) can be enforced. But in either case, the defendant won't be able to enforce any order for costs beyond the point of wiping out the claimant's awarded or agreed amount of damages and interest (and setting-off any costs payable by the defendant to that claimant).[54] And of course where the claimant has lost outright and been awarded no damages at all to enforce against, this is bad news for the defendant.

The exceptions to this rule are extremely narrow. One is where the proceedings have been struck out as disclosing no reasonable cause of action, or as an abuse of process or because the claimant's litigation conduct was likely to obstruct the just disposal of proceedings. This might happen very early on. Strike out on one of these grounds effectively amounts to the court saying either that the claim should never have been brought in the first place or that the claimant's litigation conduct was beyond the pale, and in such circumstances no permission of the court is required to

54 CPR, r 44.14, as amended by the Civil Procedure (Amendment) Rules 2023

enforce any costs order against the claimant up to its full extent.[55] In this scenario, the QOCS protection is effectively lost because either the claim or the claimant is clearly undeserving of it.

There are a few other situations where the court can *give permission* to enforce a costs order made against a claimant. One[56] is where the court finds the claim to be (on the balance of probabilities) 'fundamentally dishonest', in which case the defendant will be permitted to enforce the costs order against the claimant up to its full extent.[57]

Finally, note how limited these exceptions to the QOCS protection are. They do *not* include the claimant either having or suddenly coming into a lot of money. There is no means or financial test involved in the application of the QOCS rules.

B. MULTIPLE DEFENDANTS

When a claimant sues two defendants and is successful against one but not the other, a strict application of the general rule that costs follow the event would mean that while the claimant would get costs from the unsuccessful defendant, he would have to pay the costs of the successful defendant. But where it was *reasonable* to proceed (and continue to the bitter end) against both defendants (for example, because the defendants were blaming each other for the same harm and it was impossible to anticipate who was liable), an adaptation of the general rule *may* be possible. The court has a *discretion* to order, in effect, that the losing defendant pay the winning defendant's costs. This sort of order comes in two forms:

(i) *Bullock* Order[58]

Here the claimant (C) is ordered to pay the costs of the winning defendant, but once paid these can be recovered from the losing defendant in addition to the claimant's own costs. The order would look something like this:

55 CPR, r 44.15

56 CPR, r 44.16(1). The situations set out in r 44.16(2) are rather more nuanced, and deal with aspects of a case not covered by the QOCS rules. If the claim is not solely for personal injuries, the court will adopt a broad-brush approach to decide whether, and to what extent, costs orders may or may not be enforced. See WB para 44.16.1

57 Dishonesty is 'fundamental' if it goes to a substantial (not peripheral) aspect of the case, for example lying to the court and medical expert about the extent of injuries forming the essence of the PSLA claim. See WB, para 44.16.2 and examples there.

58 This gets its name from *Bulllock v London Transport Omnibus Co* [1907] 1 KB 264, CA.

- Judgment for C against (unsuccessful) D1 with costs
- The case against (successful) D2 dismissed; C to pay D2's costs
- D1 to pay to C the costs so paid by C to D2.

(ii) *Sanderson* Order[59]

Here the payment of the successful defendant's costs comes straight from the losing defendant, instead of being routed through the claimant. This sort of order may be appropriate, if, for example, the claimant is insolvent or protected by QOCS, as there may be greater certainty that the money will actually reach the winning defendant. Such an order might look like this:

- Judgment for C against D1, with costs.
- The case against D2 dismissed.
- D1 to pay D2's costs.

It is important to remember that whether to make such an order, and if so in what form, is entirely within the discretion of the court. A court will be mindful that the winning defendant had no option but to defend the action brought against him, and much will depend on how reasonable it was for the claimant to pursue the successful defendant to trial. But the court will also be mindful that such orders are capable of doing an injustice to the unsuccessful defendant, and if that defendant did nothing to motivate the claimant to proceed against the successful defendant, then this could militate against the making of a *Bullock* or *Sanderson* order (and vice versa). But every case is different, and some cases have a lot of parties. There are no hard and fast rules - the court's discretion is wide so as to be able to do justice in every case.[60]

59 This gets its name from *Sanderson v Blyth Theatre Co* [1903] 2 KB 533, CA.
60 See WB, para 44.2.28

Finally, the various types (and permutations) of costs orders discussed earlier can also come in particularly handy when dealing with multiple parties. They provide flexibility. In the case of *McGlinn v Waltham Contractors* (No 5)[61] the claimants sued three defendants (D1, D2, D3) for £3.65 million. The claimant lost against D1 (who had offered to settle for £300,000!). The claimant did better against the other defendants, but only just. He was awarded just under £440,000 from D2, and just under £135,000 from D3, for a grand total of about £575,000 - less than 1/7th of his claim. The costs incurred by the claimant amounted to some £2.2 million. D1's costs were £880,000 and D2's were £1.2 million (D3's costs were put over to another hearing - case No. 6, probably!). The total costs so far were about £4 million. Issue-based costs were ordered on a percentage basis between the claimant and D2 in relation to liability and quantum. The claimant was ordered to pay D1's costs, the judge declining to make a *Sanderson* or *Bullock* order. On this aspect alone, the claimant was already out of pocket, even before taking into account the fact that he would have to pay his own costs of pursuing D1. Ouch!

C. CLAIM AND COUNTERCLAIM

Where a counterclaim amounts to a total set-off (one that completely extinguishes the claimant's claim), then the defendant will have been successful and costs will (all other things being equal) follow the event. Where, however, a defendant's set-off is less than the claimant's claim (and there is no other answer to the remaining amount claimed), the defendant should either pay the difference or make a Part 36 offer on the 'balance' to protect himself on costs because, unless the set-off fails, the claimant can never 'beat' the offer.

Otherwise, where there is success 'both ways' (i.e. both claim and counterclaim succeed to an extent), the traditional rule has been that there should be two judgments

61 [2007] EWHC 1410 (TCC). Any case with a (No 5) after its name is going to be messy!

and two separate orders as to costs. This is known as the rule in *Medway Oil*,[62] which also said that in such a situation, a defendant is only entitled to costs 'exclusively referable' to the counterclaim. But this can cause hardship where much of what is referable to the counterclaim is also referable to the main claim (and so is not 'exclusive' to the counterclaim). This will happen where there is a high degree of interconnection between the actions, including a set-off claim which does not entirely extinguish that of the claimant. For a long time now, where the rule in *Medway Oil* would cause hardship, the court has been able to make a 'special order' on costs, either a single order or no order as to costs.[63] The court's options in this regard are now reinforced by the breadth of discretion in the CPR, and the various types of orders it can make. *Percentage orders are particularly helpful in these sorts of cases.* Indeed, giving the overall winner a proportion of its costs will often be preferable to orders for costs 'going in opposite directions.'[64]

D. COSTS ORDERS AGAINST THE LAWYERS

We have seen how 'conduct', in connection with the assessment of cost, can affect orders for costs between parties to litigation. By virtue of CPR, r 44.11, intentional *misconduct* (as opposed to mistakes or negligence) in connection with the assessment of costs, can result in adverse costs orders *not only* against the party in question but *also against their lawyers*. For example, if a legal representative were found to have acted improperly or unreasonably (before or during the proceedings giving rise to the assessment of costs, or during the assessment process itself) the court could order that they *personally* pay the costs which another party has incurred as a result.[65]

This power is in addition to (and somewhat overlaps with) a much older power of the court to make a party's legal representative personally liable for costs, under the Senior Courts Act 1981 s 51(6). So called 'wasted costs orders' can take

62 *Medway Oil and Storage Co Ltd v Continental Contractors Ltd* [1929] AC 88

63 *Chell Engineering Ltd v Unit tool and Engineering Co Ltd* [1950] 1 All ER 378

64 See WB, para 44.2.14, sub-paras 1 and 2

65 CPR, r 44.11(2)(b)

two forms: disallowing the costs caused by the improper behaviour and effectively making the legal advisor reimburse their client, and/or ordering the legal advisor to pay the costs of another party. Wasted costs orders are compensatory as well as punitive in that there must be a causal connection shown between the improper behaviour and the wasted costs. They are draconian orders, which need to be reported to the relevant professional regulator. They should not be made lightly and are thankfully pretty rare.[66]

E. PRO BONO COSTS

Pro bono representation is (obviously) undertaken for free. A court can, however, order a losing party to make a payment to a prescribed charity (currently the Access to Justice Foundation) in respect of pro bono representation. *Such orders are possible in all courts*, including now most Tribunals. The discretion to make such an order will be exercised by reference to whether an adverse costs order would have been made in the ordinary course of events (that is, had the successful party not had pro bono representation). In essence the loser would be ordered to pay the costs he would otherwise have had to pay - but to the charity (not to the successful party). This helps 'level the playing field', by imposing adverse costs risks on all parties, even those facing a pro bono assisted party. Fixed costs would be awarded if applicable, otherwise the court would assess the costs by a summary or detailed assessment. A summary assessment would always be preferable, to save money and get the funds quickly to the charity.[67]

66 Wasted costs orders are covered in the rules under CPR r 46.8. Do not confuse 'costs thrown away' (a common interim costs order) with a 'wasted costs' order. They both sound judgmental, but the latter is much more serious and is aimed exclusively at legal representatives. At the time of writing, CPR r 46.8 is not on the Bar exam syllabus.

67 Legal Services Act 2007, s 194(3) and s 194A and LASPO Act 2012, s 61. See generally Access to Justice Foundation website.

revision tips

- Costs is a big and broad area, so focus on the specific topics and issues covered by your examination syllabus. In this book, costs management is covered in Chapter 8.
- Make your own table of the possible orders a court might make on an interim application, including what they mean and in what circumstances they might be made. Make up little fact patterns which would lead to a particular interim costs order.
- Regarding costs orders between the parties, make sure you distinguish between these three related but distinct parts of the process, namely:
  - who pays and to what extent (CPR, r 44.2),
  - on what basis costs which are not fixed are to be assessed (CPR, r 44.3) *and*
  - how assessed costs are actually quantified (CPR, r 44.4).
- Be aware of the range and types of orders available to the court when making costs orders, including percentage orders or time-specific orders, as alternatives (or adjuncts) to straight issue-based orders. There is a very wide discretion to make costs orders which achieve the overriding objective in any given situation.
- Remember that the costs implications of Part 36 offers of settlement are covered by Part 36 and not Part 44 of the CPR.
- Keep alert to the extensions in the fixed cost regime likely commencing October 2023

It is worth reading ...

The judgment of Dyson LJ (as he then was) in ***Halsey v Milton Keynes General NHS*** [2004] EWCA Civ 576 (don't worry about the ***Steel v Joy*** component). A little unusually, the court sets out or confirms the general principles to be derived from its judgment before dealing with the cases at hand. But no harm in that. The ***Halsey*** case (which the court addresses specifically from para 36-54) is a straightforward one, and the judgment reads a bit like a mystery thriller - you will be asking yourself: *"What will the claimant's solicitors suggest next? Shall we all hold hands and sign a song?"*

Pegg v Webb [2020] Costs L.R. 1001. This is a good little case on the operation of QOCS, and in particular the effect of 'fundamental dishonesty' on the protection otherwise afforded claimants in *personal injuries claims.* The trial judge had made a strange costs order in any event, but you can ignore that and focus on the QOCS point (which the appeal court was able to do). The claimant 'forgot' to mention to the medical expert that soon after what was essentially a 'fender bender' he had fallen off his quad bike! Reading this case you can see why the rules committee wanted to try and choke off low value whiplash cases. Did the claimant go to his GP or the hospital after the accident? No - he went to his solicitors. Hmmm...

CHAPTER 19

Judgment and beyond

Most litigants assume that once judgment is given in a case, it is all over. They would particularly like to think so if they have just been successful. But they would be wrong. In particular, the loser may want to appeal, or the winner may have to enforce the judgment. These are two particularly important aspects of the litigation process, which are discussed briefly below.

1. JUDGMENTS AND ORDERS

We have seen over these pages the various orders and decisions which the court might make on interim applications; at the end of a trial, what is handed down is a final judgment on the issues in dispute. Although the context here is final judgment (we have come to the end of the book after all!), the rules discussed in this section essentially apply equally to all orders and judgments.[1]

After final judgment is pronounced, it must then be *drawn up*. The general rule is that the court takes responsibility for drawing up orders and judgments, but the court may give permission or order that a party do this (usually the winner, as they will be motivated to do so!). More particularly, however, in the KBD (including

1 As the title of Part 40 indicates! And see r 40.1. In terms of enforcement, too, there is little practical difference between an order and a judgment.

the TCC and Commercial courts, but not the Admiralty courts), the general rule is *reversed* so that unless the court orders otherwise, the judgment in those courts must be drawn up by the *parties*. A party who is required to draw up a judgment is allowed seven days to file the relevant documents (with sufficient copies for the court and all parties), failing which any other party may draw up and file them. The court will seal the judgment and serve a copy on each party, including the party who drew it up![2]

Most judgments (and orders) must state the name and judicial title of the person who made it.[3] Unless the court specifies otherwise, they take effect from the date they are *given or made*, not the date they are drawn up, sealed or served.[4] Final (like interim) injunctions must contain a penal notice (to warn of the consequences of breach), and will not be enforceable until the respondent is made aware of the order (usually by being personally served, or being in court to hear it). This is just common sense - until a party knows it has been ordered to do or not do something, how can it comply?

A judgment for the payment of money (including costs) must be complied with within 14 days of the date of judgment or order, unless the court (or the judgment or the rules) say otherwise.[5] Interest will run (usually at the judgment rate, currently 8%) from the date judgment is given (again unless the rules or the court specify otherwise).[6]

When an order imposes a time limit for doing any act, the date of compliance must be clearly expressed (including the time of day and calendar date by which the act must be done), as must the consequences of non-compliance.[7] Where the case involves a claim and a counterclaim, and the court gives judgment for specific amounts on both, then the court may simply order the party who achieved the lesser amount to pay the balance. This is just a 'short cut', and does not stop the court giving separate orders as to costs against both parties.[8]

Appealing is the main way of impugning a judgment,[9] but accidental 'slips or omissions' can be corrected by the court at any time (not surprisingly this is known as

2 CPR, r 40.3/4. Some consent orders are entered administratively and do not require judicial intervention. *See below*.

3 Exceptions include default judgments and consent judgments: CPR, r 40.2

4 CPR, r 40.7

5 CPR, r 40.11. The court can, for example, order payment by instalments. In personal injuries cases, the judgment will set out the amounts awarded under each head of loss, and the amounts which are to be 'diverted' to the state to repay relevant benefits pursuant to the Social Security (Recovery of Benefits) Act 1997

6 CPR, r 40.8

7 See CPR, PD 40B, para 8 and examples there of wording.

8 Although in most cases giving the overall winner a proportion of its costs may be preferable to separate

the 'slip rule'), either on its own initiative or application.[10] A person who is or was not a party to proceedings, but who is nevertheless 'directly affected' by the judgment (or order) may apply to have it set aside or varied.[11] Finally a party against whom judgment has been given (or an order made) may apply for a stay of execution of that judgment (or other relief) if *matters occurring since the date of judgment* warrant it, and the court may make such order as it thinks just.[12]

Many judgments or orders are made 'by consent'. As you know, parties are encouraged to settle their disputes without recourse to the courts. And even if litigation is begun, parties must remain open to the idea of a possible settlement. When the parties do agree terms, the question then arises as to how settlement is to be recorded and enforced.

The form used to record the outcome of an ADR process will depend on the process itself. For example, an arbitration will be concluded by a binding award, and be enforced much like a civil judgment.[13] If an agreement is reached privately through a non-adjudicative process, like mediation or negotiation, typically the settlement will be recorded in a written compromise agreement, which will be enforceable like any other contract and which can only be set-aside or varied on grounds rendering the contract void or voidable (for example, fraud or misrepresentation). For that reason, it will be crucial that the contractual terms are clearly set out, comprehensive, understood and accepted by all concerned. Such agreements are often stated to be 'in full and final settlement' of the claimant's claim (this is consideration flowing from the claimant and is intended to stop him litigating the action), but it is very important that it is made clear exactly what cause or causes of action are covered by these words.[14]

Settlement can also be reached once litigation has begun. There are a number of ways this could be recorded,[15] but that usually favoured by lawyers is incorporation of the settlement into a court order, staying the proceedings upon the agreed terms.

orders. See CPR, r 40.13 and WB para 44.2.14

9 As opposed to applications to set aside or vary, which are more in the nature of requests to the court which made the order to reconsider the matter, usually in view of a change of circumstances or new information or because the rules allow it. *See below* regarding appeals.

10 CPR, r 40.12 and see PD 40B, para 4

11 CPR, r 40.9

12 CPR, r 40.8A

13 See generally Jackson, para 20.01

14 See the example at Jackson, para 18.09

15 See Jackson, para 19.02

This is a form of 'consent order'. Such must be drafted carefully - the orders must *record* the agreement rather than appearing to order or compel agreement. And it is only orders which a court has *jurisdiction* to make which can appear on the face of a consent order.[16] So a court cannot compel a claimant to discontinue his action, but can record the fact that this is part of the package by saying: 'Upon the claimant discontinuing the claim ....' (this is sometimes known as a 'recital').[17] The orders should also include a provision about costs.[18] Many consent orders can be entered and sealed administratively by a court official (for example an order for the payment of money, where neither party is a child or litigant in person); otherwise judicial approval is necessary.[19] Once a consent order has been entered and sealed, a breach of any of its obligations can be enforced like any other court order.[20]

There is a special kind of consent order known as a *Tomlin* order, which you need to be aware of. These are used in complex cases, or where the settlement agreement goes beyond the original issues in dispute or where (often for commercial sensitivity) the parties want the terms of the agreement kept secret. It was invented by Tomlin J and duly named after him. The beauty of a *Tomlin* order is that the terms of the settlement agreement are *not* in the order itself, but set out in a separate *schedule* (or other clearly identified separate document). The order is a public document, but *the schedule is not.* So a true *Tomlin* order will be short and sweet - the only terms included on the face of the order itself are normally:

(i) That the proceedings be *stayed* except for the purpose of carrying out the terms set out in the schedule,

(ii) *Liberty to apply* to the court if necessary to compel compliance with the terms in the schedule,

(iii) Liability as to *costs*

---

16 See Jackson, para 19.15

17 See observations at WB, para 40.6.2 (sub-para 17) and CPR, r 40.6(7) for formal requirements for consent orders.

18 If a claim is discontinued it is particularly important to make clear what the agreement is about costs since the rules themselves require claimants to pay the costs when they discontinue their own action.

19 CPR, r 40.6(2) and r 21.10

20 *See below* and Table 20.1 in Jackson.

The confidential schedule contains the terms of the settlement agreement. This is a binding contract, and so contractual principles apply. Because it is not part of the order itself, the schedule can cover matters which go beyond the confines of the dispute or which would be beyond the court's jurisdiction to order, and it can be kept secret. These are some of the advantages of a *Tomlin* order. But because the settlement terms are not in the order itself, they *cannot* be directly enforced without returning to court on the liberty to apply provision. Essentially, a *Tomlin* order records (in the schedule) the terms of settlement agreed between the parties but those terms are not ordered by the court and so are not enforceable without further order.[21]

Two other points to make: firstly, the judge making the *Tomlin* order is not concerned with what is in the schedule and should not see it. The parties have to be careful not to accidently disclose the schedule to the court, since if this happens the terms of the agreement may well become part of the order.[22] Secondly, it is not thought that a *Tomlin* order is necessary or appropriate in cases where all that is required is that one party agrees to pay money to the other (in return for the other party discontinuing their action). But if what was agreed was the payment of money *and* an agreement to do remedial work, then this could appropriately be compromised under a *Tomlin* order (since the court would not normally be able to order a personal service like this).[23]

Sometimes the court hands down a judgment on terms to which both parties are agreeable (indeed they may have suggested the terms to the court). This is not a true consent order in the contractual sense,[24] and will be enforced like any other court order or judgment.

21 See generally WB, para 40.6.2 and para 19.10ff in Jackson.

22 *Zurich Insurance Co Plc v Hayward* [2011] EWCA Civ 641 cited at WB, para 40.6.2

23 As in *Wallace v Brian Gale & Associates* [1998] 1 FLR 1091 cited in WB para 40.6.2

24 See e.g., *Siebe Gorman and Co Ltd v Pneupac Ltd* [1982] 1 All ER 377

2. APPEALS

Litigants will want to know whether they can appeal a case they have lost - sometimes even before it has started! So it is important to have a working knowledge of the appeals structure. There are a lot of technicalities, but for examination purposes (and general understanding) the best thing to do is focus on how the system works in the vast majority of cases. The detail will then fall into place, and anomalies and exceptions can be looked up as need be.[25]

Essentially, the appeal system is designed to ensure that errors can be corrected (judges are human, after all), but without giving litigants free rein always to be able to have someone 'more senior' look at the decision in their case if they don't get the result they want the first time. The context of this chapter is appeals of final judgments, but the basic principles are the same where appeals of interim decisions and orders are concerned, with some adaptations.[26]

From the outset, it is important to *distinguish between 'first' and 'second' appeals.* You want to be clear about what these terms mean. They do not refer to how many times a party has appealed, but how many times the judgment or decision *itself* has been considered by way of appeal. So, for example, a defendant may want to appeal the District Judge's refusal to grant her application for specific disclosure. Her appeal to the Circuit Judge may succeed. If the claimant then wanted to appeal that decision, it may be her first time as appellant, but it is the *second* time the matter has been considered on appeal. So, it is a second appeal, to which (as we will see) special rules apply.

Let's start with two important observations. The first is that, as a *general rule,* appeals lie to the *next rung up* the judicial ladder (for example, District Judge to Circuit Judge, Circuit Judge to High Court Judge and so forth). There are exceptions. An

25 Be guided by your examination syllabus for the level of detail required.

26 See generally Table 1 of CPR, PD 52A

important one is second appeals - these *always go to the Court of Appeal* no matter where they come from.[27]

Secondly, *permission* to appeal is almost always required unless the liberty of the individual appealing is at stake (not common in civil cases). For first appeals, permission can be sought 'from both ends', as it were, asking the court below first.[28] If the lower court refuses, permission may be sought from the appeal court. This must be included in the appellant's *notice*, which must be filed at the appeal court within 21 days of the lower court's decision (or such other period as directed by the lower court).[29] 'Grounds of appeal' should accompany the notice. This is a separate document, which should set out the basis on which (or respects in which) it is alleged that the decision below cannot stand.[30]

Once the appellant's notice has been filed, and unless the appeal court orders otherwise, it must be served on each respondent as soon as practicable and in any event within seven days of its having being filed.[31] If permission is being sought from the County Court or the High Court, the appeal court can give permission to appeal on the basis of the paperwork alone, although (if permission is refused) the applicant can ask that the matter be reconsidered at an oral hearing (although if the case is hopeless, the court can refuse to do so).

Where permission to appeal to the Court of Appeal is sought, the procedure is a little different. Such applications are also usually determined on the papers, although a direction for an oral hearing may be made by the judge considering the application; indeed it *must* be made if it is thought that the request cannot 'fairly be determined' without one. Such a direction would identify the issues the applicant should focus on and might well ask the respondent to make written submissions or even attend the oral hearing. Such hearings must be listed no later than 14 days from the date of the direction and (as you might expect) should be heard by the judge

27 Another is the rarely invoked 'leapfrog' procedure: CPR, PD 52A, para 4.7, and see BRC, 76.3

28 CPR, r 52.3

29 CPR, r 52.12(2). The time for filing the appeal notice cannot be varied by agreement between the parties, but the court can extend time. See r 52.15

30 It is worth looking at Form N161 which makes very clear what the appellant's notice entails and the documents which should accompany it.

31 CPR, r 52.12(3)

who made the direction. If permission to appeal is granted, the court can limit the issues to be heard on appeal or impose other conditions.[32]

The *test* for being given permission to appeal *varies depending* on whether it is a first *or* second appeal. It is easier to get permission to appeal if it is a first appeal: the test is 'real prospect of success' or some 'other compelling reason' why the appeal should be heard. This should sound familiar - it is the same test that is applied in summary judgment hearings when deciding whether the defendant ought to be allowed to go to trial with his defence. As you might expect, the *test* for being given *permission* to appeal is more stringent for second appeals, since the matter at issue will have been considered on appeal once already. Permission to bring a second appeal *must* be sought from the Court of Appeal and *will only* be granted where the appeal has a real prospect of success *and* it raises an important point of law or principle, or there is some other compelling reason for that court to hear it.[33]

Not surprisingly, there is some reluctance to give permission to appeal case management decisions, since the judge who made the order will usually know best how the case in question ought to be managed. For this reason, when deciding whether to give permission, the court will also consider whether the issue is of sufficient significance to justify the costs of appeal, the procedural consequences of an appeal (for example, would a trial date be lost); and whether it would be more convenient to determine the point at or after trial.[34]

The test for *allowing* an appeal which the appeal court hears is *different yet again* (and you do not want to confuse the tests for granting permission to appeal with the test for allowing an appeal!). The appeal court will allow the appeal if it decides that the decision below was plainly 'wrong' or 'unjust through some serious procedural or other irregularity'.[35] This is a very high bar. Furthermore, and not surprisingly, in relation to an appeal, the powers of the appeal court are very wide. It has all the

32 Compare CPR, r 52.4 with r 52.5

33 Compare CPR, r 52.6 with r 52.7. Remember that it is possible for an appeal to the Court of Appeal to be a first appeal, for example if a High Court judgment is appealed against for the first time.

34 CPR, PD 52A, para 4.6

35 CPR, r 52.21(3)

powers of the lower court and then some (e.g., it can vary the order or judgment, order a new trial, make costs orders and so on).[36]

In any appeal a respondent may file and serve a 'respondent's notice'. He *must* do so if the respondent seeks permission to appeal (and so grounds must also be set out); or if the respondent wishes to ask the appeal court to uphold the lower court's decision for reasons different to those given by the lower court (in which case the different or additional reasons must be set out, since appeal judges are not mindreaders!).[37]

Skeleton arguments are obligatory in appeals going to the Court of Appeal (and above). Otherwise, they should be used where the complexity of the case justifies their use. Their content should be concise, clear and purposeful. The arguments supporting the grounds of appeal (that is, the reasons *why* the court can conclude that the decision or judgment below is wrong or unjust) should go into the skeleton (and not the grounds of appeal).[38]

It is important to note that most appeals do not involve a re-run of the trial or hearing. Rule 52.21(1) provides that *every* appeal will be limited to a *review* of the decision of the lower court, *unless* a practice direction says otherwise or the appellate court considers that, in the individual case, it would be in the *interests of justice* to hold a re-hearing. A re-hearing is basically a do-over of the hearing which resulted in the decision being appealed against; to merit a re-hearing some real injustice or omission must have occurred in the court below. By contrast, a review engages with the merits of the grounds of appeal, by reference to the documentary materials seen by the lower court and the reasons given for its decision, which will be apparent from the transcript from those proceedings.[39] A review should accord appropriate respect for the tribunal below; the greatest regard is given to findings of primary fact, where credibility is at issue (since it is the judge of the lower court who heard

36 See CPR, r 52.20

37 CPR, r 52.13

38 So there are usually three documents: the notice, the grounds and the skeleton argument. Be clear what each should contain. And see CPR, PD 52, para 5 regarding requirements of skeleton arguments.

39 Official transcripts of what went on in the court below are an important part of the process. They can be made available at public expense if the court thinks it would be in the interests of justice given the appellant's financial circumstances: CPR, r 52.14

and saw the witness) and to purely discretionary decisions (judicial discretion is not easily overturned). At the other end of the spectrum, appeal courts are more likely to interfere with decisions dependent on inferences from primary fact and/or analyses of documentary evidence.[40]

Remember too that the appellate court (unless, exceptionally, it orders otherwise) will not receive new evidence which was not before the lower court. This is so whether the appeal is conducted as a review or a re-hearing. It would, after all, be illogical to criticise the lower court's decision on the basis of evidence it had not even heard. And appeals are not intended to give parties a second chance to do a better job deploying their case![41] Thus fresh evidence will only *rarely* be permitted on appeal - for example where credible evidence was simply not available at trial, but its impact would have been very important to the outcome. This is sometimes known as the rule in *Ladd v Marshall*, which these days is applied in keeping with the overriding objective.[42] Finally note that (unless the appeal or lower court orders otherwise), an appeal does *not* act to stay the order or decision of the lower court pending the outcome of the appeal.[43]

JUDICIAL REVIEW

Judicial review is a vast subject and beyond the scope of this book. It is important, however, to distinguish it from the appeals system. Judicial review describes the process by which the courts exercise a supervisory jurisdiction over the acts and omissions of public *bodies* (including, but not limited to the courts), to ensure that they are lawful. The applicant must have sufficient standing ('locus') to invoke the Administrative Court's powers; and the grounds will have a very identifiable ring to them. Decisions of public bodies are usually attacked on one or more of three bases: illegality, irrationality, or procedural impropriety.

40 See discussion at WB, para 52.21.1

41 CPR, r 52.21(2) and see BCP, para 74.1. This is why it is important to get all relevant evidence in front of the court hearing the case.

42 See discussion at WB, para 52.21.3

43 CPR, r 52.16

Permission to apply for judicial review is always required - this in itself is an involved procedure. The time periods are tight too (compared to normal limitation periods); the application must be made 'promptly' and in any event within three months of the decision complained against. There is a pre-action protocol for such cases, and orders sought and given by way of judicial review have a very distinctive ring to them. For detail, as necessary, consult CPR, Part 54. Practitioner commentary is extensive, both in the WB and BCP. The latter also has a useful Checklist 34 which is worth consulting. Check your exam syllabus to see whether and to what extent, judicial review is assessed. In 2015 it was removed altogether from the Bar exam syllabus.

3. ENFORCEMENT OF JUDGMENTS AND ORDERS

Parties who get judgment in their favour do not automatically obtain their remedy. Once judgment is entered, the other side should do as the judgment says; in the case of money, this would be payment within a certain time (usually 14 days). Most people abide by court orders, but not all. Many a winning claimant has been distressed to find that the defendant cannot or will not obey the court's order.

'Cannot' is more of a problem than 'will not'. If, say, a money judgment has been made against someone with no money or assets, then it is probably not worth the paper it is written on. Legal advisors should be alert to such possibilities from the outset.

'Will not' leads to consideration of the powers of the court to enforce compliance, which are extensive. But bear in mind that it is for the judgment creditor,[44] not the court, to enforce judgment. Enforcement of judgments is a solicitor's area of

44 A 'judgment creditor' is a person who has obtained judgment for the payment of money. The person against whom such an order is obtained is called the 'judgment debtor'.

expertise, and so will figure most prominently on their professional examination syllabus. The Bar examination syllabus now focuses on methods of (and venue for) enforcing *money judgments*, as will I, but even these range over several parts of the CPR! Whatever the level of detailed knowledge required, start with a basic understanding of the different kinds of enforcement order and marry them up with the type of asset or circumstance to which they relate. If, for example, a judgment debtor is unemployed, it would be silly to seek to extract money from him by applying for an attachment of earnings order.

Let us then consider enforcement of a money judgment. If too little is known about the judgment debtor's financial circumstances, then it will be necessary to obtain this information, either informally or by means of a court order that the judgment debtor be required to attend court,[45] and be questioned, on oath, to provide such information.[46] Armed with this knowledge, it is then possible for the judgment creditor to decide what the most appropriate method of enforcement would be in the circumstances. If a number of options are available, a judgment creditor can use more than one method, either at the same time or in sequence. In particular, have a look at the following possibilities:

a. Control of goods

This is a longstanding and common method of enforcement, which focuses on *things* the judgment debtors *owns* which have significant and easily realisable second-hand value (e.g., cars, fine art, expensive jewellery). The language used to describe the means by which this form of enforcement is achieved (and some aspects of administration) has been modernised in recent times. In the County Court, what were known as warrants of execution are now known as *warrants of control*. In the High Court, the old-fashioned writs of *fieri facias* ('fi fa') are now known as *writs*

45 As to what can happen if the debtor fails to comply with such an order see CPR, r 71.8

46 See CPR, r 71.1, 71.2 and 71.6

of control.[47] The County Court can only issue a warrant for judgment debts below £5,000, so if a *greater* sum is involved the case will have to be *transferred* to the High Court (if it is not there already).[48] Issuing a writ or warrant of control is normally purely administrative,[49] although where more than six years has elapsed since the date of judgment, the permission of the court to enforce is required.[50]

Armed with such orders, the relevant enforcement officer of the court will, having given proper notice, call on the judgment debtor's premises (during daylight hours). No forced entry is allowed (although 'reasonable force' may be sanctioned by court order). Once inside, control can be asserted over named goods, and (failing payment of the judgment debt within a minimum period of notice) sold to satisfy the debt.[51] One way for the debtor to avoid actual removal of the goods is to enter into a so-called 'controlled goods agreement', whereby the enforcement officer agrees to leave the goods with the debtor, who promises not to dispose of them until the debt is paid. The idea here is to motivate the debtor (and give him some time) to pay the judgment debt to avoid the goods being physically removed and sold for that purpose.[52]

Be aware that certain goods are exempt for these purposes, for example, basic domestic necessities, tools of the debtor's trade (up to total value, currently £1350), and so forth. Watch out too for goods belonging to someone else (especially hire-purchase goods), which may not be earmarked in this way. You might be surprised how many things judgment debtors have which do not belong to them!

b. Charging orders (execution against an interest in property)

It may be possible to get a *charge* against land owned by the judgment debtor - this might be a good idea if he has a house.[53] Such a charge secures the debt, but does not produce any money - in respect of land it operates rather like a (or another)

47 See WB, para 83.0.3

48 See WB, para 83.0.17

49 By merely producing the correct documentation.

50 Application for permission is made without notice, unless the court orders otherwise: CPR, r 83.2(5)

51 See useful overview at WB, para 84.0.2

52 See WB, para 84.0.3

53 Such orders are not limited to real property - shares or other securities qualify. Charging Orders Act 1979, s 2

mortgage. But take care that the judgment debtor has an identifiable equity or beneficial interest - it is no good if the house is already mortgaged to the hilt! If the property is jointly owned (e.g., with a spouse), an order can still be made but the charge will only operate on the judgment debtor's interest in it.[54]

The procedure involves *two stages*. An interim order is first obtained without notice; it is only the second stage which involves a hearing and gives interested parties the opportunity to make submissions as to why the interim order should not now be made final.[55] Getting the charging order (certainly the interim order) may be easy enough - and can act as an effective incentive to the judgment debtor to settle up. It also gives the judgment creditor security. But converting the charge into actual cash can be difficult because in order for that to happen the property must be sold, which if not done voluntarily requires a court order for sale. This is yet another complex step in the process, and if the property is a matrimonial or family home the court may be very reluctant to interfere with the interests and rights of a spouse and children living there.[56] Having said that, a charging order followed by another appropriate enforcement method can make an effective combination.

c. Third party debt orders

This method is useful if someone owes money to the judgment debtor. A typical example is a bank account in the name of the judgment debtor which is *in credit*. In effect, this form of order requires the person owing money to the judgment debtor, to pay an amount directly to the judgment creditor. It is no good, however, if the account is jointly held with an innocent other (such accounts *cannot* be enforced against[57]) or if it is overdrawn (where the debtor owes the bank money, not vice versa!). Like the charging order, the third party debt order follows a similar two stage procedure.[58]

54 See WB, para 73.0.4 (point 2).

55 See good overview at WB, para 73.0.1

56 See WB, para 73.0.4

57 See WB, para 72.2.13. Compare this restriction on joint bank accounts to the position with charging orders and jointly owned land (discussed above). Examiners like to test you on this!

58 See WB para 72.0.1

d. Attachment of earnings

This may be the only option if the judgment debtor has no assets other than a salary. It is in effect an order directed to the debtor's *employer* requiring the latter to deduct, and pay to the court, a named amount from the employee's salary. These orders can generally *only* be made in the *County Court* (usually following an order for payment by installments which has fallen into arrears), so if it is a High Court judgment debt, the claim will have to be transferred to the County Court.[59] The amount deducted is limited by a formula which is intended to ensure that a judgment debtor is left with enough to live on.[60] Remember that these orders are only available against employees, so will not work against sole traders or the self-employed (who effectively just pay themselves). Similarly, an order can be made against an occupational pension, but not against a state pension. Examiners like to test these differences.

Non-money judgments (for example, injunctions) are, as you might expect, enforced by different means. When a party does not do what a court says he must (or does what he must not), this can amount to 'contempt', which requires the direct intervention of the court. If a party disobeys a mandatory order of some kind, the court can (if this is practicable) order the act to be done by someone else, but at the disobedient party's expense.[61] Otherwise, enforcement would be by way of committal proceedings. These are very different to the kinds of enforcement procedures described above - they are up close and very personal!

e. Committal Proceedings[62]

Proceedings for contempt are essentially punitive, but with the added aspiration that any sanction given will result in future compliance with the court's orders. The two main punishments are imprisonment (for up to two years), which can be suspended, and/or a fine or sequestration of assets. The court can also give a stern

59 The only exception is in the Family Division of the High Court. See WB, para 70.3.1

60 Attachment of Earnings Act 1971, ss 6(5) and 24

61 This is essentially a form of court sanctioned self-help. See CPR, r 70.2A

62 CPR Part 81 covers committal procedure, which was overhauled and streamlined significantly in 2020. At the time of writing, this topic is not on the Bar exam syllabus.

warning. That all sounds very criminal, doesn't it? It is precisely for this reason that to establish the contempt, the breach must be shown to be *intentional* (a form of mens rea, in effect) and the standard of proof is the criminal standard: beyond reasonable doubt. Similarly, it must be shown that the relevant judgment or order contained a *penal notice* (warning of the consequences of breach) and was served *personally* on the party (unless the court ordered otherwise).[63] Procedurally, committal orders are applied for using the Part 23 procedure (or Part 8 if no proceedings are underway). The application notice must set out full grounds, and this is one of the exceptional situations where the written evidence in support must be on *affidavit/affirmation* (again, because of the criminal nature of the proceedings). The hearing will be in front of a Circuit or High Court judge.

It is useful to note too that committal proceedings can also be used to punish/ enforce a breach of an undertaking (that is, a promise) given to the court by a party, which are sometimes given in lieu of an order being made.

This is just a brief introduction to the enforcement possibilities (especially where money judgments are concerned). Once you understand the basics, it should then be easier to learn the detail required by your examination syllabus.

63 CPR, r 81.4

revision tips

- Check your examination syllabus for the level of knowledge to be tested in these areas. Some aspects will just need to be memorised.
- Do not run out of steam and be tempted to leave out enforcement altogether. It is usually worth a question or two. In terms of enforcing money judgments, check which method or methods are best in the circumstances. Make a table matching up different types of enforcement to various kinds of assets etc which the judgment debtor might have. Note procedural differences. Are you in the right court?
- Regarding appeals, do not confuse the test for granting *permission* to appeal (which itself varies depending on whether it is a first or second appeal) with the basis for a court's actually granting the *substantive* appeal.
- There can sometimes be an overlap, but remember to distinguish conceptually between *appeals* (which attack the judge's decision itself) with applications *to set aside or vary* a judgment or order (which itself cannot necessarily be faulted).

It is worth reading …

The judgment in ***Singh v Habib*** [2011] EWCA Civ 599. This is a fun little case about when an appeal court will hear fresh evidence, and the application of the ***Ladd v Marshall*** principles in the CPR context. This was a second appeal (hence heard by the Court of Appeal). The evidence was admitted, the appeal allowed and a fresh trial ordered. These claimants were even worse than that in ***Pegg v Webb*** (see Ch 18), since they invented the collision as well as the injuries. One wonders if anyone ended up in the nick.

Judgment of McKinnon LJ (it is the last of three) in ***Hirschhorn v Evans*** [1938] 2 KB 801. A case so old that the KB reference is to the previous King, not the new one! Third party debt orders used to be known as garnishee orders (I know, sounds like something a chef does before sending out his main course) and the claimant's name is mis-spelled in the WB, but the principle is clear.

CHAPTER 20

Approaching the exams

Since the last edition of this book, there have been many changes to the teaching and testing of civil litigation for those training to be barristers. The examinations have been centrally set by the Bar Standards Board (BSB) for more than a decade, but during that period there has been much experimentation both with what should be tested, and how. At one point there was one single sitting, using a combination of ways to demonstrate knowledge. At present there are two papers (designated Paper 1 and Paper 2 and taken on different days), but both employing only one type of question to be answered: a manifestation of the multiple-choice question, known as the 'Single Best Answer' (SBA) question.

The examination syllabus is still very wide but is now entirely dictated and described by reference to two texts, the main one being the White Book. Much of the examinable material is found in the CPR rules themselves or in related Practice Directions or statute. These primary sources can of course all be accessed from a variety of places. But an important component of the BSB examination syllabus comes from named commentary paragraphs in the White Book, which elaborate (sometimes at great length and not always with optimum clarity!) on the parts of the rules or principles to which they relate.

The other syllabus text is Jackson's ADR Handbook, which is used to a lesser extent and for questions which directly relate to the different types and means of Alternative Dispute Resolution. This is a fairly compact and accessible book, whose worst failing may be a tendency to repeat itself. Again, the examinable material is clearly identified by paragraph number.

Paper 1 is a two-hour closed book exam, containing 50 unrelated SBA questions. These can range across the whole of the syllabus. Indeed, any questions based exclusively on the Jackson Handbook can only feature in Paper 1.

Paper 2, which was introduced in 2020, lasts for 2.5 hours and is an open book exam, but the only book you can have open is the White Book - this is why questions exclusively based on the Jackson Handbook do not appear on it. Because it is open-book, this paper is more apt to ask more nuanced and/or technical questions, and those where the answer resides somewhere in the relevant WB commentary. This is why it is important to feel very comfortable finding and extracting information from the White Book. The BSB should make clear which version of the White Book can be used for this purpose (at the time of writing only the hard-back version can used).

Paper 2 also contains a new format of question which has been dubbed the rolling-case scenario (RCS). At the time of writing, there are five of these on Paper 2, each with seven SBAs. As the name suggests, the RCS involves a series of questions which take you through different stages of the same case. For example, you might start with an application for pre-action disclosure and follow the case through various points to trial and end with an appeal. As the case progresses you are given more relevant facts, and then required to answer another SBA. Although the story develops in a logical way, each SBA is independent of the others, so that getting the correct answer on any one of them does not depend on getting an earlier question right.

The teaching institutions thus have limited (if any) input into the examination content, except to try their best to share their expertise (and keep up) with the BSB and, in particular, to prepare you for the tests, so you should make the most of the guidance, practice and information which your tutors and course leaders give you. It is important when taking these exams to be alert and in a confident frame of mind, knowing what sorts of questions you are likely to find on the papers.

1. LEARNING AND REVISION

Learning and revision are very personal things. Some people make lists, some people use index cards, some people like mind maps. *Vive la différence.* Having said that, there is some general guidance which is worth imparting.

First, you need to keep on top of your learning as your course progresses. These are not subjects that you can leave until the last minute to 'swot up'. Prepare and participate as well as you can for lessons, and be willing to listen and learn while you are there. Remember that ultimately you need to understand and get the relevant information into your head, not merely onto a piece of paper. This requires thought and effort. It is a good idea, for example, to spend a couple of hours every week or so to consolidate and review your knowledge. There is a lot to learn and when you start revising properly, you should not be confronting the material (at least not most of it) for the first time.

According to the BSB, the assessments are intended to test the 'fundamental principles, key rules and core elements of civil litigation and civil dispute resolution' to be expected of a newly qualified lawyer about to embark on a pupillage and early years of practice at the Civil Bar. The exams are challenging because the syllabus is very wide, but the questions are not directed at historical or academic points of law or matters about which there are intellectual or other differences of opinion. Nor do they test minutiae such as form numbers (although notice periods can be fair game). Similarly, the key requirements of statutory provisions, rules and practice directions are more important than the rule or section numbers in themselves. These may be referred to in a question, but usually as part of the description, not something to be tested as such. Having said that, there are several cases which you will be expected to know by name, which are identified on the exam syllabus and all of which have been mentioned in previous chapters (e.g., *Denton*, *American Cyanamid*), and you would be expected to know the most important sections of the most important legislation (e.g., s 33 Limitation Act 1980).

But it is what such cases and statutes tell us which is what really matters. You will also need to 'drill down' into the rules sufficiently to learn the relevant essentials. Sometimes synonyms will do for general principles, but at times the actual wording is crucial. For example, the overriding objective requires the courts (among other things) to deal with cases justly and at 'proportionate' cost - not reasonable or sensible or some other kind of cost.

Therefore, when reading the rules or judgments in cases or the White Book commentary as part of your study (or indeed anything from which you are attempting to extract basic information), note the gist and mark up the one or two sentences or sections which encapsulate the principles and reasoning. You must extract, and get to grips with, the *essence* of the source material.

Similarly, in terms of rules, PDs and so forth (of which there are a lot), always make a note of the *key* concepts, words and requirements. Sometimes the differences between one procedure and another seem rather subtle. Take default and summary judgment, for example (discussed in Chapter 5). If default judgment has been properly entered (under CPR, Part 12), to get that judgment set aside r 13.3 refers to the defendant having to show that he has a 'real prospect' of successfully defending the claim or that there is some other 'good' reason for having a trial. This test has obvious (and necessary) similarities to that for summary judgment, but is articulated a little differently, so that in order to get summary judgment a claimant must show that the defendant has no 'real prospect' of successfully defending the claim and that there is no other 'compelling' reason for a trial. The test is essentially the same, but the procedural prospective is slightly different, and for that reason, so too is the wording.

Do not, I repeat, do not, think you can succeed by trying to 'question spot' for these examinations. They are not predicated on your demonstrating that you understand some things well, and others not at all. You may find you do not quite get to every nook and cranny of the examinable paragraphs (you are human after all), but you should try your best. These are professional examinations, and you should aim to enter the exam room thinking like a lawyer. You wouldn't be impressed if your GP couldn't help you with your aching knee because she hadn't revised the bit of her syllabus dealing with the causes of joint pain!

The BSB sometimes issues 'guidance' as to the number of questions per topic which might appear in the assessment. This is useful, but I would not take it too literally. They have been known to change their minds. Clearly if you have a confident grasp, for example, of Part 36, limitation and disclosure of documents this could be good for 15 questions or so; but that still leaves a lot left for other topics. You can be asked anything from the 'examinable material', and it is important to note that *more than one topic can feature in one question.* If you do not have a confident grasp of the syllabus across the board, you could get side-tracked and confused by references in a question which you do not really understand.

Next, I believe it is important to review and consolidate your knowledge 'little and often' and in sensible chunks, giving yourself breaks in between and rewards for what you have accomplished. This is especially true as you approach the exams. For example, you might spend a couple of hours in the morning revising interim payments and then go out for a coffee or go for a run. Then come back and tackle interim injunctions. Take breaks, in other words, if only short ones. My own view is that the brain (well, certainly mine) can only take in so much in one sitting and it helps to let what you have covered sink in for a while before going on to the next topic. Revising just before falling asleep is supposed to be good - maybe because what you have just been working on 'marinates' all night! In any event, whenever you do it, always make sure that you really *understand* what you are revising (and why the rule or principle is as it is). It is almost impossible to learn, recall, and especially to apply information you do not fully comprehend.

As your learning and revision progresses, aim towards reducing down to a few pages the fundamentals of each area you are reviewing, noting key principles, rationale and vocabulary. These in a sense represent a 'snapshot' of the subject matter. Not only will this help you distil the subject matter, but as you approach the exams you will have a handful, rather than a file (or worse, a room) full of revision notes for a last-minute run through. This is especially important for the closed book exam, of course, but it is also essential for Paper 2 since a sound grasp of the topics will help you answer a question seeking more depth or detail.

Note also that you will not have time in Paper 2 for a leisurely stroll through the White Book in search of an answer to a question - you must be able to navigate your way knowingly through what is a rather unwieldy tome. In essence, you need to know the syllabus material and the White Book itself well enough to know where to look and how to get there quickly. You should be learning your way around this text as your course progresses, but you need to be able to access the relevant information efficiently in the exam. You will be allowed to highlight wording and/or annotate the text and/or use post-it notes to help you get to the right place (see guidance given by the BSB about this). But remember that the objective is to assist you to find and identify information, so make sure that your marking up is *purposeful*. If you highlight everything, you may be no better off than if you highlighted nothing. It is probably also a good idea to begin doing this annotating and so forth during your final revision period, once you have studied the entire syllabus.

Last but certainly not least, make sure that you are very clear about what is examinable and up to what cut-off date, since this can change from year to year. Always (and periodically) cross-check your general knowledge and understanding of the various topics you are learning against the specifics of your examination syllabus. You do not necessarily need to learn the basics from the White Book (which can be challenging for beginners), but ultimately you need to learn *how to use* the White Book (and have read the relevant commentary paragraphs). My advice is to get a good grasp of each topic you are learning, by whatever means works for you, and then focus on the examinable material for the necessary coverage as you approach the exam. However you learn the subject matter, all revision roads should lead to the specifics of your examination syllabus! Try crossing these off a list as you revise the topics.

It is also crucial to take any and all practice tests which are made available to you, and in particular the mock examinations which the BSB provides, both for the experience and to highlight any weaknesses in your understanding of the subject. It is important to know what you know (and what you still have to learn), and what to expect on the day of the test. Don't worry too much at this stage about making mistakes; this can be a good (and memorable) way to learn. The mocks, where possible should be taken *in exam conditions*, following a revision period. It is also a good idea to do (or re-do) a mock relatively close in time to the real thing.

Since the COVID-19 pandemic, the civil procedure examinations have been conducted electronically. At the time of writing, it seems that the BSB will revert to pen and paper. This could change yet again. So always be sure you are as prepared as you can be for the method and manner in which the exams are to be conducted.

2. THE SINGLE BEST ANSWER QUESTION FORMAT

The Single Best Answer test is a sophisticated form of multiple-choice test. If you have not taken even a basic multiple-choice test recently, or if you are used to exams where you can get marks for telling the assessor something you know, even if you were not asked, then you need to get used to answering this form of question. No doubt you will be given a lot of information, help and advice about this form of assessment from your tutors and course materials. Make sure you take it all on board, and get as much practice in and exposure to the sorts of questions you will have to answer. And while you are learning, there is no great harm in getting some of the answers wrong in practice tests - so long as you learn from the attempt. It is getting them correct in the actual assessments which matters. You do not have many re-sit opportunities anymore, so make the most of this attempt.

On Paper 1, each of the 50 SBAs is a stand-alone question in the form of a (sometimes very detailed) factual scenario, followed by a specific question and four possible answers [A] to [D]. Only one of these is the correct answer. One mark is awarded for selecting the right answer. No marks are given for choosing the wrong answer (obviously), or marking more than one answer, but no marks are deducted for bad answers. Paper 2 begins with five stand-alone SBAs followed by the five RCSs (discussed above), making a total of 40 questions.

SBAs can come in various permutations, ranging from the traditional MCQ to the pure-form of SBA, with various 'hybrids' in between. Thus, you might encounter any of the following:

- A case scenario, followed by a question asking which of the following is the "best" answer (or similar form of wording). The four possibilities are all legally or factually possible (if only theoretically), and you have to apply your knowledge and use your judgment to decide which, from a professional lawyer's point of view, is the best of the four. This is the pure SBA, which is well suited for questions involving judicial discretion or counsel's advice.
- A case scenario, followed by a question asking you to choose which of the four possibilities is correct. In this type of question, only one answer is correct. The other three are incorrect. This is the classic multiple-choice question, which is most suited to specific time periods, and other 'black or white' rules or requirements. (You could also be asked to identify which of the possibilities is 'wrong', but again only one of the four options will meet this description. The BSB does not seem particular fond of this variant).
- A case scenario, followed by a question asking you for the 'best' answer, where some of the possibilities are clearly wrong. Here you must eliminate the wrong answers, and then use your judgment to select the best of the remaining possibilities. This is something of a hybrid SBA - the best (or worst) of both worlds!

In all cases, you are being tested on your ability to apply what you know to a given fact pattern and to select the correct answer to the question posed.

My advice when tackling SBAs is:

(i) Read any factual scenario carefully...

... and constructively, noting key facts like type of case (e.g., personal injuries), age of the claimant (e.g., a child), whether an action has been commenced yet or not - and so forth. At times, some of the information you are given in the fact pattern is not relevant to answering the question. These so-called 'distractors' are intentional. The idea is that you can discern what facts are and are not pertinent to the issue raised by the question. As you read the fact pattern you should be able to identify what aspect(s) of procedure or evidence the question is testing; you might even anticipate the question (or answer!). Often a 'best' answer will be entirely dependent on the circumstances set out in the fact pattern.

(ii) Read *all* possible answers.

This is so even if the first one seems like the right one. It might well be, but you *must* double check that there is not a better one below it. Sometimes one choice is only *partly* correct, or another choice is more accurately worded. Watch out for words like 'never', 'always' or 'must' in a choice you are given (which leaves no room for exceptions) - this can sometimes be the one thing which makes it right or wrong. It is particularly important with the pure SBA question, where you effectively have to make a value judgment about all the possibilities, that you read each option!

(iii) Be methodical.

With a classic multiple choice type question, because you are asked to distinguish between one correct and three incorrect possibilities, it can help (mentally or otherwise) to put a mark (e.g., T or F) by each one as you go along (if unsure, put a '?'). This can make it easier to answer the ultimate question accurately. Assuming you can mark all four choices either T or F, the odd one out should be the answer.

(iv) The process of elimination can help...

... to get you to the correct answer. This is a useful device no matter which form of SBA you are dealing with. If it is a classic multiple-choice type question, you might be a bit doubtful about which answer is correct, but more confident about those which are not. Eliminating the wrong answers will leave you with the one right one.

In a hybrid SBA, eliminating the wrong answers narrows down the field, and even when having to select the 'best' answer or course of action, there is no reason why you cannot eliminate the worst (or less good) options first!

And in respect of *all* of the SBA's:

(v) Record your answers carefully.

Take a second to make sure you are doing this accurately and recording the right answer to the right question. This is especially important if you are tempted to skip a question you are unsure of, so that you can go back to it later. My advice about the latter is not to leave such answers blank, but to record the best answer you can first time round. Then, if you do go back and change your mind about the answer, just make sure you make your revised choice clear. You do not want to get out of sequence!

(vi) Treat the examiner as infallible.

If your initial reaction when you read a particular question is that there is no correct answer or there are two correct answers or it is impossible to give a correct answer, read it again. If you still feel that way, swallow your pride and choose the *best* answer you can in the circumstances. You can complain later. Mistakes can happen, but they are still more apt to be committed by students than examiners, so have a go at the question whatever you think. If there is an error in the question, it can be taken into account when the questions and answers are all analysed after the test.

(vii) Keep the momentum going.

Do not slow yourself down with unnecessarily time-consuming methods of registering detail as you read, or let a question stop you in your tracks. Some questions will be more difficult, and so will take you longer to answer than others - the two minutes or so for each question is an average. But do not linger too long over any one question or let a question derail you (there are bound to be some 'nasty' ones on the paper) so that you cannot do your best on the rest of the test. Having said that...

(viii) Do not rush.

Remember that two minutes is really quite a long time. Just because the factual scenario you are given seems a long one, read it carefully. If you have taken the detail on board (and know the subject matter), it might only take a few seconds to find and record the correct answer. You will not need the full two minutes for each question, but do not worry when you do.

(ix) If necessary make an intelligent guess.

You do not lose marks for a wrong answer, so it is always worth making an educated guess. Narrow down the field as much as you can, make a sensible choice and move on. Remember to think laterally and apply known principles and rationales when guessing - it should be as informed a choice as possible. And don't forget to use your common sense - this can be very handy when choosing 'best' options.

In any event, try not to sit your exams while sleep deprived. My own view is that a good night's sleep the night before the test is a good thing - what you do not know by 11 pm that night is either not worth knowing, or it is too late. Having said that, I appreciate that many people get exam fever and are too excited to sleep. If you are one of these people, it is especially important that you get plenty of sleep as you approach the exam dates. Do not stay up two or three nights in a row. For similar reasons, make sure you are appropriately fed - you don't want to be faint from hunger or so full that you feel sleepy. Have a reasonably hearty and healthy meal beforehand. Your best asset for these assessments is your brain, and you want that working to full capacity.

And finally, remember that the assessments, although challenging, are designed to allow you to show off what you know and the extent to which you know it - it is not (or shouldn't be) calculated to make you fail. If you are well prepared, there should be a part of you (possibly a very small part) which is looking forward to the tests. As I used to tell my students before their exams, remember:

P repare sensibly (little and often, but thoroughly)
A pply known principles when in doubt (think analogously)
S leep beforehand
S ustenance beforehand

This became known as the PASSword. Many of you, I am sure, can achieve much more than a mere pass. Now go and show them what you can do!